D1739051

"Ungraspable Phantom"

"Ungraspable Phantom"

Essays on *Moby-Dick*

EDITED BY

John Bryant,

Mary K. Bercaw Edwards,

and Timothy Marr

THE KENT STATE UNIVERSITY PRESS

KENT, OHIO

© 2006 by The Kent State University Press, Kent, Ohio 44242

ALL RIGHTS RESERVED

Library of Congress Catalog Card Number 2005034827

ISBN-10: 0-87338-860-7

ISBN-13: 978-0-87338-860-3

Manufactured in the United States of America

10 09 08 07 06   5 4 3 2 1

"Composing *Moby-Dick:* What Might Have Happened: The Astman Distinguished Lecture"
is from *The Creationists* by E. L. Doctorow, © 2006 by E. L. Doctorow.
Used by persmission of Random House, Inc.

LIBRARY OF CONGRESS CATALOGING-IN-PUBLICATION DATA

Ungraspable phantom : essays on Moby-Dick /
edited by John Bryant, Mary K. Bercaw Edwards, and Timothy Marr.

p.   cm.

Consists of a selection of revised pages presented at the interdisciplinary conference,
Moby-Dick 2001, held Oct. 18–20, 2001 at Hofstra University.
The conference was co-sponsored by the Melville Society.
Includes bibliographical references and index.

ISBN-13: 978-0-87338-860-3 (pbk. : alk. paper) ∞

ISBN-10: 0-87338-860-7 (pbk. : alk. paper) ∞

1. Melville, Herman, 1819–1891. Moby-Dick—Congresses. 2. Sea stories, American—
History and criticism—Congresses. 3. Whaling in literature—Congresses. 4. Whales in
literature—Congresses. I. Bryant, John, 1949– II. Edwards, Mary K. Bercaw.
III. Marr, Timothy, 1960– IV. Melville Society.

PS2384.M6U65 2006

813'.3—dc22   2005034827

British Library Cataloging-in-Publication data are available.

Contents

Preface

"To Fight Some Other World"

JOHN BRYANT

Lately, when thinking about *Moby-Dick*—and having nothing else in particular to interest me on shore, I keep Melville's novel in mind a great deal—I find myself dwelling on the "hug." I do not mean to suggest that the novel fills me with such exhilaration and warmth that it requires a strong moral principle to prevent me from deliberately embracing the first person I meet on the street. Of course, like many readers—including artists, scholars, and critics—I love this book and readily admit to moments of stunned awe in reading passages in the book and to having shared them in classrooms, at home, and once or twice with strangers on the street; I have even participated in marathon readings of *Moby-Dick* along with other bleary-eyed companions, up all night reading their assigned chapters out loud, hopped up on Melville's jazz. I will admit to having hugged a Melville reader in fellowship now and again. But, in fact, *Moby-Dick* is also a hard read, at times infuriating, frightening, indeed alienating; and the enthused, celebratory hug of mutual self-contentment you might expect me to offer in a preface like this to a book of essays celebrating the sesquicentennial of *Moby-Dick* is not at all the hug I am thinking of when I find myself thinking about *Moby-Dick*.

The hug I am thinking of is above all a physical act, which is not at all what one might think is central to a book that is so famously metaphysical, one that ventures beyond materiality. But, of course, the search for something spiritual, essential, ideal "beyond" our physical realm—what Melville calls the "ungraspable phantom of life," or more bravely and weirdly the extracted essence called "sperm"—occurs within, not beyond. It happens very much here and now, mixed within the stuff of nature and in our contemplation of the dull thud we hear and feel as we continually find ourselves running up against the impenetrable and finally unknowable "thing" of existence. Melville always plays this out in the dramatic difference between the lyrical transcendence of Ishmael and the tragic frustration of Ahab. Think of Ishmael's comic vision expressed in his contrasting of two whale heads in Chapters 74 and 75: The Sperm Whale, with eyes on either side of its head, each taking in a separate image, has a mind that can "subtilize" those opposing views into one; the Right Whale with a lifeless lip pressed upon the deck seems, through Ishmael's poetic expansions, "to speak of an enormous practical resolution in facing death" (335). But also think of Ahab playing Hamlet in "The Sphinx" (ch. 70), contemplating the decapitated head of a whale hanging alongside the *Pequod*, leaning upon a cutting spade impaled in the whale's cheek, soliloquizing: "O head! thou hast seen enough to split the planets and make an infidel of Abraham, and not one syllable is thine" (312). So many decapitated heads, so many blobs of flesh, once vessels of life, now inert and inanimate. Where is the spark that gave them animation? Where is the consciousness that rides that spark? What is this phantom of Being? Perhaps if we hug these blobs real hard, we can get an answer.

At the heart of *Moby-Dick* is a problem, and the problem is this: the essence of life is contained within the substance of life and cannot be "extracted" without killing life; full transcendence, therefore, is impossible. No wonder that a Sperm Whale—deep-diving, silently knowing, yet outrageously large, and therefore unhuggable—became the apt symbol for both the material thing to grab at and the essential elusive "thingness" within that cannot be grabbed. The irony, then, is that the essential meaning of life is inseparable from the stuff of life, and yet no matter how close we hold this stuff to us, we get no closer to that essence. Thus, hugging, whether it be hugging oneself, another human, the shore, the inhuman sea, or some impossible whale, is a futile act. Which is why hugging figures so prominently in Melville's book.

That Melville could take his symbol of a sperm whale, paint it white to raise the stakes and make his whale a terror signifying not death or evil but nothingness; that he could float this whale among men and other whales to raise the stakes yet again, and make it the focus of drama and meditation, tragedy and comedy; that he could fashion the conflicts around this whale to body forth flesh-and-blood ideas about sexuality, race, madness, democracy, death, and domesticity; that he could write in such a way as to give courage—as playwright Tony Kushner has put it—to other writers to think and write bravely and weirdly for themselves; that his writing has given me courage to write a hold-your-breath sentence like this; that Melville wrote so wildly well and continues to grab us is surely far more important than any image of a simple hug.

And yet the Melvillean hug is everywhere in *Moby-Dick,* in one form or another. It comes most often in association with Queequeg (earthy, silent, and profound; more centered than nervous Ishmael or sullen Ahab). In "The Counterpane" (ch. 4), Ishmael wakes up to find Queequeg's tattooed arm over him in a wedding-like embrace: "it was only by the sense of weight and pressure that I could tell that Queequeg was hugging me" (25). And it is this hug that reminds Ishmael of an episode from his childhood when, forced to bed in midday as punishment for attempting to climb up the chimney, he dozes then wakes with the sensation of "a supernatural hand" placed in his. This "phantom," as he calls it, holds him as if for ages; it is a version of the "grand hooded phantom" of Moby Dick and of the tormenting image that Narcissus saw and died trying to reach. Is it some essential thing from some other world, real but intangible, this phantom? Or is it a reflection of the self, equally real, but also (despite the intimacy of selfhood) equally intangible? It is, Ishmael concludes, "the ungraspable phantom of life" (5), and Melville wants us to know this ungraspableness in graspable ways.

What is a hug? Bodies together, arm in arm, head to toe, the full embrace, a melting of being into being, if you are lucky. But most social hugging is quite different: two people touching shoulders, three pats to the back, no chest or belly touching, please. Or perhaps a bit more daring: one arm over a shoulder, one arm beneath, the mutual cheek on cheek, yes, but hips far apart. With hugging there is always desire, the intended embrace, and always the resistance to it; we hug, but only for a moment, then push away. And some hugs mask aggression. Let's not forget the bear hug, or the time-honored parental cheer: "I could hug you to death."

Queequeg is not given to superficial hugging. For him, it is a useful tool in his survival kit. When taunted by a greenhorn on board a skiff, he catches the bumpkin "in his arms," throws him somersault over his head, landing him on his legs square upon the deck, shocked, inverted, and suddenly put in place. Queequeg's unexpected act of aggression is a safe bit of nonviolent violence that disrupts the pattern of conventional male-male harassment with an unexpected hug, the kind a parent might give an overactive child. A page later Queequeg is saving the same bumpkin's life, rescuing him (now with a life-saver's hug) from certain drowning. Witnessing all this, Ishmael says, "I clove to Queequeg like a barnacle" (61), which is to say he hugged him hard. Other hugs, or versions thereof, are the monkey rope that ties two whalers together in mutual safety or mutual demise, the accidental sensual squeeze of the hand while squeezing solid sperm oil back into a fluid, and black Pip catching Ahab by the hand and offering to stand in place of the captain's lost white leg, a tug at Ahab to abandon his deadly chase and turn him back to humanity. These hand holdings and tuggings—sexual, communal, racial, even prophetic for America—are perhaps not hugs, per se, but they will do. They combine embrace and resistance.

I do not propose that the Melvillean hug is "the key to it all" or that as an image pattern, it constitutes the one "theme" to which all of *Moby-Dick* should or even could be reduced. It is rather a thread stitching together important areas of concern—metaphysics, sexuality, and politics—that inhabit the novel. And I think I can sum it up, thusly. The Hug: A Problem. To wit: "the ungrasp-able phantom of life" expresses our inability to transcend the materiality of our being and access the all-engendering, all-connecting Being that we think is there, hope is there, but fear may not be there. In moments of hope and poetic effusion, we feel Goethe's "'all' feeling" (as Melville put it in a letter to Hawthorne just as he was completing *Moby-Dick*); we form friendships, pursue sexual attractions, get married or not, forge alliances and political unions; we invent God as a larger-than-life embodiment of the consciousness that predates Him and us; we transcend the things of nature and apperceive Nature's Ideal Over Soul in moments of Platonic and Emersonian ecstasy. And we "brace the whole brotherhood. For genius, all over the world, stands hand in hand, and one shock of recognition runs the whole circle round" ("Mosses," *PT*, 249). In short, we hug. But this "'all' feeling" never lasts, cannot last, and may be an illusion. The whiteness of the whale stands a blank before us, like the blankness of Ahab's night terrors, imaging for us the equally un-engendering, dis-connected notion of non-Being, of existential Nothingness. Friendship and sexuality end in betrayal; marriage, in alienation of affection. Heroes are charlatans and thieves. All politics comes down to mobs and manipulation. Nature paints like the harlot and is a sham. Light and life have no substance. And waking from this dream, taunted by a false sense that there is a "phantom of life" holding our hand, we turn to one another and hug, not out of love or social convention but out of desperation. Like Ishmael clinging to Queequeg's coffin life-buoy, we feel a different shock of recognition: life is a maelstrom sucking us down to nowhere. O, o, that Melvillean hug.

The power of the hug resides in its capacity to encapsulate two opposing visions, that come and go upon us in a cycle of belief and doubt that drives Ahab crazy but becomes for Ishmael a dynamo of energy fueling his lyric meditation. Ishmael's deepest insights invariably emerge, always unexpect-edly, out of his obsessive descriptions of the seemingly banal details of whale anatomy and whaling life. The strategy is to have readers stumble upon sudden coherencies in the mess and chaos and things in life. One such descriptive chapter—"Stowing Down and Clearing Up" (ch. 98)—comes toward the end of the novel's "cetological center"; it is a neglected chapter and a seemingly tiresome delay of the fearsome duel between Ahab and the white whale, and therefore understandably neglected. Of course, Melville's further strategy in stalling the forward motion of his plot is to allow readers to make the necessary metaphysical dive into the materiality of existence so that they can all the more understand, not simply the mechanics of whaling, but the frustrations in the struggle between belief and doubt, and therefore Ahab's rage. All the more frustrating, perhaps, is the seemingly paradoxical fact that the chapter in question does not contain a single hug. Even so, the perpetual "essence seeking" Ishmael engages in allows us to see that the chapter's obsessive reiteration of "cleansing" has everything to do with the kind of extraction of ideality out of materiality that hugging is also all about. Melville depicts the behaviors of everyday life—cleaning up as well as hugging—as a secret enactment of our desire to grasp the ungraspable phantom of life.

"Stowing Down and Clearing Up" relates the routine process of cleaning the ship after the butchering of the whales on deck. One day everything is blood and oil everywhere, and the next day the decks are swabbed and furbished, the sperm oil, itself, having a "singular cleansing virtue" (428) and the ashes of the incinerated carcass yielding a "ley" (or lye) that scrubs away bits of gore. The whalers also tidy up themselves, "and finally issue to the immaculate deck, fresh and all aglow, as bridegrooms new-leaped from out the daintiest Holland." This remarkable sexual image of sailors as young lovers undraping from out their honeymoon sheets is utterly unexpected—indeed, the British censored it in their version of the novel called *The Whale*—but it is typical of Ishmael's sensualizing of the material world prelusive to a deeper metaphysical dive. Ishmael imagines his sailors as parlor gentlemen, scented and coifed, so "cleansed" that they would have no idea what you would be saying to them if you gave the "hint" that they might in fact be whalers: "They know not the thing you distantly allude to." They are, in short, in comic denial of their trade. But instantly another whale is sighted, and the whole killing and cleaning process begins again, like the endless cycle of life and death, belief and doubt, that Ahab cannot stop and will bemoan later in Chapter 114, "The Gilder." But here, Ishmael speaks: "Oh! my friends, but this is man-killing! Yet this is life. For hardly have we mortals by long toilings extracted from this world's vast bulk its small but valuable sperm; and then, with weary patience, cleansed ourselves from its defilements, and learned to live here in clean tabernacles of the soul; hardly is this done, when—*There she blows!*—the ghost is spouted up, and away we sail to fight some other world, and go through young life's old routine again" (429).

The deeper dive at the end of Ishmael's finally not-so-tiresome chapter is signaled in Melville's metaphysical code. Cleansing, like hugging, is a process that participates in the larger problem of accessing or getting at the immaterial through the material. Instead of trying to grasp the ungraspable, as in a hug, the "routine" here is in "extracting" the essence of the whale, its "sperm," from blubber and then cleaning up the material mess ("defilements") left behind. (The process is not without some vestige of Puritan guilt.) Like hugging, which has its superficial as well as deep versions, this act of cleansing, once routinized, becomes merely a social grace, a "tabernacle of the soul," just a monument to the moment of extraction experienced in the extraction of the whale sperm. But the "weary" thing in all this is the recurrence of the hunt. The "ghost" (that is, the whale's spout, but also the phantom of life) is sighted; we dive again into some search for ideality within the material, "to fight some other world," and we come up with an extraction, but we are also defiled once again and ready for a cleansing return to social life: marriage, clean sheets, tabernacles. This is not hugging, precisely, but the dynamic of grasping at the ungraspable is there in the routine of extraction and cleansing, just the same.

In presenting this volume of essays entitled *Ungraspable Phantom,* we are not suggesting that *Moby-Dick,* a piece of writing first published in the fall of 1851, is itself "ungraspable," that is, too diffuse to be interpretable. In fact, the novel, which ranges in size (depending on the edition you buy) from something like a shoe to something like a Sears catalog, is quite graspable, although once read, it is susceptible, we are happy to say, to numerous interpretations. You can hug it or throw it somersault over your head however you like. By invoking the notion of Melville's "ungraspable phantom of life," the editors of this volume want to suggest that the collection as a whole acknowledges the multiplicity in Melville's novel. If *Moby-Dick* is "ungraspable," it is only because it cannot be grasped through one approach only. And the fact that the novel lends itself to multiple approaches and numerous interpretations accounts for both its appeal to some and repulsion for others.

Indeed, the history of the book's rocky reception reflects the cumulative reader responses of those finding themselves reading the book today. Since its publication 150 years ago, *Moby-Dick* has evolved from its earliest reception as a "prose-poem" too artful to sell (and it did not) to a private, cherished delight savored by a limited readership (in part gay and mostly abroad) to a rediscovered sea narrative in the early twentieth century to, quite suddenly in the 1930s and 1940s, The Classic American Novel enjoyed by a wide range of world readers deeply engaged in its artistry and radical politics. Now, the work seems so intrinsic to America's many cultures and provides such an inspiration to artists, composers, novelists, playwrights, and filmmakers that it has reached the status of cultural icon. *Moby-Dick* is enough to put the fear of god in anyone, especially younger readers, who like myself at a certain rebellious age would refuse to read something simply because it was a "classic" and an "icon." And yet, to read this novel with students, colleagues, neighborhoods, or friends is to experience not simply the delight and instructive confusion of its challenging ideas and language but also the perpetual contemporariness of its voice, conflicts, imagery, and tale. *Moby-Dick* has withstood the nation's culture wars; is lionized by conservatives and liberals, gays and straights, alike; has meaning for minority readers, male and female; appeals to readers of all races; and has followings in Asia, the Pacific, and Europe as well as the Americas. *Moby-Dick* is a fiction for the world, and an international conference celebrating the 150th anniversary of its publication in the year 2001 seemed a good idea.

The twenty-one essays collected here from that conference reflect not only a range of problems and approaches but also the cosmopolitan perspective of international scholarship. They offer new thoughts on familiar topics: the novel's problematic structure, its sources and reinvention of the Bible, its Lacanian and post-Freudian psychology, and its rhetoric. They present new thoughts in new and renewed areas of interest as well: Melville's creative process, law and jurisprudence, Freemasonry and labor, race and measurement, Latin Americanism, and the native American. They offer fresh information about contemporary "versions" of *Moby-Dick* in translation and in performances on stage by Laurie Anderson and Rinde Eckert. They forecast its appearance on the Internet.

When Melville wrote *Moby-Dick,* he created a fiction that was a world unto itself, and that world, in a century and a half, has generated for a worldwide readership a culture of reading, scholarship, and art. It was only logical, then, that in the mid-1990s, after doing some math and calculating that 2001 would indeed mark the 150th anniversary of the publication of *Moby-Dick,* I set out to secure the blessings of the Melville Society and Hofstra University to mount an international conference (the Melville Society's third such affair) devoted to one book only. We called it "*Moby-Dick* 2001: An Interdisciplinary Celebration." Serious planning began in 1999. Mary K. Bercaw Edwards and Timothy Marr, who share the editorship of this volume with me, along with Berkshire County Historical Society director Susan Eisley and my Hofstra colleague Neil Donahue made up the conference committee that helped solicit, evaluate, and select out of the scores of proposals submitted the fifty or so papers for the conference itself. In the meantime, we were able to lure into the program novelist E. L. Doctorow and Melville scholar Walter E. Bezanson as keynote speakers as well as *Moby-Dick* illustrator Barry Moser as a featured presenter. Natalie Datloff, Athelene Collins-Prince, Richard Pioreck, Joanne Flood, and the staff of Hofstra's Cultural Center organized mailings, registration, rooms, coffee, music, meals, and all the rest of the nuts and bolts that go into mounting a conference of this size and magnitude. With the help of Hofstra Museum director Dean David Christman, curator Karen Albert, and Axinn Library Dean Daniel Rubey, we were able to offer during the three-day event various additional programs: a production of Orson Welles's *Moby-Dick Rehearsed* (directed by the Cultural Center's Bob Spiotto), a book display in the Hofstra Bookstore, a poetry reading conducted by Frank Van Zant, a Melville Walkabout in Manhattan led by Jack Putnam, and three exhibits collectively entitled *Artists After* Moby-Dick: *An Exhibition of Art, Books, and Manuscripts* curated by Elizabeth Schultz, Robert K. Wallace, and myself. A full-color catalog of these exhibits (including essays by each curator) was available at the time of the conference in the form of the October 2001 issue of *Leviathan: A Journal of Melville Studies,* published with generous donations of time and money by the Hofstra Museum, in particular Mary Wakeford and Dean Christman.

Well in advance of our scheduled event, hundreds of participants sent in their registrations; *Moby-Dick* 2001 was promising to become one of Hofstra's and the Melville Society's largest events. Then September 11. The attack on the World Trade Center was a sudden shock of recognition that changed our world, but for those of us on Long Island, it was a local event. Hofstra colleagues, alumni, students, family, and neighbors were lost; and though the campus is situated twenty miles from Manhattan, the smoking ruins were visible for weeks from the library's tenth floor. Astonishingly, as calls began to come in asking about the status of the conference, we were encouraged by a solid response of support for our decision to continue and hold the conference despite the fear of terrorism. Five weeks later, the anticipated two hundred and more participants arrived from around the world and congregated in Hofstra's Cultural Center and the library's tenth floor. With the altered Manhattan skyline in view, we came to speak, listen, debate, and learn, in peace for three days, October 18–20, 2001. It was not a typical conference by any means; there was, I will say it, some hugging, too, in both celebration and despair.

In preparing this volume derived from the *Moby-Dick* 2001 Conference, the editors asked participants to submit revised versions of their papers, and from those submitted, twenty-one were chosen for their argument, vision, style, and connection to the volume's rubrics. (Excellent essays that did not fit those rubrics and therefore did not receive a berth have appeared in issues of *Leviathan.*)

Five years have passed since *Moby-Dick* 2001 and September 11th. In that time, and perhaps not surprisingly, writers have editorialized about *Moby-*

Dick and terrorism. Just as scholar Howard Vincent and artist Gil Wilson, in the early 1950s, equated the figurative power of the white whale to the ominous uncontrollable power of the atomic bomb, so too have individuals today cast Moby Dick, a nineteenth-century symbol of nature's terror and awe, as a symbol of modern political terrorism. And while that analogy is understandable, it misses the mark. *Moby-Dick* is not so much about a terrorizing whale as it is about our reactions to terror, in particular Ahab's rage and Ishmael's more useful poetic penetration to its causes. As America continues its war in Iraq, and terror begets terror, the nation seeks "to fight some other world." But it has failed to know that world, or to see its "ghost spouting," or extract its meaning, or grasp the phantom of Islam and find a hand there we can hold. Now would be a good time to read *Moby-Dick* again, and with new eyes.

Introduction

Renderings of the Whale

MARY K. BERCAW EDWARDS AND TIMOTHY MARR

"There's another rendering now; but still one text. All sorts of men in one kind of world, you see."
—Flask in "The Doubloon"

In September of 1891, Herman Melville's earthly remains were laid to rest in Woodlawn Cemetery in the Bronx. His family erected a headstone inscribed only with his name and the dates of his life. Engraved on the memorial is an unfurled but blank writer's scroll superimposed over a vine. So different from the wordy funerary tablets described in "The Chapel" in *Moby-Dick*, or the eloquent epitaphs that Melville composed for the Civil War dead in *Battle-Pieces*, the tantalizing emptiness over his tomb has led many to ponder the meaning of this bequest of a "dumb blankness, full of meaning" (*MD* 195). Is it Melville's final statement on the vagaries of a public fame that had deserted him during his later years, symbolic of his earlier acknowledgment to Nathaniel Hawthorne that he was resigned to annihilation and parallel to his obituary in the *New York Times* that mistook his name as Henry? Or does this engraving without inscription teach lessons on the wisdom of silence—his ultimate comment on the futility of words as a means of expressing truth? (Fifteen years before he died, Melville wrote in *Clarel* that the pen was a "Dead feather of ethereal life! / Nor efficacious much, save when / It makes some fallacy more rife" (*Clarel* 1.12.89–90). Cynicism and despair aside, Melville remained an active and devoted writer until his last days. So perhaps we can read Melville's preference not to condense

1

the meaning of his life into a few words on a gravestone as an invitation to measure his achievement by reexamining the body of his writing rather than the absence of its author. We can best discover the memory and the meaning of Melville by grappling with the legacy of his literature. Ishmael supplies some insight when he writes, "deep memories yield no epitaphs" (*MD* 106). He memorializes Bulkington, the mysterious sailor with a large name, not with an engraved epitaph but with one of the shortest chapters in *Moby-Dick*—a "six-inch . . . stoneless grave"—called "The Lee Shore" (ch. 23), which attests that "all deep, earnest thinking is but the intrepid effort of the soul to keep the open independence of her sea" (107). "For small erections may be finished by their first architects," Ishmael elsewhere avers, but "grand ones, true ones, ever leave the copestone to posterity" (145).

One hundred and ten years after his death and only a twenty-nine-mile drive from his grave site, a few hundred of Melville's admirers convened at Hofstra University to celebrate a different milestone of his dynamic literary life. The year 2001 marked the sesquicentenary of the publication of his most revered work, *Moby-Dick, or The Whale.* As the selected essays from this conference collected here attest, Melville's legacy, far from being effaced, has flourished more fully with the coming of a new millennium. By the time of the centenary of the publication of *Moby-Dick* in 1951, Melville's work had already been recognized as "the one undoubted classic of American Literature" (Hillway and Mansfield viii). As in Melville's poem "The American Aloe on Exhibition," in which a plant that blooms only after the passage of a century adumbrates the resurrection of his literary reputation, the work of Melville's life has begun to see its most redolent fruition only in our times. One measure of the burgeoning recognition of *Moby-Dick* is the global prominence that Melville's book has achieved. The sesquicentenary occasioned the third international conference since the Melville Society of America (founded in 1945) first gathered abroad in Volos, Greece, in 1997, and proclaimed itself the Melville Society of the World. One of the great strengths of *Ungraspable Phantom* and the conference from which it grew resided in the contributions of scholars from Italy, Japan, Germany, and Brazil. Unlike the silence of the scroll at his grave, posterity has been both voluble and expansive in its attempts to fathom Melville and his mighty book.

Part of the symbolic power of *Moby-Dick* emerges from the confusion between the text and its central creature. Commentators regularly confound the book *Moby-Dick* (indicated by the hyphen) with the white whale Moby Dick itself—a conflation that is built into the title of the book, *Moby-Dick, or The Whale.* By naming his book after the white whale that had survived all human efforts to destroy him, Melville prefigured (and perhaps exulted in) his readers' inability to grasp the profundity of his own creation. Both whale and book are ungainly creatures that have circumnavigated the globe, whose bulk and legend have made onlookers and readers alike tremble with apprehension. And just as the white whale's power is premised on fabulous narrations about its immortality and ubiquity (for the whale as well as Ishmael presumably survives the battering and sinking of the *Pequod*), so Melville's book has itself become an icon of literary power, both to those who dive in and explore its rich language and to those who stay on the surface and respond to its spectral authority and reputation. Even though scholars—including deep divers with bloodshot eyes—have attempted to get at the beating heart of *Moby-Dick* with their critical lances, Melville's *Whale* still retains its elusive vitality as it breaches before new generations of readers. Ishmael mightily strives but ultimately fails to be "omnisciently exhaustive" in providing "a large and thorough sweeping comprehension" of the whale; similarly, these essays throw out new lines into the *Whale* that reveal anew both how majestic and how ultimately unfathomable Melville's creation remains (*MD* 455, 448).

Ungraspable Phantom incorporates twenty-one revised and expanded essays drawn from the seventy papers originally presented at the sesquicentenary conference. These various forays to measure the meanings of Melville's masterpiece are gathered into seven sections, each of which pursues the wonders of *Moby-Dick* along different tacks. The volume launches by exploring in its first two sections the compositional challenges that Melville confronted in creating his story and the ways that writing enabled him to author an antidote to the disruptive forces that threatened Ahab with madness. The next portion examines how the experience of reading *Moby-Dick* constitutes a commentary on the ethics of interpretation as well as a critique of conventional paradigms of cultural power. This criticism is amplified in two sections that historicize Melville's creative appraisal of how hierarchical inventions of law and race have systematically worked to destroy human community. The final two parts go beyond Melville's own words and century to measure the opportunities and challenges of translating *Moby-Dick* into German and Portuguese, as well as staging Melville's work within the multimedia venues of the theater, the cinema, and the World Wide Web. Collectively, these essays reveal a crew of contemporary Ishmaels who have arisen to chart afresh the significance of *Moby-Dick* in new critical waters.

"Modern American literature . . . begins with *Moby-Dick*," confides the novelist E. L. Doctorow after launching his insightful surmises into why Melville's book so drastically subverts the conventions of the novel. Examining the book through the eyes of a fellow master craftsman, Doctorow celebrates

Melville's "technical effrontery" and "perverse romanticism," discovering again the vibrant exuberance of a literary creation that issues forth more from poetic excess than from conventional plan. Doctorow observes how Melville found it necessary to stop the passage of time in order to fill the volume of *Moby-Dick*—"We expand to its bulk," narrates Ishmael (456). Continuing the section entitled "Constructing *Moby-Dick*: Breakdown and Redemption," Lori N. Howard explores other reasons why Melville, the pilot of *Moby-Dick*, may have chosen to tack back and forth between the ocean drama of Ahab's pursuit of the white whale and seemingly digressive "breakout" chapters devoted to cetological lore. Howard expands upon Elizabeth Renker's interpretations of Melville's anxiety about the vacancy of the white page to suggest that the jumbled form of *Moby-Dick*'s "intellectual chowder" was integral to finding the "sea-room" necessary to balance his desire to speak the truth with the realization that words could never intimate such a consummation. Giorgio Mariani's illuminating essay engages with the works of René Girard to explore Melville's paradoxical engagement with the sacrificial logic that necessitates violence in the service of the sacred. On the one hand, Melville employs the biblical book of Jonah and the relationship between Ishmael and Queequeg to denounce the vengeful ethic of scapegoating. Nevertheless, by the end of the book, Melville reconstitutes its "victimage mechanism" with the sacrifice of the *Pequod*, an act that leaves Melville ironically exulting in the feeling of being "spotless as the lamb." Melville himself partakes in the circular logic of scapegoating when he sacrifices Queequeg and destroys Ahab, confirming Doctorow's acknowledgment that "the story of Ahab is realized as the universal punishment."

The second group of essays compresses this inquiry into Melville's strategic authorship from a reflection on writerly pragmatics and religious ethics into an exploration of psychological interiority. During the centennial celebration at Williams College in 1951, Harvard psychologist Henry A. Murray presented "In Nomine Diaboli," which lauded *Moby-Dick* as Melville's "wicked" staging of the elemental Freudian battle between Ahab as a satanic "Captain of the Id" and the white whale as an oppressive cultural superego. Fifty years later, and in the second section of *Ungraspable Phantom*, "Man, Mind, Whale," we offer three essays that reexamine the subject of Melville's internal strife from different critical angles of analysis that dramatize the changing registers of psychoanalytic criticism. Dennis Williams interrogates Ahab's obsessive and perverse negotiations with the void from a Lacanian perspective. Diagnosing Ahab's attempts to construct a strong self that might alleviate his traumatic suffering, Williams explores how Ahab's defiant desire to raise the white whale renders the beast into such a fetish of fantasy that in a powerful sense

Ahab becomes Moby Dick. Taking a less clinical approach, Wendy Stallard Flory interprets Melville's moods of self-destructive depression by examining their manifestation in *Moby-Dick*'s "psychosymbolic" characterization. Focusing on the three mates (Stubb, Flask, and Starbuck), two harpooneers (Queequeg and Fedallah), and the cabin boy Pip, Flory explores how these symbolic characters represent different means of weathering the dark gales of suicidal moods represented by Ahab's monomania. Only Queequeg's healing model of calm self-reliance, adopted by Ishmael, engenders an openness to the inscrutable that enables Ishmael to survive Ahab's murderous fury and tell his symbolic story. Sanford E. Marovitz attends to the realistic register of how mental derangement is expressed in Melville's descriptions of Ahab and Pierre. Marovitz demonstrates how Melville developed his understandings of insanity from his historicist context beginning with psychological disturbances in his own family genealogy; and then ranging from his reading of Hawthorne, Shakespeare, and an entry on "insanity" by Dr. James C. Pritchard in the *Penny Cyclopaedia;* and also from his relationships with the authors Charles Fenno Hoffman and Dr. George J. Adler (his companion when he crossed the Atlantic in 1849), both of whom suffered from psychological aberrations. These models informed Melville with a realism of perception about mental trauma that enabled him to create the intensity of his tortured characters.

Melville navigated his own maelstrom of psychic distress in his works; he also examined the inability of the constructed discourse of law to create a just society. The essays by Kathryn Mudgett and John T. Matteson featured in "*Moby-Dick* and Law" situate *Moby-Dick* in the context of Melville's ambivalent relationship to the legal traditions of his time. Melville's father-in-law Lemuel Shaw (on whom he depended at times for financial assistance) held the post of Chief Justice of the Supreme Court of Massachusetts and, in his obedience to the law during the time of *Moby-Dick*'s composition, he ordered the return of fugitives to southern slave owners. Through her analysis of the confrontation of Starbuck and Ahab, Mudgett explores the larger cultural tension between the letter and spirit of the law in the formation of social order—the clash between the positive statutes of man-made law (represented by Oliver Wendell Holmes) and the moral authority of natural law (embodied in Abraham Lincoln's discourse). Sailors at sea could be considered as being in a sort of "situational slavery" because of the powers invested in a captain's legal authority. Ahab, taking advantage of his hegemonic ascendancy, violates the established social contract by instituting an extralegal mobocracy on board the *Pequod.* His skill at gaining the consent of the crew members highlights the limits of Starbuck's lawful resistance, and his internal crisis of moral authority reflects larger national dilemmas. Matteson expands this inquiry into

Melville's reckless lawlessness by analyzing the ways that *Moby-Dick* can be read as an "outlaw text." Like Melville's blank gravestone, *Moby-Dick* refuses to participate in the logic of commemoration upon which national memory was established. Matteson finds that systems of moribund precedents offer no stable location for inventing more vital traditions of memory. His essay ends by suggesting that an alternative ethic of living fellowship is perhaps best found in the community of readers who have gathered in broader and more diverse circles around *Moby-Dick* since its publication.

Ishmael poses the question, "And what are you, reader, but a Loose-Fish and a Fast-Fish, too?" (398). With this question, embedded within a chapter of legal discussion, Melville ponders the complex relationship that links the lines of his text with the freedom of interpretation he grants to his readers. The three essays in the section on "Reading and Mapping" explore the ramifications of Melville's creative pedagogy, one that is not only critical of confining conventions but also constitutive of more open and democratic alternatives. Michael Kearns considers the moral efficacy of Melville's book as a reading experience. Engaging with the critical ethics of Peter Levine and Lynne Tirrell (among others), Kearns discusses how Melville's narration refrains from determining moral evaluation. Rather, by inviting ethical contemplation, the thick narrative rhetoric of *Moby-Dick* elicits the experiential engagement of the reader and thereby dramatizes the challenges of individual agency. Kearns proposes the existence of a contextual moral sense premised on a commitment to empathy that invites readers into the shared ethos of the story. "All men live enveloped in whale-lines," asserts Ishmael, including the reader whom he imagines as "seated before your evening fire with a poker, and not a harpoon, by your side" (281). Carol Colatrella also examines how Melville's *Moby-Dick* valorizes and conditions the power of reading. Ahab's awe-inspiring authority over his crew and his unwillingness to alter his behavior in the face of new evidence signifies to Colatrella the failure of the antebellum project of reading as a rehabilitative reform. However, Ishmael (for whom "a whale ship was my Yale College and my Harvard" [112]) offers an alternative model of how reading can elevate moral character. His heterogeneous narration and consideration of the multivalent perspectives of others exemplifies the challenging ambiguity of the interpretative process and its unpredictable outcomes. Anne Baker's quite different approach to Melville's process of reading explores his ironic measurement of the cultural enterprise of mapping. She interprets Ishmael's attempt to quantify the whale skeleton in "A Bower in the Arsacides" and Ahab's obsession with mapping the migrations of the sperm whale in "The Chart" in light of Charles Wilkes's five-volume narrative of his circumglobal naval expedition of 1838–42. Baker insightfully elucidates Melville's involvement with the changing authority of religious and scientific discourses in her critical assessment of the incorporative process of national expansion.

Race, language, and society are the overarching concerns of the final three sections of this volume. *Moby-Dick* contains many figures representing race and language, with the largest number of such figures appearing in "Midnight, Forecastle" (ch. 40)—a chapter Wyn Kelley discusses at length in the concluding essay in this volume. This richness renders *Moby-Dick* an especially difficult text to translate, as Daniel Göske and Irene Ruth Hirsch illustrate so well. But it also allows the book to expand beyond literature and express itself in other media and arts, as Samuel Otter, Robert K. Wallace, and Wyn Kelley articulate from varying perspectives. The diverse essays on race and language locate the intersections between race, language, and perceived difference and reveal a deeper commonality.

Race—or rather our perception of human difference—is often perceived as a gulf between peoples. Observable features and characteristics have served as a basis for conflict, misunderstanding, and the glorification of one people over another. As humans attempting to share a complex world, we must ultimately choose to believe one of two things: either that humans are fundamentally capable of achieving deep understanding of each other despite cultural, ethnic, or linguistic differences, or that they are not. If one believes the latter, then one shuts the door on humanity—and takes a road that leads to Hitler or bin Laden. On the other hand, assuming that language, culture, and the historical and personal experience of a particular ethnic community can be easily understood leads to a mere cultural relativism that ignores the powerful influence of these factors. Melville explores the shifting sands of these options, observing throughout his work that individual personality, temperament, and experience often have a more marked effect on intersubjective understanding than broader cultural, linguistic, or ethnic variations.

Melville uses Queequeg to explore questions of race and language. Ishmael reacts with fear in his first encounter with Queequeg. Initially Queequeg seems hideous to Ishmael. "Landlord, for God's sake, Peter Coffin!" he shouts. "Watch! Coffin! Angels! save me!" (*MD* 23). But Ishmael overcomes his fear and replaces it with love and respect. Henceforth, he says, he "clove to Queequeg like a barnacle" (61). Melville portrays Queequeg as a figure that simultaneously perceives, seeks, and embodies underlying truth. The question for truth is exemplified in his life story. He has left the isolation of his native islands to seek understanding. Away from home, Queequeg must express his humanity in a tongue alien to himself, and to us as well. "You gette in," he tells Ishmael, "motioning to me with his tomahawk, and throwing the clothes to one side." Queequeg's humanity—and not Ishmael's, not that of the non-"savage" native speaker—crosses the gulf of race and language. "He really did this," Ishmael writes, "in not only a civil but a really kind and charitable way" (24).

In "Flood-Gates of the Wonder World: Race and the Americas," Mark K. Burns, Susan Garbarini Fanning, Rodrigo J. Lazo, and Yukiko Oshima explore various problems of race, language, and culture. Burns links the taxonomy of cetology to those of race. "Cetology" (ch. 32) establishes the futility of creating a system of classification—whether that system is based on cetological or racial differences. Like Burns, Fanning is interested in what she calls Melville's decentering of racial prejudice. She explores Melville's use of the satiric device of the feast, which he employs to invert hierarchy. For instance, in "The Cabin Table" (ch. 34), the official feast presided over by the white officers is followed by an inverted feast in which nonwhite harpooneers are served by the white Dough-Boy. Melville, Fanning argues, finally leaves glints of hope in *Moby-Dick* that a regeneration from the evil of racism is possible.

Lazo's essay investigates Melville's engagement with Latin America. *Moby-Dick*, Lazo argues, approaches difference by playing with stereotypes and raising questions about them. Melville's narrators set up stereotypes and then force us to recognize the problems with our too facile acceptance of those stereotypes. Lazo contends that Melville's fiction calls into question the very designation of the Hispanic, or Spanish American, world as a unitary entity. In a similar vein, Oshima considers Melville's encounter with Native Americans. In particular, she investigates the ties between *Moby-Dick* and Catharine Maria Sedgwick's novel of the 1676–77 King Philip's War, *Hope Leslie* (1827). Oshima draws parallels between the vengeful leaders of the Pequot tribe and *Pequod* crew, between the interracial marriages of Oneco/Faith and Queequeg/Ishmael, and between the arms of Sedgwick's Magawisca and Melville's Queequeg (that literally, sacrificially, and symbolically save the lives of their beloved). The more strongly the reader feels the sense of unfairness in not seeing Queequeg survive, she argues, the more strongly we question the validity of our preconception of the incompatibility or coexistence of the races. All four of these essays, then, ask readers to reconsider the degree to which perception constructs race.

In "Very Like a Whale: *Moby-Dick* in Translation," Daniel Göske and Irene Ruth Hirsch turn our attention from race to language. The very difficulty of translating *Moby-Dick* speaks to both the profound differences between languages and the deeper commonality of the humanity set forth by Melville in *Moby-Dick:* the "Anacharsis Clootz deputation from all the isles of the sea, and all the ends of the earth" (121).

Language represents a much greater diversity than race. Consider, for example, Melville's own multilingual derivations of the word "whale" in "Etymology" (*MD* xv–xvi). Language conjoins and enables thought, meaning, expression, and understanding; it serves as the structure through which humans shape their experience of the world. Entire vocabularies and grammars, the very construction of one's sense of self, vary from language to language. Hence, differences among individual languages may exert a more profound influence on consciousness than those between the putative races.

Linguists seek the unifying deep structures of language—the connections between language, symbol, and grammar. What part of language is hard-wired in the brain? What part is shaped by individual culture? Linguists have yet to find the structuralist's universal formula for all language. The links between language as used and the core of meaning it transmits remain veiled. The linguists' quest echoes Ahab's. He, too, searches for the "unknown but still reasoning thing [that] puts forth the mouldings of its features from behind the unreasoning mask" (*MD* 164). Among biologists, the human genome project is another attempt to articulate the hidden structures of our being: it is an extraordinary, epoch-making example of humans wrestling with "the ungraspable phantom of life" (*MD* 5). Linguists and geneticists alike grapple with what it means to be human. They seek out deep structures—a core humanity—through individual forms of expression: words and genes, language and race. People in their individual races express the same core humanity; similarly, all languages are expressions of this same core. Language and race are the human translation of meaning.

Melville knew only the early manifestations of modern linguistics and biology, but like Emerson, he knew that expressions of our core humanity in both word and flesh are symbols. Queequeg's physiognomy is covered with symbols. He represents the intersection between race, language, and culture. Pip does likewise. The novel's black cabin boy is distinguished not only for his race, but also, as Wyn Kelley reminds us, for the ways he uses language. And it is Pip, lowliest of the crew aboard the *Pequod,* who is paired with Captain Ahab, "lord over the Pequod" (*MD* 474). Pip dies in madness, but as most cultures aver, madness can open the gateway to ultimate truth. Pip passes through that gateway, but he is restricted by language and race from expressing what he has seen. Pip "saw God's foot upon the treadle of the loom, and spoke it; and therefore his shipmates called him mad" (414). Speaking only the nonsense of irrationality, Pip cannot fully articulate his encounter, and as a small black boy, he is limited by the invisibility conferred upon his race, "daft with weakness" (522), as the old Manxman says. Yet his nonsense symbolizes our own inability to translate truth: Pip's most penetrating words are "I look" (434).

Göske writes eloquently of the difficulties, challenges, and joys of translating, in the words of critic Richard Brodhead, "a book in love with language" (*New Essays* 6). The translator must be playful and inventive as well as disciplined and subservient. It is not whether a translation *ought* to recreate an author's idiosyncratic use of language, but *how* it should do so. As editor of the Hanser edition, the first complete German translation of *Moby-Dick* in fifty years, Göske and fellow translator Matthew Jendis resisted the temptation to diminish Melville's "thumping rhetoric" into something bland and prosy. Toward the end of his essay, Göske considers the difficulties of rendering the phrase "Call me Ishmael" in another language. Göske's essay inspires the reader afresh with the wondrous language of *Moby-Dick*.

Hirsch, too, reflects on translation in her study of Portuguese renderings of *Moby-Dick* for the Brazilian market. She posits three types of translations: an integral, faithful version of the text; a covert translation, in which omissions and suppressions are not acknowledged; and an illustrated adaptation for children, which is clearly labeled as such. In her discussion of the integral, faithful version of the text, Hirsch, like Göske, considers the pitfalls of being "faithful" to the original text. Both note that a faithful translation can flatten ambiguities and destroy idiomatic expressions. How faithful can a translator be, Hirsch asks, to Melville's endless semicolons? All three of Hirsch's categories of translation are problematic, and her inquiry addresses many of the same questions previously asked by Göske.

As Göske and Hirsch indicate, *Moby-Dick* circles the globe in translation. It is confined neither to the American market nor to the English language. In "Modern Breachings: *Moby-Dick* on Stage and Web," Samuel Otter, Robert K. Wallace, Elizabeth Schultz, and Wyn Kelley consider other ways in which *Moby-Dick* is freed from confinement. In essence, they offer other forms of translation: the adaptation of *Moby-Dick* onto stage, Web, and, to a lesser extent, film. Such translation is not, of course, in Hirsch's words, an integral, faithful version of the text. Cultural translation allows *Moby-Dick* to free itself and float away from the text and to incorporate interpretation. *Moby-Dick* has become a resource that enables other types of cultural work in other media. This volume does not include the astounding range of artwork displayed at the *Moby-Dick* 2001 conference nor the panel discussion presented by the artists about their work. These materials appear in two issues of *Leviathan:* the October 2001 exhibition catalog (vol. 3, no. 2) and the March 2003 *Moby-Dick at 150* issue (vol. 5, no. 1). Through art, stage, film, and Web, the message of *Moby-Dick* is updated in contemporary contexts, reaching larger audiences and causing them to reconsider the text itself. Translations into other art forms render *Moby-Dick* accessible to many who may not have attempted reading it out of fear of its size or its linguistic complexities. They also enable those familiar with the work to reconsider the text in imaginative ways. "I look, you look, he looks; we look, ye look, they look," Pip says at the end of "The Doubloon" (ch. 99; *MD* 434).

Otter argues that the most straightforward responses to *Moby-Dick*, like the 1956 film starring Gregory Peck, are the least interesting. Instead of discussing these, he concentrates on Laurie Anderson's *Songs and Stories from Moby-Dick* (1999) and Rinde Eckert's *And God Created Great Whales* (2000). Interestingly, Anderson in *Songs and Stories* is drawn to the cetology chapters of *Moby-Dick,* chapters that are often slighted in film and stage. She mistrusts the narrative tantalizations in *Moby-Dick* (about which Göske has written so eloquently) and is especially leery of the line "Call me Ishmael": there is no Ishmael in Anderson's cast of characters. In a discussion encompassing not only Anderson and Eckert, but also Orson Welles, Charles Olson, Frank Stella, and C. L. R. James, Otter writes that with "Call me Ishmael," the narrator invites, enjoins, seduces—and apprehends his readers.

In Rinde Eckert's *And God Created Great Whales* (2000), Wallace finds two dramas: the immediate drama of whether Nathan, a piano tuner who is writing an opera based on *Moby-Dick,* will complete his opera before he loses his mind and the deeper drama of whether he will be humanized by Olivia, the diva who is his Muse. Eckert's homage to Melville fuses audacity and reverence by avoiding Melville's vortex. "You can get caught in Melville's vortex," Eckert told Wallace, "because it's so compelling. At some point I had to respectfully put him at arm's length and say the only way I'm going to do service to his book is if I absorb it and make it mine." Like Eckert, women have tried to absorb *Moby-Dick* and make it "mine," as Schultz illustrates in "Feminizing *Moby-Dick.*" She notes: "What I term the feminizing of *Moby-Dick* represents a cultural impetus propelled primarily by women artists asserting their rights to claim *Moby-Dick* for women as well as to critique it on their behalf." Schultz concentrates on Patty Lynch's *Wreck of the Hesperus,* JoAnne Spies' "Me & Melville," Bill Peters' *Hunting for Moby Dick,* and Ellen Driscoll's *Ahab's Wife, or The Whale.*

Absorbing *Moby-Dick* and making it "mine" also forms the subtext of Kelley's essay. Kelley created an electronic archive of images, music, and film for "Midnight, Forecastle" (ch. 40). Her students could use this archive to make *Moby-Dick* "mine." Kelley's most compelling argument is her own multimedia essay, "Pip's Soliloquy," which centers on both race and language. Pip, Kelley writes, performs the fear—of the whale, of God, of Ahab, of whiteness—that the men have not dared give a name or recognize in themselves. As a boy in the liminal space of adolescence, Pip is free to utter the men's fears and to challenge the great white God above. The use of multimedia allows for a more flexible, less thesis-driven form of argument.

As collected here, these essays (from the Latin word *exagium* meaning a weighing) attempt to capture and ponder the meaning of Melville's textual and biological whale. They are the equivalent of the process of "trying-out" on a whaleship. Just as a whale's blubber is sliced into pieces and boiled in large pots where it is rendered into a valuable essence—sperm oil—to be stored and later sold, so the reader "tries out" the language of *Moby-Dick*. While parts of the whale's body are fed to the very fire used to boil down other parts from the same body, the result is a substance that produced in Melville's time the very light that illuminated the reading of *Moby-Dick*. The word *render*, literally meaning to give back, has other meanings beyond the melting down of flesh. To render also connotes both retributive transaction as well as the actual process of artistic representation and critical interpretation. Melville exhaustively anatomizes the whale from its wrinkled brow to its flexile tail, from its translucent skin to its dry bones. Yet despite such prodigious effort, Melville cautions us: "you had best not be too fastidious in your curiosity touching this Leviathan" (264). He confesses that "there is no earthly way of finding out precisely what the whale really looks like" (264), asserting that it "is only to be seen at sea in unfathomable waters, . . . [and] out of that element it is a thing eternally impossible for mortal man to hoist him bodily into the air, so as to preserve all his mighty swells and undulations" (263). In reexamining the bones and sinews of Melville's book, these essays serve as illuminating afterwords that rehearse, in the surviving spirit of Ishmael's resistless inquiry, the incapacity of lines of hemp to raise the mystery of the white whale, or lines of language to measure the meaning of *Moby-Dick*. But as the intricacy and inclusivity of Ishmael's narration demonstrates, it is in the assaying that the very ungraspability of the whale is itself even comprehended. "I try all things; I achieve what I can" (345), wrote Melville of Ishmael's search to interpret the face of the Sperm Whale: "I but put that brow before you. Read it if you can" (347). These essays attest that Melville's accomplishment was a mighty one that is signified most fully by the ways that his *Whale* still inscrutably swims the seas of the wonder world.

Constructing *Moby-Dick:*
Breakdown and Redemption

Composing *Moby-Dick*

What Might Have Happened

The Astman Distinguished Lecture

E. L. Doctorow

I for one, appreciate my courage in speaking here this evening. For what can I presume to say about Melville's *Moby-Dick* to a congregation of literary harpooners who have heaved their darts time and time again into the textual hide of this Leviathan? I suspect that while I seem to be standing in an academic setting facing a company of scholars, I am actually in the foc'sle of the *Pequod* with the oil lamp swinging from the headbeam and throwing lights and shadows over the faces of a crew of savage old salts who have lit their pipes and downed their drams of literary theory and await the words from me that will persuade them to throw me to the sharks.

For we know from Melville that we are never in one place alone at any given minute, but in two—in the present that is the past, or on the land that is the sea, or in the sea that is the soul, or in the novel that is God's ineffable realm.

There is only one recourse for me, and that is to speak of *Moby-Dick* as a working writer looking at another writer's work. I will leave the profoundly ambiguous art object to you. I will leave the thematics, the influences, the symbols, the historico-ideological contexts to you. I will attempt to see what is being done in this book and perhaps why it is being done. I think that is the only way I can sensibly and truthfully go about this talk, as a writer seeing the writerly things, making the practical if awed, and envious observations in presumptive colleagiality of one literary tradesman with another.

I can claim a personal relationship to Melville and his works, having read *Moby-Dick* three and a half times. The half time came at the age of ten when I found a copy in my grandfather's library. It was one of a set of great sea novels all bound in green cloth, and it was fair sailing until the cetology stove me in. I first read the book in its entirety, (and *Typee, Omoo, Billy Budd,* and "The Encantadas," and "Benito Cereno," and "Bartleby," for that matter) as an undergraduate at Kenyon College. Later, as a young editor at the New American library, a mass-market paperback publisher, I persuaded a Kenyon professor, Denham Sutcliffe, to write an afterword to the Signet Classic edition of *Moby-Dick,* and so read the book again by way of editorial preparation. In anticipation of this evening I have after too many years read *Moby-Dick* for the third time. And the surprise to me, at my age now, is how familiar the voice of that book is, and not merely the voice, but the technical effrontery, and not merely the technical effrontery, but the character and rhythm of the sentences. And so with some surprise, I've realized, how much of my own work, at its own level, hears Melville, responds to his perverse romanticism, endorses his double dipping into the accounts of realism and allegory, as well as the large risk he takes speaking so frankly of the crisis of human consciousness, that great embarrassment to us all that makes a tiresome prophet of anyone who would speak of it.

Hawthorne I have always understood as a writer who affected me deeply and I have realized my sometime inclination to write romances in the Hawthornian sense—novels set in the past that would cure up real life into a gamier essence. But whatever rule breaking I have done in my work I probably owe to Melville, Hawthorne's devoted admirer, but also his saboteur, in taking the elements of the well-constructed novel and making a cubist composition of them.

Literary history finds among the great novelists a few who achieved their greatness from an impatience with the conventions of narrative. Virginia Woolf composed *Mrs. Dalloway* from the determination to write a novel without a plot or indeed a subject. And then Joyce, of course: Like Picasso who was an expert draftsman before he blew his art out of the water, James Joyce proved himself in the art of narrative writing before he committed his assaults upon it. The author of the sterling narrative *Typee* and *Omoo* precedes Joyce with his own blatant subversion of the narrative compact he calls *Moby-Dick.* Yet I suspect that, in this case, the subversion may have been if not inadvertent, then only worked out tactically given the problem of its conception. I would guess that what Melville does in *Moby-Dick* is not from a grand preconceived aesthetic (Joyce: I will pun my way into the brain's dreamwork; I will respect the protocols of grammar and syntax but otherwise blast the English language all to hell) but from the necessity of dealing with the problem inherent in constructing an entire nineteenth-century novel around a single life-and-death encounter with a whale. The encounter clearly having to come as the climax of his book, Melville's writing problem was how to pass the time until then—until he got the *Pequod* to the Southern Whale fisheries and brought the white whale from the depths, Ahab crying "There she blows—there she blows! A hump like a snow hill! It is Moby Dick!" She blows, I point out to you not until page 537 of a 566-page book—in my old paperback Rhinehart edition.

A writer lacking Melville's genius might conceive of a shorter novel, its entry point being possibly closer in time to the deadly encounter. And with maybe a flashback or two thrown in. A novelist of today, certainly, would eschew exposition as far as possible, let the reader work out for herself what is going on, which is a contemporary way of maintaining narrative tension. Melville's entry point, I remind you, is not at sea aboard the *Pequod*, not even in Nantucket: he locates Ishmael in Manhattan, and staying in scene every step of the way, takes him to New Bedford, has him meet Queequeg at the Spouter Inn, listen to a sermon, contrive to get them both to Nantucket, meet the owners of the *Pequod*, endure the ancient hoary device of a mysterious prophecy; and it isn't until Chapter 20 which begins "A day or two passed" that he elides time. Until that point, some ninety-four pages into the book, the writing has all been a succession of unbroken real time incidents. Another ten pages elapse before the *Pequod* "thrust[s] her vindictive bows into the cold malicious waves" (ch. 23).

I wouldn't wonder if Melville at this point, the *Pequod* finally underway, stopped to read what he had written to see what his book was bidding him to do.

Now this is sheer guesswork, of course. I have not read the major biographies, and I don't know what Melville himself may have said about the writing of *Moby-Dick* beyond characterizing it as a "wicked book." Besides, whatever any author says of his novel is of course another form of the fiction he practices and is never, never, to be trusted.

Perhaps Melville had everything comfortably worked out before he began, though I doubt it. Perhaps he had a draft completed of something quite conventional before his writer's sense of crisis set in. The point to remember is the same that Faulkner once reminded his critics of: that they see a finished work and do not dream of the chaos of trial and error and torment from which it has somehow emerged.

No matter what your plan for a novel—and we know Herman was inspired by the account of an actual whaling disaster (the destruction of the ship *Essex* in 1819) and we know whaling was a subject he could speak of with authority of personal experience, and we know he understood as well as the most commercial practitioner of the craft, that a writer begins with an advantage who can report on a kind of life or profession out of the ken of the ordinary reader—nevertheless, I say that no matter what your plan or inspiration, or trembling recognition for an idea that you know belongs to you, the strange endowment you set loose by the act of writing is never entirely under your control. It cannot be a matter solely of willed expression. Somewhere, from the depths of your being you find a voice: it is the first and most mysterious moment of the creative act. There is no book without it. If it takes off it appears to you to be self-governed. To some degree you will write to find out what you are writing. And you have no sense of possession for what comes onto the pages–what you have is a sense of discovery.

So let us propose that having done his first hundred or so pages of almost entirely land-based writing, Melville stopped to read what he had written. What have I got here?—The author's question.

"This Ishmael—he is logorrheaic! He is entirely confident of holding my attention whatever he writes about, and whatever he writes about, *he takes his time.* With this Ishmael, I have a hundred or so land-based pages, so if I am to keep the proportion of the thing, I will need five hundred at sea. And if the encounter with the Whale is my climax it will need—what?—maybe four hundred and fifty pages of sailing before I find him? Migod."

So there was the problem. His sentences had a texture that could conceivably leave his book wallowing with limp sails in a becalmed narrative sea.

I will not speculate that there may have come to Melville one of those terrible writer's moments of despair that can be so useful in fusing as if with lightning the book so far with the book to come. In any event he would for his salvation have to discover that his pages manifested not one but two principles of composition. First, a conventional use of chronological time and a narrator, Ishmael, whose integrity was maintained. And that in this extended opening or land prelude there was dutiful attendance to the dramatic necessities of conventional fiction—e.g. the biblical Elijah figure who issues his cryptic prophecy, the suspenseful non-appearance above deck of Captain Ahab—and surely at this early stage, as we readers can see, the use of humor, good abiding humor of language, and loving character depiction, that suggests the shrewdness of a writer who knows his story will end in horror. (Perhaps the least of the things Shakespeare taught Melville was the value of tangential humor to the bloodiest stories: it establishes the hierarchy of human souls that brings the few at the top into tragic distinction.)

All well and good. Melville could project from these traditional storytelling observances a whole series of narrative tropes. Ahab would have to allow the crew the hunting of other whales. So there was that action. Bad weather and worse could reasonably be invoked. There might be the threat of piracy. As Ahab's maniacal single-mindedness became apparent to the crew, some of them, at least, might contest his authority. Other whalers were abroad around the world. They could be met and inquired of. As indeed there are what?—perhaps eight or nine such encounters—the *Albatross,* the *Town-Ho,* the *Virgin,* and on to the *Bachelor,* the *Rachel,* the *Delight*—each ship the occasion for a story, and depending on the usefulness to Ahab's passion, a matter for his approval or rejection. Given this pattern, a habitual recourse of the narrative, we readers today can make a case for *Moby-Dick* as a road novel. (This is not a misnomer when we constantly find through the text equivalences between sea and land, the representation of the one by means of the other. When Ishmael takes up the *Town-Ho* story of Steelkilt and Radney, he steps out of the time of the book and takes us to Peru to tell it, at which point we know he has read *Don Quixote* and perhaps *Jacques the Fatalist.*)

But while in these first 105 pages, Ishmael's integrity as a narrator is maintained, and the setup for the voyage suggests an assiduous, and conventional narrative, there is something else, possibly less visible, a second principle of composition lurking there. It would come to Melville incipiently as a sense of dissatisfaction with his earlier books, and their gift for nautical adventure. While we may know that there is nobody, before or since, who has written better descriptions of the sea and its infinite natures and the wrathful occasions it can deliver, to Melville himself this talent would be of no consequence as he contemplated the requirements of his *Moby-Dick,* and felt the aching need to do this book, to bring it to fruition out of the depths of his consciousness—to resolve into a finished visionary work, everything he knew.

So he looks again at his Ishmael. And he finds in him the polymath of his dreams: "Yes Ishmael tells a chronological story well enough. But look how he does it. He breaks time up into places, things, like someone planting the stones of a mosaic one by one. He has read his Shakespeare. He knows European history. He is conversant with biblical scholarship, philosophy, ancient history, classical myth, English poetry, lands and empires, geography. Why stop there? He can express the latest thinking in geology (he would know about the tectonic plates), the implications of Darwinism, and look, his enlightened cultural anthropology (that I have lifted from *Typee*) grants Queequeg a system of belief finally no more bizarre or less useful than Christendom's."

"I can make this fellow an egregious eavesdropper, so talented as to be able to hear men think, or repeat their privately muttered soliloquies verbatim. See when he finally gives me some action on the schooner from New Bedford to Nantucket—when Queequeg first roughs up a mocking passenger and then saves him from drowning—and this is a nautical adventure despite all—see how when he finally allows a physical action, Ishmael hurries through it to get back to his contemplative ways. My Ishmael was born to be a tactless writer of footnotes—yes, I will make him the inexhaustible author of my water world."

And it is a fact that no sooner are we at sea, in Chapter 24, "The Advocate," does Ishmael step out of time in a big way and give us the first of his lectures on whaling. Melville's big gamble has begun—to pass the time by destroying it, to make a new thing of the novel form by blasting its conventions.

I know this to be true: Herman Melville may have been theologically a skeptic, philosophically an Existentialist, personally an Isolato, with a desolation of spirit as deep as any sea dingle—but as a writer he is exuberant.

Even if my scenario is false, and Melville did not need to stop and read what he had written at the point the *Pequod* goes to sea, even so, at a hundred or so pages into a book that is working, it begins to give things back to you, it begins to generate itself from itself, a matter, say, of its stem cells differentiating into the total organism. Even with a completed draft of conventional storytelling before him, when the author reads to see what he has done, the lightning strikes early on, it is the book's beginnings that tell him what finally he must do by way of revision. Thus, from Father Mapple's pulpit like a ship's prow, a rope ladder its means of access, from the story of Jonah as a seaman's sermon, from the Try Pots chowder house, and the whalebone tiller of the *Pequod*, we derive a landless realm; and by the time much later in the book, when the ship and its crew are four hundred and fifty pages at sea, Ishmael tells us we—*we*—are still in Noah's flood, that it is eternal, with only the whale able to "spout his frothed defiance to the skies" (ch. 105), we need no persuading—the story of Ahab is realized as the universal punishment.

It interests me that Ishmael who is the source of Melville's inspired subversion of the narrative compact must therefore be himself badly used by the author. Ishmael is treated with great love but scant respect—he is Ishmael all right in being so easily cast out, and if he is called back, it is only to be cast out again. I wonder if it was not a private irony of his author that the physically irresolute Ishmael, with roughly the same protoplasm of the Cheshire cat, is the *Pequod*'s sole survivor. I can't help feeling that he would not be so, if his continued life was not factually necessary to give voice to the tale—Melville's grudging deference to the simple Job-ic logic of storytelling.

In any event what Ishmael certainly knows about is whaling—despite his greenhorn status aboard the *Pequod*. He represents himself as having been new to the practice at the time, but by way of compensation, has become well versed in the scientific literature. Like E. A. Poe, he has a habit of citing extra-literary sources. Now let me talk about Poe, for a moment. I don't know whether Melville read Poe, or what he thought of him, but among Poe's bad writing habits is his attempt to provide authority for the tale he is about to tell by citing factual precedents for it. He begins "The Premature Burial," for example, by citing three or four newspaper stories about people buried prematurely—just to establish that this sort of thing can happen. He would give his tale then the authority of borrowed fact. He argues from scientific authority in "Descent into the Maelstrom" that the Nordic waters are known to be susceptible to just such terrifying phenomena as he will describe. Poe likes to argue his way into his stories. It's the fiction writer's admission after all that he is not a factualist, that he stands outside the culture of empirical truth. And as such it is a fatally defensive move. On occasion, especially at the beginning of *Moby-Dick,* Melville might seem to be doing the same defensive thing: In the very first chapter, "Loomings," he cites men on Manhattan docks fixed in "ocean reveries" and argues the narcissistic attraction of rivers, lakes, and oceans to make Ishmael's decision to take to the sea more than just a personal matter. He cites authorities for the existence of albino whales. And in "The Advocate" chapter, of course, he argues for the social beneficence, the respectability, the grandeur, and so forth of the whaling profession. This sort of non-narrative case-making to justify the telling of the tale would be as much of a mistake as it is in Poe—if that was as far as Melville took it. But of course, unlike Poe, Melville doesn't stop there, he will load his entire book with time stopping pedagogy—he will give us essays, trade lore, taxonomies, opinion surveys; he will review the pertinent literature,—he will carry on to excess outside the narrative. It is indisputable in my mind that excess in literature is its own justification. It is a sign of genius, and in this case, turns the world on its head so that just what is a weakness when done in modest proportion is transformative as a consistent recourse and persuades the reader finally into the realm so nakedly proselytized.

And then of course the excess touches every corner, every nook and cranny below deck, every tool and technical fact of the life aboard the *Pequod,* and everything upon it from Ahab's prosthesis, to the gold doubloon he nails upon the mast, from Queequeg's tattoos, to the leaking oil barrels in the bowels of the ship. The narrative bounds forward from the discussion of *things.* So finally we look at the details and discover something else: whatever it is, Melville will provide us the meanings to be taken from it. The doubloon upon the mast will be described in such a way, its zodiac signs, its Andean symbols, a tower, a crowing cock, and so forth, as to affirm Ahab's rumination that it is emblematic of an Ahabian universe, the given horror of the half-known life. Queequeg's hieroglyphic tattoos are a "complete theory of the heavens and the earth, and a mystical treatise on the art of attaining truth; so that Queequeg in his own proper person was a riddle to unfold; a wondrous work in one volume" (ch. 110) though he himself could not hope to understand it. And of course Moby Dick's color is lifted from him to show "by its indefiniteness" (not a color so much as a visible absence of color) "the heartless voids and immensities of the universe," white being the "colorless, all-color of atheism from which we shrink," a "mystical cosmetic" colorless in itself that paints all Nature like a "harlot" (ch. 42).

Melville's irrepressible urge to make the most of everything suggests the mind of a poet. The significations, the meaningful enlargements he makes of tools, coins, colors, existent facts are the work of a lyric poet, a maker of metaphorical meanings, for whom unembellished linear narrative is but a pale joy. So I will say here Melville's solution is not a novelist's solution; it is a poet's solution. *Moby-Dick* can be read as a series of ideas for poems. It is a procession of ideational events. Melville's excesses are not mere pedagogical interruptions of the narrative; nor are they there to provide authority for the tale. They burst from the book as outward flarings or star births, as a kind of cosmology, finally, to imply a multiplicity of universes, one inside another, endlessly and each one of which could have its novel as the sea has this one.

At this point however I see that I am in danger of breaking the rules of this talk and am threatening to come up somewhat off the ground level observation of the writer at work. You will notice I have avoided the autonomy-of-literature argument, or the temptation to speak of the recurrent theme in Melville of the perversities of captainship, the rule of law, the law of men, in the universe of a ship, or of Ahab as an archetype, for example, and to find him today in such beings as Slobodan Milosevic, and so forth. I have not done any of that, but when I talk about the book as a procession of ideational events, or a metaphoric cosmology, I begin to get nervous.

So let me veer off here to another claim I can make in my homage to Herman Melville. Many years ago I bought a home in Sag Harbor. Now, you know Sag Harbor, at the east end of Long Island, was a whaling town, and for some years in the nineteenth century with the whaling industry booming, its denizens had reason to believe that someday with its deep water harbor it would rival New York as a major port. Melville mentions Sag Harbor, gives Queequeg a funny anthropological moment there, and even today it has maintained its village character; a town that time has fortunately forgot: preserved are the larger Main Street homes with their widows' walks built by the whaling captains, as well as the smaller more modest cottages on the side streets where the ordinary seamen left their families when they went to sea. The village cemetery on Jermain Avenue provides gravestone records of the lost captains, the sunken ships, in this most dangerous of trades (so dangerous that it makes the age of Ahab the single most unlikely fact of the tale—most of the captains of the Sag Harbor whaling fleet were quite young, and if they were lucky enough to live to the age of forty or forty-five, they were likely to be burned-out and land-bound forever after—it was a young man's get rich quick game, whaling, in my understanding). But as I say, with Sag Harbor certainly a busy active whaling community, Melville chose to work his fleet out of Nantucket. Now, I know the *Essex* hailed from Nantucket, and he himself went whaling out of Fairhaven right next door and that he knew the area well enough. But I would like to believe he chose Nantucket because he brilliantly realized the Quaker speech that predominated there was his means of access, his bridge, to the Elizabethan diction he so exuberantly exercises in his Shakespearean riffs. I will make that my theory of why he chose Nantucket over Sag Harbor where the Quakers were very small in number, and there were no thees and thous and dosts to segue him into the soliloquies and dramatic dialogues that he cannot resist. And why would he? Perhaps you know—I don't—any other writer in history as uncannily able to iterate Shakespeare—at moments apt to be equal to him—with his monologues and scenes—but also to so successfully adopt the social structuring of his characters, their hierarchies of rank, comedy and tragedy, their parallel relationships to those in the master's plays all of which I assume you have annotated in your scholarship—this is the exuberance in one of its manifestations, the irrepressible love of language that causes Melville to be so eccentric, quirky, inconstant, toward the narrative demands of fiction as to render his book on publication unsaleable.

Certainly *Moby-Dick* is a very *written* book. If I may be crude for a moment, I'll distinguish those writers who make their language visible, who draw attention to it in the act of writing and don't let us forget it—Melville, Joyce, and Nabokov in our own time, the song and dance men, the strutting dandies of literature—from those magicians of the real who write to make their language invisible, like lit stage scrims that pass us through to the scene behind so that we see the life they are rendering as if no language is producing it. Tolstoy and Chekhov are in this class. Clearly, neither one nor the other method can be said to be *the way*. But the one is definitely more reader-friendly than the other. And Melville in his journey from *Typee* to *Moby-Dick* abandons the clear transparent pools of the one, for the opaque linguistic seas of the other.

In case you are curious: had I aspired to a scholarly position this evening, I would have invoked Northrop Frye's category of Menippean Satire. For after all, it can be argued that *Moby-Dick* is that—an Anatomy—a big kitchen sink sort of book into which the irrepressible author, a writing fool, throws everything he knows, happily changing voice, philosophizing, violating the consistent narrative, dropping in every arcane bit of information he can think of, reworking his research, indulging in parody, unleashing his pure powers of description—so that the real *Moby-Dick* is the voracious maw of the book swallowing the English language.

By way of conclusion, let me admit finally what you may by now have realized—that in interpreting Melville's writing process, perversely applying textual analysis of a sort to read from the finished book what it might have gone through to become itself, I am insisting not so much on the literal truth of my claims but on their validity as another kind of fiction.

I confess I have given you tonight not a speech so much as a story—a parable of the grubbiness and glory of the writer's mind.

We celebrate this evening the hundred and fiftieth anniversary of a revolutionary novel. Its importance is not negated by the fact that our culture has changed and we now no longer hunt the whale as much as we try to save it. In fact, according to newspaper reports, whale watching—not hunting—is now the greatest threat to their well-being, or whalebeing. Going out in sightseeing boats to frolic with the whales is a bigger industry now, producing more income than fishing for them, and threatens to disrupt their migratory patterns and thus their organized means of survival. In fact, one can imagine *Moby-Dick* as possibly a prophetic document, if one day a Leviathan rises from the sea in total exasperation of being watched by these alien humans, humans who once at least in hunting them were marginally in the natural world, but now in only observing them are in that realm no longer, and so rightly destined for the huge open jaw, and the mighty crunch, and the triumphant slap of the horizontal flukes.

But whatever the case, I can assure you Ernest Hemingway was wrong when he said modern American literature begins with *Huckleberry Finn.* It begins with *Moby-Dick,* the book that swallowed European civilization whole. And we only, are escaped alone on our own shore, to tell our tales.

"Ungainly Gambols" and Circumnavigating the Truth

Breaking the Narrative of *Moby-Dick*

LORI N. HOWARD

Since water still flows though we cut it with swords
and sorrow returns though we drown it with wine
since the world can in no way answer to our cravings
I will loosen my hair tomorrow and take to a fishing boat
—Li Po

Writing *Moby-Dick,* Herman Melville takes to his fishing boat and then perhaps dreads completing this particular voyage or changes destinations, dragging out the composition longer than he did in writing any of his previous books. When he slams hard into the white whale wall of the page, possibly despairing at what words to write or how to get at the elusive truths deep below the tale, Melville apparently writes anything pertaining to the grand venture of whaling regardless of whether it relates closely to the project of *Moby-Dick.* The novel contains much more than the stories of Ishmael or mad Ahab. The massive text begins with "Etymology" and quotes "Extracts" before reaching the famous opener of Chapter 1, "Call me Ishmael." In this manner, Ishmael's tale begins after a two-part delay, and his narrative is repeatedly broken by chapters such as "The Advocate," "Postscript," "Cetology," "Of the Monstrous Pictures of Whales," "Less Erroneous Pictures of Whales," and so forth. Throughout the book's 150-year history, these breakouts have been interpreted in numerous and often unsatisfying ways.

Commencing with *Moby-Dick*'s initial reception and continuing through the Melville revival of the twentieth and now twenty-first centuries, critics have been questioning, deriding, and apologizing for the breakout, nonnarrative sections of the work. Melville's friend Evert Duyckinck wrote one of the early American reviews of *Moby-Dick* in November 1851. He praised the book overall but not its mixed form, calling it "a most remarkable sea-dish" but also "an intellectual chowder" (in Hayford and Parker 613–14). In *John Bull*, October 1851, *Moby-Dick* was hailed as being "far beyond the level of an ordinary work of fiction. . . . The author has succeeded in investing objects apparently the most unattractive with the most absorbing fascination." The *London Morning Post* seconded this view in November 1851, finding "wild and wonderful fascination in the story against which no man may hope to secure himself."[1] Can the encyclopedic whale-detail and the particulars of sperm whale butchery possibly hold an intrinsic fascination for both Melville and these readers?

In the twentieth century, readers continue to react in diverse ways to *Moby-Dick*'s jumbled form. As Betsy Hilbert explains, "Analysts of *Moby-Dick* have commonly worked to demonstrate that the cetological information functions to forward a thematic or structural unity of one kind or another. . . . Thus was developed the Ballast Theory of Cetology in *Moby-Dick,* an idea that persists today that, though the nonfiction in the book is dull and difficult, still every story must have its slow parts" (825). Hilbert's dismissal of the nonfiction sections disregards many potential purposes of the breakout chapters. Not all critics follow Hilbert's ballast theory. David Ketterer, for example, suggests connections between the nonfiction and *Moby-Dick*'s organization, while Harrison Hayford uses the nonfiction as a way to decipher Melville's compositional process. Alternatively, the nonfiction breakouts may be vital elements of the act of writing and of the reader's experience of the novel.

Justifications for the cetology chapters have taken a new turn in recent years. Ketterer offers a more complex explanation for the inclusion of these chapters, organizing *Moby-Dick* into "24 books depend[ing] upon the identification of 23 time breaks" (Ketterer 301), whereas the more typical structures of the novel have four, five, and six parts. The nonnarrative sections do not weigh heavily in Ketterer's division of the novel. He explains: "The numerous informational or explanatory chapters . . . cannot be said in themselves to consume any of the horizontal narrative time line. In effect, they are dropped vertically into the ongoing action, temporarily suspending that action. . . . A time-break cannot, then, occur before a *purely* informational chapter; it can only occur after one." In Ketterer's scheme, these time-suspending, breakout chapters attach themselves to the preceding "action" chapters on the horizontal narrative time line. This is an interesting idea, and for Melville, these breakout chapters may indeed be the result of, or material fallout from, the preceding action chapters. Melville's reluctance to move forward with the narrative and his need to break up the text with cetology and other ballast may very well be born from a fear of the white page, its kin, the white whale, and maybe even from a fear of the consummation of blankness that would come at the project's completion. After all, he describes this novel as an endless work, "the draught of a draught" (*MD* 145).

Hayford offers another intriguing explanation of *Moby-Dick*'s narrative breaks. He finds that many of the novel's "compositional elements seem, in ordinary fictional terms, to be 'a mob of unnecessary duplicates' . . . [and] these duplicates give us a new key . . . as we keep trying to open some of the interlocked complications of the book's genesis, to which there is no master key we know of" (128).[2] By dissecting what he considers the novel's duplicate characters—such as Bulkington and Queequeg, and the prophets Elijah and Gabriel—and repeated events such as inn-seeking, signing-on, and gams, Hayford hypothesizes the stages in which Melville added bulk to the novel and then changed course without eliminating previous additions. For example, in the case of the mysterious Bulkington, who is expediently replaced with pagan harpooner Queequeg, Hayford proposes that the duplicate characters signal different stages in Melville's writing. When Melville revised his work with Queequeg filling the role he initially planned for Bulkington, he did not remove Bulkington's initial chapter. This theory raises questions, though. If Melville has gone to the trouble to dismiss Bulkington from the narrative and substitute Queequeg in the role of Ishmael's whaling comrade, why doesn't he write Bulkington completely out of the novel? Likewise, if the cetological and other nonnarrative sections are largely plagiarized whale facts that have been stuffed into the text as mere ballast or time-outs, why didn't Melville remove them before going to press?

Hayford gives a possible answer when commenting on the strange ripples added to the text when Queequeg "comes out of hiding" to replace Bulkington. He writes: "I believe some of the book's most awkward anomalies were induced and some of its best passages inspired in just these ways" (140). Hayford's positive appraisal of the text introduced or left over by what he considers duplicate characters and events is a step toward recognizing the potential importance of the variety of nonnarrative, breakout sections of the novel. It seems that despite Melville's initial reasons for repetitions, partial plagiarisms, and long breaks from the Ishmael and Ahab narratives, by the time *The Whale* goes to press these arabesques and ballasts have become integral parts of the text that he does not choose to edit out. As Hershel Parker contends, "authorial intentionality is built into the words of a literary work during the process of composition, not before and not afterwards."[3]

Hayford's examples of frequent duplication in the novel support his theory that at a crucial third stage in the writing process, four major characters undergo what he calls a "multiple reassignment of roles" (145). Thus, it seems, building on Hayford's theory one could suggest that the retained duplicates throughout *Moby-Dick* that support Hayford's compositional theory also point to a balance of doubles or multiples in the cetological breakout chapters. These chapters about whaling are not necessary to the advancement of the plot, but like the character and plot twinnings, they have been left in the novel by the author. Small doublings such as contradicting details of the *Pequod*'s design may be explained away as minor oversights, but chapter "duplicates" such as "Of the Monstrous Pictures of Whales" and "Less Erroneous Pictures of Whales" or "The Sperm Whale's Head" and "The Right Whale's Head" or "The Fountain" and "The Tail" do not appear to be slips of the pen. They seem to be part of a balanced, orchestrated design, and to serve some vital purpose in Melville's white whale project.

Melville himself provides some explanation for the breakouts. In a May 1850 letter to Richard H. Dana Jr. in which he downgrades the grandeur of his work in progress, Melville hints at the basis of its mixed form, writing that it "will be a strange sort of a book, tho,' I fear . . . to cook the thing up, one must needs throw in a little fancy, which from the nature of the thing, must be ungainly as the gambols of the whales themselves. Yet I mean to give the truth of the thing, spite of this" (*Cor* 162). What if this whalish ungainliness is precisely the matter, and the method, that makes possible his truth-telling, rather than simply expansiveness adding to the grandeur and "bigness" of the book? The encyclopedic breakouts bulk up the novel but also add to its intellectual weight, and writing the breakouts may have been central to Melville's method of telling the truth.

If Melville sought symphonic balance and ultimate truth in a novel that would not mesh with the marketplace, if he was unsure of how to proceed directly, it makes sense that he would provide double or multiple sidesteps from the narrative to further the balancing act between the find-and-kill-the-whale plot and that higher truth he was also pursuing. It seems highly unlikely that Melville mistakenly left some partially plagiarized chapters in *Moby-Dick* because he needed a mere exercise to jump-start his writing hand. Rather, the reams of cetology furthering other seemingly "unnecessary duplicates" might fit perfectly with the grand project of Melville's hand. Maybe he worked through his peculiar form of writer's block—by moving his pen, initially copying words until he was able to rejoin the stream of the "story." Once he recovered from the blockage Melville remodeled these plagiarisms into structural necessities, and they formed part of the delicate balance of this massive text. These copied words became digressive paragraphs that became brilliant chapters, often placed at heightened sites in the text, where Melville needed to break away from the intensity of the story so that he could circle around and get at his truths from other directions. Further, these dual chapters serve the reader as well as the writer, functioning as a sort of psychological "lee side" for the explosive, dangerous chapters where the reader can recover before returning to the Ishmael narrative.

In *Strike Through the Mask,* especially the chapter "Fear of Faces: From *Moby-Dick* to *Pierre,*" Renker illuminates connections between the two texts' recurring faces and imagines Melville's relationship to the page. She explains that "Melville's repeated figuration of faces is symptomatic of the terms of his material and conceptual engagement with the process of writing, and more specifically, with the chronic frustrations and blocks that characterize his engagements with the page" (xv). Although *Moby-Dick* has mainly the one horrible blank face—that of the white whale—the following passage seems as relevant to *Moby-Dick* as to his next novel, the face-saturated *Pierre.* Renker writes that "Melville's irruptive faces emerge concomitant to his conflicted desire for truth-telling, simultaneously and insistently figuring moments of blockage, suspension, and fear. These faces stage 'within' Melville's texts the scene of blocked writing constitutive of those texts. When I speak about writer's block, I do not mean that Melville was unable to produce . . . but rather that he chronically experienced the page as [an] obscuring, frustrating, resistant force against whose powers of blankness he battled as he wrote" (xviii). While *Moby-Dick* is not as face-haunted as the novel *Pierre,* Melville does make specific references to the face of the sperm whale as a "dead, blind wall" (*MD* 336–37), while Moby Dick's face, of course, stands out in its inscrutable whiteness—a white wall, a blank page. The unseeable face of the white whale and its inscribed, unreadable hieroglyphics when the sailors finally do view it are a horrifying specter in the novel, but Moby Dick's blank face is not the only sign of Melville's frustration with language and the white page. Perhaps Melville wrestled with pen and page—and dodged difficult passages and truths—by dredging safe harbors into the text.

In *Moby-Dick,* Melville dodges sideways when he is unable to plunge toward the whale. He skirts the horizontal plane of the page by writing away from the tale when depth and truth are hard to reach on it. He moves at these times to side-texts as though he had them printed, laid out next to his writing page, and he uses these sources to slide back onto his own page. Melville incorporates Thomas Beale's *Natural History of the Sperm Whale* [4] and other texts, for example, weaving them into his manuscript as safe rigging to hold on to in the violent wash of his imagination when faced with the white page. Regaining his footing with these borrowed facts, he converts encyclopedic data on whales into part of the book of the white whale, quarto and folio folding into his text, until he can again dive back into the narrative. He not only restarts the narrative but comes back into physical contact with the page, encouraging the flow of ideas from his mind to his hand to his pen rather than from another writer's work.

Melville himself, in the role of critic, explains why this might be necessary. In his laudatory review of Hawthorne's *Mosses from an Old Manse,* Melville writes that "[y]ou must have plenty of sea-room to tell the Truth in" (*PT* 246). This essay was written in 1850 during the composition of *Moby-Dick,* and its statement on truth-telling should be applied to Melville's seafaring novel rather than to its supposed subject, Nathaniel Hawthorne's landlocked stories, which were published four years previously. Melville, not Hawthorne, writes voluminously about the sea, plunging ever deeper in his attempt to write the truth. In light of Renker's theory on writer's block, this quotation applies perfectly to *Moby-Dick*'s cetological chapters. The possible connections between the cetological chapters and their preceding chapters may hint at why Melville added "sea-room" where he did. Examining several of the breakout chapters can highlight revealing connections between these chapters and their possible catalysts in previous chapters.

Chapter 24, "The Advocate," begins with Ishmael saying, "As Queequeg and I are now fairly embarked in the business of whaling" (*MD* 108), but then immediately jumps ship to defend whaling's cleanliness, nobility, influence, discoveries, authors, "good blood," respectability, and so forth. Did the even briefer previous chapter somehow send Melville into this defensive catalog about the good of whaling? Chapter 23, "The Lee Shore," serves as the duplicate harpooneer Bulkington's "stoneless grave" and ends with one of the novel's vast climatic statements: "But as in landlessness alone resides the highest truth, shoreless, indefinite as God—so, better, is it to perish in that howling infinite, than be ingloriously dashed upon the lee, even if that were safety! . . . Take heart, take heart, O Bulkington! Bear thee grimly, demigod! Up from the spray of thy ocean-perishing—straight up, leaps thy apotheosis!" (107).

Choosing to write about the sea, perhaps the transcendental apotheosis of "the highest truth," may have challenged the bravest writer to take a few steps back into safety. For Melville, this highest truth hiding beneath the white page may have been nearly unbearable. Alfred Kazin writes that "even when Melville laughs at himself for trying to hook this Leviathan with a pen . . . we know that he not merely feels exhilaration at attempting this mighty subject, but that he is also abashed, he feels grave."[5]

The second breakout under consideration is the epitome of Melville diversions, Chapter 32 on "Cetology," which descends from the likes of Sterne and Fielding. Though it should not be impugned as merely therapy for writer's block, for the method of whale categorization is a heady attempt at binding Linnaean taxonomy, this chapter breaks mightily from the *Pequod*'s journey. The previous chapter, "Queen Mab," ends not with a mighty statement on truth like "The Lee Shore," but rather with an impending confrontation that is avoided by abandoning ship. Stubb here explains to Flask the problem of Ahab and the white whale, then abruptly ends their conversation with foreboding by saying, "Look ye—there's something special in the wind. Stand by for it, Flask. Ahab has that that's bloody on his mind. But, mum; he comes this way" (*MD* 133). Instead of seeing what happens in the next moments on deck with the bloody-minded Ahab, we get the full chapter of "Cetology" and then a disquisition on the officers of whale craft, only to rejoin the *Pequod* in Chapter 34, "The Cabin-Table," for a ship officers' dinner. Is it too early for Stubb and Flask to have words with Ahab? Perhaps Melville had a great scene in mind that he was unable to put on paper at once, so he went on writing and found himself returning to the story too far downstream for this meeting of Stubb, Flask, and Ahab. Or, perhaps he felt unable to mark the page with the truth of that unwritten scene about "that that's bloody" on Ahab's mind, so he avoided the confrontation by penning something infinitely easier.

A particularly interesting breakout occurs with Chapter 45, "The Affidavit," in which the narrator comments, metatextually, on the very act of breaking the narrative. This breakout follows a crescendo in the plot in Chapter 36, "The Quarter-Deck." Ahab has made clear his quest and compelled the crew to swear to join him. "The Quarter-Deck" is followed by chapters detailing the sailors' gathering dread: Starbuck in "Dusk"; Stubb in "First Night-Watch"; Pip in "Midnight, Forecastle"; and Ishmael in "The Whiteness of the Whale," and "Moby Dick," the chapter in which he learns and shares the specific history of the white whale. In the lattermost, Ishmael explains that "[a]ll truth with malice in it; all that cracks the sinews and cakes the brain; . . . all evil, to crazy Ahab, were visibly personified, and made practically assailable in Moby Dick" (*MD* 184). Ishmael also reports Ahab's "undeniable delirium at sea" (186) that is detailed firsthand in two chapters that depict Ahab brooding, "Sunset" and "The Chart."

Chapter 43, "Hark!" which immediately precedes "The Chart," builds up to the captain's true obsession by hinting at the sailors' growing feeling that they are hosting stowaways. In "Hark!" seamen Cabaco and Archy argue about the source of noises that the first man hears emanating from under the *Pequod*'s hatches. At the conclusion of this brief chapter, Archy vows that "there is somebody down in the after-hold that has not yet been seen on deck; and I suspect our old Mogul knows something of it too. I heard Stubb tell Flask, one morning watch, that there was something of that sort in the wind" (*MD* 197). Sandwiched between "Hark!" and "The Affidavit," Chapter 44, "The Chart," moves on from hints of Fedallah to the "old Mogul" himself, brain burning over his charts, firing up his strategy for finding one particular sperm whale on the surface of the vast watery planet by hunting him during the Season-on-the-Line.

The narrator reports that sometimes when Ahab's monomania overwhelms him after a night of scouring his charts and tossing feverishly in his hammock, "this hell in himself yawned beneath him, a wild cry would be heard through the ship; and with glaring eyes Ahab would burst from his stateroom, as though escaping a bed that was on fire" (*MD* 202). This fleeing creature is actually Ahab's spirit, seeking "escape from the scorching contiguity" of his reeling mind. The crashing final statement of this chapter reads, "God help thee, old man, thy thoughts have created a creature in thee; and he whose intense thinking thus makes him a Prometheus; a vulture feeds up on that heart for ever; that vulture the very creature he creates" (202). After all this buildup, the revelation of the quest, and the glimpse of the hell that Ahab inhabits, Melville himself may need a break from the narrative's intensity, or he may need to provide one for the reader.

The break follows immediately with the opening words of the next chapter, "The Affidavit," which goes so far as to announce itself as a departure from the story proper. The irruptive first sentence begins: "[S]o far as what there may be of a narrative in this book; and, indeed, as indirectly touching one or two very interesting and curious particulars in the habits of sperm whales, the foregoing chapter, in its earlier part, is as important a one as will be found in this volume" (*MD* 203). The narrator refers to the portion of the previous chapter that details the practice of charting a whale's cruising patterns with precision so that it can be relocated, as contrasted with the ever-worsening state of Ahab's mind and his suffering soul. After the disclaimer that he does not want to provide his cetological affidavits "methodically," the narrator then descends into pages of annotated accounts of sailors reuniting with whales from earlier combats and the real possibility of recognizing specific leviathans from earlier whale hunts.

After "The Affidavit," the novel returns to Ahab and the specific business of the *Pequod* with Chapter 46, "Surmises," but once again Melville has floated further down the narrative stream to a place where the captain is not mired in monomania, but has actually chosen to revisit the practical venture of whaling for profit rather than obsession and revenge. Once more, the narrative has superheated only to be cooled by a cetological breakout and is rejoined only after the surface of the linear text has calmed. As with the previous breakout examples, this tack may signal Melville's need to build some "sea room" into the narrative, perhaps to give himself or the reader enough space in which to process the truth of the tale.

The following narrative chapters, 47–52, include "The Mat-Maker," when the crew first sees Ahab "surrounded by five dusky phantoms that seemed fresh formed out of the air" (*MD* 216) who are to man his whaleboat, and further chapters dealing with Fedallah and the other hideaways, including "The First Lowering," "Ahab's Boat and Crew—Fedallah," and "The Spirit-Spout." Ishmael realizes the precariousness of life on a whaler, and on the *Pequod* in particular, during the first lowering. In Chapter 49, "The Hyena," he concludes that "considering in what a devil's chase I was implicated, touching the White Whale . . . I thought I might as well go below and make a rough draft of my will" (227). With Queequeg as his witness, Ishmael finds relief in ordering his affairs before his seemingly imminent death.

The final chapter in this narrative series, "The *Pequod* Meets the *Albatross*," contains a series of ill omens that weigh upon the sailors more than their day-to-day proximity to death. The *Pequod* encounters the *Goney*, which has clearly been at sea for many years and is "bleached like the skeleton of a stranded walrus" (*MD* 236). The *Goney*'s crew is ragged and ghostlike, its captain "strange" (237). When Ahab asks his burning question, "Have ye seen the White Whale?" (237), the *Goney*'s captain drops his speaking trumpet into the water and cannot be heard over the wind. While Ahab is yelling out his ship's name and destination to the passing whaler, the schools of fish that had been swimming alongside the *Pequod* abandon her for the *Goney*, distressing him. The narrator explains that "there seemed but little in the words, but the tone conveyed more of deep helpless sadness than the insane old man had ever before evinced." The crew does not miss the ill omens resulting from Ahab's first mention of Moby Dick to another whaler.

Ahab's secret crew and the depths of his monomania are revealed to the *Pequod*'s sailors in this series of chapters. Instead of dealing directly with the events foreshadowed in this section laden with ill omens, the narrative takes another break with chapters 53–57. Chapter 53 introduces the traditional practices of the whaling gam, perhaps as an alternative to the *Pequod*'s encounter with the *Goney*, and a segue into Chapter 54, "The *Town-Ho*'s Story (As told at the Golden Inn)." The *Town-Ho* chapter is not a complete break from the narrative, as it relates information about Moby Dick that the harpooner

Tashtego learns during the gam between the *Pequod* and the *Town-Ho*. In relating the intelligence from this gam, however, Melville builds in several removes from the main narrative. The chapter does not include the uneventful discussion between Ahab and the *Town-Ho*'s captain. Neither does it feature the discussion between Tashtego and the three whalemen who shared their story, "which seemed obscurely to involve with the whale a certain wondrous, inverted visitation of one of those so called judgments of God which at times are said to overtake some men" (*MD* 242). The narrator relates the story in "the style in which [he] once narrated it at Lima" (243), a circumstance completely divorced from Tashtego's secretive retelling on the *Pequod*.

Cetological chapters 55–57 follow this oddly told story of Moby Dick's dark nature without transition. Chapter 55, "Monstrous Pictures of Whales," takes a rambling tour through sub-par whale art, connecting briefly with the narrative in the penultimate paragraph by quoting "humorous Stubb" on whale anatomy (*MD* 264). The next two chapters, "Less Erroneous Pictures of Whales" and "Of Whales in Paint, In Teeth, &c.," make no specific references to the main narrative.

When the reader finally rejoins the *Pequod* with Chapter 58, the shadow of Fedallah has shrunk into hiding and the sailors are in the midst of "vast meadows of brit" and grazing right whales (*MD* 272). The narrator reminds the reader that "man has lost that sense of the full awfulness of the sea which aboriginally belongs to it" (273), but the level of horror has returned to that typical of a whaling voyage. Chapter 59 brings another ill omen, the "strange spectre" of the giant squid, which the crew members mistake for Moby Dick. After the squid sank out of sight, Starbuck "with a wild voice exclaimed—'Almost rather had I seen Moby Dick and fought him, than to have seen thee, thou white ghost!'" (276). He then explains that the apparition was "the great live squid, which, they say, few whale-ships ever beheld, and returned to their ports to tell of it."

The squid, both the largest and most ominous of omens, inspires another break. Chapter 60, "The Line," explains the similarly "magical, sometimes horrible whale-line" (*MD* 278). After this step back from the portentous nature of the squid, Chapter 61, "Stubb Kills a Whale," delves back into the narrative and even reinterprets the giant squid as a positive sign of the nearness of sperm whales. A successful, uneventful whale hunt follows, and then two chapters of explanatory cetology, Chapter 62, "The Dart," and Chapter 63, "The Crotch." The narrator even offers up an explanation for this nonnarrative section: "Out of the trunk, the branches grow; out of them, the twigs. So, in productive subjects, grow the chapters" (289). While this explanation may be satisfying in some instances, it falls short when applied to some other breakout chapters. Sometimes Melville appears to add nonnarrative chapters to provide background or additional information that follows naturally on the subject of the previous chapter. Alternatively, when emotions, especially Ahab's, run wild, the ensuing nonnarrative sections may provide a breather from the narrative's intensity for the author or perhaps the reader. Chapters 62 and 63 follow an easy chapter aboard the *Pequod*, lacking talk or sightings of Moby Dick, Fedallah, or crazed behavior from Ahab. Chapters 64 and 65 show a similar connection, with the latter, "The Whale as a Dish," providing background for the former, "Stubb's Supper."

The next series of chapters proceeds in like fashion, intermingling shipboard and narrative chapters with explanatory chapters, none of which deal with the dangerous hunt for Moby Dick. In Chapter 70, "The Sphynx," Ahab mutters somewhat madly to the head of a whale, only to be distracted by the sighting of another ship. The shadow fully returns in Chapter 71, "The *Jeroboam*'s Story." During this gam the *Pequod*'s sailors encounter Gabriel, a crazed hand that holds sway over the rest of the *Jeroboam*'s crew, and Ahab finally meets a captain who has news of Moby Dick. Gabriel intersperses Captain Mayhew's tale, which recounts an encounter he had with Moby Dick, with warnings about the whale, whom Gabriel considers "no less a being than the Shaker God incarnated" (*MD* 316). Despite Gabriel's warnings about the sacrilege involved in hunting the white whale, one of the *Jeroboam*'s crew had sighted the white whale, and Macey, the chief mate, convinced a crew to join him in its pursuit. The deity-attacking officer "was smitten bodily into the air" by Moby Dick; "[n]ot a chip of the boat was harmed, nor a hair of any oarsman's head; but the mate for ever sank." The mate's death proved Gabriel's prophetic abilities to the rest of the mutinous crew. As the gam between the *Pequod* and the *Jeroboam* concludes, the ranting Gabriel continues to intercede in the captains' conversation, telling Ahab that he will soon be dead.

This "wild affair" contributes to the uneasiness of the *Pequod*'s crew while they are busy with the business of whaling in chapters 72 and 73 (*MD* 318). By the end of the latter chapter, the crew is speculating about Fedallah and "all these passing things" (328). Before the crew can possibly band together in response to the changes in Ahab or the ascendancy of Fedallah, the narrative predictably sidesteps the issue by breaking into cetological chapters 74–77. Chapter 78 returns to the narrative to deal with a different type of crisis; Tashtego falls into a whale's head, nearly drowning in spermaceti before Queequeg rescues him. Chapters 79 and 80 provide explanatory cetology. Chapter 81 brings both a gam with the *Jungfrau*—a clean, virgin ship—and a successful whale hunt that ends badly when the elderly victim sinks without being harvested. The shifting between narrative chapters that do not focus directly on Moby Dick and explanatory chapters continues, with occasional shifts into chapters dealing directly with Ahab's hunt or mania, which are often followed by diversionary breakout chapters.

In conclusion, this sea hash of action and digression, tale-telling and tale-avoiding, may be a part of Melville's master plan for *Moby-Dick* as an epic striptease of a novel. Admittedly many of the nonnarrative chapters appear to serve an explanatory function and to add to the epic richness of the novel by adding history, religion, philosophy, nobility, and art to the pursuit of the whale. The pattern of the breakout chapters, which break the progress of the novel when the reader expects climactic narrative release, may well indicate that part of Melville's plan was to cope with and write through his blocks, to keep stabbing at the white page until he could face the next chapter and ultimately the ending, sinking the *Pequod*, killing Ahab, and leaving the sea's surface calm and blank once more, indifferent to his futile quest for truth. Perhaps the cetological ballast in *Moby-Dick* was not excised because Melville recognized how these chapters functioned during the writing process and decided to preserve them to function similarly for the reader. The mixed content may also be evidence of Melville's struggle between writing what he wants and what he must. He explained, "What I feel most moved to write, that is banned,—it will not pay. Yet, altogether, write the *other* way I cannot. So the product is a final hash, and all my books are botches" (*Cor* 191).

Notes

1. *John Bull* and the *London Morning Post* are both quoted in Sheila Post-Lauria, "'A Philosophy in Whales . . . Poetry in Blubber': Mixed Form in *Moby-Dick*," *Nineteenth-Century Literature* 45 (1990): 315.

2. See also A. Robert Lee, "*Moby-Dick*: The Tale and the Telling," in *New Perspectives on Melville*, ed. Faith Pullin (Kent, Ohio: Kent State Univ. Press, 1978), 86–127.

3. Hershel Parker, *Flawed Texts and Verbal Icons: Literary Authority in American Fiction.* (Evanston, Ill.: Northwestern Univ. Press, 1984), 23.

4. See Honore Forster, "Melville and the Whaling Doctors," *Melville Society Extracts* 85 (1991): 6–9 for information on sources in Beale and Frederick Debell Bennett's *Narrative of a Whaling Voyage Round the Globe, from the Year 1833 to 1836.* See also Robert K. Wallace, "Melville, Turner, and J. E. Gray's Cetology," *Nineteenth-Century Contexts* 13.2 (1989): 151–75.

5. Alfred Kazin, "'Introduction' to *Moby-Dick*," in *Melville: A Collection of Critical Essays*, ed. Richard Chase (Englewood Cliffs, N.J.: Prentice Hall, 1964), 47.

"Chiefly Known by His Rod"

The Book of Jonah, Mapple's Sermon, and Scapegoating

GIORGIO MARIANI

There! the ringed horizon. In that ring Cain struck Abel. Sweet work, right work! No? Why, then, God, mad'st thou the ring?
—*Moby-Dick,* Chapter 40

Order leads to Guilt
(for who can keep commandment)
Guilt needs Redemption
(for who would not be cleansed)
Redemption needs a Redeemer
(which is to say, a Victim!).

Order
Through Guilt
To Victimage
(hence: Cult of the Kill)
—Kenneth Burke, *The Rhetoric of Religion* [1]

In the final chapter of *Violence and the Sacred,* René Girard discusses the biblical book of Jonah to recapitulate the central argument of his study.[2] The tempest sent by the Lord against the ship Jonah boarded in his attempt to escape from his prophetic duties is read by Girard as a textbook sacrificial crisis. The crisis brings about a breakdown of the religious order—"then the mariners were afraid, and cried every man unto his god" (Jon. 1:5)—and it can be solved only through the ritual expulsion of a scapegoat.[3] The crew wonders "for whose cause this evil is upon us" (Jon. 1:7) and goes on to cast lots to identify the culprit. The lot falls on the wayward prophet, yet the sailors are reluctant to sacrifice him and they attempt to reach the shore by their own efforts. When they fail, they finally cast Jonah into the sea, and the tempest subsides. Only Jonah's sacrificial expulsion saves the community. Jonah is, in Girard's terms, the surrogate victim whose sacrifice prevents the community from disintegrating and plunging into the utter chaos of reciprocal violence.

As we all know, Father Mapple preaches upon the book of Jonah in Chapter 9 of *Moby-Dick*. Thus the book of Jonah forms one of the stories-within-Ishmael's-story about which much has been written but whose sacrificial logic, at least to judge from the scholarship, has never been properly discussed. The connection between violence and the sacred forms a major concern of both the sermon's narrative strategy—especially when the latter is considered in light of the major discrepancies between Mapple's reading of Jonah and the original biblical text—and of its relation to the novel as a whole. Focusing on this theme accomplishes a threefold purpose. First, Father Mapple's manipulation of biblical discourse warrants further attention. The differences between the text of Jonah and Mapple's sermon have often been noted. Some critics see Mapple's emendations as Melville's utterly serious attempt to provide the reader with a moral yardstick to judge his characters; others believe that Melville ironically undercuts Mapple's sermonizing. Yet both groups have to a greater or lesser extent ignored the fact that the best commentary on Mapple's sermon is to be found in the book of Jonah itself. Secondly, Girard's theories help to illuminate an aspect of the book of Jonah that (somewhat surprisingly) he neglects to mention in his brief discussion of this biblical text. Finally, by evaluating the understanding of scapegoating implicit in both the biblical and Mapple's texts, we may be in a better position to map out, on the one hand, Ahab's and his crew's relation to the White Whale and, on the other, Ishmael's role in the overall narrative scheme of the novel.

1

In his recent *The Errant Art of Moby-Dick*, William Spanos claims that the majority of Melville critics have avoided discussing Father Mapple's sermon because of the subversive implications of Ishmael's reading of it (87–114). However, Spanos's lengthy discussion of Mapple's sermon and its place within the overarching narrative of *Moby-Dick* proves to be in several ways merely

an elegant though perhaps predictable updating of "antibiblical" interpretations of the sermon and Melville's mighty book first proposed by Lawrance
Thompson in his *Melville's Quarrel with God*. In his book, Thompson took
issue with the then dominant "Christian" readings of Melville that, at least
since Nathalia Wright's *Melville's Use of the Bible*, set out to prove that, even
though in his sermon Mapple completely disregards the fourth and last chapter
of Jonah—where the Lord shows His kindness and mercy by sparing the city
of Nineveh—"the structure of *Moby Dick* calls for the sermon and narrative
to agree" (Wright 83–84). Thompson argued, instead, that Mapple's sermon
"is ridiculed and burlesqued" by both Ishmael and Melville and that, unlike
Mapple's Jonah, the biblical one was a "headstrong, recalcitrant, God-challeng-
ing prophet" who obeyed divine authority "only after God had scared poor
Jonah witless" (Thompson 164). Yet Thompson's belief that Melville's texts
nearly always call for anti-Christian, antibiblical readings ignored the extent
to which the story of Jonah, and especially its fourth chapter, can be read as
an implicit critique of the very sermon that Mapple preaches.

Mapple makes of Jonah a man who, in boarding the ship on which he
wishes to run away from the Lord, is terrified of being "discovered" and treated
as a criminal. "So disordered, self-condemning is his look, that had there
been policemen in those days, Jonah, on the mere suspicion of something
wrong, had been arrested ere he touched a deck" (*MD* 43). Here he clearly
manipulates the original text, where things stand in exactly the opposite way.
In the Bible the narrator points out that "the men knew that he fled from the
presence of the Lord, because he had told them" (Jon. 1:10). Mapple adds that,
once on the ship, Jonah fears that God will soon punish him. Yet in the Bible
we read that, despite the agitation certainly caused by the "mighty tempest"
sent by God, "Jonah was gone down into the sides of the ship; and he lay,
and was fast asleep" (1:5). The passage contains no indication that Jonah is
troubled by his conscience. Mapple goes on to argue that once Jonah is cast
into the sea and swallowed by a "great fish" he "does not weep and wail for
direct deliverance. He feels his dreadful punishment is just. . . . And here,
shipmates, is true and faithful repentance; not clamorous for pardon, but
grateful for punishment" (*MD* 46–47). In the Bible, however, Jonah wastes
no time in invoking God's help—"out of the belly of hell cried I, and thou
heardest my voice" (Jon. 2:1)—and yet he can in no way be said to become
"a model for repentance," as Mapple dubs him, because even once he finally agrees to preach to the Ninevites he remains, in his own words, "angry,
even unto death" (4:9) vis-à-vis God. Summing up, there can be little doubt
that Melville's irony is not directed so much at the Bible as at the particular
reading of the book of Jonah offered by Mapple.

Spanos denounces Mapple's sermon as a perfect type of the Puritan Jeremiad, "teleological and logocentric with a vengeance" (100), and proceeds to juxtapose Ishmael's befriending of the pagan Queequeg to Mapple's orthodoxy. Like Thompson, Spanos ignores that the biblical Jonah—far from being, as Mapple argues, grateful for his punishment—is incensed by God's decision not to punish Nineveh; that is, Jonah can conceive of divine authority only in terms of sacred violence, thus joining hands with Mapple in praising a God chiefly known to him for His "rod." Yet the biblical narrator casts a critical light on Jonah's behavior by showing that Jonah fled from his mission not because, as Mapple maintains, he was "appalled at the hostility he should raise," but because he suspected all along that the Lord would eventually forgive the Ninevites, thus undermining the continuum linking prophetic Truth and sacred violence. "Therefore I fled unto Tarshish: for I knew thou art a gracious God, and merciful, slow to anger, and of great kindness, and repentest thee of the evil" (Jon. 4:2). The Bible makes clear beyond any shadow of doubt that Jonah has no fear whatsoever of the Ninevites—he fears only God's mercy.[4]

Jay Holstein has rightly seen that the book of Jonah's "core teaching ... [points to] the boundlessness of divine compassion even for pagan humanity." Holstein, however, believes that Melville is out to attack such a teaching everywhere in *Moby-Dick* by affirming "a paganism which sees man at the mercy of powers either alien and malevolent (in the case of the white whale) or indifferent (in the case of the sea) to man" (20). Spanos and Holstein overlook that Ishmael's "pagan" response to Mapple's sermon is cast not only in strong biblical and Christian language but also in terms that clearly articulate some of the preoccupations of the biblical narrator of Jonah, beginning with the latter's blurring the distinctions between "heathens" and "children of God," as well as his preference for a peaceful resolution of conflict contra Jonah's invocation of God's wrath.

In "A Bosom Friend," the chapter following Mapple's fiery sermon, we see the pagan Queequeg and the Christian Ishmael become "cronies . . . a cosy, loving pair" (*MD* 52). It would be hard not to take Ishmael's words in this chapter as a rather explicit critique of Mapple's misreading of the Bible, especially when the delicate issue of Queequeg's idolatry is discussed. Ishmael comically concludes that to be a good Christian by doing to his fellow man what he would have his fellow man do to him, he must turn idolator. Similarly, when Ishmael pleads with Bildad and Peleg to hire Queequeg, he mentions "the great and everlasting First Congregation of this whole worshipping world" as a community in which "we all join hands" instead of fighting one another. In both cases Ishmael's rhetoric turns its irony not so much against Christian ethics as against those institutional forms that turn religion into unquestionable dogma, and in some sense, as highlighted by Peleg's words, Ishmael becomes a sort of anti-Mapple: "Young man, you'd better ship for a missionary, instead of a fore-mast hand; I never heard a better sermon. Deacon Deuteronomy—why Father Mapple himself couldn't beat it" (88). Yet Ishmael's language cannot be described as antibiblical: like the narrator of the book of Jonah, Ishmael appeals to mercy for and tolerance of the Other and, most importantly, juxtaposes the violent mimicry of revenge, which would justify the destruction of Nineveh, with an ironic but thoroughly peaceful imitation of the idolator's behavior that is in some sense deeply Christian. Ishmael's sly critique of Mapple's sermonizing is by no means "pagan"; instead, its logic depends heavily on the antisacrificial message at the center of the biblical book of Jonah, where God not only forgives the Ninevites but repents himself for having contemplated at some point the evil prospect of revenge.[5]

As noted previously, Girard, focusing exclusively on the first chapter in his brief reading of the book of Jonah, overlooks a fundamental feature of the story—fundamental, that is, precisely in terms of Girard's own scapegoat theory. The crew expels the victim chosen by Chance, thereby restoring order on the ship and placating Nature's fury, but the God unto whom Jonah is sacrificed does not kill him. The book of Jonah can thus be seen as a nearly perfect illustration of that "revelation of the structuring power of victimage" that Girard sees as first taking place in the Hebrew Bible, before reaching its climax in the Gospels.[6] The book of Jonah depicts a world in which men still resort to scapegoating, while the Lord not only spares Jonah's life but goes on to grant the salvation of Nineveh, thus severing the connection between violence and the sacred. The Lord of the book of Jonah is a largely peaceful and tolerant God—the God whom Ishmael seems implicitly to invoke, especially when describing his relationship with Queequeg. Indeed, just as the Bible shows that the "heathens" can be more God-fearing than the Hebrews, Ishmael juxtaposes his genuine friendship with the pagan Queequeg to contemporary Christians' "hollow courtesy." Yet *Moby-Dick* does not end in New England. While Ishmael at this stage in the novel appears to share the biblical narrator's hope of overcoming the primitive equation between violence and the sacred, it remains to be seen whether the overall story he tells succeeds in doing so or whether, as seems to be the case, Ishmael's own rhetoric is ultimately imbricated in the victimage mechanism he appears to contest in the early part of the novel.

2

By analyzing Ahab's relation to the White Whale through Girard's interpretive lenses, one immediately realizes that it illustrates what Girard calls "mimetic desire," the perverse relation linking the desiring subject and his "monstrous double." According to Girard, desire is always mimetic and "triangular"—always directed toward an object that is desired by a model one feels compelled to imitate. In other words, there is no such thing as a "pure" or "spontaneous" desire: in Girard's view one desires something because someone else also wants it and, by so doing, ignites the spark of desire.[7] In our case, Ahab perceives the White Whale as the custodian of some awful secret that must be wrestled away from him, and Melville carefully represents the struggle between the two as one in which the antagonists end up mirroring each other. Ahab famously declares that he sees in Moby Dick "outrageous strength, with an inscrutable malice sinewing it. That inscrutable thing is chiefly what I hate; and be the white whale agent, or be the white whale principal, I will wreak that hate upon him" (*MD* 164). In this sentence Ahab identifies the whale's malice with a hateful "strength" that can hardly be distinguished from the hate he feels toward the whale. This equation between what Ahab hates and the force that makes him hate it is reinstated in the final pages of the novel, when Ahab defines as equally "inscrutable" and cruel the mysterious force that compels him to seek revenge (545). Ahab, therefore, learns his desire for revenge mimetically, by imitating his model Moby Dick; appropriately enough he wishes "to dismember my dismemberer" (147), to do to his rival what the latter has done to him. Ahab desires, that is, to be like the whale, to which he is often implicitly compared and which he resembles even in physical and symbolical details.[8] The model of Ahab's desire thus becomes, literally, his "monstrous double." The "wall" that Ahab sees incarnated in Moby Dick, and that he wishes to dismantle, can be considered a fit emblem of the Girardian *skandalon:* "the model exerting its special form of temptation, causing attraction to the extent that it is an obstacle and forming an obstacle to the extent that it can attract. The *skandalon* is the obstacle/model of mimetic rivalry; it is the model in so far as he works counter to the undertakings of the disciple and so becomes an inexhaustible source of morbid fascination."[9]

According to Girard, only "generative" or collective violence can transform the monstrous double into a savior and its killing into a sacrifice, and by appealing to the generative qualities of violence Ahab justifies to the crew, and to himself, his revenge mission. Ahab himself sees the whale precisely as a scapegoat in two senses: that "all evil . . . [is] visibly personified, and made practically assailable in Moby Dick" and that he "piled upon the whale's white hump the sum of all the general rage and hate felt by his whole race from Adam down" (*MD* 184). Ahab here stands out as the typical Nietzschean man of resentment who, trapped in the "it was," "lives his past in the future ... and can hope to will only by directing his power towards revenge."[10] His preoccupation with the past, however, transcends the temporal and spatial boundaries of his own person and grows into a collective rage that comes to include all time and humanity. His hunt can thus easily be read as a classic attempt to rid a violent world through violent means. Indeed, Moby Dick's status as scapegoat in the Girardian sense goes a long way in explaining why the White Whale is perceived as both malicious and sacred: his nature is the ambivalent one of the sacrificial victim, who is said to be responsible for the violence at large in society but whose sacrifice will also grant the return to a state of peace. It is no accident that Ahab insists maniacally on the *ritual* aspect of the hunt for Moby Dick, which he distinguishes from the commercial goals of the *Pequod*, vainly invoked by Starbuck. Yet Melville, for all the emphasis he places on Moby Dick's monstrosity, never turns his novel into a mythical allegory. As a whole, that is, the novel does not make of the White Whale a monster deserving punishment and annihilation. By repeatedly calling attention to the fact that the hunter and the monster are really one and the same being, Ishmael can be said to be following, at least up to a point, the example of the biblical narrator of Jonah and the latter's attempt to unveil the paradoxical, circular logic of scapegoating.

3

Of course, Ahab's attempt to sacrifice Moby Dick fails. On the other hand, one could say that the sacrificial crisis described in the novel is ultimately brought to a close by the act of sacrificing. In a fascinating reversal of the traditional scapegoating mechanism requiring one victim to perish so that the rest of the community may be saved, both Ahab and his crew, minus Ishmael, are sacrificed to the captain's monstrous double. Obviously the sacrificial outcome of the novel could be seen as the consequence of a purely arbitrary chain of events—a fortuitous outcome of the *Pequod*'s adventure and nothing else. This would be at odds, however, with how Ishmael describes the climactic moments of his story. His rhetoric resurrects time and again throughout the novel, and especially in the end, the religious, sacrificial logic embodied in the sailors' behavior in the book of Jonah. Even though in "The Mat-Maker" Ishmael identifies Chance as the force that "has the last featuring blow at events" (*MD* 215), when it comes to describing Moby Dick's last blow at the *Pequod*, he sees it as the working of Fate—of a retributive Violence that for all of its possibly nihilistic shadings still obeys some mysterious, superhuman logic. As even a cursory glance at the language employed by Ishmael in the epilogue will show—from the Job epigraph to the evocation of what "the Fates ordained" and the mention of "unharming sharks" and sea-hawks "with sheathed beaks" (573)—the narrator strives to read some degree of logic and justice into the whale's "swift vengeance."

In this regard Priscilla Wald has rightly argued that "[w]hen Ishmael ends *Moby-Dick* with Rachel's searching for her children he paraphrases a gospel that itself repeats Jeremiah in fulfillment of the prophecy. Repetition, in Matthew, is authorizing and authenticating. But in *Moby-Dick* it is a reflection of Ishmael's internalization of Ahab, his need, that is, to find meaning in chance events, such as his survival."[11] Equally significant in Ishmael's search for meaning, and further proof that his narrative cannot rid itself of a jeremiadic rhetoric ultimately akin to the one employed by Father Mapple, is Ishmael's choice of epigraph for his epilogue. The identical lines from Job—"And I only am escaped alone to tell thee" (1:14–19)—appear in the introductory paragraph of Mary Rowlandson's captivity narrative, one of the best examples of the Puritan Jeremiad. If it is difficult to deny the critical and satirical dimension of several of Ishmael's narrations, it would be equally wrong to overlook the novel's continuity with those traditions from which Ishmael works hard to distance himself but can never break away completely. Ishmael's use of the Job quotation contains no apparent irony. On the contrary, Ishmael is the sole survivor of a massacre through which a divine agency avenges itself. Ishmael is no less terrified by witnessing Moby Dick's revenge than Rowlandson is in the punishment dispensed by an angry God to His backsliding children: the violence through which the sacred makes itself known wears, like the Indian violence described by Rowlandson, a fearsome, diabolical mask. But just as Rowlandson's infernal Indians ultimately manifest God's wrath, also Moby Dick's "eternal malice," in Ishmael's rhetoric, represents a manifestation of the sacred.

A close reading of the "Chase" chapters will further sustain a skeptical approach to one of the strongest commonplaces of post–World War II Melvillean criticism, according to which the main action of the novel can be traced in Ishmael's progressive withdrawal from Ahab's deadly and fatalistic vision. If Ahab declares that "we are turned round and round in this world . . . and Fate is the handspike" and that he himself is "The Fates' lieutenant" (*MD* 545, 561), when Ishmael notes that "The hand of Fate had snatched all their [the crew's] souls" (557), he places an equal emphasis on Fate as the ultimate cause of events.

The world of the novel, as Ishmael describes it, is quite unlike the "alien and malevolent," or simply "indifferent," universe depicted by Holstein. It is a world ruled by a Fate whose revenges and punishments are seen by the narrator not as gratuitous acts but as embodiments of a supernatural violence. In Moby Dick's furious aspect a moment before the final charge, Ishmael not only reads the same hateful traits always seen by Ahab, but the features of a being bent on taking revenge: "Retribution, swift vengeance, eternal malice were in his whole aspect" (571). In the universe of *Moby-Dick* a divine agency powerfully reasserts the connection between violence and the sacred against the theological outlook presented by the book of Jonah. Ishmael's rhetoric makes of the White Whale's revenge against Ahab and his crew one of those "judgments of God" that—as seen in "The *Town-Ho*'s Story"—are Moby Dick's prerogative. In the novel's apocalyptic ending, "God's burning finger" (506)—evoked by Ishmael in "The Candles"—touches once again the "fated" *Pequod*'s quarter-deck.

Ishmael, therefore, does not resign himself to seeing his adventure and his own salvation as utterly void of meaning and, as narrator, he ends up in a position the biblical Jonah would have certainly envied. Ishmael becomes a sort of "resurrected" Jonah who can tell the story of how a wicked leader and his community were eventually punished and annihilated. Wai-chee Dimock's suggestion that Ahab is doomed from the start and set up by the novel's logic as the designated victim on whose shoulders all blame will have to fall does contain some degree of truth.[12] Ahab is after all marked by moral and physical abnormalities that, as Girard explains, have always been typical features of mythic victims, from so-called primitive mythologies all the way to Oedipus and beyond.[13] To the extent that Ishmael's narrative responds to Ahab's construction of Moby Dick as a scapegoat by casting Ahab in the role of the deserving victim, one can argue that Ishmael is writing what Girard calls a "text of persecution"—a text that, by blaming all violence on the victim, blinds us to our own participation in the violence of scapegoating.

What must be added, however, is that the novel's final act of victimization takes place only after the text has staged, and to a large extent demystified, the logic of scapegoating. The absurdity of revenge—on a "dumb brute," moreover—is certainly highlighted at various points in the text, and yet by the end Ishmael seems incapable of letting go of the logic of revenge and he conceives the whale's act as one of "divine retribution"—the same divine retribution that is renounced in the book of Jonah. The novel appears divided between, on the one hand, the critique of the victimary mechanism and its cathartic effects and, on the other, the need nevertheless to provide its readers with an obligatory scapegoat, which entails a recanting of the former critique.

Thus Melville provides us with an insight into the perverse contradiction into which not only revenge but the critique of revenge itself is always in danger of running; he alerts us, that is, to the fact that, in Girard's own words, "the indignant or ironic denunciation of the hunt for scapegoats, may constitute a new kind of scapegoating." This moral double bind is further illustrated when the very crowd that should have witnessed the execution of the White Whale is turned by the novel into the real victim of a "redoubled and inverted theater"—of a blow-back in which the reader's complicity with Ishmael is predicated on a thinly disguised act of sacrificial violence.[14] Those readers who, like Spanos, insist on seeing Ishmael as an uncomplicated, well-rounded subversive character and focus on the "peaceful" resolution of the narrative, whereby even a symbol of death like Queequeg's coffin is turned into a life buoy, seem to forget the bloodbath required by the novel's "redeeming" ending—a redeeming ending in which, if on the one hand what was originally singled out as the designated surrogate victim escapes alive from the hands of a barbaric crew equivalent to Girard's enraged mob, on the other hand an enraged Moby proceeds to annihilate his own antagonist and his associates.[15] The resolution of Melville's book occurs in an inescapably violent way, utterly unlike the peaceful and jocose ending of the book of Jonah.

4

The sacrificial dimension of *Moby-Dick*'s ending may be further highlighted by showing the extent to which it amounts to a rewriting of what can be considered the primal scene of Melville's lifelong obsession with victims, scapegoats, and sacrifice: the ending of *Typee*.[16] To understand the victimary mechanism displayed in the final pages of Melville's first novel, however, we must take a close look at the third paragraph of its first chapter. There we can find in a nutshell the theme to which Melville's narratives would return time and again. Tommo's first words in the novel describe the ship's microcosm in a state of crisis: virtually no food is left on board and, as we learn in more detail in a subsequent chapter, the crew is comprised "of a parcel of dastardly and mean-spirited wretches, divided among themselves, and only united in enduring without resistance the unmitigated tyranny of the captain" (*T* 21). Yet what prevents the social crisis from turning into a full-fledged sacrificial crisis is not only the fear inspired by the captain's absolute authority. As we learn in the novel's third paragraph, a more suitable scapegoat figure than the captain comes to the crew's rescue:

There is but one solitary tenant in the chicken coop, once a gay and dapper young cock. . . . [T]here he stands, moping all the day long on that everlasting one leg of his . . . He mourns, no doubt, his lost companions, literally snatched from him one by one, and never seen again. But his days of mourning will be few; for Mungo, our black cook, told me yesterday that the word had at last gone forth, and poor Pedro's fate was sealed. His attenuated body will be laid out upon the captain's table next Sunday, and long before night will be buried with all the usual ceremonies beneath the worthy individual's vest. Who would believe that there could be anyone so cruel as to long for the decapitation of the luckless Pedro; yet the sailors pray every minute, selfish fellows, that the miserable fowl may be brought to his end. They say the captain will never point the ship for the land so long as he has in anticipation a mess of fresh meat. This unhappy bird can alone furnish it; and when he is once devoured, the captain will come to his senses. I wish thee no harm, Peter; but as thou art doomed, sooner or later, to meet the fate of thy race; and if putting a period to thy existence is to be the signal for our deliverance, why—truth to speak—I wish thy throat cut this very moment; for, oh! How I wish to see the living earth again! (*T* 4)

On a first reading the story of Pedro/Peter the cock would seem only a way to describe comically the desolation onboard the *Dolly,* but if we reconsider this passage after reading the whole novel we cannot fail to realize that here the narrator traces the contours of the human drama running through the entire narrative. And at the heart of such drama stands not only the contradictory nature of human desire, but also the function of violence within the network of human relations.

The narrator tells us that Pedro, the sole survivor of his tribe, walks on one leg as he awaits to be devoured by the captain: this obviously foreshadows Tommo's predicament in the Typee valley. As we know, Tommo's injured leg hurts, especially when he is afraid he will be eaten up by the alleged cannibals. But Pedro is much more than a metaphor for Tommo's captive condition. We are told that the price to pay for the "deliverance" of the crew from both the misery and the tyranny onboard the ship requires Pedro's sacrifice: only after eating the fowl will the captain agree to touch land. Even though the passage has a comical tone, the sacrificial nature of the cock's "decapitation" is strongly underlined. The cock will be eaten on the Lord's day and then "buried" with all the proper rites. Even though he claims he has nothing against Pedro, addressing the cock with the "thou" and "thy" reminiscent of the King James Bible, the narrator admits he would be willing to slit the cock's throat any time if that could convince the captain to put an end to the voyage. Pedro is therefore a typical sacrificial victim, a "scapecock" who, like the classical scapegoats studied by Girard, is both despised and revered. He is marked by a physical defect readable as the external sign of some mysterious sin (Pedro limps—like Oedipus and dozens of other designated victims, including, of course, Ahab) and he is also the convenient target of a hatred that, as it cannot be directed toward the one most directly responsible for the crew's sufferings, must be deflected on a substitute victim.

Melville's analysis of the nature of sacrifice, however, contains an important, though less explicit, commentary on Christian discourse. It is no accident that when Tommo addresses him directly, he turns the cock's name into the anglicized Peter, thus underlining its religious implications. To the extent that in Christian tradition Peter's crucifixion is a sort of mirrorlike repetition—Peter was nailed to the cross upside down—of Christ's own crucifixion, the text seems to suggest that even such an apparently innocent killing as that of the last cock on board must be read as the attenuated or allegorical version of a more deadly serious sacrifice in which the target of communal resentment is not a fowl but a human being.[17] Moreover, once we are alerted to the Christian dimension of the narrator's language, we can hardly miss the reference to Christ's famous warning to Peter: "the cock shall not crow this day, before that thou shalt thrice deny that thou knowest me" (Luke 22:34; John 13:38). Peter provides, in Girard's view, "the most spectacular example of mimetic contagion" in the whole Gospel narrative—a textbook demonstration of how irresistible is the mimetic desire to unite against the victim (*I See* 19). Even Peter, who has been up to this point the first of Christ's disciples, cannot resist the crowd's violent unanimity.

To arrive at an adequate understanding of why Melville brings up such an intricate knot of religious references, we must turn to the end of the novel. After three months on the island, Tommo feels every day more a captive than a guest of the Typees. Ironically, while at the beginning of the narrative his desire was to touch land, now he seems ready to do anything to sail again. If initially the ship was the prison and the island the object of his and his companions' desire, now things are reversed. Yet the way in which the fulfillment of desire and the road to "freedom" are paved with violence remains unchanged. The Typees do not want Tommo to leave, and when the latter reaches the shore and jumps into the sea to board a nearby boat, the native Mow-Mow, along with other warriors, rush into the water in pursuit. At this point Tommo performs his Peter-like betrayal. To prevent Mow-Mow from seizing one of the oars, Tommo seizes the boat hook and, "exerting all

[his] strength," he strikes Mow-Mow "just below the throat" (*T* 252). One can hardly fail to see the resemblance between this blow against the islander and the earlier one against Pedro the cock. Both Mow-Mow and Pedro are construed by the novel as the last obstacle between the narrator and his, albeit temporary, deliverance; both are marked by physical defects (the cock limps, Mow-Mow is one-eyed) that qualify them as scapegoat figures; both are the target of terrible blows "just below the throat" described as regrettable but ultimately necessary forms of violence.

These connections between the novel's ending and its opening shed new light on how, from the very beginning, Tommo is implicated in the sacrificial logic he wishes to criticize. Notwithstanding the narrator's pose as a critic of colonialism and the white man's violence—"the white man [is] the most ferocious animal on the face of the earth" (*T* 125)—as a whole the text presents Tommo as an individual ready to resort to violence whenever his desires meet with resistance.[18] If at the beginning the only throat to be slit on the road to deliverance is that of Pedro the cock, by the end the throat to be cut is that of a human being whom Tommo needs to demonize in order to justify his behavior. The reason why the cock is named Peter is by now clear. Peter is not only the Christlike victim of communal violence but also the disciple incapable of resisting the crowd of persecutors. At the end of the novel, by presenting himself as a potential victim of Typee violence, Tommo—like Peter—chooses the side of violence because he is afraid of becoming himself the target of violence. When Tommo tries to run away, the tribe is for the first time shaken by an eruption of internal violence: "a new contest arose between the two parties [those who wished Tommo to leave and those who wished him to stay] who had accompanied me to the shore; blows were struck, wounds were given, and blood flowed" (*T* 250). The novel portrays a textbook sacrificial crisis, an explosion of violence that subsides only when Mow-Mow and his warriors run after Tommo.

It seems only appropriate that Tommo depicts his pursuers, and especially Mow-Mow, as bloodthirsty savages capable of swimming while holding a "tomahawk" between their teeth—a weapon that suddenly brings us back from Polynesia to America and its own savages and favorite scapegoat figures. In brief, Tommo gains his freedom only thanks to an intensification of the violence he originally needed to escape from the tyranny of the ship and, most importantly, by construing his act of violence as a necessary act of self-defense—as a form of "good," legitimate violence in opposition to the frenzy of a mob of hostile savages. Yet if we read carefully enough between Tommo's words, we can see that he has selected a scapegoat figure who—just like Pedro acting as the captain's surrogate—will turn the sacrificial crisis around and lend justification to the narrator's use of violence. Mow-Mow, in other words, provides Tommo with a mimetic model that will allow him to mitigate the "horror" he feels at the moment he strikes the islander.

After this detour through the South Seas and the early days of Melville's writing career, we should be able to appreciate the extent to which the ending of *Moby-Dick* is, structurally speaking, a rewriting of the victimizing scenario found in the last pages of *Typee*. A student of sacrificial strategies would find the ending of *Moby-Dick* striking because, instead of depicting the unanimous killing of a single, designated scapegoat (the Whale) and the deliverance of the entire community, in the ending of this novel the entire community is sacrificed while a single individual survives. Girard would call this an "inverted mimetic crisis," examples of which are to be found in several mythologies.[19] A biblical example would be, of course, the story of Noah, a story evoked, in fact, by Ishmael when he writes that "the great shroud of the sea rolled on as it rolled five thousand years ago" (*MD* 572), thereby reminding the reader that what he or she has just witnessed is a miniature reenactment of the Flood. Just as in the ending of *Typee* a band of savages unites in pursuing a human victim whose limping and marginal status as a foreigner make him a likely scapegoat, in the final pages of Melville's major novel a crew that has been repeatedly described as savage and barbaric directs its hate toward an animal victim. Yet in both cases the mimetic crisis is suddenly reversed as the would-be scapegoaters are turned into scapegoats themselves. Both Tommo and Moby Dick strike back against their pursuers. Significantly enough from this point of view, Ishmael directs his attention to Tashtego, the last visible crew member of the sinking *Pequod*. Tashtego, an American Indian, embodies an updated version of Mow-Mow: a savage perceived as the member of a doomed race (like the Typees and like Pedro the cock), represented as fierce as any one of Mrs. Rowlandson's Indians, and brandishing to the end his hammer (the whaling equivalent of Mow-Mow's tomahawk). Tashtego, in short, metonymically underlines the status of Ahab and the entire crew as appropriate victims of the Whale's revenge.

Once we have fully grasped the sacrificial dimension of this final scene, we are in a position to read Ishmael's deliverance through different lenses. Like Tommo—and unlike the Ishmael of the early chapters—Ishmael is saved only to the extent that he denies his former link with the "savage" world. The pagan harpooners have by the end become so many metaphors of the doomed, vanishing savages of America, "fixed by infatuation, or fidelity, or fate, to their once lofty perches" (*MD* 572) as the *Pequod* is inexorably drawn into a deathly vortex. That Ishmael is saved by taking a hold of Queequeg's coffin-canoe is from this perspective deeply ironical, and we have had to wait for an American Indian critic and novelist to point out that Ishmael's seizure of the coffin should be interpreted as an act of "white" appropriation of a formerly "red" space. As one of the Indian characters in Louis Owens's *The Sharpest Sight* reminds us, "When that white storyteller come bouncing up on the Indian's coffin, he killed off half of himself and he lost his power but didn't know it."[20] Even though Ishmael, unlike Tommo, does not seize a boat hook to kill off his "savage" half, the deaths of such figures as Tashtego and Queequeg are definitely presented by the novel as sacrificially necessary to the providential plot that leads to Ishmael's miraculous survival.

In the end the *Pequod*, which Ishmael in "The Try-Works" had already described as a ship "freighted with savages, and laden with fire ... and plunging into that blackness of darkness" so as to seem "the material counterpart of her monomaniac commander's soul" (*MD* 423), has become nothing less than an incarnation of Satan himself, sinking not to the bottom of the ocean but to hell. The sacrificial scope of the last pages of the novel is thus properly underlined by Ishmael's religious rhetoric, which stages the scapegoating of the *Pequod* as a casting out of Satan. Yet this choice inevitably raises the issue of how an agent of "eternal malice" like the White Whale can accomplish the ritual expulsion of an equally malicious entity; Ahab and his crew, as Ishmael stresses more than once, by the end are hardly distinguishable—to borrow a phrase from "The Doubloon," "all are Ahab" (*MD* 431). Here Ishmael's narrative amounts to an implicit, unwitting reply to one of the key questions raised by Jesus in the Gospels—a question to which Girard has in fact devoted much attention: "How can Satan cast out Satan?" (Mark 3:23). If we take Satan as another term for the violence of the mimetic crisis, to expel Satan through Satan means to expel violence through violence thanks to the sacrificial mechanism, by turning the violence that threatens to destroy a community into the violence of all against a single victim. *Moby-Dick* literally ends with the satanic expulsion of Satan, with the *Pequod* that, "like Satan," "sink[s] to hell," dragging along with her "a living part of heaven" (*MD* 572)—the seahawk nailed to the main-mast by Tashtego's hammer, a sort of emblematic portrait of the victimary mechanism itself. Yet Ishmael's narrative makes clear beyond any doubt how the violent and vengeful world of the ship is brought to an end by a creature described as equally violent and vengeful. It can be read as a virtual textbook illustration of Girard's notion that "the Satan who expels and reestablishes order is really identical to the Satan who foments disorder" (*I See* 44). Ishmael's story expels Ahab's violence only through a confirmation of that violent, revengeful, and "sacred" nature of Moby Dick on which Ahab's vision depends.

5

If one agrees that Ishmael's voice parallels the rhetoric of the Jeremiad and its victimizing ideology, what remains to be seen is what degree of distance from the narrator is granted to the reader by *Moby-Dick* as a whole. According to James Duban, scholars should not confuse Melville with Ishmael. By arguing against those who wish to make of Ishmael a "cultural hero" who speaks for Melville as well as against those who impute to Melville himself the flawed vision of his narrator, Duban insists that Melville employs Ishmael in order to *critique* the latter's ideological assumptions (see "Chipping with a Chisel"). Similarly, one of the best-known New Americanists, Donald Pease, also attempts to exonerate Melville from Ishmael's blindness. Pease convincingly argues that Ishmael's discourse is implicated in Ahab's totalizing scenario but, like Duban, he refuses to see in the narrator's contradictions a reflection of the author's own impasse. Pease rejects the novel's logic of mutual destruction and thus resorts to Melville's correspondence with Hawthorne in order to find at least a modicum of the "genuine fellow feeling" lacking in the catastrophic world of the novel. But while in the letter from which Pease quotes, Melville does speak of the "infinite fraternity of feeling" that has overtaken him on account of his friend's understanding of *Moby-Dick,* in that same letter Melville also famously states: "I have written a wicked book, and feel spotless as the lamb" (*Cor* 212).[21] These words—in a letter exceedingly rich with references to religion and sacrifice—provide a telling instance of that "new mood of harmony and peace" ("Generative" 91) following a successful scapegoating. The novel's scapegoat is of course, first and foremost, the would-be scapegoater himself, Captain Ahab. Melville stages in the letter what another student of ritual violence, Walter Burkert, calls a "comedy of innocence": by expressing at once guilt (that he has written a wicked book) and disclaiming his responsibility (he feels spotless as the lamb), Melville himself acknowledges his novel's participation in the logic of sacrifice.[22]

Pease and Duban rightly underscore a position already brilliantly argued by Walter Bezanson nearly fifty years ago, thus reminding us of the dangers involved in any simplistic identification of Ishmael with Melville ("Work of Art" 31–58). However, one can hardly believe that the author can completely and fully transcend the merciless, revengeful world inhabited by Ishmael. It certainly seems plausible, as Duban notes, that Melville created a narrator "whose assumptions, sincerely advanced, the reader is independently left to analyze, judge, and perhaps find inadequate" ("Chipping with a Chisel" 365). But if the reader may—to confine ourselves to the theme at hand—see the limitations of Ishmael's sacrificial reading of the novel's ending, the latter is the work of an author fully aware of its victimizing mechanism. To an extent, Ishmael can tell the tale of sin and punishment denied to Jonah precisely because Ahab, unlike the Ninevites, never repents, thus paving the way to his well-deserved condemnation.[23] In the second chapter of the biblical book of Jonah, however, the Lord is also willing to forgive those who, like Jonah himself, do not repent. In *Moby-Dick,* instead, Ahab does not repent, nor does he receive any forgiveness, and this results from both the sacrificial rhetoric embraced by Ishmael and, in part, Melville's own narrative choices.

This conclusion should not be understood as an implicit moral condemnation of Melville. On the contrary, also on this score one must admire his "Shakespearean" stature: like the "divine William," Melville knew all too well the difficulty of conceiving a tragic path that did not lead up to the cathartic effect granted by the victimage mechanism.[24] Just as Hamlet's drama is, in Girard's eyes, an attempt to highlight and subvert the logic of revenge tragedy without depriving the public of the customary sacrificial ending, *Moby-Dick* can be seen as the, inevitably flawed, critique Melville mounts against our victimizing propensities. *Moby-Dick* does not rest content in offering us one or more victims who receive the punishment they deserve. Instead, the novel tries hard to cast light on how any desire for revenge and any effort at solving contradictions by having recourse to violence can only reinstate what Kenneth Burke, in the poem quoted in the epigraph above, describes as "the cult of the kill." By offering us an anatomy of the contradictory and circular fascination that violence exerts upon the individual and society at large, the novel lays bare the sacrificial logic that underlies it.

Melville, as both Pease and Duban have rightly seen, cannot be identified wholesale with Ishmael, and the narrative does, to an extent, allow the reader to take an independent perspective toward the narrator. From the very beginning of the novel Ishmael's voice is clearly fraught with tensions and contradictions. Far from being a narrator who talks to us from the heights of his complete redemption, Ishmael has attained no long-term psychological and existential balance from the cathartic ending of the adventure he begins to narrate. Ishmael declares, in fact, in the very first paragraph of his narrative that "Whenever I find myself growing grim about the mouth; whenever it is a damp, drizzly November in my soul; whenever I find myself involuntarily pausing before coffin warehouses, and bringing up the rear of every funeral I meet; and especially whenever my hypos get such an upper hand of me, that it requires a strong moral principle from deliberately stepping into the street, and methodically knocking people's hats off—then, I account it high time to get to sea as soon as I can" (*MD* 3). As the insistent use of "whenever" clearly indicates, Ishmael's "hypos" is not an occasional but a recurrent condition, and since the Ishmael who talks to us here can only be the one who survived the *Pequod*'s disaster, what he has gone through has obviously not managed permanently to heal his soul. On the contrary, Ishmael seems condemned to go to sea any time his depression grows so severe that he is tempted to find some relief in violence. The jovial tone of this opening chapter should not distract us from seeing that going to sea is Ishmael's only cure. Only in this way can he find an outlet to a violent impulse he may direct toward others or himself: "This is my substitute for pistol and ball. With a philosophical flourish Cato throws himself upon his sword; I quietly take to the ship" (*MD* 3). As an account of Ishmael's sea-adventures, *Moby-Dick* therefore also qualifies as a "substitute for pistol and ball": an act of imaginative violence capable of healing to the extent that it can provide its narrative "pistol" with a legitimate target. The novel therefore theorizes the usefulness of the victimage mechanism from the very start.[25] But if on the one hand Melville grants Ishmael his "wicked book," on the other *Moby-Dick* does not hide the fact that what we call "spotlessness" is often nothing but the paradoxical effect of our participation in the violence of sacrifice. From Ishmael's viewpoint his "mighty book" can indeed function as a means to exorcise the violence that surrounds him and, most importantly, to expel—for a time at least—the violence he harbors within himself. From the point of view of a reader able to distance himself or herself from the narrator, *Moby-Dick* is best compared to Queequeg's famous tomahawk-pipe, "which, it seemed, had in its two uses both brained his foes and soothed his soul" (100). By reminding us that what soothes our souls is all too often what hurts those we have chosen as our enemies, Melville, without transcending it, unveils the mis(t)ery of the victimage mechanism.

Notes

1. Kenneth Burke, *The Rhetoric of Religion: Studies in Logology* (Boston: Beacon Press, 1961), 4–5. I wish to thank Masturah Alatas and Gordon Poole for their precious readings of earlier versions of this essay. I dedicate this piece to the memory of Dick Wasson, without whose encouragement and support my graduate school days at Rutgers University would have not been the same.

2. René Girard, *Violence and the Sacred* (Baltimore: Johns Hopkins Univ. Press, 1977), 312–14.

3. Here and elsewhere all scriptural quotations are from the King James Bible.

4. Biblical scholars have often commented on the ironic and satirical elements of the Jonah story. For a reading of the story as an example of classical satire see James S. Ackerman, "Jonah,"

in *The Literary Guide to the Bible,* ed. Robert Alter and Frank Kermode (Cambridge, Mass.: Harvard Univ. Press, 1987), 234–43.

5. Also Elisa New has detected a "sacrificial imperative" at the heart of Mapple's sermon. New, however, fails to see that even such a champion of what she calls "Hebraic prolixity" as Ishmael is ultimately implicated in a sacrificial rhetoric.

6. René Girard, "Generative Scapegoating," in *Violent Origins. Ritual Killing and Cultural Formation,* ed. Robert G. Hamerton-Kelly (Stanford: Stanford Univ. Press, 1987), 117.

7. Even though in most of his work Girard has emphasized the dangers of mimetic desire as the breeding ground of the sacrificial crisis, he does by no means deny that humanity's imitative propensities can often have positive effects. For Girard's comments on what we may call the bright side of mimetic desire see especially his *Origine della cultura e fine della storia.* Dialoghi con Pierpaolo Antonelli and João Cezar de Castro Rocha (Milan: Raffaello Cortina, 2003).

8. Both Ahab and Moby Dick are marked by a "wrinkled brow"; the whiteness of the whale is matched by Ahab's "white hair," his "white mark," and his "barbaric white leg" (made of whalebone, of course); both are marked with scars and wounds; both are compared to a pyramid, and both Ahab and Moby Dick are called "King of the sea." Moreover, even the *Pequod* is compared by Ishmael to a whale. Of course the idea that Ahab and Moby Dick are "doubles" is not a new one: it can be found, for example, in Richard Slotkin's discussion of the novel in *Regeneration through Violence: The Mythology of the American Frontier, 1600–1860* (Middletown, Conn.: Wesleyan Univ. Press, 1973), 545. However, while Slotkin's notion of the double is functional to his reading of *Moby-Dick* as yet another incarnation of the "myth of the hunter," Girard's concept of the monstrous double allows one to go beyond a purely mythological-psychological reading, and to demystify the "sacredness" of Ahab's hunt. Indeed, Melville's narrative alerts us to the fact that, however monstrous, as a proper scapegoat figure Moby Dick is also in many ways humanized. Scapegoats must be marked by abnormalities, but they can never be felt to be too far from the human community their sacrifice is destined to purge.

9. René Girard, *Things Hidden Since the Foundation of the World* (Stanford: Stanford Univ. Press, 1987), 416. As Moby Dick's double, Ahab shares the Whale's scandalous nature. Interestingly, Girard reminds us that "the Greek word *skandalizein* comes from a verb that means 'to limp.' What does a lame person resemble? To someone following a person limping it appears that the person continually collides with his or her own shadow." René Girard, *I See Satan Fall like Lightning,* trans. and with a foreword by James G. Williams (Maryknoll, N.Y.: Orbis Books, 1999), 19. This etymology is worth bearing in mind also in connection to Tommo's limping in *Typee,* which is commented upon below.

10. "The greatest danger to the self is the past, for disappointment may transform the will to power into the desire for revenge. The will does not easily learn to forget or to pass by. 'This, indeed this alone,' Zarathustra concludes, 'is what *revenge* is: the will's ill will against time and its 'it was.'" Tobin Siebers, *The Ethics of Criticism* (Ithaca, N.Y.: Cornell Univ. Press, 1988), 138.

11. "Ishmael, traditionally considered a foil for Ahab's megalomaniacal acts of interpretation, is in fact finally, although subtly, seduced by Ahab's point of view; his mirroring ultimately submits, to a large extent, to a reflection of rather than on Ahab." Priscilla Wald, "Hearing Narrative Voices in Melville's *Pierre,*" *Boundary* 2 17 (Spring 1990): 125.

12. Dimock 109–39. Dimock's comparison of Ahab's destiny to the fate of the American Indian as an example of "negative individualism" is, though, not altogether convincing. More importantly, Dimock argues that "Ahab can have only one narrative, not a narrative of vengeance, but a narrative of doom," but it seems to me that his narrative is one of doom (like that of a Macbeth or a Hamlet) precisely *because* it is a narrative of vengeance. In other words, it cannot be ignored that the man who is scapegoated by the novel is himself a great would-be

scapegoater. What the narrative does to him is no more and no less what he would have done to the White Whale.

13. As in the case of the White Whale, Ahab's scapegoat status helps to explain his ambivalent characterization. As an embodiment of the "sacred" he is both divine and infernal, a figure to be both revered and loathed. He can be represented as a Christ figure metaphorically wearing the Crown of Lombardy and yet also as an ally of the satanic Fedallah.

14. René Girard, "Hamlet's Dull Revenge," *Stanford Literary Review* 1–2 (1984–85): 183.

15. One of the best arguments in defense of Ishmael as "redeemed hero" is to be found in Christopher Sten, *Sounding the Whale: "Moby-Dick" as Epic Novel.* It is well known that Melville drew on the legendary tales of "Mocha Dick: or the White Whale of the Pacific." However, what prompted Melville to choose the name "Moby" for his whale apparently has never been established. If we keep in mind the whale's magnitude as well as how Moby Dick "tasks" and "heaps" Ahab, it might not be farfetched to imagine that Melville wanted to exploit the semantic value of both the noun "mob" and the verb "to mob." Along these lines it is worth noting that during "The Chase—Second Day" Starbuck yells at Ahab that "all good angels [are] *mobbing* thee with warnings" (*MD* 561, my emphasis). Simply put, the angels' "mobbing" of Ahab cannot outweigh the perverse attraction of Moby Dick's mobbing.

16. In addition to *Moby-Dick* and *Typee,* a preliminary list of Melvillean narratives that are brought to a close only through violence and the expulsion of sacrificial figures would include "Benito Cereno," with its execution of the rebel Babo; "Bartleby," with the gradual but nonetheless inexorable casting out of the eccentric scrivener; *Pierre,* with its tragic trajectory of the writer-as-outcast; the "Indian hating" section of *The Confidence-Man,* with the scapegoating of the Indian Mocmohoc; and *Billy Budd,* with its execution of the "handsome sailor."

17. After describing the situation on board the *Dolly,* as soon as the narrator mentions that the ship is heading toward the Marquesas, he immediately thinks of "*heathenish rites and human sacrifices*" (*T* 5, emphasis in the original). In a sense, he has been talking about that from the beginning of his story.

18. Here D. H. Lawrence's commentary still proves valuable: "So Melville escaped, and threw a boathook full in the throat of one of his dearest savage friends, and sank him, because that savage was swimming in pursuit. That's how he felt about the savages when they wanted to detain him. He'd have murdered them one and all, vividly, rather than be kept from escaping. Away from them—he must get away from them—at any price." *Studies in Classic American Literature,* in *The Shock of Recognition,* ed. Edmund Wilson (New York: The Modern Library, 1955), 1038.

19. On this see *Origine* 176–77. Girard does not explain in detail how to interpret such inversions of the mimetic crisis. Yet the Boroboro myth from Levi-Strauss's *The Raw and the Cooked* to which he refers bears a striking resemblance to the ending of *Moby-Dick.* After a deluge the earth's population is growing too fast and Meri, the sun, orders the entire population to cross a river by walking over a tree trunk. Under such great weight the trunk collapses and all the people perish except Akaruio Bokodori, who was lagging behind because of his deformed legs. Akaruio, however, will resurrect everyone thanks to his drum and his magic. Akaruio is obviously a scapegoat figure—deformed, endowed with unusual powers, and at some distance from his community. He is therefore an embodiment of the sacred, the one capable of restoring harmony to a community plagued by a "crisis of indifferentiation" (that is, a mimetic crisis in which social differences disintegrate and the group is ridden with violence) represented by the two consecutive floods. In the case of *Moby-Dick,* the reversal of the mimetic crisis results, on the one hand, in the confirmation of the "sacred" status of the Whale, and, on the other, in the miraculous survival of Ishmael who is himself, like Akaruio, an outcast, the "orphan"

picked up by the *Rachel.* Obviously, as Ishmael ultimately inhabits a novelistic rather than a mythic universe, his "ressurection" of the community can only be a purely narrative feat.

20. "But you know, it was a white man's book. There was a Indian man in it who smoked the pipe with the storyteller. . . . At the end, the white-man storyteller come bouncing up to the surface of the ocean on that Indian's coffin. You know grandson, us Choctaws signed nine treaties with the government, smoking the pipe nine times, and every time it's like this book. The white man comes riding to the surface on a Indian's coffin." Louis Owens, *The Sharpest Sight* (Norman and London: Univ. of Oklahoma Press, 1992), 90–91.

21. Donald Pease, *Visionary Compacts: American Renaissance Writings in Cultural Context.* (Madison: Univ. of Wisconsin Press, 1987). The Melville letter to Hawthorne is the famous November 17 [?], 1851 letter.

22. Walter Burkhert, "The Problem of Ritual Killing," in *Violent Origins: Ritual Killing and Cultural Formation,* ed. Robert G. Hamerton-Kelly (Stanford: Stanford Univ. Press, 1987), 166.

23. It is no accident that Ahab tells Captain Gardiner: "may I forgive myself, but I must go" (*MD* 532). In his monomaniacal, self-referential logic, Ahab conceives forgiveness as something coming not from the Other, but from himself.

24. Shakespeare's influence on *Moby-Dick* has been one of the traditional themes of Melvillean studies, especially after Charles Olson's and F. O. Matthiessen's investigations. Yet, despite the fact that Matthiessen entitled his *American Renaissance* chapter on *Moby-Dick* "The Revenger's Tragedy," the sacrificial dimension of Ahab's revenge has gone largely unnoticed.

25. In other words, the early scenes of *Moby-Dick* are also structurally similar to the opening of *Typee,* just as the ironic, circular nature of Ishmael's desire to go to sea is a recasting of Tommo's longing for adventure, first, and for "Home" and "Mother," later.

Man, Mind, Whale

⸎

Filling the Void

A Lacanian Angle of Vision on *Moby-Dick*

DENNIS WILLIAMS

In one of the funniest moments of the now-venerable television special *A Charlie Brown Christmas*, Lucy, sitting at her psychiatrist's booth, says to a depressed Charlie Brown, "If you can tell us your fears, we can *label* them." No doubt some literary scholars' assessment of the psychoanalytic enterprise derives from a scene such as this one: "psychoanalysis" (broadly and monolithically conceived) consists of a quasi-scientific discourse that attempts to explain away the richness of "human experience" in difficult, jargon-ridden, reductive language. Unfortunately, certain theoretical and interpretive attitudes and abuses—particularly in early, "vulgar" psychoanalytic readings—have contributed to this perception. Furthermore, various forms of cultural studies and the New Historicism continually insist upon the culturally determined and reductive nature of psychoanalytic discourse (even as they ignore their own culturally determined status and philosophical issues concerning sufficient causality, thus leading to their own forms of sociological and historical reductionism). The result, on the intellectual scene, has become rather predictable. As Slavoj Žižek, whose own work is deeply indebted to both psychoanalysis and ideology critique, has wryly noted, "One of the seasonal rituals of our intellectual life is that every couple of years, psychoanalysis is pronounced *démodé*, surpassed, finally dead and buried."[1] Alas, despite numerous stakes in the heart and the *ex cathedra* pronunciamentos of critics who, as a matter of theoretical pride, excoriate *ex cathedra* pronunciamentos, the monster will not stay quite dead. Perhaps it has assumed, at the very least, a crepuscularlike existence in the region of the "undead."

Whatever its current status may be in the ongoing contestations for intellectual legitimation, psychoanalysis continues to provide a conceptual framework capable of producing provocative insights into the complexities of human experience and its artistic representations, and Herman Melville's monumental novel *Moby-Dick* is a perfect candidate for just such a reconsideration. Ever since Henry A. Murray's groundbreaking "In Nomine Diaboli" and Newton Arvin's seminal reading of *Moby-Dick,* the use of specific psychoanalytic concepts or a hermeneutic frame at least partially indebted to psychoanalytic thinking has proven crucial in exploring, among other things, the symbolic, mythic, and oneiric dimensions of the novel. This essay will employ psychoanalysis—here, specifically, the work of French psychoanalyst Jacques Lacan—as a kind of hermeneutic frame to explore the importance of the void, a critical concept in both Melville's novel and Lacan's theorizing, with respect to existential positioning, the constitution of the subject, behavioral manifestations, intersubjective dialectics, and the role of fantasy. *Moby-Dick*'s length and richly textured complexity would require a full-length study to attempt anything like a comprehensive psychoanalytic reading; hence, this approach, of necessity, will be much more modest and arbitrary in its choice of topics. The first two sections will address how, in Lacanian terms, the void functions in the character and behavior of Ahab, and the third section will analyze the pivotal role that it plays in the relationship between Ahab and Moby Dick. The complexity of Lacanian analysis will not be reductive but will, in fact, help us appreciate the depth and density of Melville's characterizations and conceptions, many of which are remarkably prescient in their proto-analytic specificity. As has been amply documented and as Freud readily acknowledged, literature has influenced psychoanalysis as much as psychoanalysis has influenced literature.

Ahab as Obsessive: "What Am I?"

For obvious reasons, the attempt to define or delineate the contours of the void is precarious at best, impossible at worst. Neither a commonsense "thing" as an epistemology of realism might suggest, nor a phenomenon as such given in terms of sensory intuition, nor available for a noetic or noematic analysis from a phenomenological point of view, the void or absence can only be approached indirectly, from descriptions and analyses of its effects. Such effects often point to its structural or functional presence, the presence of an absence, so to speak; but the analyses themselves are potentially subject to a certain undoing or ambiguity resulting from the operation of the void within the system of discursivity or signification. Our approach, then, can only be indirect and epistemologically humble, tentative at best. How could one possibly be certain about nothing?

From a psychoanalytic perspective, particularly the psychoanalysis of Jacques Lacan, the presence of this nothing is best traced through some-things, in this instance, one's fundamental positioning as a subject and one's symptomatic behaviors. And as the most dramatic, fully realized character in *Moby-Dick,* Ahab provides the most striking instances of the manifestation and function of the void.

Ahab's intense and tempestuous monomania certainly qualifies him as clinically "neurotic," but the use and connotations of this word need to be modulated carefully here. Lacan's major nosological categories (psychosis, perversion, neurosis), although useful for delineating symptomatology, more importantly mark psychic structures and existential-ontological subject posi-tions[2] representing a particular kind of response to the primordial losses that, from a psychoanalytic point of view, constitute the subject.[3] Thus to call Ahab "neurotic," for our purposes, does not reductively place him in a diagnostic category and foreclose further inquiry; instead, the designation indicates in a general manner a fundamental stance or orientation toward the void produced by the subject's primordial traumas. Such a designation provides a kind of propaedeutic investigatory tool allowing for the further examination of the specific, complex psychic elements that constitute literary "character."

Psychological responses to something as indefinite as the void are likely to be equivocal or even contradictory; and the obsessional economy that characterizes Ahab, at least in part, is no exception. For example, although obsessives exhibit considerable self-reliance and thus often appear self-as-sured and sovereign, the subject position of neurosis in general (obsession and hysteria are the major subdivisions) is characterized at another level by extreme doubt concerning the nature of one's identity.[4] Indeed, Bruce Fink even suggests that "Lacan views the fundamental question involved in neurosis as the question of being: 'What am I?'" clearly emphasizing the existential-ontological dimension of subject positioning (121). Ahab's com-plex and tortured personality powerfully demonstrates this tension between megalomaniacal self-assurance and anxious uncertainty about one's most fundamental being.

This existential anxiety is dramatically illustrated in Chapter 132, "The Symphony." In response to Starbuck's entreaty to abjure the monomaniacal quest for the whale and rejoin the human community, Ahab lapses into what appears to be a primarily metaphysical meditation on the nature of personal agency and the ineluctability of Fate; but his meditation, in fact, reveals, in compressed and somewhat oblique form, Ahab's existential-ontological apprehensions: "What is it, what nameless, inscrutable unearthly thing is it; what cozening, hidden lord and master, and cruel, remorseless emperor commands me; that against all natural lovings and longings, I so keep pushing, and crowding, and jamming myself on all the time; recklessly making me ready to do what in my own, proper, natural heart, I durst not so much as dare? Is Ahab, Ahab? Is it I, God, or who that lifts this arm?" (*MD* 545). The heart of the passage seems to be a straightforward enough question—"Is Ahab, Ahab?" the interrogative form of the basic philosophico-logical formula of identity: A=A, Ahab is Ahab. But a closer look reveals a more complex scenario.

The nature of the self, for both Melville and Lacan, significantly problematizes simple specular identification, which, for the latter, in fact, signals the fundamental *mis*identification or *méconnaissance* of the ego in the image of an "other."[5] Employing the paradigm of identity (Ahab=Ahab), even in the interrogatory mode, generates an empty tautology and presumes precisely what is at stake in the interrogation: the identity (in the sense of a comprehensive definition or an enumeration of predicates) of "Ahab," whatever that might be. *What is* an "Ahab"? *What* is subsumed under the identity? Beginning with the paradigm of identity, formulating the question in this manner, produces only a superficial answer: yes, Ahab is, or no, Ahab is not, Ahab. But it provides no substantive information and serves only as a kind of psychological security blanket that substitutes the mollification of mere formal, specular identity for meaningful conceptual elaboration and, in this instance, psychological self-comprehension.

This conception of identity, A=A, in fact conceals the necessary split upon which any subsequent claim of identity depends—there must be, at the very least, a minimal differentiation between something and itself in order for the statement, then, of its identity, of that jointure, to be feasible.[6] The possible conceptual recuperation of the self (Ahab=Ahab) veils the void that lurks just beneath—that *is*—that ever-so-slight, minimal differentiation; but this recuperation may be as conceptually misleading as it is psychologically comforting. At the heart of Ahab's deceptively simple question lurk certain assumptions of Western thought concerning the imperative of identity thinking that Melville's explorations of the self in *Moby-Dick,* including those concerning Ahab, will problematize.

This issue of the ontological gap or void is highlighted even further if we are allowed some hermeneutical liberty in considering the syntax and diacritical markings of Ahab's question. The question reads, "Is Ahab, Ahab?" and at issue here is the diacritical function of the comma. Technically unnecessary, although permissible and perhaps even preferable, the comma serves merely a clarifying function, separating adjoining *Ahab*s. (Interestingly, without it, Ahab's question threatens to collapse into a meaningless stutter yet also mimetically reproduces more closely ["Ahab Ahab"] the desired identity, a specular reflection, with, presumably, no interference or mediation.) But if we are allowed to pressure the question a little, the emphasis now shifts to the verb: "*Is* Ahab, Ahab?"—that is, does Ahab, in fact, even *exist,* and if so, in what mode? The status of the "is" commutes, then, from the "is" of identity to the "is" of ontology, and the context shifts from the empty tautology of identity to the ontological question of being. But note also that, in this form of the question, the subject interrogated (the existence of Ahab) must simultaneously be presumed in the mode of address (Ahab as addréssee of the question—"*Is* Ahab, *Ahab?*) *as* a subject (in the other sense of that word). So the question either answers itself by presupposing the existence of the very subject whose existence is being questioned, or it collapses in a performative contradiction. What appears initially as a relatively simple question in fact turns out to be a complex interrogation concerning the possibility of self-identity (or the identity of the self—presumably, but not necessarily, the same thing), the nature of this "self" subsumed under the proper name "Ahab," and the even more fundamental question of its very existence.

One last aspect of the obsessional economy deserves particular attention, both because it accurately reflects Ahab and because the scene of its exemplification in *Moby-Dick* elegantly links obsessionality with what we have been calling "the void" as it appears in and traverses both psychoanalytic and philosophical registers. A dominant, perhaps fundamental, characteristic of the obsessive is the need for total control and mastery. As Joël Dor points out, "Obsessionals are mighty conquerors in this respect, mobilizing the most insane and protracted means to win this fantasized mastery" (121). This need for mastery is invariably accompanied by a great deal of frenetic activity, ironically often devoted to maintaining the status quo, keeping the world in order.[7] These characteristics, in turn, tend to be accompanied by another: an extreme emphasis on consciousness, that is, on the conscious mind. Because the need for control produces a consequent distrust of anything that might threaten it, phenomena such as sleep and the unconscious generate anxiety precisely because they signal loss of consciousness and thus the loss of control that the obsessive so dearly craves. "The obsessive," Bruce Fink notes, "is convinced that he is, that he *exists,* only when he is *consciously* thinking" (122, my italics). The essentially defensive orientation here should be obvious—those things that are uncertain, that suggest indeterminacy, are to be avoided at all costs because they suggest loss of control; and loss of control, for the obsessive, points directly to the voiding of the category of the self.

This crucial linkage between obsession, the decentering of the self, and the void is impressively demonstrated in a scene from Chapter 44, "The Chart."[8] After a day of "intense thoughts" "whirled ... round and round in his blazing brain" (*MD* 201) concerning the great White Whale and his (Ahab's) mono-maniacal plan of revenge, Ahab's sleep is disturbed and fitful, and he awakens, bursting forth from his quarters: "For, at such times, crazy Ahab, the scheming, unappeasedly steadfast hunter of the white whale; this Ahab that had gone to his hammock, was not the agent that so caused him to burst from it in horror again. The latter was the eternal, living principle or soul in him; and in sleep, being for a time dissociated from the characterizing mind, which at other times employed it for its outer vehicle or agent, it spontaneously sought escape from the scorching contiguity of the frantic thing, of which, for the time, it was no longer an integral" (202). Once again, the passage explicitly raises the issue of "agency": who—or if the use of this pronoun is already too tendentious, what—is Ahab? Here, he is dichotomized as a "soul" and a "mind" that appears to supervene upon it, the word "contiguity" emphasizing the apparently arbitrary connection between the two.

The passage goes on to indicate what we might call the composition of this "mind": "But as the mind does not exist unless leagued with the soul, therefore it must have been that, in Ahab's case, yielding up all his thoughts and fancies to his one supreme purpose; that purpose, by its own sheer inveteracy of will, forced itself against gods and devils into a kind of self-assumed, independent being of its own. Nay, could grimly live and burn, while the common vitality to which it was conjoined, fled horror-stricken from the unbidden and unfathered birth" (*MD* 202). This passage portrays a remarkable combination of eighteenth-century facultary psychology and protopsychoanalytic insight. The mind, as a result of its intense obsessions, has developed a life of its own, independent from its animating principle, the latter so appalled that it flees in horror. Translated, *mutatis mutandis*, into Lacanian terms, the ego (roughly the equivalent of "mind" here) appears as a product, a construction, a "thing," an alienated and alienating agency that attains independence from the animating force of the life dynamism (roughly, the "libido").[9] The ensuing relation between the agencies of mind and soul, far from being synergistic, is tense and antipathetic. Although the passage closely links "mind" and will, the union, from a certain perspective, is rather unorthodox: many (particularly Romantic) conceptions of the psyche coun-terpose the (rational) mind to the will and tend to align the latter with the life dynamism. The resultant "unfathered birth" in this passage underscores the will's tendency toward autogenesis and the concomitant occlusion of elements necessary to realize its intentions—here, the "mind" as an essential partner upon which it supervenes. The will's potency, however, does not eventuate in a sufficiently realized birth. Note Melville's qualifier: the mind assumes "a *kind of . . .* independent being" (my italics), a quasi-independence necessarily relying on the animating life force while simultaneously resisting and even undermining it—the operation of what Freud will call the death drive, that in the psyche which impels toward dissolution and ultimately self-destruction. Thus Melville's theatrical and somewhat unorthodox allegory of the psyche underscores the internal divisions, the fundamental decenteredness, of the "self" as it reveals the intrapsychic manifestations of the notorious strength of will that ultimately will lead to Ahab's destruction.

The passage concludes: "Therefore, the tormented spirit that glared out of bodily eyes, when what seemed Ahab rushed from his room, was for the time but a vacated thing, a formless somnambulistic being, a ray of living light, to be sure, but without an object to color, and therefore a blankness in itself. God help thee, old man, thy thoughts have created a creature in thee; and he whose intense thinking thus makes him a Prometheus; a vulture feeds upon that heart for ever; that vulture the very creature he creates" (*MD* 202). Excavating "below" this thing created by thoughts, insisting that sufficient analytical labor will reach an origin, a pristine *fundamentum* of the "self," we find . . . what? "A vacated thing," "a formless, somnambulistic being," "blankness in itself." Describable but not comprehensible (what would "blankness in itself" *mean?* What would the experience of this *be?*), this self-as-void bears remarkable resemblance, at least in part, to the Hegelian self of absolute negativity, the Kantian self as transcendental apperception, and the Lacanian self as the gap between two signifiers.[10] That is, it requires a thinking of the "self" in terms other than that of "substance," its formal categorization in Western culture at least since Descartes (the self as *res cogitans,* a thinking *thing*), and implicitly since Plato and Aristotle. The "self" is, indeed, ineffable—and in this sense, the Romantics may have been surprisingly accurate. In this Melvillean-Kantian-Hegelian-Lacanian conception, the "self" is a trace or a mark appearing phenomenally only in the process of a continual disappearing. Because of historical sedimentation, however, it is almost impossible for us to think "self" without substantializing it; and, consequently, the idea of a "formless" self tends to engender anxiety and horror, "formlessness" being associated with lack of foundation or anchoring. That psychotics routinely report feeling the loss of "self" to be a powerful indicator of incipient psychotic collapse inspires no confidence in this "blankness" as something one might appropriate or celebrate.[11] Melville wishes to capitalize on precisely this horror in the scene under discussion. No wonder, then, that Ahab, Ahab-as-obsessive, so distrusts sleep. It allows—better, it forces upon him—an experience of who he is at the "deepest level" (although, as we have seen, this designation is something of a misnomer since one can never get to the "originary" level): a paradoxical experience of nothingness, a total loss of control (in contradistinction to the control the ego in general and the obsessive in particular so desperately crave). This "blankness," via the implications of the well-known "whiteness of the whale," adumbrates the presence of Moby Dick; and although understandable and affectively unsettling enough as a kind of existential marker for the "self" in this passage, it will come to have a psychoanalytically precise and more complex function in the third section of this essay. But first another aspect of Ahab's psyche needs to be addressed.

AHAB AS PERVERT: "NOT THY WILL, BUT MINE BE DONE"

Lacan's diagnostic categories, as noted above, are less shorthand designations of behavioral symptoms than existential-ontological positions that mark, in a general manner, a subject's basic orientation to the fundamental losses experienced in early life—most notably, the original, traumatic separation from the mother. These fundamental positions, for Lacan, are the neurotic, the perverse, and the psychotic. One might reasonably assume that such orientations to something as potentially elusive and equivocal as "loss" or its metonymic/philosophical extension, "the void," are not strictly categorical (although clinically, such orientations do exhibit a certain statistical regularity). That is, a subject's behaviors may manifest a certain amount of "bleed" between positions. Certain obsessive neurotics may manifest perverse tendencies or even psychotic symptoms, such as hallucination; nevertheless, their fundamental psychic orientation remains "neurotic." These facts suggest a perhaps banal yet still important cautionary truth: that human experience and behavior are extremely complex and elusive and that psychoanalytic categories are imperfect and best employed with a certain nuance and sensitivity to their fluid or even provisional nature.

Critically regarded as one of the most complex and enigmatic characters in American literature, Ahab, perhaps more than anyone, threatens to escape any categorical reductionism, psychoanalytic or otherwise.[12] Although his negotiations with the void can be elaborated partly through the category of obsessional neurosis, other aspects of his behavior and its relationship to the void are best conceived via Lacan's category of the perverse subject.

Both the neurotic and the perverse structures—and herein lies the potential for confusion—exhibit minimal Oedipal triangulation.[13] However, while neurotic structure, which represents statistical "normality," results from the relatively successful interruption of the mother-child dyad by the "third" (someone exercising the Paternal function), perverse structure, clinically relatively rare, results from a less-than-satisfactory intervention. Consequently, the child remains "too close" to the mother, at risk of being her mere libidinal extension and not able to establish an independent identity in the Symbolic dimension (that of language, law, and social mores).[14] This results, to syncopate rather quickly a complex series of events and positions, in what Freud calls a splitting of the ego (*Ichspaltung*): the pervert simultaneously accepts and rejects the possibility of castration (for Lacan, Symbolic castration). For our purposes, two possible results of this impossible scenario prove significant: the perverse subject establishes a fetish object, a kind of apotropaic idol, as a defense against having to acknowledge the possibility of castration; yet he[15] simultaneously desires to stage the very castration he fears in order to obtain some "breathing space," the separation from the mother necessary for establishing his identity. He wishes to resist or transgress the Law (of paternal interdiction) yet also, paradoxically, to institute that Law. This paradoxical relationship will be the concern in this section; the issue of the fetish object will be taken up in the third.

With respect to Ahab's desire to be *the* law, to establish a complete autocracy, contemporary criticism has fully documented its political impact aboard the *Pequod*.[16] The concern here, however, is somewhat more abstract, structural, and properly psychological—namely, Ahab's desire to become a law unto himself, to establish himself as a complete autarky. Such a desire characterizes the perverse subject position and manifests itself as an almost compulsive need to defy and transgress not only sexual boundaries—the popular conception of the "sexual pervert"—but boundaries and limits of all kinds.

This type of extreme defiance and transgression appears in Chapter 119, "The Candles," one of *Moby-Dick*'s most dramatic chapters. After lightning strikes the *Pequod*, producing corposants at the top of the masts,[17] Ahab, with Fedallah kneeling at his feet, takes the main-mast links in his hand in order to "feel this pulse" (*MD* 507) of the electricity move through him and addresses the fire:

> Oh! Thou clear spirit of clear fire, whom on these seas I as Persian once did worship, till in the sacramental act so burned by thee, that to this hour I bear the scar; I now know thee, thou clear spirit, and I now know that thy right worship is defiance. To neither love nor reverence wilt thou be kind; and e'en for hate thou canst but kill; and all are killed. No fearless fool now fronts thee. I own thy speechless, placeless power; but to the last gasp of my earthquake life will dispute its unconditional,

unintegral mastery in me. In the midst of the personified impersonal, a personality stands here. Though but a point at best; whencesoe'er I came; whencesoe'er I go; yet while I earthly live, the queenly personality lives in me, and feels her royal rights. (507)

The passage dramatically portrays both "defiance" (specifically named) and transgression (a necessary ramification). Ahab challenges a putatively superior and dominating power—an entity equally physical and metaphysical—and in so doing necessarily transgresses both natural and supernatural laws. The scenario's power, dramatic enough in itself, will resonate throughout the novel—Ahab here establishes himself as a kind of proto-*Übermensch*, in the vulgar sense, a classically Romantic rebel of Promethean proportions whose conception of "self" will determine the fate of both himself and his crew.

This defiance, however, is complicated by an important rhetorical gesture. Defiance requires something to defy. That Ahab personifies his adversary, the fire, a natural phenomenon, via the prosopopoeia of address has significant implications. First, such a gesture "humanizes" nature, places a human face on an impersonal phenomenon, and thus assumes the possible intellectual or emotional response of a human interlocutor.[18] A remnant of animism, such a gesture "makes sense" of the universe, allows for comprehensible, ostensibly intersubjective interaction (even if that interaction appears in the mode of negation) with impersonal forces. The struggle with a "humanized" superior foe generates less anxiety than the possibility of utter indifference—better to have a clearly delineated adversary than to flail helplessly and impotently against an impersonal and unresponsive void. Furthermore, later in the speech, Ahab identifies the power as his "fiery father." His fervent rejection of its authority—his refusal to concede any dominance or hegemony—mirrors the perverse subject's refusal to acknowledge the Law of the Father that would result in the subject's Symbolic castration and thus introduce loss, an avatar of the void, into the mother-child subjective economy. When Ahab states, "I own thy speechless, placeless power," "own," of course, means "acknowledge"; but through a paronomastic slippage, he comes to "own" the power in the quite different sense of appropriating it. In this Oedipal-scenario-gone-wrong, the "son" does not typically abjure the struggle for power in exchange for a secondary or ultimate identification with the "father," thus ensuring his (the son's) identificatory stability; there is no gain/loss economy here. Instead, the act of supersedure *is* the act of identification. Manifesting a convoluted logic of identity and beyond-identity, of the identity of identity and the beyond of identity, engaging in a classically defiant gesture, Ahab, by disputing the fire's "unconditional, unintegral mastery" over him and arrogating its power, simultaneously becomes and overcomes the father.

But Ahab's rhetorical gesture is even more daedal in that Ahab is *aware* of it *as* a rhetorical gesture. By referring to "the personified impersonal," he calls explicit attention to the very troping of nature that constitutes his interlocutor. Normally, one takes objects, including one's adversaries, as "real," as simply given in the nature of things, a belief suggesting a naive, unreflected empiricist or "realist" epistemology. However, if the object is engendered by tropological constitution, the means of that constitution—here, the functioning of prosopopoeia—must remain unconscious: one cannot truly believe in a fire god's existence and simultaneously suspect that linguistic legerdemain has constituted its ontological status. But in this passage, Ahab acknowledges the fire spirit's reality yet explicitly betrays his own creative rhetorical gesture. This kind of "double vision" ("I know perfectly well, but nevertheless . . .") reflects precisely the logic of *Ichspaltung* characteristic of the perverse position—the capacity to entertain consciously two contradictory positions. Ahab seems to be saying, "I know very well that nature is an impersonal force capable of no personal intentions toward its creations; nevertheless, it is personal, it is intentional and willful, and as a result of its encroachment upon my personality, I must rebel against its might and the laws it would impose upon me." Such double vision nicely illustrates the oxymoronic logic of the "supreme fiction"—as soon as one recognizes, on whatever level, its "fictional" status, it can no longer reign "supreme." It cannot sustain the epistemological and ontological weight of "reality," since one registers, however subliminally, the "merely" fictional quality—even if the idea functions as an ostensibly "necessary" fiction—imaginatively framing any "reality." F. Scott Fitzgerald famously suggested that the ability to entertain two contradictory ideas simultaneously in consciousness distinguishes genius. It also distinguishes the schizoid state, a precursor to madness.

Another aspect of Ahab's defiance also reflects the convoluted logic of the perverse position, specifically with respect to the Law. In a sense, Ahab's rhetorical gesture of prosopopoeia, by "creating" his adversary from the formless flux of nature, *brings into being* the very Law he must then transgress. Such a paradoxical relationship to the Law characterizes the logic of perversion. On the one hand, the pervert disavows castration and thus the intercession of the Law of the Father yet, on the other, desires to "prop up" the Law, desires actually to establish it.[19] That is, he denies the Father's Law of separation in order to maintain the pleasures of the mother-child dyad yet at the same time realizes that without the Law, without that separation, without a "space" in which to breathe and establish his own identity, he will remain merely a libidinal extension of the mother. He therefore desires simultaneously to disavow and to institute the Law. Ahab's instantiation of this paradoxical logic is especially complicated and reveals, in the process, the aporetic deadlock involved in "self-identity." With the "creation" of a "fiery father" via the trope of prosopopoeia, Ahab establishes the very agency of the Law that will provide the "space" to create his identity; yet the same Law, viewed from a different perspective, requires his submission, a situation that appears to preclude the establishing of any "true" *self*-identity. In a final dialectical turn, however, he can now rebel against this Law of the Father and ostensibly fashion his own identity, a minimal component of which will be "the one who rebels against the Law." Chasing its tail at every turn, the Law of perversity reveals the perversity of its Law—the need for the Law and the simultaneous need to disavow the Law. His attempt to resolve this dilemma firmly establishes Ahab in the grand Promethean-Romantic lineage and underscores his intense obsession with sovereignty and autarky: he becomes the Law; he becomes a Law unto himself.

Or so he thinks. Sovereignty attempts to deny both the necessary relationship to an Other or Others that constitutes any "self," and the relationship to the void that marks, from a psychoanalytic perspective, our originary losses and, from a certain philosophical perspective, the human condition. These relationships need to be further explored.

Ahab as Moby Dick: "I Is an Other"

If the operation of loss or the void in existential-ontological positioning has significant implications both for an understanding of Ahab and for an understanding of how Ahab's complexity exceeds reductive categorization, the same operation has perhaps even more significance in a consideration of Ahab's relation to the great White Whale. Like the novel itself, the images and tropes of which allow for plurivocal and multivalent readings, the relationship between Ahab and the whale, while significant enough in its more literal aspect as the driving plot mechanism,[20] has implications that exceed the "local" context, so to speak. The relationship dramatically exemplifies the nature of the subject-object link in general—a crucial paradigm in psychoanalysis in which the operation of the void plays a pivotal role—and thus leads to a more general, philosophically inspired meditation/speculation on the void as a basic ontological (or a- or preontological) operator.

On a certain commonsensical level, Ahab's monomaniacal intensity with respect to Moby Dick is fueled simply by revenge: Ahab wishes to exact a kind of Old Testament revenge upon an assailant who has brutally injured him. However, beyond the obvious fact of the revenge motif, continually emphasized throughout the novel, Moby Dick exerts a wholly disproportionate fascination for Ahab, the other mariners, and most readers. For Ahab, part of this fascination no doubt results from projecting upon the whale all of "his intellectual and spiritual exasperations" (*MD* 184), as perspicuously noted in Chapter 41—the frustrations and aggressions resulting from his profound questioning of existence and identity. Thus we sense that beyond his mere physical presence as an object of revenge, the whale has become the flashpoint for Ahab's psychic energies (and, even beyond Ahab, for the psychic energies of the other mariners and for us as readers).[21] The mesmeric intensity of Moby Dick's presence, then, exceeds the commonsense explanation of simple revenge; in fact, Moby Dick has become a phantasmatic object, a kind of fetish object at the center of Ahab's libidinal economy, one that both occasions obsessive psychic interest yet also deflects attention from a "deeper" problematic. This function largely explains his considerable psychoanalytic import.

One index of the void, of the absence around which everything in this novel has been vertiginously spinning, is suggested by the nature and symbology of Ahab's injury. The references to the loss of Ahab's leg as a "dismast[ing]" (*MD* 163) and to the remnants of it as a "bleeding stump" (79) suggest castration, as critics, both psychoanalytic and otherwise, have noted, a suggestion provocatively reinforced by a certain ambiguity surrounding the injury itself: we are never told which leg Ahab has lost; and it appears that nothing in the novel suggests an answer. From a Lacanian perspective, this perhaps somewhat too literal gesture of castration signals the loss of primordial *jouissance,* the initial trauma, loss, or original "cut" that then precipitates the entire panoply of desires, defenses, and compensations that will mark the lifelong attempt to "fill" this gap, to assuage this moment of initial trauma. So while simple revenge propels the novel's literal narrative action—and Melville fully exploits many conventions of the revenge tragedy to heighten the novel's drama—in the psychoanalytic register, "another story" is taking place. The narration seems to bifurcate here and create, within the *sjužet*, a quasi-allegorical narration recounting the elements of psychoanalytic subject formation—the tale of Ahab's attempt to exact revenge upon the whale functioning also as a tale of subject formation and of the void as a constitutive element of that operation. The nature of the infliction and the character of Ahab's injury make Moby Dick not only the object of revenge but also, via metonymic slippage, the object of fantasy, Ahab's phantasmatic *object petit a.*[22]

Initially, the possibility of Moby Dick as phantasmatic object, of fantasy object for Ahab, appears counterintuitive. Fantasy objects are usually positively valorized and intensely desired; and although Ahab certainly "desires" revenge upon the whale, in a manner of speaking, this desire is not the kind usually associated with fantasy objects.[23] The explanation requires a more comprehensive assessment of the complicated role that fantasy plays in psychic development: although it frames and coordinates the vicissitudes of desire, fantasy also functions as a *screen*, as a psychic covering or papering over of the void that subtends it.[24] Thus beneath the preoccupations of fantasy lurk the originary losses that have set the mechanism into motion. Ahab's monomaniacal obsession with the whale, however much rooted in empirical "reality," also obfuscates this more originary relationship to the void. In a particularly interesting way, this void becomes a primary thematic in the novel and links Ahab to Moby Dick.

One key to this final association between the void, Ahab, and Moby Dick lies in the symbology of whiteness, one of the novel's most important intellectual legacies[25]—"whiteness" and "blankness" play a crucial psychoanalytic role in fashioning the link. *Moby-Dick* criticism, from the beginning, has often pursued the whale's "meaning," since virtually all readings have assigned to Moby Dick a greater or lesser symbolic function. But unlike most symbols, which, because of their "motivation" (that is, the necessary connection between their empirically proper and ultimately figural meanings) have a certain necessity built into them, the whale has remained maddeningly ambiguous—he has symbolized virtually everything, from the innocence of nature to the "motiveless malignity" of pure evil.

Ishmael's extended meditation on the ambiguity of whiteness in "The Whiteness of the Whale"—the difference between many of its most common cultural appropriations and his own reading of it—powerfully underscores this ambiguity. Due to space limitations, the following discussion of Ishmael's lengthy analysis focuses only on aspects of his justly famous conclusion: "Is it that by its indefiniteness it shadows forth the heartless voids and immensities of the universe, and thus stabs us from behind with the thought of annihilation, when beholding the white depths of the milky way? Or is it, that as in essence whiteness is not so much a color as the visible absence of color, and at the same time the concrete of all colors; is it for these reasons that there is such a dumb blankness, full of meaning, in a wide landscape of snows—a colorless, all-color of atheism from which we shrink?" (*MD* 195). On the one hand, one aspect of Ishmael's extraordinarily Nietzschean reading corroborates the Lacanian psychoanalytic emphases on the void and absence—the whiteness of the whale directly symbolizes nothingness, the emptying or evacuation of nature; the meaning of the whale is, in essence, meaningless-ness—and these ontological pronouncements on the ultimate meaning of reality provide a kind of philosophical basis, then, for understanding the psychoanalytic operation of the void. On the other hand, we should avoid a precipitate reading that forces a "choice" between white as "meaningful" and white as "meaningless." It is precisely the ambiguity *itself* generated by these conflicting readings—*ambiguity* "itself"—that, from one perspective, constitutes the very "meaning" of "whiteness."[26] And the phrase "the meaning of meaninglessness" signals precisely the aporia or self-canceling logical dead-lock involved here: if all things are evacuated of meaning, there still remains, as a kind of shadow or negative image, the meaning of that evacuation, the meaning of the assertion of meaninglessness. The psychoanalytic function of the "void" evokes precisely this tension and oscillation: any "meaning" or semantic depth necessarily supervenes upon the "meaninglessness," the void, of the originary losses that constitute the subject.

Another aspect of this conundrum emphasizes less the hermeneutic riddle of the whale as such and more the issue of how meaning itself is generated, the fundamental *dispositif* that *produces* "meanings." In other words, the problem "what does the whale mean?" becomes reconfigured as "how are things structured such that the whale appears to have a mean-ing?" or "how is 'meaning-in-general' generated?" The answer involves the nature of fantasy projections, and here "whiteness" and the perception of a Sperm Whale's head as a "dead, blind wall" (*MD* 336–37) become particularly significant. From a Lacanian perspective, "reality"—the "facts" of everyday, empirical existence—is subtended by various fantasy projections.[27] That is, fundamental fantasies "frame" our experience and thus determine, in large part, what we will or can consider as meaningfully "real." In a complex literalization of the figural and figuring of the literal, the "blankness" and "whiteness" associated throughout the novel with Moby Dick, semantic indeterminacy, and even possible semantic evacuation become the screen upon which fantasy projections appear and thus create the space for empirical "meanings": Moby-Dick-*as*-fantasy-screen for Ahab and the other charac-ters. In so projecting—most importantly—Ahab and the others constitute themselves as subjects, as the Lacanian formula for fantasy indicates (the $\math$ in $\mathⲔa$—the divided or split subject in reciprocal relation to the *object petit a*). As a result, then, Moby Dick plays a complicated dual role here: there is a kind of short circuit between the meaning of Moby Dick and Moby Dick as the possibility of meaning. The novel depicts not only a phantasmatic Moby Dick—Moby Dick as the focus of Ahab's libidinal economy, the object-cause of his "desire," the metonymic substitute for the *a* in $\mathⲔa$, the formula for fantasy—but also (via the whale as the essence of "whiteness," "blankness," the "wall," indeterminate and enigmatic) what we might call the formal operation of the screen itself: Moby Dick *as* the screen of fantasy, upon which Moby-Dick-as-phantasmatic-object will be projected—the phantasmatic projection of the formal ground of the projection of phantasms.

The crucial final move in this investigation establishes the manner in which the void functions to effect the linkage between Ahab and Moby Dick via some subtle negotiations of the psychoanalytic subject-object paradigm. This linkage is accomplished by Melville's characteristically adroit manipulation of the logic of images and tropes. It has long been a commonplace of *Moby-Dick* criticism that Ahab and Moby Dick bear an uncanny resemblance to one another[28]; and Melville establishes this semicryptic identity through a series of descriptions in which the prominent features of one mirror, *mutatis mutandis,* those of the other, the most noteworthy elements being the "high," "furrowed," and/or "wrinkled" brow or forehead and the associations with various aspects of whiteness. But perhaps the most important similarity harkens back to the passage that was addressed in the first section of this essay in which Ahab bursts forth from his cabin in an indeterminate state of consciousness, suspended between sleep and wakefulness. He was described there as "a vacated thing," "formless," and "blankness in itself" (*MD* 202)—exactly the attributes associated with Moby-Dick-as-fantasy-screen.

Beyond suggesting the ambiguous penumbra of fate that overshadows the novel, a vague, atmospheric, Gothic/Romantic doubleness, and/or the dialectic of inner and outer (the physical similarity between Ahab and Moby Dick reflecting a characterological similitude), Melville's most penetrating proto-analytic insight is that, in a very real sense, Ahab *is* Moby Dick, that they represent the two "slopes" of the mutually constituted subject-object relationship. On this reading, Moby Dick as "sea-monster," as terrifying, sublime "Thing" (ergo "formless," exceeding cognitive boundaries) is located not "out there" in the world that is considered objective "reality"; rather, he represents—he *is*—the most interior aspect of Ahab himself, the essential traumatic kernel or "shadow" at once paradoxically internal and external to Ahab, what Lacan in his later seminars called "extimate," confounding the border between internal and external.

As Rimbaud famously remarked, "I is an Other." So the identity of Ahab and Moby Dick intimated by Melville goes beyond a simple enumeration of ontic predicates. Both subject and object share an essential lack of essence, an essential relation to the void, or "blankness," so to speak, revealed in their mutual constitution. As Slavoj Žižek notes in a discussion of the relationship of the subject to the object-as-Thing, "The subject is the nonsubstance, he exists only as nonsubstantial self-relating which maintains its distance from inner-worldly objects; yet in monsters, this subject encounters the Thing which is his impossible equivalent—*the monster is the subject himself, conceived as Thing.*"[29] This passage reveals a conception of the subject indebted to the German Idealistic tradition ("nonsubstantial self-relating," a Kantian-Hegelian conception) grafted, in Žižek's inimitable style, onto a Freudian-Lacanian conception of the subject's relation to *Das Ding,* the sublime object, emphasizing the mutuality of their constitution—Ahab as the "blankness" or void of the subject and Moby Dick as, literally, his "white shadow" (*MD* 548), metonym of *object petit a,* object of desire, simultaneously marking, substituting for, and occulting the place of lack or the void. This penetrating exploration of the nature of subjectivity is one of the greatest legacies of Melville's monumental novel. And Melville's final tableau prior to the epilogue provides a haunting and fitting conclusion to his study of the void: "Now small fowls flew screaming over the yet yawning gulf; a sullen white surf beat against its steep sides; then all collapsed, and the great shroud of the sea rolled on as it rolled five thousand years ago" (572).

Fade to white.

NOTES

1. Slavoj Žižek, *The Metastases of Enjoyment* (London: Verso, 1994), 7.

2. Joël Dor nicely explicates the concept of "psychic structure" in chapter 1 of *The Clinical Lacan* (New York: Other Press, 1999), esp. 16–17; and Bruce Fink explains the concept of "subject position" in *A Clinical Introduction to Lacanian Psychoanalysis* (Cambridge, Mass.: Harvard Univ. Press, 1999), esp. 115–35. Both emphasize Lacan's structural orientation in discussing the constitution of the subject.

3. The most important of these, of course, is castration, an issue to which the present discussion will return. From a Lacanian perspective, "castration" means Symbolic castration, that is, the division that occurs when the Father (not necessarily the biological father but someone or something occupying the position and carrying out the function of the "third," the Father function—hence, the capital F) effects a division within the previously uninterrupted mother/child continuum. Such an intercession introduces the child into the register of the Symbolic (language and law) and creates a space for the child to begin forming a separate identity. But this only happens at a price—the price of having to relinquish the jouissance, or enjoyment, of the primordial union. The (unconscious) stance or position that the subject assumes with respect to this fundamental, lost jouissance determines how he or she negotiates the traumatic rupture and thus which clinical category he or she occupies. This fundamental stance, then, consists of considerably more than a mere delineation of empirical symptoms.

4. Excellent extended discussions of the Lacanian reading of obsession and its psychic mechanisms can be found in Fink (112–45) and Dor (59–68, 109–30).

5. Such specular identification—the identification of the nascent subject with its image in the mirror (which comes to represent, falsely, psychic unity)—results from the "mirror stage," perhaps the most widely known Lacanian theoretical formulation. It is elaborated in "The

Mirror Stage as Formative of the Function of the I as Revealed in Psychoanalytic Practice," in Jacques Lacan, *Écrits: A Selection*, trans. Alan Sheridan (New York: Norton, 1977), 1–7.

6. This statement represents, in overly compressed and simplified form, the basis for Jacques Derrida's nonconcept of différance. See "Différance," in *Margins of Philosophy*, trans. Alan Bass (Chicago: Univ. of Chicago Press, 1982), 1–27.

7. That is, the obsessive wishes to "fix" the world in its place in order to avoid that most anxiety producing of elements, the desire of the other: "The universe of the other must remain scrupulously regimented, and it is through this total regimentation that the obsessional controls and masters the death of the desirous other" (Dor 126). Obsession, then, clearly relates to the classical Freudian conception of the "anal character."

8. Space limitation necessitates some editing, but one should read the entire final paragraph of the chapter to appreciate the full emotional impact and perspicuity of Melville's descriptions. As is the case throughout *Moby-Dick*, the compelling descriptions of Ahab's mental states present the divisions and conflicts in Ahab's psyche with considerable power and subtlety.

9. For a discussion of the formal or thing-like quality of the ego, see "The Mirror Stage" (*Écrits* 1–7). The equation here between libido and life dynamism is loosely colloquial at best and should not be confused with any kind of Jungian monism—a more detailed account would need to address the relations between libido and the death drive as theorized by Freud in *Beyond the Pleasure Principle* and in Lacan's reading of that text. For the purposes of the present essay, the significant issues are the problematic identification of one's sense of self with a hypostatized "ego" or "mind," and the intrapsychic tension between that hypostatization and the other elements and forces constituting the "self."

10. In each case, the "self" is a void, a kind of "x" that one can approach asymptotically but never fully reach "in itself": the "ontological crack" produced by absolute negativity as the restless, relentless engine of the dialectic (see Slavoj Žižek, *Tarrying with the Negative* [Durham, N.C.: Duke Univ. Press, 1993]), 9–44, only one of his many insightful readings of the Hegelian dynamic); transcendental apperception as the "I or he or it (the thing) which thinks" but of which nothing can be predicated (Immanuel Kant, *Critique of Pure Reason*, trans. Norman Kemp Smith [1929; New York: St. Martin's, 1965], §A 346); and the self as inverse corollary of Lacan's famous definition of the signifier—"that which represents the subject for another signifier" ("The Subversion of the Subject and the Dialectic of Desire in the Freudian Unconscious" [*Écrits* 316]).

11. One might think, in this respect, of the politically celebratory atmosphere surrounding the notorious "schizo-analysis" of Deleuze and Guattari (see especially Gilles Deleuze and Félix Guattari, *Anti-Oedipus* [Minneapolis: Univ. of Minnesota Press, 1989]). While the hesitation here about celebration is rooted in clinical fact (psychotics invariably describe their experiences as tortured and painful, not freeing and liberating), it is important also to note that Deleuze and Guattari carefully qualify their use of "schizo" and do not equate it with the schizophrenic experience in toto.

12. The critical literature is much too voluminous to list, and many excellent recent readings of Ahab have been proposed. One should not forget, however, the classic, early studies of the novel, which offer richly detailed accounts of Ahab's character. See, among many others, F. O. Matthiessen, Richard Chase, and Arvin.

13. Danny Nobus (*Jacques Lacan and the Freudian Practice of Psychoanalysis, Makers of Modern Psychotherapy* [London: Routledge, 2000], 37–48) traces the complicated history of Lacan's formulations of perversion and Lacan's attempts to distinguish it clearly from neurosis. His formulations—clear, fully informed, yet largely nontechnical—are particularly recommended for readers not well versed in the technicalities of Lacanian thought.

14. Space restrictions and a desire to avoid a reductive psychoanalytic reading prevent extended speculation here, but it is not insignificant that Ahab's only parental contact was with his "crazy, widowed mother" (*MD* 79), and that for only a year. This sort of background could conceivably produce the intersubjective constellation that leads eventually to the position of the perverse subject.

15. The male pronoun is being used only because statistically the vast majority of perverts are male. The complex psychoanalytic explanation of this skewing is beyond the scope of this paper; the reader may consult Fink and Dor for detailed explanations.

16. See, for example, Michael Paul Rogin's *Subversive Genealogy: The Politics and Art of Herman Melville* and Larry J. Reynolds's *European Revolutions and the American Literary Renaissance* (New Haven. Conn.: Yale Univ. Press, 1988). Leo Bersani's "Incomparable America" incisively traces the contradiction involved in the novel between Melville's championing of a democratic ideal (as represented in the crew of the *Pequod*) and his clear affection for the kind of Übermensch or "hero"-figure represented by a strong, "superior" personality such as Ahab.

17. Spelled "corpusant" in the text, it is a luminous electrical phenomenon produced by the lightning. St. Elmo's fire is the best-known example.

18. Relating to "nature" in this manner creates a multitude of possible respondents and virtually infinite possibilities for figural substitution, to which Romantic poetry eloquently attests. This substitutability of respondents is very important; and in the next section, we will see how Moby Dick, in a manner, comes to occupy this "slot."

19. A typically lucid discussion of this phenomenon is found in Fink (180–81).

20. Many critics, including, for example, Walter Bezanson ("*Moby-Dick:* Document, Drama, Dream" 181–82), quite naturally see Ishmael as the narrative center of the novel. But here, the Ahab–Moby Dick axis is more suggestive for thematic purposes. Of course, one could also approach Ishmael's character psychoanalytically or, perhaps more provocatively, take advantage of his centrality as the narrator to explore aspects of psychoanalytic narratology.

21. A detailed analysis of this effect on the reader, for example, would provide an excellent psychoanalytic entrée into the novel via a consideration of the transferential effects of reading, one of the more sophisticated alternatives to the traditional, "vulgar" psychoanalysis of character and, particularly, author.

22. Castration in this context concerns the initial traumatic divisions that produce the loss of "pieces of the Real" that separate from the body; Lacan's list includes the breast, feces, the Imaginary phallus, urine, the gaze, the voice, and the Nothing (*Écrits* 315; "The Subversion of the Subject"). This moment of traumatic separation results in a loss of jouissance yet, paradoxically, the production of a surplus jouissance (as a kind of pleasure-pain "beyond the pleasure principle"). Such an "object," however, is predisposed to metonymic slippage and substitution, which accounts for the fact that the object in our fantasies (the formula for fantasy is $\$\Diamond a$, the divided or split subject in relation to the *object petit a*) is never the initial "object" as such but always a substitute.

23. One could, however, still make the argument that Ahab's revenge fantasy is so heavily libidinally cathected that it becomes, in fact, a source of jouissance and that Moby Dick really does function as a quasi-conventional fantasy object.

24. See n. 22. In the formula for fantasy ($\$\Diamond a$), the fantasy object (metonym of the *object petit a*) stands in for and attempts to fill the void produced by originary separation. This void both constitutes and de-constitutes the subject, as indicated by $\Diamond$, the symbol for the reciprocal relation of constitution/de-constitution, and $\$$, the symbol for the split subject.

25. Once again, the critical literature here is voluminous. Some examples: in *Ishmael's White World,* a phenomenological reading of *Moby-Dick,* Paul Brodtkorb emphasizes the ontological

aspects of the color white. Edgar Dryden (*Melville's Thematics of Form* 100–104) nicely traces the narratological and existential implications of whiteness; and Christopher Sten in *Sounding the Whale: Moby-Dick as Epic Novel* calls attention to how whiteness contributes to Ishmael's seeing Moby Dick as a "blank screen" (35).

26. This reading would certainly make sense in terms of the trajectory of Melville's biography, for his next book, in many ways a logical extension and working through of this idea, would be *Pierre, or, the Ambiguities*.

27. Slavoj Žižek eloquently articulates this idea in virtually all of his work. See esp. *The Sublime Object of Ideology* (London: Verso, 1989), 44–47, 118–19, and *The Plague of Fantasies* (London: Verso, 1997), 7–8. In both of these analyses, he provocatively likens the role of fantasy to the role of Kant's transcendental schematism in *The Critique of Pure Reason* as fundamental "frames" of our empirical experience.

28. For example, Bainard Cowan goes so far as to suggest that Ahab is the "double" of Moby Dick and even makes some interesting, nonpsychoanalytic speculations concerning the importance of the subject-object relation (*Exiled Waters* 97). And David Simpson, among many others, has noted some of the imagistic parallels between Ahab and Moby Dick (*Fetishism and Imagination,* in *Ahab,* ed. Bloom, 47–48). The resemblance between Ahab and Moby Dick will have a very specific, somewhat more technical psychoanalytic import in our reading.

29. Slavoj Žižek, *Enjoy Your Symptom!* (New York: Routledge, 1992), 37, original italics.

Melville, *Moby-Dick,* and the Depressive Mind

Queequeg, Starbuck, Stubb, and Flask as Symbolic Characters

WENDY STALLARD FLORY

Moby-Dick's superabundant symbolizing is hospitable to a wide range of critical approaches. Melville's obtrusive biblical, mythological, literary, and artistic references have provided plenty of scope for "myth-and-symbol," or allegorical, or psychoanalytic readings. The approach taken here (which is quite different from Charles Feidelson Jr.'s approach in *Symbolism and American Literature*[1]) provides an alternative to psychoanalytic ones. It focuses, as they do, on the psychological-symbolic dimension of the work, but without importing Freudian, or Jungian, or Lacanian theories of mind. This new approach that I have labeled "psychosymbolic" addresses the symbolizing dynamics of the unconscious mind in a demystifying and accessible way. It pays close attention to the crucial connection between romance symbolizing and mood and to what I have called "symbolic characters." The sustained psychological-symbolic significance of these characters gives them an important role in addition to the obvious part that they play on a romance's "realistic"[2] level. In developing their symbolic attributes and presenting their actions and interactions with one another, the romance author creates a fully developed level of symbolic significance, one that stages a dramatization of the mind's unconscious workings. *Moby-Dick*'s main psychological-symbolic focus is on the moods of depression and manic depression and the attitudes that follow from these. Given space constraints, I will focus mainly on Ahab's three mates (rather than Ahab himself, whose symbolic role is more immediately evident) and Queequeg (in his relationship with Ishmael).

The terms "manic depression" and "madness" are not being used interchangeably here. Many critics have written on the theme of madness in

Melville, the most comprehensive survey being Paul McCarthy's *The Twisted Mind: Madness in Herman Melville's Fiction* (1990). McCarthy presents a descriptive and enumerating account that is not concerned with the characters' symbolic significances. Where he is analytical, the author follows Henry Nash Smith's "The Madness of Ahab" in focusing mainly on theories of "madness" from Melville's own time. To consider the characters of *Moby-Dick* with reference to mood (and specifically manic-depressive moods) rather than the very general topic of madness is to arrive at a far more particularized reading of their symbolic significances. Depression (in fact suicidal depression) is alluded to right away in the opening paragraph of Chapter 1. Here, Ishmael speaks of "driving off the spleen," "growing grim about the mouth," having "a damp, drizzly November in my soul," "pausing before coffin warehouses," "bringing up the rear of every funeral I meet," having the "hypos get such an upper hand of me," and deciding to go to sea as a "substitute for pistol and ball." The manic takes the form of his almost irresistible urge to go "methodically knocking people's hats off" (*MD* 3).

Depression—and in the characterization of Ahab, self-destructive manic depression—is a major, symbolically developed theme in *Moby-Dick*. It is also one that was of pressing personal interest to Melville. His own experience was bound to have made him seriously concerned about the status and nature of the mental aberrations associated with depressive dread or manic flights, about the extent to which they could be said to constitute "insanity," and, even more disturbing, about whether they would become permanent states. At the age of twelve, Melville had been in the house during the whole three weeks that his father, Allan Melvill, was dying there. During this period Allan "by reason of severe suffering" was, in the words of his wife, "deprive'd of his Intellect" and, according to his brother's account, had fallen into a state of mental derangement that was "at times fierce, even *maniacal*."[3] That Melville himself suffered from hereditary depression seems certain. In his correspondence with Nathaniel Hawthorne, Melville alludes several times to their experience as fellow depressives. In a letter of June 29, 1851, he refers to "certain crotchetty and over doleful chimaeras, the like of which men like you and me and some others, forming a chain of God's posts round the world, must be content to encounter now and then, and fight them the best way we can" (*Cor* 195). In a letter of July 22 he proposes that they "go and vagabondize" on Mount Greylock and then adds, "But ere we start we must dig a deep hole and bury all the Blue Devils, there to abide till the Last Day" (199–200).

In her 1993 study *Touched With Fire: Manic-Depressive Illness and the Artistic Temperament*, the eminent psychiatrist and MacArthur fellow Kay Redfield Jamison (who herself suffers from bipolar disorder) chooses Melville as one of the twelve artists whom she profiles in her chapter on the hereditary nature of manic-depressive illness. Identifying people on both sides of his family who suffered from manic depression, she notes his mother's depressive episodes and "nerves," the extravagant temperaments of his father and his brother Gansevoort (and the extreme mental derangement of their last days), the legal insanity of his father's nephew Henry (and, we could add, his niece Lucy), and the suicide of his son Malcolm.[4] Jamison also quotes the revealing letter that Melville wrote to Evert Duyckinck on April 5, 1849, about the collapse into insanity of their mutual friend Charles Fenno Hoffman. Calling this "but the sequel to a long experience of morbid habits of thought," Melville wrote, "This going mad of a friend or acquaintance comes straight home to every man who feels his soul in him,—which but few men do. For in all of us lodges the same fuel to light the same fire." He ventures that the "sort of sensation permanent madness is may be very well imagined" and his analogy—"It is the climax of a mad night of revelry when the blood has been transmuted into brandy" (*Cor* 128)—obliquely links madness and alcohol (a connection to be taken up below). Jamison takes the title of her chapter "Genealogies of These High Mortal Miseries" from Chapter 106 of *Moby-Dick*, in which Ahab reflects on how "both the ancestry and posterity of Grief go further than the ancestry and posterity of Joy" and that "the gods themselves are not for ever glad" (464). In concluding this chapter she writes: "The genetic basis of manic-depressive illness provides ... the constitutional core of a determining temperament, one providing in part the sealed orders with which so many sail," and she follows this with the passage (from the final chapter of Melville's *White-Jacket*) that ends: "Thus sailing with sealed orders, we ourselves are the repositories of the secret packet, whose mysterious contents we long to learn. There are no mysteries out of ourselves" (Jamison 237).

The hereditary nature of manic depression is a prominent theme in *Pierre; or, the Ambiguities.* Pierre, whose father, like Melville's, "died a raver," agonizes over his "own hereditary liability to madness"—the "black vein" of the Glendinnings (*Pierre* 287, 358). In *Moby-Dick,* it is of course Ahab who suffers from black depression and ungovernable manias. Here, the idea of manic depression as an inherited curse is conveyed symbolically by the prophecies about Ahab's self-destruction. Melville shows symbolically that Ahab is "born into" his fate by emphasizing his naming at birth by his "crazy widowed mother." That he is named after the biblical Ahab who, by defying God, brought his own doom upon himself, was said by "the old squaw Tistig" to be prophetic (*MD* 79). This prophecy, together with Elijah's, Gabriel's, and Fedallah's, are examples of an obtrusive and often melodramatic strain of symbolizing that is in a different register from the work's more subtle, psychosymbolic techniques. To a great extent, Melville characterizes Fedallah and Pip in this obtrusive "allegorical" way.

"Myth-and-symbol" or allegorical approaches can be used very effectively in analyzing much of the obtrusive symbolizing associated with Fedallah and Pip. An allegorical mode also fits well with Ahab's hyperbolic and "pre-destinarian" way of conceptualizing his situation. Yet the melodramatically elaborated symbolic characterization of Fedallah and Pip differs greatly from that of the three mates. Psychosymbolically their role also differs. Fedallah and (eventually) Pip personify versions of a psychological state beyond manic depression. They "body forth" actual insanity—the inescapable, irreversible psychological condition in which Ahab's manic depression culminates. Fedallah has qualities of the manic and Pip has features of the depressive.

Ahab's signing on of Fedallah and his Asian crew symbolizes the point at which his eventual insanity is ensured. The sinister nature of this boat's crew and their hidden presence in the after-hold during the first part of the voyage correspond to the "sinister" potential for permanent insanity that lurks "beneath" the ebb and flow of Ahab's depressive and manic episodes. In Ishmael's opinion, the "vivid, tiger-yellow complexion" of Fedallah's crew identifies them as "aboriginal natives of the Manillas" who, according to "some honest white mariners" are "the paid spies . . . of the devil, their lord" (*MD* 217). In characterizing the "tall and swart" Fedallah, Melville draws on demonizing stereotypes of people from several different "oriental" cultures. He calls Fedallah a Parsee, an Indian Zoroastrian, yet the "Allah" component of his name evokes Islam. Although his "glistening white plaited turban" is, in fact, made of his own hair, this "turban" reference links him to a range of eastern cultures, from Turkey to India, in which turbans are worn. His "Chinese jacket of black cotton" extends the range of his associations even further—to the Far East. Ahab's "diabolical" boat's crew aptly personifies the "hell-bent" nature of his mania at its insane extreme. Driving Ahab's boat toward the whale like "trip-hammers" (220), they personify the headlong, relentless force with which his manic extremity drives him onward to his psychological catastrophe.

Pip, once he is insane, can be seen as a very tangible symbolic representation for Ahab of Ahab's own insanity. After Pip has gone mad Ahab allows him to take his hand and to share his cabin. Their psychosymbolic bond is made very clear when Ahab says to Pip, "Thou touchest my inmost center, boy; thou art tied to me by cords woven of my heart-strings" (*MD* 522). This "embrace" of Pip symbolizes Ahab's acceptance of his own insanity and is all the more poignant on this account. In the context of mood, Pip's blackness has two opposite significances. Before he becomes insane (and on the story's realistic level) his African skin color is associated with happiness, as in Ishmael's (racist) description of him as full of "that pleasant, genial, jolly brightness peculiar to his tribe" (411). This is Pip with his tambourine. Once Pip has gone mad, his blackness symbolizes depression and sadness. Now, with his "brightness" gone, Pip resembles Ahab in "lack[ing] the low, enjoying power" (167). To Pip, in his mad state, "Pip" forms a separate being from himself. He asks the (apparently) dying Queequeg to "Seek out one Pip" and adds, "I think he's in those far Antilles. If ye find him, then comfort him; for he must be very sad; for look! he's left his tambourine behind" (479).

Ishmael, so he tells us, ships out on the *Pequod* as an alternative to suicide and yet, although he refers several times to the seriousness of his recent depressive mood—his "splintered heart and maddened hand" (*MD* 51)—and makes clear that such moods recur periodically, it is hard, as we come to know him in the course of the story, to think of him as someone who is potentially suicidal. Ahab rather than Ishmael has manic-depressive moods that drive him to self-destruction and the destruction of his crew. The drama of "overmastering" depression is most fully played out not on the realistic level of the story (on which Ishmael suffers from depressive moods) but on its psychological-symbolic level, and with Ahab rather than Ishmael as the protagonist. The *Pequod* serves as the stage for this drama in which key members of her crew play the supplementary roles of "symbolic characters." On this psychological-symbolic level Ahab personifies fatal manic depression (with its range of symptomatic feelings, attitudes, and behaviors). His three mates personify three different kinds of moods, attitudes, or temperamental tendencies that provide ways of "managing" depression, but, for Ahab, they fail. Queequeg, vis-à-vis Ishmael, personifies a mood that makes it possible to survive the potentially fatal onslaught of manic depression. All these characters personify dimensions of Melville's own psychological experience—his depressive "Ahab moods," his inevitably unsuccessful attempts to use the power of conscious resolve (represented by Starbuck) to avert these moods, the temporary relief from them that the moods created by "self-medication" (personified by Stubb and Flask) would bring, and the capacity for mental calm (Queequeg) that allowed him to survive them.

Ishmael's role is somewhat different from that of these characters. As the narrator and "writer" of the story, he has a symbolic significance of a more straightforward kind, that of "Melville-surrogate." He stands at a certain remove both from Melville and from the psychological-symbolic drama that the symbolic characters enact. He watches it, reflects upon it, learns from it, and "puts it into words." This degree of separation from the other characters is made clear by his status as sole survivor of the tragic drama that Ahab "stages" and in which he plays the leading role. As the survivor of this catastrophe and the writer of its story, Ishmael is closest to the Melville who is the survivor of his own depressions and the writer of *Moby-Dick*. Ishmael's identity as established by his commentaries is fluid and comprehensive. Writing from the survivor's retrospective vantage point, he has a privileged overview. Melville gives Ishmael access to what he himself knows. He often allows his narrator to speak for him in an only minimally mediated way, so that the reader often feels that the narrative voice is Melville's as much as or even more than Ishmael's. When Ishmael is being reflective he generally says "what is on Melville's mind" and says it in a highly Melvillean way.

Reading Psychosymbolically

Of fictional works in the American romance tradition, the psychological-symbolic romances (those that, on one level, dramatize the mind's unconscious workings) are among the most dramatic and memorable. To discuss the psychological-symbolic significances of such works is necessarily to address the mind's unconscious workings. Previous psychologically oriented literary-critical approaches have relied on, or been influenced by, elaborately developed "theories of mind," particularly the Freudian, the Jungian, and the Lacanian. Critics of romance symbolizing who work with reference to these theories have to divide their attention among the details of the literary text, the extensive and complex corpus of Freud's, Jung's, or Lacan's own writings, and the commentaries of other critics working with these theories. What they can discover in that symbolic tour de force *Moby-Dick* is likely to be either determined or strongly colored by the psychological hypotheses upon which they rely. Geoffrey Sanborn, for example, in *The Sign of the Cannibal,* presents a fascinating and thoughtful reading of Queequeg's significance. His book is a very significant contribution to postcolonial studies, yet his Queequeg is a cannibal "lacanianistically developed." The qualities of Queequeg that Sanborn identifies as most important are ones upon which postmodern and Lacanian theory place a premium. "The essence of Melville's ideal of savagery," Sanborn writes, has "three major components: the Queequegian virtues of inconsistency, irreverence, and gameness."[5]

My aim has been to find an approach that allows a reader to focus on the details of the romance texts with a minimum of distractions. I explain this approach in detail in a book-length project.[6] This study treats the mind's symbolizing as a perpetual, constantly reconfiguring dynamic that is the primary mode of unconscious mental activity, the "traces" of which can readily be seen in what we can recall of dream activity and in highly symbolic works of art—such as the psychological romance. A major simplification was to move beyond hypotheses such as Jungian "archetypes" and a "collective unconscious," the Freudian "Oedipus complex" and "death-drive," or the Lacanian "mirror stage" and "Symbolic Order" and to focus, as current psychological science does, on mood. My focus is not on the biological bases of mood, as a scientist's would be, but rather on how mood manifests itself symbolically—both routinely, in the experience of any individual, and, most particularly, in the form of the symbolic characters that are the hallmark of the psychological romance. My criterion for my own hypotheses about symbolizing was simply that they not conflict with the most reliable, current findings of psychology and neuroscience.

Symbolic Characters

The "symbolic characters" of the romance operate simultaneously on both the realistic and symbolic levels of the story. What makes them readily recognizable as symbolic characters are the obvious aspects of their characterization that are at odds with realistic representation. They may, like Ahab, be "larger than life" and characterized very hyperbolically, or, like Stubb, with disproportionate emphasis on one idiosyncratic characteristic. The limitations of their "realisticness" may make them seem "otherworldly," as in the case of Billy Budd's strange childlikeness or Bartleby's eerie detachment. Queequeg has several kinds of symbolic significance and the various signs of his psychological-symbolic significance are not likely to be overlooked. One set (his symbolic tattoos) is quite literally "written all over him." Symbolic characters personify not only a variety of unconscious dynamics, particularly moods and the attitudes that stem from mood or temperament, but also the potential for emotional growth as well as mental faculties such as the creative imagination. In romance works where there is a "primary symbolic character" (one whose characterization is "un-realistic" in highly obtrusive ways) we find a sustained level of symbolic significance within which the other main characters of the book are seen to play an important symbolic role, in addition to their role as "realistic" characters. To realize this is to discover a fully developed, additional level of symbolic significances in many of the best-known and most powerful American romances.

To think of the works of writers such as Poe, Hawthorne, and Melville with reference to mood is certainly appropriate. In the case of all three, the moods associated with depression or manic depression are of particular interest, and no romance writer has dramatized the experience of manic-depressive mood swings more comprehensively than Melville in *Moby-Dick*. In other works, Melville has created characters who can be seen as personifying aspects of depressive mood. Bartleby, for example, unforgettably embodies the affect-lessness, lethargy, and finally catatonia of severe depression. Ahab, however, stands out because of how—with his irresistible coercive power, black moods, metaphysical agonizing, paranoia, rage, obsession with revenge, grandiosity of self-concept, and headlong rush to self-destruction—he embodies such a wide range of the feelings, attitudes, and behaviors characteristic of manic depression.

Nonhuman symbolic "characters" (for example, Poe's black cats) can also play important roles in romance fiction. The cock in "Cock-A-Doodle-Doo!" and the whale in *Moby-Dick* are both instances of "symbolic creatures" that embody a mood or temperamental tendency. Ahab's depressiveness and mania are elaborately presented and specifically linked to the presence of the Whale. Melville is very explicit about the psychological dynamic (later labeled projection) that is involved in Ahab's attitude toward Moby Dick: "The White Whale swam before him as the monomanic incarnation of all those malicious agencies which some deep men feel eating in them." "All that most maddens and torments . . . all that . . . cakes the brain . . . were visibly personified, and made practically assailable in Moby Dick" (*MD* 184). Psychosymbolically, the Whale embodies Ahab's own manic and depressive moods, the attitudes that he falls into (and agonistic metaphysics that he adopts) as a result of these, and the monomaniac theory about being hunted *by* the Whale that he seizes on as an unconscious rationalization of his attitudes.

As Melville knew from his own experience and as his writing of *Moby-Dick* shows, to be overcome by depressive moods is often, for a reflective person, to become obsessively preoccupied with depressing thoughts about one's own mortality and also with unanswerable, eschatological questions. To be preoccupied in this way is to feel constantly trapped, able, as Hawthorne said of Melville, "neither [to] believe, nor be comfortable in [one's] unbe-lief" (*Journal* 628). The real "enemy" is the mood, yet the conscious mind can more easily grasp the patterns of thinking that follow from the mood and so the problem seems, certainly for Ahab and perhaps, to some extent, for Melville also, to originate with the unanswerability of the questions that obsess him—with the inscrutability of the universe as the individual, turning inward, confronts this. The malice that Ahab sees in the Whale is the projec-tion of Ahab's rage at himself for being unable to stand the strain of living with inscrutability. He believes that Moby Dick is "hounding" him out of an active malice and that he has no alternative but to kill it. Yet, as the symbolic representation of radical inscrutability, the Whale cannot be destroyed and

Ahab's fate shows his murderous fury to be suicidally self-destructive.

A psychological-symbolic reading of Ahab's hunting of Moby Dick reveals the intimately personal significance for Melville of his group of mariners. It lets us see not just Ahab but other important members of the crew also as personifications of moods or attitudes that Melville had, consciously or unconsciously, identified within himself as dimensions of the psychological dynamics of manic depression. In his characterization of the crew, Melville explores various options, familiar to him from his own experience, for attempting to "weather" the moods of manic depression—for managing (or failing to manage) them. That Ishmael's psychological strategy for dealing with his depression proves more effective than Ahab's is made clear by Ishmael's survival. That Queequeg plays an indispensable role in Ishmael's psychological survival strategy is conveyed by Melville's decision to make Queequeg's coffin-lifebuoy the means of Ishmael's rescue. Before considering Queequeg as a particularly important psychological-symbolic character in the book, I will show how the three mates can also be seen in this way. Melville identifies Starbuck's "mere unaided virtue or rightmindedness," Stubb's "invulnerable jollity of indifference and recklessness," and Flask's "pervading mediocrity" (*MD* 186–87) as incapable of turning aside Ahab's headlong rush to destruction, and we can consider the characteristic attitudes, temperaments, and behaviors of the three mates as ways of attempting to deal with depression. Even if some of these ways offer some short-term relief, their ultimate limitations are made clear by the destruction of all three of the mates.

As authority figures on the *Pequod* (ranked, in descending order, immediately below Ahab himself), the mates are associated with the idea of control. In their professional capacity they are described as excellent: "Three better, more likely sea-officers and men, each in his own different way, could not readily be found" (123). Seen with regard to temperament (rather than professional competence), Stubb, with his "indifferent air" and dedication to comfort, and Flask, with his complete lack of imagination, are unlikely to be thought of as linked to Melville himself. Yet in their role as symbolic characters they *can* be thought of in this way. Just as Starbuck is incapable of, and Stubb and Flask are uninterested in withstanding Ahab's psychological coercion—the "spiritual terrors [of] the concentrating brow of [that] enraged and mighty man" (*MD* 117)—so the moods and attitudes that the mates personify are ultimately and inevitably ineffectual in counteracting the black mood and dangerous obsessiveness that Ahab represents.

Stubb's pipe makes it easy to link him to a mood of Melville's own and to the theme of "dealing with depression." Smoking is one of the two most common, traditional kinds of "self-medication" for depression and the pleasure that Melville derived from tobacco is constantly reflected in his work.[7] This is evident from *Typee* on. Some important instances are his poetic paean to tobacco, "Herba Santa," his stories "I and My Chimney" and "The Paradise of Bachelors," and Chapters 10 and 11 of *Moby-Dick* in which the sociable smoking of the tomahawk pipe is a prelude, first to Queequeg's embracing of Ishmael as a "bosom friend" for life, and then to Queequeg's telling of his life story. Melville's description of the "good-humored, easy, and careless" Stubb is a kind of treatise on the anxiolytic or psychologically calming effects of nicotine. Awake, Stubb is never without his pipe and Melville may even have named him for it, in that his pipe *is* a "stub," the "short, black little pipe" that "like his nose . . . was one of the regular features of his face." Ishmael explains Stubb's "almost impious good-humor" in the face of "the burden of life" as the result of his pipe. "Stubb's tobacco smoke might have operated as a sort of disinfecting agent," he suggests, against the depressing effects of "the nameless miseries of the numberless mortals who have died exhaling [this earthly air]" (*MD* 119). That Ahab can no longer experience the alleviating mood that Stubb personifies is enacted psychosymbolically when Ahab verbally lashes out at Stubb with "Down, dog, and kennel!" (127). His spurning of Stubb is symbolically finalized when, in the following chapter, Ahab throws his own pipe into the sea (130).

Flask is described as a "short, stout, ruddy young fellow" who is "very pugnacious concerning whales" (*MD* 119). Read as a symbolic character, he also can be linked to the theme of countering depression. In several oblique ways, Melville associates him with that other traditional self-medication for depression, alcohol. This fits with Martha's Vineyard as his place of origin, his "ruddi[ness]," and his "pugnacious[ness]." Most important, it explains "Flask" as Melville's choice for his name—as in the "dark flask" of "strong spirits" that Stubb gives to the exhausted, blue-lipped Queequeg (in place of ginger-jub) after the dangerous operation of attaching the blubber-hook to the floating whale in "The Monkey-Rope" (322). Melville himself used alcohol to try and alleviate his depressions. Laurie Robertson-Lorant writes in her biography of Melville that "it seems certain that during the mid-1850s he came to rely on alcohol for relief of his physical pain and emotional distress" (370). "Would the Gin were here!" we find him writing to Hawthorne in the letter of June 1850 in which he declares, "Dollars damn me" and "all my books are botches" (*Cor* 191).

As a symbolic character, Flask represents not "a man who drinks" (as does Perth, the ship's alcoholic blacksmith), but rather the elevated and devil-may-care *mood* that drinking can create and that can, temporarily, hold at bay the dark, icy mood of depression. Despite the unimaginative Flask's limitations, Melville encourages his readers to take Flask as they find him, and he acknowledges Flask's staying power, calling him a "wrought [nail]; made to clinch tight and last long." His nickname, King Post, also links him to the attempt to withstand the crushing oppressiveness of black and icy depression. The king post is the "short, square timber . . . in Arctic whalers" that holds the struts that "brace the ship against the icy concussions of those battering seas" (*MD* 119). Yet Ahab's extreme depressive and manic moods can no more be alleviated by alcohol than by tobacco. He uses liquor, instead, to stir up his crew into a frenzy of aggressiveness, ordering his harpooneers to drink the "fiery waters" from their harpoon-sockets as they swear to "hunt Moby Dick to his death!" (166).

While Melville shows Flask as too unimaginative to have any "finer feelings," he does not make him a strongly negative character. One episode, however, does point toward the darker side of the use of alcohol—the abusive lashing out that can be a consequence of drunkenness. Flask's "ignorant, unconscious fearlessness" makes him "a little waggish" as a hunter of the whale, which he sees as no more than a "magnified mouse, or at least water-rat." His "waggishness" takes the form of impulsive, gratuitous cruelty as he lances the abscess on the old, dying whale with the fin-stump. Here he is called "cruel Flask" and Ishmael tells how "humane Starbuck" protests this tormenting of the whale with "Avast! . . . there's no need of that!" (358).

As Wyn Kelley was presenting, at the "*Moby-Dick* 2001" conference, a selection of some of the whaling illustrations from her Web-based "Melville Project," one drawing immediately recalled Flask. This was one of a set of twelve cartoons of whaling crewmen, drawn by E. C. Snow in 1844, now in the collection of the Kendall Institute of the New Bedford Whaling Museum.[8] It shows a head-and-shoulders profile of a red-nosed man labeled "Irish 3rd Mate." It would be interesting to know whether the similarity between the representation of this cartoon figure of the Third Mate and Melville's characterization of Flask is simply a coincidence or whether Snow's decision to make his Third Mate an alcoholic Irishman conformed to some popular stereotype about third mates. Unlike the other cartoons, this one appears to have been "elaborated upon" by someone other than the artist. The word

Courtesy of the New Bedford Whaling Museum.

"[F]inegan" has been written vertically, along the right-hand margin, and where the "F" should be are lines that (clumsily) extend the beard from the tip of the chin. As this, in rebus fashion, makes the word "[Chin]inegan," it is probably intended as a play on a well-known old street rhyme. The version that I learned as a child is, "There was an old man called Michael Finnegan. /

He grew whiskers on his chinegan. / The wind came out and blew them in ag'in. / Poor old Michael Finnegan, begin ag'in."

Starbuck has more depth of character than Stubb or Flask. While the moods that the latter embody are the result of external stimulants, his symbolic role is to represent the contribution of the reasoning, conscious mind to withstanding the depressive mood. His thoughts, as he reflects on his distress at having his "soul . . . overmanned" by that "madman," Ahab, help to establish his psychosymbolic role as the personification of sane reasoning: "Insufferable sting, that sanity should ground arms on such a field! But he drilled deep down, and blasted all my reason out of me!" (*MD* 169). Starbuck's inability to withstand the "spiritual terrors" of Ahab's "concentrating brow" is a dramatic enactment of the inevitable ineffectuality of conscious will and resolve against the overmastering moods of manic depression. To grasp Starbuck's role as a symbolic character is to be able to concede him the kind of dignity that Melville writes about in his initial description of him, a dignity denied him by critics who choose to see his conscientiousness as a failing. There is much psychological truth to Melville's characterization of Starbuck, more even than Melville was able consciously to know, given the lack of understanding of the causes of manic depression in his own time. The onset of major depression or of manic episodes cannot be turned aside by any conscious act of will, no matter how determined and "resolute." And Starbuck is resolute. The tally of his strengths of character is impressive. He is courageous, "earnest," "steadfast," a person of "hardy sobriety and fortitude" who is "uncommonly conscientious for a seaman, and endued with a deep natural reverence" (115–16).

Starbuck's one "shortcoming" is his inability to stop Ahab, yet Melville has made it clear that Ahab cannot be stopped by anything short of murder. It is surely reasonable to see Starbuck's inability to kill Ahab in cold blood as a sign, not of any blameworthy inadequacy in Starbuck, but of the irresistibility of the destructive power of the mood that Ahab personifies. Starbuck (unlike Stubb and Flask) is dignified with a scene of dramatic testing. In this scene, which is as poignant as it is anticlimactic, Melville shows the impossibility of Starbuck's situation. At the climactic moment, when Starbuck is about to kill Ahab, Melville's wording is eerily precise: "The yet levelled musket shook like a drunkard's arm against the panel" (*MD* 515). It is not Starbuck's own arm, but the musket he holds that is compared to a "drunkard's arm," that is, to something that is completely alien to Starbuck and his "hardy sobriety." The gun (and the potential act of murder that it signifies) is not a "natural extension" of Starbuck's arm, but something with all the negative connotations of drunken behavior—impulsive, deadly action taken at a time of "unreason" and likely to be regretted in retrospect.

In dramatizing Starbuck's predicament vis-à-vis Ahab, Melville is taking on a troubling issue—the question of how far one should blame a person for depressive or manic behavior. In Melville's day, to be seen as "giving way to" depression or "giving in to" manic compulsions was likely to be thought of as demonstrating either a shameful lack of will or self-control, or, even worse, some constitutional moral or spiritual weakness. Self-blame is a common feature of manic depression and, although Melville would have known from his own mood swings how unavailing conscious attempts to deflect them were, he would probably not consider this as excusing what could all too easily seem to be moral weakness. Melville's uncertainty on this score betrays itself in an unmistakable indecisiveness in the attempt to identify those limitations of Starbuck's that make him unable to withstand Ahab's malign power. Vague mention is made of "certain qualities in [Starbuck] which at times affected, and in some cases seemed well nigh to overbalance all [his strengths]." Yet all that is specified is a strong inclination to "superstition" and even this is immediately qualified by the observation that it was "that sort of superstition, which . . . seems rather to spring, somehow, from intelligence than from ignorance" (*MD* 116).

Melville chooses the term "superstition" to label what it is that holds Starbuck back from "the gush of dare-devil daring" necessary for challenging Ahab. Yet rather than "superstition," it seems closer to a reliable intuitiveness and a heightening of sensitivity and imaginativeness that Starbuck has "grown into." For Starbuck, an attentiveness to "outward portents and inward presentiments" and, "much more . . . his far-away domestic memories of his young Cape wife and child" have moderated the "original ruggedness of his nature." A further refining influence is his distress at the tragic deaths of his father and brother (an experience that Melville shares). "It was not in reasonable nature that [for] a man so organized, and with such terrible experiences and remembrances as he had . . . [such] things should fail in latently engendering an element in him, which, under suitable circumstances, would break out from its confinement, and burn all his courage up." Yet the sentence that follows contradicts the idea that Starbuck loses "all" his courage. "And brave as he might be, it was that sort of bravery, chiefly visible in some intrepid men, which, while generally abiding firm in the conflict with seas, or winds, or whales, or any of the ordinary irrational horrors of the world, yet cannot withstand those more terrific, because more spiritual terrors, which sometimes menace you from the concentrating brow of an enraged and mighty man" (*MD* 116–17). These "irrational horrors" are nonhuman forces of potentially lethal power in the external world. The "spiritual terrors" are psychologically terrifying forces.

Melville is, then, of two minds about Starbuck. He is drawn to describe the mate's ineffectuality as a limitation and even a kind of cowardice, but he keeps retracting this idea, as here: "But were the coming narrative to reveal, in any instance, the complete abasement of poor Starbuck's fortitude, scarce might I have the heart to write it; for it is a thing most sorrowful, nay shocking, to expose the fall of valor in the soul. . . . That immaculate manliness we feel within ourselves, so far within us, that it remains intact though all the outer character seem gone; bleeds with keenest anguish at the undraped spectacle of a valor-ruined man" (*MD* 117). Presumably then, as Melville does go on to complete the narrative of Starbuck, what is shown is not the "complete abasement" of his "fortitude." Starbuck is "poor" in the sense of "unfortunate" or "to be commiserated with" rather than "weak" or "cowardly."

QUEEQUEG

Psychosymbolically, Queequeg and Ahab are opposite. They personify, respectively, the healing and the destructive power of the mind's unconscious symbolizing. Melville's choice of a South Sea islander as Ishmael's "bosom-friend" can be partly explained by Melville's own experience in the Marquesas and it happens that the "South-Sea attribute" of Queequeg's tattooing fits perfectly with his psychological-symbolic role. Ishmael can weather his own bouts of depression because the attitude he adopts, under Queequeg's influence, is so different from Ahab's. The inscrutability embodied in the White Whale goads Ahab into ever more extravagant and finally suicidal monomaniac rage. Ishmael's association with Queequeg has a calming influence on him that deflects the kinds of moods that Ahab is trapped in and Melville makes this clear early in the story with Ishmael's memorable statement, "No more my splintered heart and maddened hand were turned against the wolfish world. This soothing savage had redeemed it" (*MD* 51). Queequeg can be seen as symbolizing both a saving attitude of calm open-mindedness that can adjust to living with inscrutability and also the psychological dynamic of symbolizing itself. He embodies what is indispensable for both Ishmael's and Melville's survival.

Queequeg's symbolic status is conveyed in several ways, for example, in Melville's decision to make him an islander of Kokovoko, an imaginary place, "not down in any map [as] true places never are" (*MD* 55). Seen from a psychosymbolic perspective, this is not taken as undermining the reader's sense of Queequeg's substantiality on the story's realistic level, but rather as drawing particular attention to the great importance of his additional role on its symbolic level. He has a symbolic significance that continues to be very resonant through the whole extent of the story and one that the reader is reminded of (for example, by the coffin-lifebuoy) even when Queequeg himself is not directly focused on. Sanborn approaches what he sees as Queequeg's "disappearance" from the text, from a Lacanian's orientation toward "loss," "lack," and "the void." "When it comes time to address the fact that Queequeg fades rather suddenly into the margins of the text," he writes, "most critics fall back on a quasi-theological conception of Queequeg as a symbolic figure shedding goodness without end, even at those times when Ishmael seems to have forgotten that he exists." (It is worth noting that a psychosymbolic reading can be very un-Lacanian without being at all "quasi-theological.") "It makes much more sense," he continues, "to recognize in this disappearance a second waning. The values of savagery, as revealed by the light of the 'natural sun,' are simply an attractive prospect; as Queequeg's disappearance suggests, and as Ahab's quest will demonstrate, our only true ground is the fact that light and life wane" (Sanborn 134). Sanborn reiterates this sentiment in his book's closing words (before his afterword): "the echo of nothingness, the only voice of our God" (200).

To Ishmael, Queequeg personifies an attitude of calm self-reliance: "some twenty thousand miles from home . . . thrown among people as strange to him as though he were in the planet Jupiter . . . he seemed entirely at his ease; preserving the utmost serenity; content with his own companionship; always equal to himself." His intimate relationship with Ishmael is presented as exceptional. Ishmael had noticed that Queequeg "never consorted at all, or but very little, with the other seamen in the inn [and] made no advances whatever" (*MD* 50). The suddenness, intensity, exclusiveness, and permanence of his attachment to Ishmael fits well with Queequeg's symbolic significance as a positive and ultimately life-saving attitude that Ishmael, by virtue of his own responsiveness, is given the opportunity to embrace and "be embraced" by. Queequeg personifies openmindedness in that he responds to the tentative overtures of the to-him-alien Ishmael by swearing lifelong loyalty to him and by dividing with him all his worldly possessions. In the reciprocity of their relationship they mirror one another so that Queequeg can easily be seen as the embodiment of a psychological dimension both of Ishmael and of Melville-as-Ishmael.

Where Ahab's monomania leads to death and destruction for everyone other than Ishmael, Queequeg's calm is associated with healing and rescue and with

Ishmael's survival. Early in the book we see Queequeg spontaneously save the life of the drowning bumpkin even though the man had just been mocking him. To mock and recoil from Queequeg's "alien" appearance is the most likely reaction, and Ishmael's openmindedness in being able quickly to overcome his instinctive prejudice shows him to be an exception. This earns him Queequeg's devotion and special protection. Queequeg embodies healing and rescue in other ways also, as in his often-noted, underwater "delivery" of Tashtego from inside the sperm whale's head. Even Melville's initial description of Queequeg and his tattoos brings in the theme of healing in a telling way. Ishmael at first misreads his mysterious bedfellow's appearance according to his own depressive mood. He sees the stranger's shaven head as "like a mildewed skull." He also assumes, from the appearance of the man's face, that he has been "dreadfully cut" in a fight and patched up with "sticking plasters" by a surgeon. Ishmael's response to the sight of the tattoos on the man's torso and arms is to think that he has "been in a Thirty Years' War, and just escaped from it with a sticking-plaster shirt" (21–22). Reading Queequeg from his own depressive viewpoint, Ishmael may be doing so on behalf of Melville also. The choice of this particular war is probably no coincidence. Melville, who turns thirty shortly before writing *Moby-Dick,* has good reason to think of his own "embattled" life to date as itself a "thirty years' war." Yet even as Ishmael's mood leads him to think in terms of death, wounds, and war, he also associates Queequeg's appearance with healing and recovery with his references to a surgeon and plasters.

The tattooing that covers his body also links Queequeg to the related themes of inscrutability and symbolizing. At their first meeting, he confronts Ishmael with the challenge of how to respond to inscrutability, much as Moby Dick confronts Ahab, and Melville develops the link between Queequeg and the White Whale in some intricate ways, as in his paired references to "Chaldee." Moby Dick's inscrutability is symbolized by "the awful Chaldee of the Sperm Whale's brow" (*MD* 347), yet, when "Chaldee" is used with reference to Queequeg, it is with a very different emphasis. Although Queequeg dies on the *Pequod,* Melville sets him apart from the rest of Ahab's victims by providing him with a very positive "death-bed scene" before his actual death. Ishmael sees in the expression of Queequeg's eyes, as he seems to be dying of fever, "a wondrous testimony to that immortal health in him that could not die, or be weakened." Queequeg's calm acceptance of his imminent death prompts Ishmael's comment that "no dying Chaldee or Greek had higher and holier thoughts than those [that crept] over the face of poor Queequeg" (477).

Queequeg's tattooings are directly connected to the story's major theme of metaphysical inscrutability and to the challenge of preserving a calm and open-minded attitude in the face of this. This "twisted tattooing" is described as "the work of a departed prophet and seer of his island, who, by those hieroglyphic marks, had written out on his body a complete theory of the heavens and the earth, and a mystical treatise on the art of attaining truth." Queequeg, we are told, "in his own proper person was a riddle to unfold; a wondrous work in one volume; but whose mysteries not even himself could read, though his own live heart beat against them" (*MD* 480–81). Ishmael is saved by clinging to the coffin upon whose lid Queequeg has carved some of the mysterious figures from his own body; that is, by being able to hold fast to the self-preserving attitude of calm acceptance of inscrutability that Queequeg embodies.

Inscrutability is never anything but enraging to Ahab, whether it is symbolized by the White Whale or by Queequeg's unreadable tattoos that Ahab calls the "devilish tantalization of the gods!" (*MD* 481). Once Ishmael embraces Queequeg in all his alienness, inscrutability—rather than seeming only devastating—becomes something that one responds to as best one can. In Ishmael's (and Melville's) case, this means writing the story of it. As the seer "inscribes" the symbols on Queequeg's body, so Queequeg copies them onto the lid of the coffin-lifebuoy that will save Ishmael who, in turn (and courtesy of Melville's creative imagination) will write down, in heavily symbolic form, the story of the hunting of the White Whale. In this way, Queequeg, with his tattooed body ("that wondrous work in one volume"), is linked to the symbolizing power of the mind itself that remains largely inscrutable yet makes it possible to write creatively and symbolically about inscrutability both metaphysical and psychological—that of the universe and that of the unconscious mind.

Notes

1. Feidelson wrote primarily as an intellectual historian with a philosophical orientation. One of his definitions of "Symbolism" is "the coloration taken on by the American literary mind under the pressure of American intellectual history" (43) and his commentaries are strongly influenced by the epistemological inquiries of the day into "the meaning of meaning" (214). He could be unduly negative about the artistry of nineteenth-century romance authors because of his tendency to judge them according to their *intellectual* grasp of the symbolism-related issues that were his own particular concern. He discussed their symbolic practice with reference to more fully theorized kinds of symbolism, both that of the French Symbolist movement and "Modern symbolism," which he called "the literary consequence of certain basic problems of modern thought" (43). These priorities are clear from his comment that, "Melville, Hawthorne, [and] Poe . . . wrote no masterpieces . . . [although] as symbolists they look forward to one of the most sophisticated movements of literary history; however inexpert, they broaden the possibilities of literature" (4).

2. I use the term "realistic" (as the antonym of "symbolic") for that level of significance in the romance that follows from taking the details of character, action, and setting "at face value," as though they were realistic representations. The term "literal," in that it is etymologically tied to the letter of the written word, applies less well to imaged forms.

3. See the accounts of Allan Melvill's death in Parker 1:57–59 and Robertson-Lorant 47–49.

4. Kay Redfield Jamison, *Touched With Fire: Manic-Depressive Illness and the Artistic Temperament* (New York: The Free Press/Simon & Schuster, 1994), 216–18. Jamison has written about her own experience with bipolar disorder and suicidal depression in *An Unquiet Mind* (1995) and her book *Night Falls Fast* (1999) is a highly important study of suicide. Lucy Melville, Allan's daughter, died in an asylum at the age of twenty-nine. Hershel Parker describes her in his biography as having been "long, perhaps congenitally, weak in mind and body" (2:868).

5. Sanborn 140. The description of Queequeg as "game" is the mad Pip's. He is fixated on the "old Pip's" cowardice and so, on its opposite.

6. My working title for this manuscript (now completed) is "Inside Stories: A New American Romance Criticism." Part I describes the nature and strategies of and the rationale for the new, "psychosymbolic" approach that it proposes. This is followed by chapter-length readings of eleven works of romance fiction from the nineteenth and twentieth centuries, mainly full-length romances but also some short stories and two children's books. One chapter discusses *Pierre; or, the Ambiguities,* and another, *Billy Budd, Sailor.*

7. *Melville Society Extracts* 121 (July 2001) has two articles on Melville and smoking: "Tobacco, Melville, and the Times" (1–6) by Collamer M. Abbott and "Dutch Pipes and Stubb's Pipe" by Bernard J. Lyons and Thomas F. Heffernan (1–2).

8. These twelve cartoons are titled "Yankee Captain," "English First Mate," "Irish 3rd Mate," "Dutch 4th Mate," "Turk," "Mexico" (a Mexican sailor), "Chinese Cook," "Jap," "Turk Carpenter," "The Far North" (an Inuit sailor), "A Dead Whale" (showing a smiling man [presumably the artist] dancing on the up-pointing head of a sperm whale floating in its blood), and "Home at Lust (*sic*), from a Foreign Shore" (the artist's winking self-portrait). Three further drawings in this group by Snow are whaling scenes: "Stove Boat," "A Long Stroke" (showing a boat's crew at the moment of harpooning a sperm whale), and "Fast Boat" (showing a boat being towed by a whale, but not the whale itself).

Correspondences

Paranoiac Lexicographers and Melvillean Heroes

Sanford E. Marovitz

In Memory of Harrison Hayford

In nearly all his major fiction, Herman Melville portrayed characters suffering from various types and degrees of mental abnormality. Where he gained such profound insight into psychological aberration has long been a subject of critical investigation, largely through research into the author's life and reading, but the answers remain partly conjectural. In his estimable study of madness in Melville's fiction, Paul McCarthy observed that Melville's depictions of mental derangement are more detailed and dramatic in *Redburn* (1849) and *White-Jacket* (1850) than in his earlier narratives (McCarthy 35–36, 138). Then, with the publication of *Moby-Dick* (1851) less than two years after he had completed *White-Jacket,* and *Pierre* (1852) less than a year after that, Melville's psychological portraits intensified and diversified dramatically. Such striking and rapid development warrants further attention.

Although madness unquestionably relates to moral issues raised in the novels, the focus of this investigation is not on morality or symbolism but on the phenomenon of insanity. Melville perceived insanity partly through his reading but particularly from his experience and then imaginatively transformed what he had learned by incorporating it into his fiction, especially into the characters of Ahab and Pierre. The following exposition should be thought of as two sections, *text* and *subtext*. The text sets out familiar passages, predominantly from *Moby-Dick* but also from *Pierre,* to provide a textual exposition for the next section. The subtext discusses the most likely sources for Melville's ideas on insanity, including observations he made in his family, drew from his reading, and gained through his acquaintance with lexicographer Dr. George J. Adler. The description of Adler will be supplemented with that of another semanticist of a sort, Dr. William Chester Minor, whom Melville did not know but whose psychological state complements and illuminates Adler's.

First, the *Text*. Both Ahab and Pierre manifest delusions of grandeur in their dementia. From his initial appearance on the quarterdeck, the "supreme lord and dictator" over the crew, as Ishmael describes Ahab, "stood before them with a crucifixion in his face; in all the nameless regal overbearing dignity of some mighty woe" (*MD* 122, 124). Much later, in Chapter 96 ("The Try-Works"), Ishmael expands upon the terms of this stark portrait when he relates truth first to woe then to madness, and Ahab's image reappears almost magically in the mind as if on a scrim over the imagination: "[T]hat mortal man who hath more of joy than sorrow in him, that mortal man cannot be true—not true, or undeveloped. With books the same. The truest of all men was the Man of Sorrows, and the truest of all books is Solomon's, and Ecclesiastes is the fine hammered steel of woe. . . . There is a wisdom that is woe; but there is a woe that is madness" (424–25).

Ishmael implies that Ahab has looked "too long in the face of the fire," the same fire that had caused the narrator's own "unnatural hallucination of the night" and nearly brought the *Pequod* to founder while he was at the helm (*MD* 424). But if Ishmael emerges from his trance in time to save the ship, Ahab in his pride and indomitable dedication to the fire plunges with it into the "blackness of darkness, [that] seemed the material counterpart of her monomaniac commander's soul" (423), thus leading the vessel with its crew to destruction. For Ishmael, "the glorious, golden, glad sun" is "the only true lamp," the sun that lights the spaces over the mountain peaks where the Catskill eagle can soar into invisibility; "all others but liars!" (424). Indeed, Ahab would "strike the sun if it insulted" him; he challenges the "great gods" to impede him, asserting that he has an "unconquerable captain in [his] soul" (168, 164, 560). To them, he says: "[C]ome and see if ye can swerve me. Swerve me? ye cannot swerve me, else ye swerve yourselves! man has ye there. Swerve me? The path to my fixed purpose is laid with iron rails, whereon my soul is grooved to run. . . . Naught's an obstacle, naught's an angle to the iron way!" (168). Much later, as the first day of the final chase ends, Ahab declares: "Ahab stands alone among the millions of the peopled earth, nor gods nor men his neighbors!" (553).

As for Pierre, he echoes Melville's own ambition and frustration as expressed in several letters written to Hawthorne in 1851. In the spring, for example, Melville identified with a man that is "a sovereign nature (in himself) amid the powers of heaven, hell, and earth. He may perish; but so long as he exists he insists upon treating with all Powers upon an equal basis. If any of those other Powers choose to withhold certain secrets, let them; that does not impair my sovereignty in myself" (Letter of [April 16?], 1851; *Cor* 186). About six weeks later, Melville wrote again but in a darker frame of mind: "Though I wrote the Gospels in this century, I should die in the gutter.—I talk all about myself, and this is selfishness and egotism" (Letter of June [1?], 1851; *Cor* 192). Pierre appears to take his cue from such language in his own egocentric rhetoric. Preparing for exile from God and man, he will declare himself "an equal power with both; free to make war on Night and Day, and all thoughts and things of mind and matter"; later he determines to "gospelize the world anew, and show [the gods] deeper secrets than the Apocalypse!" As his madness increases, he awakens from a wild dream and envisions "his own duplicate face and features" magnified on the colossal armless trunk of Enceladus; finally, freed of inhibitions on receiving an insulting letter from his cousin and a former friend, he exclaims: "I defy all world's bread and breadth . . . and challenge one and all of them ["the drawn-up worlds in widest space"] to battle!" (*Pierre* 107, 273, 346, 357).

Moreover, both Ahab and Pierre are driven men on quests for ends both ideal and worldly. Ahab is impelled by a metaphysical hatred of the "inscrutable malice" and sum of all human "rage and hate" embodied in the white whale as well as by an intense emotional craving for vengeance over the loss of his leg (*MD* 164, 184). Likewise, Pierre's dedication to Absolute Truth and Virtue pressures him toward attempting to realize them through his commitments to Isabel, Delly, and authorial brilliance, while simultaneously he knowingly lusts for the girl he assumes is his half sister. His "foetal fancy" (*Pierre* 51), the image in his imagination, corresponds with the "half-formed foetal sugges- tions of supernatural agencies" that enhance the mythic component of the white whale and exacerbate Ahab's drive to destroy him (*MD* 181). Whereas Ahab's mind takes him to ever-lower layers of thought and thus deeper into his insatiable ego, Pierre is trapped amid dizzying "infernal catacombs of thought," "mysteries" that impel him to smash himself "against the wall, and [fall] dabbling in the vomit of his own loathed identity" (*Pierre* 51, 142, 171). Later in despair and confusion, he roams the dingiest, darkest streets alone until one night he collapses: "When he came to himself he found that he was lying crosswise in the gutter, dabbled with mud and slime" (341).

Although Ahab burns with silent rage at night, he never sickens this way in self-disgust over his identity. Yet Pierre's degrading falls do have a precedent in *Moby-Dick,* for not long before the *Pequod* sails on its final cruise, Ahab is found one night lying on the ground unconscious, victimized by "some unknown, and seemingly inexplicable, unimaginable casualty, his ivory limb having been so violently displaced, that it had stake-wise smitten, and all but pierced his groin." In his "monomaniac mind," Ahab attributes his anguish to "a former woe"—implicitly associated here with Moby Dick—whereas for the few who learn of it before the *Pequod*'s crew does, the misfortune "invested itself with terrors, not entirely underived from the land of spirits and of wails" (*MD* 463–64).

Aware of his state as "demoniac, . . . madness maddened," Ahab retains enough rationality to maintain his crew's confidence as a responsible commander whose eccentricities may be fearful yet are rarely so out of control that he must be bound in his hammock (*MD* 168, 185). Knowing in his more rational state not to disregard the fundamental monetary purpose of the cruise lest he alienate the crew and lose his ship, Ahab shrewdly succumbs to Starbuck's insistence on unloading leaking casks from the hold to avoid further loss of oil and ultimately revenue. But, says Ishmael, "Human madness is oftentimes a cunning and most feline thing. When you think it fled, it may have but become transfigured into some still subtler form. Ahab's full lunacy subsided not, but deepeningly contracted . . . as in his narrow-flowing monomania, not one jot of Ahab's broad madness had been left behind; so in that broad madness, not one jot of his great natural intellect had perished" (185). Instead, the aim of his "special lunacy," the killing of Moby Dick, gains dominance over his "general sanity," and in the "larger, darker, deeper part" of his psyche, Ahab realizes that his "means [are] sane" but his "motive and . . . object mad" (185–86).

When the white whale is sighted again, however, Starbuck's pleas to abandon the chase are futile despite Ahab's knowledge that his first mate is right. Ahab asks: "What is it, what nameless, inscrutable, unearthly thing is it: what cozening, hidden lord and master, and cruel, remorseless emperor commands me; that against all natural lovings and longings, I so keep pushing, and crowding, and jamming myself on all the time; recklessly making me ready to do what in my own proper, natural heart, I durst not so much as dare? Is Ahab, Ahab? Is it I, God, or who, that lifts this arm?" (*MD* 545). Not knowing what drives him to oppose what his heart would otherwise forbid, Ahab seems driven by what Edgar Allan Poe called "the imp of the perverse."[1]

Compelled to fulfill their quests at any cost, both Ahab and Pierre die consequent to futile actions: Ahab, attempting to resolve his metaphysical hatred and worldly desire for vengeance, is slain by his nemesis, and Pierre, imprisoned after irrationally murdering his cousin and perhaps his assumed half sister as well, dies by his own hand in a rage. Ultimately, Pierre is under the same compulsion as Ahab, whose soul is directed as if on rails toward his unshakable end. By the time rage alone governs his actions, Pierre, too, is "[b]ent . . . on a straightforward, mathematical intent" (*Pierre* 359).

The preceding parallels exemplify Melville's representations of madness in Ahab and Pierre independent of the symbolic value that Wendy Stallard Flory examines in the preceding essay.[2] These correspondences attest to the authenticity of the portraits because, as the following *Subtext* will show, he based their psychological aspects firmly on a combination of what he had recently gained from his readings about insanity and his experiences with it as a somewhat fearful, careful observer.

Now the *Subtext*. First, Melville's empathic reading, early in 1849, of Shakespeare's four major tragedies in which madness occurs—*Othello, Macbeth, Hamlet,* and *King Lear*—was instrumental in the deepening of his tragic portraits. All four expose the disintegration of an apparently sound, noble mind. Prodded toward vengeance and deluded by Iago, the noble Othello transforms from a stable hero into a hallucinating psychopath in less than twenty-four hours. From *Macbeth,* Melville drew not only the magic of witchcraft and prophecy to cast deep shadows over *Moby-Dick,* but more pertinent here, he perceived how forcefully the ego, in its quest for self-aggrandizement, can inexorably drive even the most systematic of minds to delirium and death.

From *Hamlet,* too, Melville adapted specific incidents and passages of dialogue for use in *Moby-Dick,* but no less important was the contrast displayed in that tragedy between Ophelia's authentic insanity, which leads to her death, and Hamlet's affected "antic disposition," exhibited as if the prince in his right mind were behind a mask of madness that deceives all but his friend Horatio and the audience. Ahab is similarly portrayed as exposing an eccentric but controlled public self to the crew while the full extent of his egocentric grandeur and its essential role in his quest for Moby Dick are suspected by Starbuck but known to the reader alone.

However much Melville may have perceived in, conceived from, and reflected on the nature of insanity in Shakespeare's writings, the play to which he was most indebted in that respect was *King Lear.* From *Lear* he learned to tear off the mask, not Hamlet's purposeful falsity, but the mask that inhibits, prevents, all access to vital truth as Melville saw it. Raging on the inside, writing desperately on the outside, he attempted to convey in *Moby-Dick* the truth that Shakespeare helped him discover deep in the recesses of his own mind and imagination, a truth that he still may have believed Hawthorne had discovered before him and, to some limited extent, had infused in his tales. But with all Hawthorne's admiration for Shakespeare and the subtlety of his own mind and art, he never apprehended the "sane madness of vital truth" (*PT* 244) that Melville perceived in the Elizabethan's tragic drama and invested particularly into the character of "crazy Ahab," at times "a raving lunatic," and by his own admission, "madness maddened," for whom "Truth hath no confines" (*MD* 184–85, 168, 164).

Second, reading Hawthorne's fiction the following year together with establishing a close personal relation with his Lenox neighbor soon afterward affected Melville's psychological portraiture at midcentury decisively. He brings Hawthorne and Shakespeare together in his review of *Mosses from an Old Manse* in August 1850, where Melville emphasizes the power of Hawthorne's "mystical blackness...that so fixes and fascinates" him, a power that "furnishes the infinite obscure of his back-ground,—that back-ground, against which Shakespeare plays his grandest conceits" (*PT* 243–44). Yet this is also the blackness that less than a year later would become "the invisible spheres . . . formed in fright" described in Chapter 42 of *Moby-Dick,* the inscrutable realm of "nameless things" and the source "of the demonism" within the world of light we see and know (*MD* 195, 194). From such thoughts and images as these, it was only a short step for Melville to conceive the central contrast and conflict of *Pierre* in which Isabel's dark world of visions, mysteries, and lies rapidly superimposes itself over the naive hero's heretofore glorious life of light.

Third, in addition to reading Shakespeare early in 1849 and Hawthorne the following summer, Melville studied many entries in the *Penny Cyclopaedia,* a set of twenty-nine volumes edited by Charles Knight and published in London from 1833 to 1843.[3] When he met and dined with Knight in December 1849, Melville was impressed with the editor's voluminous publications for the dissemination of popular information, including the *Cyclopaedia.*

Melville's depictions of psychological abnormality in *Pierre* suggest that his debt to the *Cyclopaedia* in those novels is a significant one because, as McCarthy has persuasively shown, he seems to have had the long entry on *insanity* in mind while drafting them. The article is heavily based on the observations and definitions of Dr. James C. Pritchard and others whose definitions are quoted there. Of the "many forms of insanity" itemized and described in that article, three are relevant here: "moral insanity," "monomania," and "mixed forms of madness."

Moral insanity "consist[s] in a morbid perversion of the [moral] feelings, affections, and active powers, without any illusion or erroneous conviction impressed upon the understanding; sometimes co-existing with an apparently unimpaired state of the intellectual faculties.... An inordinate degree of pride and vanity is often the prevailing characteristic of the feelings of a disordered mind; and it is generally attended with some delusion."[4] Monomania, then still a recent word that the *Oxford English Dictionary* records as first used in 1823, is described by the *Cyclopaedia* as a mind "occupied by some illusion or erroneous conviction, the individual still retaining the power of reasoning correctly on matters unconnected with the subject of his delusion. . . . It is rarely that the mind of the monomaniac is otherwise perfectly sound; there is generally combined with the delusion a morbid state of the moral feelings, and in many instances a great weakness of the reasoning faculty." Some deluded individuals "fancy that they have lost their head, others that their legs are not their own, but belong to some other person." Monomania is also said to be "very rare" in its "pure form." Note that the "moral feelings" are adversely affected in the minds of those suffering from monomania and moral insanity alike. The category of mixed forms combines the other two and includes brief definitions of both (*PC* 12:484–85).[5]

At times, Ahab and Pierre alike manifest symptoms of both "moral insanity" and "monomania," according to these descriptions; this suggests they might best be categorized under the heading of "mixed forms." Although ultimately both characters are also governed by delusions inflamed by hate and rage, Ahab alone represents monomania in its "rare" "pure form" that reveals no "further disorder of the intellect" when he dies knowing that his "topmost greatness" coincides with his "topmost grief" (*MD* 571). As Henry Nash Smith notes, Ishmael makes it clear "that Ahab is suffering from a disease of his moral powers, not his intellect."[6] Although it is no delusion of Ahab's that he has lost a leg to the white whale, Pierre's envisioning his own face and features on the armless torso of Enceladus on awakening from a dream does correspond with the symptomatic belief of some monomaniacs in a loss or transference of bodily parts, according to the *Penny Cyclopaedia*.

After writing two full-length narratives in the summer of 1849 for which he had drawn a few details from the *Penny Cyclopaedia*—*Redburn* and *White-Jacket*—Melville badly needed to give his mind a rest. He had seen his father die some seventeen years before in a state of psychological distress—severe enough that to a family member the dying man appeared maniacal (Parker 1.58–59). He knew as well that his older brother, Gansevoort, had recently died young, suffering from intellectual confusion and nervous excitement. On reading the "Insanity" entry in the *Penny Cyclopaedia*, Melville also had confirmed that "a tendency to mental and other cerebral affections is often observed to prevail in families, and to be transmitted from parents to offspring" (*PC* 12:485). He might well have felt, then, a latent threat from the mental instability he witnessed in his own family as he drafted an oft-cited Hotel de Cluny passage in Chapter 41 of *Moby-Dick*. There Ishmael identifies Ahab's "root of grandeur, his whole awful essence [seated] in bearded state;

an antique buried beneath antiquities [far below earth's surface], and throned on torsoes," with a captive king on a broken throne mocked by the gods; Ishmael tells "ye prouder, sadder souls" to go below and "question that proud sad king! A family likeness! aye, he did beget ye, ye young exiled royalties" (*MD* 185–86). Fearing that he himself might be subject to inherited insanity, Melville had acquired both an interest in and a sensitivity to mental illness in others that made him a particularly keen observer of details related to it.

When preparing to board the *Southampton* for the crossing to England and the Continent in October 1849, Melville was introduced, probably by Evert Duyckinck's brother George,[7] to Dr. George J. Adler, an adjunct professor of language, literature, and philosophy at New York University. Adler was important as an extraordinarily well-read traveling companion to Melville,[8] but on another level he was even more than that because his proximity over several weeks gave Melville an opportunity to observe firsthand the behavior of a seemingly perfectly rational mind yet one that was in fact seriously deranged.

Adler had just finished compiling a massive German-English dictionary that he had worked on for years and that, as he acknowledged to Melville soon after the ship left port, had nearly destroyed his sanity. By then, however, he was already a hopeless paranoiac. Melville did not yet realize the seriousness of Adler's distress, but he could readily sympathize with the man, having just completed a marathon writing project of his own, and the two travelers became closely acquainted during their journey.[9]

Among the letters Adler included in his small collection, *Letters of a Lunatic,* privately published in 1854 after he had been institutionalized at Bloomingdale Asylum, was one written to an unnamed recipient on December 26, 1853, only three months after he was admitted there. He describes in great detail how he had been persistently harassed and finally "driven away from New-York" while struggling to complete his dictionary in 1848, and about six months after finishing it elsewhere, he complains of being harried again by "a malevolent espionage over [his] peregrinations even in Paris."[10] One type of delusion suffered by the monomaniac, according to the *Penny Cyclopaedia,* is a conception of "unreal events which the individuals believe to have occurred, or consists in a belief of some absurdity which has no foundation except in the patient's imagination" (*PC* 12:485). All indications suggest that Adler suffered from precisely this form of delusion, although he seems to have suppressed it in Melville's company. Time references connote that his illness began over a year before he sailed for Europe to restore his health, but the letter also reveals that his travel therapy was ineffective because he mentions being hounded on his return by "the same odious conspiracy"

(Adler 18). By then, he had become suspicious of nearly everyone, which is also symptomatic of "moral insanity" as described in the *Cyclopaedia:* "sometimes jealousy and suspicion are the prevailing passions, causing their subjects to shun their dearest relatives and to live in constant misery, though at the same time they are able to reason correctly on any topic" (*PC* 12:484). Indeed, that Adler's intellectual powers did not seem adversely affected for at least a few years after traveling with Melville may be confirmed by some of his published letters, which state that he continued teaching a variety of courses at New York University from the time he returned to the United States until he entered the asylum, where he remained until his death in 1868. A list of his substantial publications from the 1850s verifies the state of his intellectual capacity even under the influence of his paranoia.[11]

It is not known how much Duyckinck told Melville about Adler's state of mind before they sailed,[12] nor does Melville reveal in his journal if he perceived traces of the doctor's mental instability. Yet it is difficult to believe that he neither knew in advance about Adler's precarious psychological condition nor noticed indications of it as they talked and traveled together over a period of several weeks. Adler's share of his intellectual conversations with Melville and his actions during their talks and rambles marked him as an agreeable traveling companion in Melville's eyes rather than an eccentric or otherwise abnormal one, which suggests how sane the lexicographer appeared to him over an extended time.

Melville may have regarded him differently in retrospect, however. Reviewing their association after the voyage, he may have become aware of signs he had observed earlier but left unattended, as readers respond to previously unheeded details in a text with the aid of an informative afterword. This modified assessment could be attributable partly to what Melville may have later learned about Adler's behavior from others. However, it may also have emerged when he remembered two incidents of delirium and insanity he had witnessed aboard the *Southampton* as well as the shock he suffered in learning that an old friend, Charles Fenno Hoffman, was institutionalized for madness earlier in 1849. If Melville later saw Adler differently, however, and if his latent fear of insanity and his reading on the subject led him to notice through hindsight indications of peculiar behavior during the voyage, he revealed Adler's insanity only through his penetrating characterizations of Ahab and Pierre among others but did not comment on it directly.

Melville's response to Adler resembles that of Prof. James Murray, originator and editor of the *Oxford English Dictionary,* to Dr. William Chester Minor, after Murray had accepted thousands of meticulously drafted entries for the new dictionary from the doctor, born a year after the twelve-year-old Adler had immigrated to the United States from Leipzig. Those who have read Simon Winchester's astonishing portrait in *The Professor and the Madman* (1998)[13] will be familiar with Dr. Minor's mental state, which the doctors then called *monomania*, later a form of paranoia, and now schizophrenia (Winchester 69–70, 209, 211). Although more extreme, Minor's mental disorder had much in common with that of the German lexicographer.

Dr. Minor was a young surgeon in the Civil War. Born in Ceylon in 1834 as the son of Congregationalist missionaries from New England, he was sensitive to the beauty of music and art, intellectually acute, and highly literate. He was also paranoid and obsessed with sex since childhood. A shock he experienced during the Civil War appears to have undermined his mental health to the extent that he could no longer maintain control of his lascivious behavior at times. Consequently, he was honorably discharged and temporarily hospitalized. Soon after his release from the asylum, Dr. Minor, like Melville and Adler before him, traveled to England in an attempt to regain control of himself, but in London early one morning he shot without reason a workman he did not know and immediately allowed himself to be arrested. By virtue of a precedent-setting decision in the English court, he was acquitted by reason of insanity and sentenced to an indefinite term at Broadmoor Insane Asylum outside London.

In the asylum, Dr. Minor had access to books in abundance, and he responded enthusiastically to Professor Murray's published requests for words with usage contexts. Years of receiving them at Oxford with great appreciation finally led Murray to visit his most reliable contributor; on arriving at Broadmoor, he was stunned to learn that the doctor was an inmate there, not a member of the staff. After first meeting him, Murray wrote: "Dr. Minor seemed as sane as myself, a much cultivated and scholarly man, with many artistic tastes, and of fine Christian character" (Winchester 176). As far as we know at present, Melville gained much the same impression of Adler while traveling with him over a period of several weeks. Murray and Dr. Minor met again on many occasions and maintained a cordial relationship.

But alone at night in his locked room, Dr. Minor was obsessed with the delusion of being sexually attacked by imps and demons. His state of mind could have served as a case study in the *Cyclopaedia* to exemplify the monomaniac suffering from "demonomania . . . a belief in the presence of invisible beings whom the lunatic sees"; they may be angels or, in contrast, persons or creatures bent on harm (*PC* 12:485). At length in despair Dr. Minor cut off his offending penis with his pocket knife and threw it into the fire, the only means he knew to overcome the fiends he imagined. As a surgeon he had learned how to stanch the blood and treat the wound, which he did so well it healed rapidly. The rational mind held up perfectly after the mad impulse that could have destroyed him.

Nothing in the record suggests that Adler's paranoia eventuated in violence but only in an extended barrage of verbal assaults and formal accusatory letters. The similarities between Drs. Adler and Minor, however, are their ostensible sanity to perceptive observers like Melville and Professor Murray, their extraordinary intelligence, their discipline in matters apart from their delusions and obsessions, and their scholarly productivity—all ultimately undermined by the devastating psychological illness that made it impossible for them to exist in society as "normal" human beings.

Ahab's rational mind could not likewise save him, after his mad thrust into the creature that had offended him and bundled him speechlessly into Eternity beneath the blue Pacific. Melville felt "spotless as the lamb" after writing what he called "a wicked book" (*Cor* 212) that he expected would achieve a far more positive critical reception than it did. When the novel that followed, *Pierre,* met ridicule and failure in the market, Melville shifted to a new methodology in his art by writing short fiction developed with quiet irony that is often comic but with tragic undertones. He was not about to follow the same route as Ahab and Pierre himself.

In a recent and as yet unpublished paper read at the fourth international Melville conference in Maui in 2002, Christopher N. Phillips posits that Melville "wrestles in *Redburn* with his desire to preserve ties to his dead father and to the culture that he represents—but his failure to get beyond philosophy and fetishized objects is the painful result of culture shock, first into the Pacific and then away from it."[14] Phillips goes on to say, "This Atlantic-Pacific cultural trauma emerges most clearly in *Moby-Dick*" (6), an observation he develops persuasively with cartographic references, on which his paper focuses.

To extend upon Phillips's argument, I suggest that Melville's "cultural trauma" on leaving his native Atlantic world for the Pacific realm still unknown to him, then returning home awakened to an altogether different way of life, was more intensely represented in *Moby-Dick* because of a further revelation—on the order of epiphany—after experiencing European travel for the first time. During his nearly two months with Adler, first aboard the *Southampton,* then in London and Paris, the gates of a new wonder-world literally swung open to Melville. After that, he would be a "thought-diver" to a greater depth than ever before, and his writing would mature accordingly. As an author, he no longer dwelled in Starbuck's earthly world; he had descended into Ahab's tragic, woeful, and inscrutable one. Starbuck cries to Ahab, "I came here to hunt whales, not my commander's vengeance. How many barrels will thy vengeance yield thee even if thou gettest it, Captain Ahab? It will not fetch thee much in our Nantucket market," and Ahab answers:

"Nantucket market! Hoot! But come closer, Starbuck; thou requirest a little lower layer. . . . My vengeance will fetch a great premium *here*" [striking his chest].

"Vengeance on a dumb brute!" cried Starbuck. . . . "Madness! To be enraged with a dumb thing, Captain Ahab, seems blasphemous."

"Hark ye yet again,—the little lower layer. All visible objects, man, are but as pasteboard masks. But in each event . . . some unknown but still reasoning thing puts forth the mouldings of its features from behind the unreasoning mask. If man will strike, strike through the mask!" (*MD* 163–64)

With *Moby-Dick,* Melville struck through the mask, and with *Pierre,* he struck through again. Only in those two major romances did he explore the world of mind at a level of consciousness equivalent to which none but the great whales might dive into the chaotic depths of the vast Pacific. Ishmael praises the imagination's creativity at heights where the Catskill eagle flies, but he conveys far more dramatically those lower levels of consciousness that are home to drives and urges that can and do overwhelm the rational state and lead to a thunderous self-annihilation: so Ahab, so Pierre. Melville found neither resolution nor silence, but he did find a new, more subtle and ironic approach to wrestling with old truths in the writings that followed his disappointment over the abysmal failure of *Pierre.* Ahab, knowing that his final thrust of the harpoon at the white whale would bring his "topmost grief," commits in effect a suicidal act as Moby Dick takes the thrust and pulls him under; similarly, in a low dungeon Pierre swallows the poison he knows will kill him. Both strike through the mask and die for their efforts, however noble they feel they are or mad we may assess them to be. Fortunately, Melville himself suppressed his disaffection and did not follow them,[15] although such later writings as, for example, "Bartleby," "Benito Cereno," *Clarel,* and *Billy Budd* confirm that he never lost sight of their quest for truth regardless how mad it may have seemed.

With the knowledge of mental derangement in his own family, his reading of Shakespeare, Hawthorne, and especially contemporary psychological theory pertaining specifically to insanity, and his weeks of travel to and in Europe with a brilliant, seemingly sane paranoiac, Melville had gained all the information and insight he needed to create his psychologically authentic portraits of Ahab and Pierre. These were not intended to be case studies of insanity, of course, but powerful, innovative characterizations that dramatically represent two complementary faces among the "company of selves" that Henry A. Murray perceived in the depths of Melville's psyche.[16] "What a revelation," Melville printed in the margin of Hawthorne's "Monsieur du Miroir."[17] Reflecting on Ahab and Pierre, we may say the same of his own tormented heroes.

NOTES

1. Poe's story of that title was first published in *Graham's Magazine* in July 1846, but whether Melville had read it or not is unknown.

2. See Wendy Stallard Flory, "Melville, *Moby-Dick,* and the Depressive Mind: Queequeg, Starbuck, Stubb, and Flask as Symbolic Characters."

3. The full title is *The Penny Cyclopaedia of the Society for the Diffusion of Useful Knowledge.*

4. "Insanity," in *The Penny Cyclopaedia* (London: Charles Knight & Co., 1838), 12: 484; hereafter *PC.*

5. These definitions may be related to the murder trial of one Abner Rogers in 1844 with Justice Lemuel Shaw, who later became Melville's father-in-law, as presiding judge. The defendant had committed the murder, but his attorney defended him on the grounds that he was insane when he did it. The insanity defense was relatively new, but Shaw agreed that despite Rogers's apparently normal conduct much of the time, he was under a delusion when he killed the victim and acted uncontrollably by impulse, not by will (McCarthy 53). Rogers's knowing right from wrong did not prevent the murder because he was compelled unwillingly to act against his moral judgment, as if Poe's future imp of the perverse had been driving him then as it would deal with Ahab a few years later. Although the Rogers trial occurred before Melville's writing career began, he is likely to have known of it by then and to have spoken with Justice Shaw about it sometime before describing Ahab's insanity in *Moby-Dick.*

6. Henry Nash Smith, "The Madness of Ahab," in *Democracy and the Novel: Popular Resistance to Classic American Writers* (New York: Oxford Univ. Press, 1978), 39.

7. Dwight A. Lee (citing the *Dictionary of American Biography* [1928]) and Parker (without documentation) aver that Evert himself made the introduction, but Leon Howard says it was George. Melville's entry for October 11 in his journal mentions that George was on the wharf when the ship sailed, not Evert (*Journals* 4). Lee had noted that Evert's alleged introduction occurred on October 11, 1849, the date of departure, but Melville's explicit reference only to George on the dock makes this appear doubtful; see Parker 1:663; Dwight A. Lee, "Melville and George J. Adler," *American Notes and Queries* 12 (1974): 139, 141 n. 5; and Leon Howard, *Herman Melville: A Biography* (Berkeley and Los Angeles: Univ. of California Press, 1951), 140.

8. Sanford E. Marovitz, "More Chartless Voyaging: Melville and Adler at Sea," *Studies in the American Renaissance 1986*, ed. Joel Myerson (Charlottesville: Univ. of Virginia Press, 1986), 373–84.

9. Only one comment in Melville's journal of the voyage refers to Adler's fright, and that pertains to his fear over attending a production of the Penny Theatre in London; even that, however, was probably less evidence of Adler's paranoia than of a normal reaction to the flimsy seating structure of the theater and the unruly audience to which playgoers there were subject, as Eleanor Melville Metcalf documents in her edition of the journal. Melville's maritime experience precluded his worrying over such trifles himself. See Eleanor Melville

Metcalf, ed., *Herman Melville: Journal of a Voyage to England and the Continent* (Cambridge, Mass.: Harvard Univ. Press, 1948), 27, 106–07.

10. G[eorge] J. Adler, *Letters of a Lunatic; or, A Brief Exposition of My University Life, during the Years 1853–54* (n.p.: privately printed, 1854), 17–18.

11. See a partial list of Adler's accomplishments under "The University of the City of New York," *Cyclopaedia of American Literature,* by Evert A. Duyckinck and George L. Duyckinck, ed. M. Laird Simons, 2 vols. (Philadelphia: William Rutter & Co., 1880), 2:753–54. The entry indicates that Adler continued to publish until his death, having brought out two pamphlets between 1866 and 1868, one on Von Humboldt's linguistic studies and the other a lecture on the poetry of Arabs in Spain.

12. Melville was possibly informed of it by Dr. Augustus Kinsley Gardner, whose book *Old Wine in New Bottles* (1848) included descriptions of asylums and other mental institutions he had seen in Paris as a medical student there. Gardner gave Melville a copy before his journey. As a friend of the Duyckincks and a physician with an interest in insanity, although it was not his specialty, Gardner probably knew of Adler's mental state whether or not he was acquainted with the man himself.

13. Simon Winchester, *The Professor and the Madman: A Tale of Insanity and the Making of the Oxford English Dictionary* (New York: HarperCollins, 1998). I gratefully acknowledge my dependence on this biography for my brief account of Dr. Minor

14. Christopher N. Phillips, "The Epistemology of Mapping in Herman Melville's Pacific Fiction," paper presented at Melville and the Pacific Conference; June 4, 2003, Lahaina, Maui, Hawaii, 5–6. I am grateful to Mr. Phillips for sending me a copy of his unpublished paper.

15. Hershel Parker observes that in mid-1867 Melville's wife, Elizabeth, "seemed convinced her husband was insane," probably because she and others believed he had been mistreating her for some time. Although this view was expressed some fifteen years after the publication of *Pierre,* it does reflect on Melville's temperamental and at times eccentric behavior as he drafted his major romances. Parker 2:599–600, 629–35.

16. Henry A. Murray, ed., introduction to *Pierre; or, The Ambiguities* by Herman Melville (New York: Hendricks House, 1962), xcv.

17. Quoted from Melville's copy of *Mosses from an Old Manse* at the Houghton Library, Harvard University.

Moby-Dick and Law

"Deadly Voids and Unbidden Infidelities"

Death, Memory, and the Law in *Moby-Dick*

JOHN T. MATTESON

Herman Melville was a bad driver, and his driving seems to have worsened while he was writing *Moby-Dick*.[1] Hershel Parker writes that, during the creation of his whale, Melville was frequently obliged to leave his manuscript to run family errands in town. He developed the habit of driving his horses "hell for leather" to his destination and back, anxious lest a more leisurely pace should deprive him of even a few minutes of writing time (1:792). Melville's disregard of the laws against recklessness serves as an apt metaphor for the struggles of art against law in general. The rules that make for a peaceable and orderly society—even those pertaining to so mundane a subject as traffic safety—can sometimes be seen as a barrier in the path of creative energy. Both Melville and his work stand in a vexed relation to law. In both his style and his opinions, he was lawless in ways that extended far beyond his tendency to drive a fast wagon.

It is fruitful to think of *Moby-Dick* as an outlaw text in a variety of senses. The book, as we know, ignores narrative convention and flouts the traditional boundaries of genre. Melville also wrote nonsequentially, observing no rule in his method of composition other than the law of his own fitful inspiration, and the eccentricities of his writing habits augment the other peculiarities of the book's structure. Lawless in both its poetics and the process of its creation, *Moby-Dick* takes a critical stance toward the existing role of law in society, especially as the book addresses the cultural nexus that unites law, death, and memory. Melville thought we should be careful both about how we remember the past and how we legislate for the future. He did not desire for memory to be static and rehearsed, and he did not want for law to be formulated as a mere series of cold, mechanically followed precedents. Rather, Melville in *Moby-Dick* rejects the traditional formalities of memory and moves toward an alternative conception of law, cryptically founded on living values of friendship and fellow feeling. If the terms of Melville's proposed code remain obscure, they remain so because his novel legislates for the spirit rather than for the state.

Melville's dominant metaphor for dead law and inert memory was the image of the sepulchre. The tomb symbolized for him not only physical death but the deadening effects of memory imprisoned in ritual and of law weighed down by formalism. In contemplating the sepulchre, Melville was reacting against an already-pronounced tendency among the Americans of his time to enshrine their cultural memories within a forbidding sanctity. The generations that followed the Revolutionary fathers sometimes assumed without argument that they would never rise to match the brilliant achievements of their forebears. This anxiety of filial inferiority extended past the middle of the century. In 1855, for instance, a reviewer of George Bancroft's *History of the United States* lamented, "One by one they totter and die, the remnants of that sturdy race . . . Those who fought the great battle—better, alas! than we could fight it!"[2] The same concern had already served as a subtext for two indispensable documents of the period: Daniel Webster's 1825 address at the dedication of the Bunker Hill Monument and the opening lines of Ralph Waldo Emerson's *Nature*. These texts contain many of the underpinnings of Melville's reflections on the sepulchre in *Moby-Dick*.

Even before the speech at Bunker Hill, Webster's voice had been associated with the gravity and darkness of the tomb. In February 1820, in his earliest known journal, a sixteen-year-old Emerson, who, it seems, had already embarked on three decades of Webster worship, recorded the following description of the great man's voice: "His voice is sepulchral—there is not the least variety or the least harmony of tone—it commands, it fills, it echoes, but is harsh and discordant."[3] Webster characterized Bunker Hill, not principally as a scene of military triumph and glory, but as a place of mass death and burial. Only moments into his speech, in his grave, gravelike voice, Webster told his audience, "We are among the sepulchres of our fathers."[4] The word that carries the most meaning is "sepulchres"; incalculable power would have been lost had Webster opted instead for "graves" or "tombs." The word "sepulchre" is essentially removed from daily speech. It raised the site of the soldiers' burial to a level of austere majesty. Webster's more attentive listeners would also have noted in the word "sepulchre" an allusion to William Cullen Bryant's "Thanatopsis," originally published eight years earlier. Bryant had told his reader that, at the end of life, "Thou shalt lie down / With patriarchs of the infant world—with kings, / The powerful of the earth—the wise, the good, / Fair forms, and hoary seers of ages past, / All in one mighty sepulchre."[5] Bryant's solution to anxiety over the lost legacy of the fathers had been figuratively to transform the entire earth into a single sepulchre, a place of eventual reunion and shared honor with past patriarchal heroes. Similarly, Webster's invocation of the sepulchre establishes communication with a legacy of wisdom and virtue, but he forges a more immediate link than Bryant does. Whereas Bryant's reunion with the heroic past must wait until death, Webster implies that, through the public consecration of a particular piece of ground, the living as well as the dead can participate in the past.

For Webster and his audience, the occasion had intensely biblical connotations. Part of Webster's mission on this day was to confirm the sacredness of the ground on which he stood; indeed, the audience had begun the ceremonies by singing a hymn that began, "O! Is not this a holy place?"[6] The "sepulchre" of Webster's speech connoted the most sacred place in Christendom, namely the Holy Sepulchre where the body of the crucified Jesus had been laid. Conflating the crucifixion with the military sacrifice of the colonists, Webster infused the soldiers of the Revolution with a similar, though lesser, quality of holy martyrdom. Moreover, the sepulchre of Jesus was the tomb from which an everlasting life had arisen. Thus Webster's invocation of the sepulchre called to mind the possibility of a figurative resurrection of Revolutionary virtue—indeed a resurrection that must be performed if America were to preserve the moral vitality of its origins.

Yet death, not resurrection, predominates in Webster's oration. The tomb, however glorious, remains a tomb, and Webster's rhetoric brings the speech back again and again to ideas of death. "Monuments and eulogy," Webster reminds his listeners, "belong to the dead" (Address 24). In his appeal to the public memory, Webster made clear that the first duty of Americans was to tend the sepulchres of past heroes. Descendants of the Revolution were obliged above all else to honor and preserve the memory-bearing relics of the past; to improve upon the Revolutionary legacy was deemed hardly possible. The speech became wildly popular. Even Webster himself, however, seemed to have sensed that his vision lacked something vital. He complained beforehand that he had written a strangely dead speech, with "no more tone in it, than the weather in which it was written." His remarks, he feared, were "perpetual dissolution and thaw."[7] Webster's oration had glorified the past, but it had found no constructive way to vivify the present.

The sepulchre into which America risked falling was not only the tomb of memory but also the tomb of outmoded, confining legal forms and institutions. The fear that a reflexive reverence for the past would frustrate efforts to invent a distinctly new and independent American culture was on Emerson's mind in 1836 when he borrowed Webster's trope for the opening lines of *Nature:* "Our age is retrospective. It builds the sepulchres of the fathers."[8] Emerson's intent in repeating Webster's words in *Nature* was both to broaden Webster's meaning and reverse it. The sepulchres in Webster's speech are meant to inspire; they are pristine monuments to a sacred historical past. To Emerson the sepulchres are a cautionary image; they emblematize a culture that risks its own premature death if it insists on paying too much homage to the past. If, in choosing the trope of a sepulchre, Emerson aimed only to score some rhetorical points off Webster, the passage would be clever enough. But to Emerson the ex-minister, the image of the sepulchre must have suggested an intriguing scriptural echo as well. The image is a linguistic link to Jesus's warning to the Pharisees in the eleventh chapter of Luke: "Woe unto you! for ye build the sepulchres of the prophets, and your fathers killed them. Truly ye bear witness that ye allow the deeds of your fathers: for they indeed killed them, and ye build their sepulchres."[9] Almost certainly, Webster had had this passage in mind when he wrote his Bunker Hill oration, but it remained for Emerson to catch its subversive irony—an irony that Webster could hardly have intended. In his journals, Emerson had fretted over the tendency of law to produce outward conformity while failing to educate and improve the inner spirit.[10] Using Webster's own probable source, Emerson now attacked the "whited wall" of legalism and the morality of mere appearances. The full identity of Emerson's target, however, is not evident until the broader context of the biblical passage becomes known. Christ begins his admonition with the cry, "Woe unto you . . . ye lawyers" (Luke 11:46).

That the precursor of Emerson's indictment was addressed to lawyers suggests Emerson's frustration with lawyerly, formalistic thinking. He saw that the law, like the broader culture in which he lived, was more concerned with preserving established forms and customs rather than creatively adapting those forms to new uses. The antilawyer subtext is strengthened by the fact that Emerson is also alluding to Webster, whom many considered the preeminent lawyer of his day.

Emerson's allusion to the sepulchre also would have called to his reader's mind Jesus's metaphor of the whited sepulchre from Matthew 23:27, which likens the Pharisees to structures "which indeed appear beautiful outward, but are within full of dead men's bones, and of all uncleanness." The sepulchre of the scripture is symbolic of the person who dedicates his or her life to conforming to external morality and convention. Such a person may present a charming façade to the world but will lead an inner life of rot and decay. The old dispensation, Emerson implies, leads inevitably to a heap of dry bones. It is fitting that *Nature*'s first paragraph ends with an appeal for establishing "our own . . . laws" (*Nature* 7).

As Michael Kammen has demonstrated the 1850s voiced its own ironic reaction to the affirmative Revolutionary tradition and the practice of monument making, a reaction typified, in Kammen's view, by the work of Herman Melville.[11] Indeed, Melville's *Pierre* may be read as a horror story of the national psyche—a tale of the terrors that may arise when the Revolutionary past refuses to remain safe and sanitized in its whited tomb and reasserts itself in morally threatening forms. Interestingly, Melville mockingly dedicates his most protracted treatment of the Revolutionary tradition, *Israel Potter,* to "His Highness the Bunker-Hill Monument" (*IP* vii). Modeled on an actual veteran of Bunker Hill who had been, to his outrage, denied a military pension, Melville's title character is curiously excluded from the effusive patriotic memory. Indeed, *Israel Potter* resists every opportunity to add to the mythos of Bunker Hill and to partake of positive, traditional commemoration. The battle that defines the hero's life is the work of a single paragraph, in the midst of which Melville writes with dismissive impatience, "But everyone knows all about the battle" (13).

After being wounded at Bunker Hill, the historical Potter spends almost fifty years in exile from America before returning in 1823. Melville slyly alters this chronology, choosing for his hero to return too late to hear Webster's address at the old battleground. Instead, the fictitious Potter returns to Boston on July 4, 1826, a day that, because it marked the fiftieth anniversary of the Declaration of Independence and saw the deaths of both Thomas Jefferson and John Adams, was perhaps the quintessential American day of patriotic death and remembrance. Half an hour after landing, Israel narrowly escapes being flattened by "a patriotic triumphal car" in the Fourth of July parade. Above the car flies a banner that bears the words, "Bunker Hill 1775. Glory to the heroes that fought" (167). This car presents an apt emblem of the American Republic. The thing it does most efficiently is to move steadily and rapidly forward, and woe to him or her who stands in the way. The car bears the emblems of commemoration, but perhaps only as a justification for its endless and reckless forward press. Always preaching glory, it is madly indifferent to the very persons on whom its glory rests.

In the final chapter, after his brush with death under the wheels of the patriotic car, Potter at last comes in view of the Bunker Hill Monument, still far from completion and difficult to see from afar. And, significantly, Potter's vantage point is from a distance. He is sitting on a mound of dirt in another graveyard on Copp's Hill, which, Melville reminds us, was occupied by the enemy on the day of the battle. Potter is pointedly remote from the scene of glory and the designated place of public commemoration. The patriotic memory takes no account of Potter's own contributions, which do not seem to belong in the story that the culture wants to tell. Underneath the unfinished monument lie the remains of nonconforming memories.

More generally enlightening on the subjects of monuments, memory, and law, however, is *Moby-Dick*. Despite its pervasive concern with death, *Moby-Dick* refuses to participate in traditional forms of mourning and commemoration. The novel shows that funerals and epitaphs are in themselves empty and meaningless; they serve only as points for jumping off in the direction of deeper and more elusive meanings. Melville's novel rejects customary rituals of memory; Ishmael embarks on the *Pequod* in an attempt, in part, to escape the trappings and formalized habits of mourning. He goes to sea because he finds himself "involuntarily pausing before coffin warehouses, and bringing up the rear of every funeral I meet" (3). It would be illogical to suppose that Ishmael goes to sea to escape death; he fully understands that whaling is a deadly business. He is repelled, however, by the ways in which the rituals of death have absorbed and preoccupied his consciousness and how conventional efforts at commemoration fail to say anything of value about the dead or about dying.

As Neal Tolchin has convincingly shown, *Moby-Dick* is permeated by unresolved grief (see *Mourning, Gender, and Creativity* 117–37). Nevertheless, despite its preoccupation with death and its verbal expansiveness in virtually all other directions, *Moby-Dick* refuses to eulogize. The abrupt ending of the novel leaves no room for funeral oratory. The closest Melville's novel comes to the eulogistic mode is in the "six-inch" chapter titled "The Lee Shore," in which Ishmael makes his truncated farewell to Bulkington. The chapter is "the stoneless grave of Bulkington," who shuns the conventional hearthstones and headstones of the port to seek truth (and find burial) in the "howling infinite" of the sea (*MD* 106, 107). He leaves behind him on the dry land "all that's kind to our mortalities" (106). In the case of Bulkington, at least, death acquires more significance apart from these kindnesses and conventions, and the soul of the man would be only poorly comprehended within the traditions of remembrance. Ishmael remarks, "Deep memories yield no epitaphs" (106). The things people incline to speak about the dead touch only on superficialities, and they are perhaps best left unsaid.

In *Moby-Dick*, the problem of establishing not only the proper convention but also the place of grieving becomes problematic because the grave is both everywhere and nowhere. The story produces corpses aplenty, but they tend not to be where one expects to find them, and they are never disposed of in an orthodox manner. Although the shadow of death lies thick over the novel, none of the apparently appropriate places for entombment, from the black-bordered marble cenotaphs in Father Mapple's church to Queequeg's airtight coffin, actually contain dead bodies. Instead, the "grave" that engulfs the bodies is the ocean, a grave that covers 70 percent of the earth's surface but is devoid of burial markers.[12] Paradoxically, although Melville's ocean harbors "the ungraspable phantom of life," it is also a place of universal cannibalism where people go in multitudes to die (*MD* 5). The melancholy of the end of the novel is accentuated by the placelessness of the *Pequod*'s disaster, the impossibility of fixing the location of the sinking: "Then all collapsed, and the great shroud of the sea rolled on as it rolled five thousand years ago" (572). The sea, described here with the funereal image of a shroud, conceals all traces of the horror that has occurred. It remains unchanged and inscrutable despite all the death it has absorbed. On Melville's ocean, one sails each day among the graves of the fathers, but those sepulchres are hauntingly mute, anonymous, and invisible. Emerson had sought an escape from the sepulchral in the ever-renewing life of Nature. Melville seals off this escape route by declaring all the natural world to be a deceptive screen for pervading, all-consuming death: "All deified Nature absolutely paints like the harlot, whose allurements cover nothing but the charnel-house within" (195).

The visible sepulchres in the novel all seem calculated to deceive us and to raise questions about the accuracy of our perceptions of death and burial. Tombs and coffins turn out to be vacant, and images of death and birth promiscuously commingle. The first apparent graves one encounters in *Moby-Dick*, the marble tablets in the Whaleman's Chapel, appall Ishmael with their emptiness:

> Oh! ye whose dead lie buried beneath the green grass; who standing among flowers can say—here, *here* lies my beloved; ye know not the desolation that broods in bosoms like these. What bitter blanks in those black-bordered marbles which cover no ashes! What despair in those immovable inscriptions! What deadly voids and unbidden infidelities in the lines that seem to gnaw upon all Faith, and refuse resurrections to the beings who have placelessly perished without a grave. (*MD* 36)

Making monuments does not avail against grief and despair; like the pasteboard masks that Ahab sees in all visual realities, these monuments have nothing in back of them. Instead of bolstering faith in a continuing social project, or the possibility of eternal life, they cruelly mock the possibilities of belief and resurrection. Their emptiness recalls an anxiety rooted at the core of Christian belief, the despair of the vacant tomb. In the Whaleman's

Chapel, widows and orphans feel with perpetual acuteness the anguish of Mary Magdalene, who lamented, "They have taken away the Lord out of the sepulchre, and we do not know where they have laid him" (John 20:2).

It is perhaps no coincidence that the last of the cenotaphs observed by Ishmael in the Whaleman's Chapel is dedicated to a captain named Ezekiel Hardy. In the contexts of burial and bereavement, the captain's name conjures images of the Valley of Dry Bones that God reveals to Ezekiel the prophet. Despite its initially grim appearance, this biblical valley is a trope of optimism; the Lord shows Ezekiel how the power of the Holy Spirit can restore flesh and skin to the desiccated, scattered remains and breathe new life into lifeless bodies (Ezek. 37:1–10). The dry bones of the valley attest, not to the finality of loss, but to the miraculous power of the Lord to bring new life to the spiritually desolate. Melville, however, renders darker prophecies than Ezekiel. In his narrative, the prospect of resurrection is thwarted because Captain Hardy has left no bones to rejoin and return to the flesh. The bones of Melville's Ezekiel lie not in a dry valley, but beneath the waters of the Pacific; the wherewithal for the performance of the miracle has been lost.

When one bears in mind the political subtext of the biblical Ezekiel's prophecies, the absence of Captain Hardy's bones becomes all the more ominous. The astounding rehabilitation described by the prophet is meant as a metaphor for a spiritually exhausted nation, which God and prophecy have the power to restore to a righteous army. As God tells Ezekiel,

> Son of man, these bones are the whole house of Israel; behold, they say, "Our bones are dried, and our hope is lost; we are cut off on our part." Therefore, prophesy and say unto them, "Thus saith the Lord God: 'Behold, O my people, I will open your graves, and cause you to come up out of your graves, and bring you into the land of Israel.'" (Ezek. 37:11–12)

Open the graves in the Whaleman's Chapel, however, and one will find nothing out of which to reconstruct the shattered nation. More distressingly still, these cenotaphs look out upon people divided by grief, not united by it: "Each silent worshipper seemed purposely sitting apart from the other, as if each silent grief were insular and incommunicable" (MD 34). The bleak monuments in Mapple's church and the griefs they represent produce no community of shared remembrance. The atmosphere of grief in the book is omnipresent, but one must grieve as an Isolato.

Like Emerson before him, Melville identified physical death and burial with the deadening aspects of legal orthodoxy. Ishmael finds in his discourses on whaling a surprising range of opportunities for commentary on law and legal customs, and these commentaries almost always arise from images of death. Of the chapters that contemplate the peculiarities of legal orthodoxy, two have a particular power to fascinate: "The Funeral" and "A Bower in the Arsacides." In the former chapter, Ishmael's reflections on law come at an incongruous moment, when the headless carcass of a sperm whale, still colossal despite having had all its worldly value extracted from it, is jettisoned into the waves. A "hideous sight," the carcass nevertheless remains an imposing object, and Ishmael relates how cruising vessels will often mistake the floating body for a tiny island: "straightway the whale's unharming corpse, with trembling fingers is set down in the log—*shoals, rocks, and breakers hereabouts: beware!*" (*MD* 308, 309). For years thereafter, Ishmael reports, ships avoid the spot of such a sighting for fear of breaking up on the spurious "rocks." Ishmael sees this phenomenon as an emblem of unthinking conformity and the common law: "There's your law of precedents; there's your utility of traditions; there's the story of your obstinate survival of old beliefs never bottomed on the earth, and now not even hovering in the air! There's orthodoxy!" (309). The law of precedents, so dear to Webster, is here likened to a dead whale: massive, aimlessly drifting, bereft of its brains, but still curiously capable of inspiring awe and commanding obedience. "The Funeral" seems not only to describe the melancholy last rites of the whale but also to call for the burial of a lifeless body of law. Significantly, Ishmael observes that the whale's corpse "flashes like a marble sepulchre" (308). The trope looks back both to the Bunker Hill oration and the whited sepulchres of Matthew. In the sepulchral image of the dead whale, Melville condemns both slavish adherence to precedent and the hypocrisy of those who adhere outwardly to law while harboring unseen corruptions within.

One gets a sense of what Melville finds absent from law by comparing the treatment meted out by nature to the whale's carcass with that which it later accords to Ishmael, afloat on Queequeg's coffin. In "The Funeral," the whale's corpse "floats more and more away, the water round it torn and splashed by the insatiate sharks, and the air above vexed with rapacious flights of screaming fowls, whose beaks are like so many insulting poniards in the whale" (*MD* 308). Another false sepulchre presented by Melville, the waterproof coffin of Queequeg, also ends up adrift on the ocean, surrounded by sharks and seahawks. The coffin, however, represents a principle entirely distinct from the deadness of precedent, and its fate differs accordingly: "Buoyed up by that coffin, for almost one whole day and night, I floated on a soft and dirge-like main. The unharming sharks, they glided by as if with padlocks on their mouths; the savage sea-hawks sailed with sheathed beaks" (573). The dead whale, emblematic of a moribund orthodoxy, seems the outcast of nature, and all the scavengers of the sea and air descend upon it with a seeming purpose to destroy it.[13] By contrast, Ishmael, afloat on the empty coffin that is the legacy of his bosom friend Queequeg, enjoys a miraculous immunity. The key difference lies in what the two bits of flotsam respectively symbolize. The marble sepulchre of the whale, "that great mass of death," as Ishmael calls it, represents a principle of social organization based on traditions and precedents that are all form and no substance (308). Queequeg's coffin, even though it is a coffin, paradoxically stands for an idea having much more to do with life: the friendship and love of a departed comrade.

The metaphorical relationship between the dead whale of "The Funeral" and Queequeg's coffin contains an additional complexity: the coffin is a kind of quasi-legal text. It bears a transcription of the tattooing that covers Queequeg's body—markings that were put there by a departed prophet of Queequeg's island, who inscribed Queequeg's body with "a complete theory of the heavens and the earth, and a mystical treatise on the art of attaining truth" (*MD* 480). To a lawyer, a treatise is a formal, detailed exposition of legal doctrine. *Moby-Dick* and its discussion of Queequeg's tattooed treatise came only a few years after Supreme Court Justice Joseph Story completed a series of nine major treatises on American law—the first such works of legal scholarship in America. Story's treatises, like the tattoos on Queequeg's body, were strikingly comprehensive—and numbingly opaque. Grant Gilmore writes that Story's prodigious knowledge was "obscured by a style which . . . is one of intolerable prolixity."[14] Story's efforts were symptomatic of the desire of antebellum lawyers for a codification—and hence a simplification—of the law. A basic tenet of the uncodified common law had always stated that no precedent is ever overruled. Any subsequent case that cannot be distinguished on the facts must be decided according to the existing body of case law.[15] This aspect of the common law gave the system its peculiar charm and fascination. The precedents gave it a degree of certainty, but an able mind could interpret and reapply the precedents in such a way as to create a virtually new rule to govern novel circumstances. Yet the common law also led into a thicket of obscurity, since every precedent soon developed its own niceties of interpretation and distinction. Thus the profession, at least in the United States, yearned for codification; lawyers lived in hopes that the principles that underlay cases, in their thousands, might be reduced to a written, connected series of reasoned propositions (Gilmore 27). The American movement toward codification cannot be separated from the society's impulse toward democracy; the laws could not belong to the people unless those laws were accessible and comprehensible virtually to everyone.

The strange figures on Queequeg's body are also an attempt at codification; the seer who inscribed Queequeg was trying to preserve in written form a system of heavenly, earthly, and spiritual laws, available to anyone who might read them. Like Story's, however, the seer's project becomes ensnared in its own complexities; he concocts a symbology so abstruse that not even Queequeg can read it. As a codification of eternal principles, the carvings on Queequeg's coffin are a failure, since the knowledge they strive to impart is communicated to no one. Nevertheless, the inscribed coffin finally proves capable of sustaining human life in a way that the dead whale of "The Funeral" cannot. Instead of being weighed down by dead orthodoxy, Ishmael is buoyed up by clinging to a text that, in its first "edition," was written on a living body. This text is both a codification and, because it is illegible, an emblem of incommunicable truth. Remarkably, Ishmael's life buoy affirms the need for a codified approach to law and truth without disclosing what the fixed principles ought to be. Melville teases us by intimating that the truths that save Ishmael are knowable (at least the seer knew what they were) while holding the content of those truths beyond our reach. Earlier in the novel, Ahab is exasperated to learn that Queequeg's illegible tattooing purports to unravel the mysteries of life, and he calls this possibility the "devilish tantalization of the gods" (*MD* 481). Melville's novel, which also purports to offer truth while at the same time withholding it, tantalizes in the same way.

Although the inscriptions on Queequeg's body illustrate the seeming impossibility of expressing truth, they are not the first treatment of this kind of uncertainty in the novel. Some chapters earlier, Ishmael attempts an exegesis of the laws of fast-fish and loose-fish—a code that can be stated in two lines and seems apparently straightforward. We soon learn, however, that even this slender body of law "necessitates a vast volume of commentary to expound it" (*MD* 396). In their efforts to render their code more perfect, the wise judges of England have argued themselves into the absurd position that, in some circumstances, a whale can become the legal "owner" of a harpoon and line. The two chapters devoted to the law of whaling end in bemused skepticism, as Ishmael says with a shrug, "there seems a reason in all things, even in law" (401). It must be noted, however, that all his criticisms of the abstruseness and absurdity of the law did not make Melville an anarchist, any more than his jibes against religion made him an atheist. He knew that no code was perfect, but that an imperfect code was preferable to what he termed "the Coke-upon-Littleton of the fist" (396). As the character of Ahab profoundly illustrates, Melville knew well that freedom must be kept within limits, and the society that has no ready answer for Ahab's "Who's over me?" is a potential breeding ground for monsters.

Melville broadens his sepulchral commentary in "A Bower in the Arsacides," one of the last of the so-called cetological chapters of *Moby-Dick*. Ishmael here recalls a visit to the island of Tranque, which Ishmael locates in the Arsacides Islands. Tranquo, the king of the island, is remembered by Ishmael as "being gifted with a devout love for all matters of barbaric vertù," chief among which is the enormous skeleton of a sperm whale which, arbored in tropical vines, serves as a chapel for the pagan islanders (*MD* 449). The bony chapel offers not only a trellis for the leafy tendrils that embrace it but also a framework for Ishmael's most incisive discussion of the nature of religious orthodoxy.

Melville uses the word "vertù" to describe the king's collection of bric-a-brac. "Vertù," also spelled "virtù," is one letter short of the word "virtue," to which it is etymologically related. Indeed, "vertù" is an incomplete sort of virtue: the lover of vertù prizes the thing instead of the talent that made it or the spirit it represents. Although Tranquo's love of his objects is decidedly materialistic, Melville describes this love as "devout," deliberately blurring the distinction between religious feeling and the desire to possess religion's emblems. Writing a few years after *Moby-Dick,* Thomas Carlyle punningly complained in *Frederick the Great* that Italy was a "noble Nation sunk from virtue to virtù."[16] Melville hints at a similar decline in the kingdom of Tranque, where God has devolved into "the great, white, worshipped skeleton" of a dead whale (450).

Melville's pun expands in another direction as well. When Ishmael marvels that Tranquo "should regard a chapel as an object of vertù," his wonderment has two distinct edges (*MD* 450). His more obvious meaning expresses his surprise that the king should see the chapel as a mere collector's item. But Melville also invites us to hear the suppressed "e" at the end of vertù. We are meant to ask whether, in an era of debased religiosity and in a place where devotion is rendered within a corridor of dead bones, one can rightly view a chapel as a place of virtue, rather than as the bleached skeleton that, for the people of Tranque, it has both literally and figuratively become. In "The Funeral," Melville had derided legal orthodoxy by likening it to a dead whale. In "A Bower in the Arsacides," the image is recapitulated, though to a more devastating effect. The orthodoxy now being critiqued is religion, and the dead whale has been stripped even of its flesh. The apparition of the skeletal whale recalls once more Emerson's whited sepulchre in *Nature,* but in Emerson's image, at least, the bones and the spiritual aridity they connote are at least obscured from view. In Melville's bower, whited death is the very structure within which worship occurs.

But the chapter goes beyond clever wordplay or reiterating the image from "The Funeral." Melville has larger ideas. Far from simply condemning the religious orthodoxy represented by the whale's skeleton, Melville also indicates the useful attributes of such a structure. The ribs of Tranque's chapel do not simply emblematize death; even though they are in themselves lifeless, they offer support to the green, fresh vines of the island's jungle vegetation. Moreover, an unextinguished flame burns within the skull. Melville's image conveys a truth about fixed ideological structures, be they religious dogmas or the precedents of the common law; although they themselves may appear sterile or lacking in vitality, they provide the framework upon which an active, vibrant being can live, change, and grow. Ironically, Ezekiel's vision comes closest to fulfilment not in the Whaleman's Chapel, but on the pagan island of Tranque; here dry bones are restored to a kind of living form, though nature, not God, performs the miracle. Melville's text, however, declines to rest on this point. The smoke produced by the flame is still an "artificial" smoke, not a breath of genuine life, and Ishmael observes that the skeleton "seemed the cunning weaver" (*MD* 450; emphasis added). The role of the skeleton in bringing forth new life may be only a trick of appearances after all. The ability of the skeleton to produce life seems more likely an illusion as Ishmael, Dædalus-like, threads his way through the ribs of the sepulchral chapel and discovers "no living thing within; naught was there but dry bones" (450). When Ishmael seeks to measure the whale's skeleton, he commits a type of blasphemy in the eyes of the priesthood of Tranque. That his search leads him inside a skeleton raises an anxious, though subliminal question: can law and religion, like the inner dimensions of the whale, be comprehended only after they are dead?

The cataclysmic ending of *Moby-Dick* rejects the conventions of mourning by rendering true "commemoration" impossible. The word "commemoration" means "being mindful together." With whom can Ishmael be "mindful together" if all the other witnesses to his adventures have been killed? Rather than being commemorative in the literal sense, Ishmael's tale presents a single memory of a fictitious collective experience. Melville's novel offers memories that are finally individual and unshareable. Whereas Webster had celebrated the sepulchres of fathers, Melville ends *Moby-Dick* on a note of fatherlessness; the last word of the book is "orphan." Having no one left with whom to be mindful together, Ishmael, it would seem, can only choose to be mindful apart.

And yet one other does survive the wreck—the reader of Ishmael's narrative, the person who shares the adventure not through lived experience but through the absorption of the text. And because reading is a living activity, in a sense always ongoing and never really completed, it forms the basis for a type of commemoration that does not lead solely backward into the dead past but also forward into new interpretation and thought. The act of reading brings us together in commemoration because we all read the same words on the page, but this act also separates us and preserves our individuality because we all read with different aptitudes, expectations, and beliefs. Melville's aptest emblem of memory is not any of the sepulchres that haunt his novel, but Ahab's doubloon, which, despite its fixity of place and worldly value, elicits a different interpretation from all who gaze upon it.

NOTES

1. Portions of this essay appeared in somewhat different form in an article titled "Grave Discussions: The Image of the Sepulchre in Webster, Emerson, and Melville," *New England Quarterly* 74 (Sept. 2001): 419–446. The author gratefully acknowledges the assistance of Robert Ferguson, Andrew Delbanco, Linda Smith Rhoads, and Timothy Marr.

2. "The Causes of the American Revolution," *North American Review* 80 (Apr. 1855): 389, 390.

3. Ralph Waldo Emerson, *The Heart of Emerson's Journals,* ed. Bliss Perry (Boston: Houghton Mifflin, 1926), 2. Emphasis added. According to the journal entry, the description had originally been made by a Boston lawyer, identified only as "K."

4. Daniel Webster, *An Address Delivered at the Laying of the Corner Stone of the Bunker Hill Monument,* 5th ed. (Boston: Cummings, 1825), 3.

5. William Cullen Bryant, "Thanatopsis," in *American Poetry: The Nineteenth Century* (New York: Library of America, 1993), 123.

6. Maurice G. Baxter, *One and Inseparable: Daniel Webster and the Union* (Cambridge, Mass.: Harvard Univ. Press, 1984), 82.

7. Daniel Webster, "To George Ticknor," June 15, 1825, *The Papers of Daniel Webster, Correspondence* (Hanover, N.H.: Univ. Press of New England, 1976), 2:54.

8. Ralph Waldo Emerson, *Nature,* in *Essays and Lectures* (New York: Library of America, 1983), 7.

9. Luke 11:47–48. Should there be any doubt that Emerson had Jesus' dialogue with the Pharisees on his mind when he wrote *Nature,* that doubt may be lessened by the fact that Emerson also concludes his book with a reference to that discourse. In the final sentence of *Nature,* Emerson describes "the kingdom of man over nature, which cometh not with observation." The phrase "cometh not with observation" is borrowed from the seventeenth chapter of Luke, in which Jesus, rejecting the demand of the Pharisees that he give the date for the coming of God's kingdom, replies, "The kingdom of God cometh not with observation." Addressing a cultural audience that, as he knew, placed more faith in forms than in revelations, Emerson deliberately frames his book with allusions to another prophet and his audience of skeptics.

10. See, e.g., Ralph Waldo Emerson, *Journals and Miscellaneous Notebooks* (Cambridge, Mass.: Harvard Univ. Press, 1964), 4:46.

11. Michael Kammen, *A Season of Youth: The American Revolution and the Historical Imagination* (Ithaca, N.Y.: Cornell Univ. Press, 1978), 43.

12. One suspects that Melville would have delighted in Marianne Moore's line, "The sea has nothing to give but a well excavated grave." Marianne Moore, "A Grave," in *The Complete Poems of Marianne Moore* (New York: Macmillan, 1981), 49.

13. It may, of course, be persuasively argued that the whale carcass is as much a part of nature as its outcast, providing as it does a rich food source to the many scavengers that feast on the

remains. Certainly, the dead whale is one of the many tropes in the novel that represent the interdependency of life and death. This interweaving can be seen as well in Melville's representation of the ocean, which teems with life but is also a mass grave, and the skeleton-bower in the Arsacides, in which "Life folded Death; Death trellised Life" (450). Like Ahab, the novel itself walks upon two legs, the one dead, the other living.

Extending the argument further, one might observe that the only creatures that derive a living from the dead whale are scavengers. It is worth wondering whether Melville intended a commentary on the nature of lawyers, suggesting that they glean sustenance from a "body" whose significance the average person can only misread.

14. Grant Gilmore, *The Ages of American Law* (New Haven, Conn.: Yale Univ. Press, 1977), 28. Indeed, Gilmore writes, "nothing like them [Justice Story's treatises], in English, had ever been seen before."

15. The rule that no precedent could be overturned persisted in England until 1968. George D. Gopen, "The State of Legal Writing: Res Ipsa Loquitur," *Michigan Law Review* 86 (1987): 333, 336.

16. Thomas Carlyle, *History of Friedrich II of Prussia, Called Frederick the Great,* bk. 3, ch. 8 (London: Chapman and Hall, 1869), 1:266.

"I Stand Alone Here upon an Open Sea"

Starbuck and the Limits of Positive Law

Kathryn Mudgett

When the *Pequod*'s casks of whale oil begin to leak in the China Sea, Starbuck appeals to Captain Ahab's conscience to save the ship's hard-earned cargo for the owners' sake by raising the damaged casks with tackles and repairing them. Ahab responds by saying that the owners are not his conscience: "the only real owner of anything is its commander; and hark ye, my conscience is in this ship's keel" (*MD* 474). He then orders Starbuck on deck, but the chief mate continues to argue with his captain, venturing further into the cabin. Ahab takes up a musket from the rack and levels it at Starbuck, exclaiming: "There is one God that is Lord over the earth, and one Captain that is lord over the *Pequod*.—On deck!" (474). Faced with Ahab's autocratic edict, Starbuck retreats.

Starbuck's confrontation with his commander is a paradigm of the relationship between master and seaman in the nineteenth-century maritime world. Shipboard society was set apart from civilized society on land by positive—man-made—law that granted the captain greater powers than those permitted to any landsman. The law gave the captain "undisputed power"[1] to control the ship and its crew, including the right to punish seamen physically for "disobedience or disorderly conduct."[2] The captain's authority was justified by the exigencies of life at sea, which required subordination of seamen to the captain's "lawful" orders and permitted even unreasonable punishment if it did not rise to the level of "cruelty and oppression" (Abbott 188).

On an open sea, an abused sailor had virtually no redress against a tyrannical captain, other than the promise of retrospective succor in the admiralty courts on land. Only in the limited circumstance where the seaman's "life or limbs" were threatened by the captain's actions could he resort to self-defense.[3] Forcible resistance in such cases was legally justifiable, but any action of the captain threatening less than imminent death or permanent bodily injury must be submitted to, "*even to evident injustice, waiting for redress from the home tribunals*" (*Givings,* 25 F. Cas. at 1332; emphasis added). Shipboard society existed in a state of suspension from the benefits of civil society enjoyed—and taken for granted—by landsmen. If the nineteenth-century ship could be analogized to the "ship of state," it could not be deemed an equivalency under law. Civil rights were suspended away from land, and democratic ideals and guarantees were an unfulfilled promise. Positive law,[4] sanctioning the subjugation of the common sailor, diverged from natural or higher law;[5] "law as it is" conflicted with "law as it ought to be" in an ideal society.[6]

Starbuck experiences this disjunction from the protections afforded to citizens of a democratic society in a late episode in *Moby-Dick* when he takes into his own hands the musket Ahab once leveled at him. Starbuck's thoughts turn murderous as he contemplates dispatching Ahab as the captain lies in his hammock asleep. The *Pequod* has just survived a typhoon, and Ahab sleeps, dreaming of his nemesis the white whale. Starbuck, mind racing, recognizes the "crazed old man['s]" willingness "to drag the whole ship's company down to doom with him" (*MD* 514). Starbuck's internal debate in "The Musket" is his dissection of the dilemma raised by the conflict between positive and natural law. Positive law is a creation of civil society, the statutory and case law bearing the imprimatur of the state and setting forth paradigms of behavior. Natural or higher law is that set of moral principles antecedent to man-made law. Starbuck's position as a subordinate to Ahab aboard ship casts him far from the protections—and constraints—of positive law. As he says: "I stand alone here upon an open sea, with two oceans and a whole continent between me and law" (515).

The musket that reminds Starbuck of Ahab's authority and tyranny over him and that now shakes in his own hands is a visceral manifestation of Starbuck's murderous thoughts and simultaneous moral hesitation. In making us privy to Starbuck's thought process—"I'll hold the musket boldly while I think"—Melville emphasizes Starbuck's belief that positive law cannot be separated from morality, that a legal system ignorant of the moral and social consequences of written law is fatally flawed and can lead only to lawlessness and revolution. In debating with himself, Starbuck chooses thought over spontaneous, unlawful action: "—wait. I'll cure myself of this" (*MD* 514). Starbuck reasons that if he permits Ahab to live, the captain will be "the wilful murderer of thirty men or more" (515). Murdering Ahab will save the captain's immortal soul, for if "he were this instant—put aside, that crime would not be his" (515). The only "death" would be Starbuck's, in his choice to act outside the bounds of both positive law and higher law by shooting a sleeping man through a "bolted door" (514). In saving Ahab from himself, Starbuck would save the entire crew but set himself up for prosecution under man's law and retribution from God for breaking His commandment not to kill.

Starbuck can think of "no lawful way" to save them all, rejecting the idea of imprisoning Ahab until the return home, fearing that he himself would go mad at the sight and sound of the "caged tiger" if, indeed, he were even able to capture the old man in the face of the crew's resistance. Starbuck's untenable position is geographic as well as psychic. He knows that even if he could resort to human law, its protections would come too late: "The land is hundreds of leagues away, and locked Japan the nearest" (*MD* 515). Beyond the aid of positive law, Starbuck turns to natural law, seeking justification for Ahab's destruction: "'Is heaven a murderer when its lightning strikes a would-be murderer in his bed, tindering sheets and skin together?—And would I be a murderer, then, if'—" (515). What stops him, as he holds the leveled musket against the door to Ahab's cabin, is the voice of Ahab speaking in a dream as he imagines Moby Dick in his clutches. Starbuck cannot defend his annihilation of the now defenseless old man by either law or conscience when it is yet uncertain "to what unsounded deeps Starbuck's body this day week may sink, with all the crew" (515).[7] Starbuck's renunciation of homicide requires a monumental physical as well as psychic struggle as his grip on the musket shakes and he appears to be "wrestling with an angel" before "plac[ing] the death-tube in its rack" and resigning himself to the possible destruction of the ship and crew (515). Thrown back on his own devices in the absence of a governing societal force that could bring Ahab to submission, Starbuck rejects the reflexive, violent act that would save his own life, unwilling to violate positive law or the moral tenets of higher law.

The same legal authority that relegates the seaman to "situational 'slavery'" in virtual bondage to an autocratic captain restrains Starbuck in his contemplation of Ahab's death.[8] Positive law, as Starbuck sees it, permits no moral ambiguity such as the chief mate confronts in his internal monologue. The episode of "The Musket" reflects the nineteenth-century debate about the separability of law and morality. Oliver Wendell Holmes, who framed the debate in his essay "The Path of the Law," did not dispute that the "law is the witness and external deposit of our moral life. Its history is the history of the moral development of the race."[9] Nonetheless, Holmes did not find moral rights coextensive with legal rights,[10] and he concluded that it would be "a gain if every word of moral significance could be banished from law altogether, and other words adopted which would convey legal ideas uncolored by anything outside the law" ("Path" 464). In placing the musket back in the rack without spilling its powder, Starbuck does not bow before the idea of purely mechanical law that denies him the technical right to defend himself from a madman. Rather, he recognizes that to engage in lawlessness himself in the face of intransigent law is to engage in anarchic and self-defeating action. Once we have taken Ahab's vow, "all of us are Ahabs.—Great God forbid!" (*MD* 515).

A dozen years before the *Pequod*'s fictional voyage, Abraham Lincoln addressed the danger of the growing "disregard for law ... pervad[ing] the country," manifested by the "disposition to substitute the wild and furious passions, in lieu of the sober judgements of Courts; and the worse than savage mobs, for the executive ministers of justice."[11] Lincoln spoke of the danger to political institutions posed by mob law, cautioning that the only way for the political community to guard itself was to "let every man remember that to violate the law, is to trample on the blood of his father, and to tear the character of his own, and his children's liberty" (Lincoln 32). He warned that even bad law must not be transgressed.[12] Law may evolve by repeal or amendment, upon a "change in the habit of the public mind" (Holmes 466), but in no instance can a law, however egregious in its effect, be subjected to mob intervention without endangering the body politic itself (Lincoln 33). Starbuck is the model citizen of the polis envisioned by Lincoln, one who practices "strict observance of all the laws," even to his own disadvantage (33).

Lincoln believed "reverence for the laws" must "become the *political religion* of the nation" (32; emphasis in original). He understood that without such reverence shared by all, "the innocent, those who have ever set their faces against violations of law in every shape, alike with the guilty, fall victims to the ravages of mob law" (31). Lincoln could have been speaking of Starbuck when he described "good men, men who love tranquility, who desire to abide by the laws," seeing "their lives endangered ... by the operation of this mobocratic spirit" (31). It is as if Lincoln contemplated the savage mob gathered on the quarterdeck of the *Pequod* to bind their lot with Ahab in an extralegal contract.

In the psychological battle between the captain and chief mate of the *Pequod,* in which Ahab plots to keep "his magnet at Starbuck's brain" and control his "coerced will," Melville forms an implicit debate about the consequences of disregarding the moral element of law to the detriment of both individual and community (*MD* 212). It is a dramatization of the nineteenth-century debate about the clash between the letter and the spirit of the law, between the positivist stance of a Holmes and the natural-law bent of a Lincoln, played out in the spiritual battle between Ahab and Starbuck.

Holmes defined law as the "prediction of the incidence of the public force through the instrumentality of the courts" ("Path" 457). As a means to "point out and dispel a confusion between morality and law," Holmes distinguished the way in which a good man and a bad man approach the law. The "bad man . . . cares only for the material consequences which . . . knowledge [of law] enables him to predict," while the "good one . . . finds his reasons for conduct, whether inside the law or outside of it, in the vaguer sanctions of conscience" ("Path" 459). The bad man relies on the purely mechanical aspects of law to avoid suffering the consequences of breaking it; the good one recognizes the moral component on which civil society and its laws are founded and acts accordingly. Ahab takes a mechanical, positivist approach to avoid the sanctions of law in his unauthorized search for Moby Dick.

Under Holmes's definition of a legal duty as "nothing but a prediction that if a man does or omits certain things he will be made to suffer . . . by judgment of the court," it becomes clear that "a bad man has as much reason as a good one for wishing to avoid an encounter with the public force" ("Path" 458, 459). According to Holmes, the bad man's reasoning in choosing to follow the law illustrates the distinction between morality and law: for "[a] man who cares nothing for an ethical rule which is believed and practised by his neighbors is likely nevertheless to care a good deal to avoid being made to pay money, and will want to keep out of jail if he can" (459). He chooses to adhere to an objective rule or prohibition solely to avoid the consequences, without any consideration of the morality on which the law may be founded. The law "always, in a certain sense, measure[s] legal liability by moral standards," but the bad man is only concerned with the "transmut[ation of] those moral standards into external or objective ones" and their legal effect on him should he transgress them.[13]

Ahab knows as well as Starbuck that the seaman, under law, has the right to self-defense or the defense of others when the captain's orders would endanger "life or limbs" (*Givings*, 25 F. Cas. at 1332). Ahab's self-imposed task throughout the voyage is to sail at the bounds of positive law without driving Starbuck to act and thereby exert moral force on the crew to resist Ahab's purpose: "[I]n reveal[ing] the prime but private purpose of the *Pequod*'s voyage, Ahab was now entirely conscious that, in doing so, he had indirectly laid himself open to the unanswerable charge of usurpation; and with *perfect impunity, both moral and legal,* his crew, if so disposed, and to that end competent, could refuse all further obedience to him, and even violently wrest from him the command" (*MD* 213; emphasis added). Ahab determines as a matter of "prudential policy" to "observe all customary usages" and continue the pretense of the "nominal purpose of the *Pequod*'s voyage" (475, 213). Such prudent calculation leads Ahab to execute orders to repair the leaky oil casks after first threatening Starbuck with the musket and belittling the rights of the faraway owners of the *Pequod* by suggesting that they "stand on Nantucket beach and outyell the Typhoons" if they disagree with his command of the vessel (474). To do otherwise than capitulate on the issue of the casks would be to risk an "open relapse of rebellion" by Starbuck, the one person onboard ship representative of the values and constraints of civil society and capable of summoning Ahab's own "humanities" to the fore (212, 79). Only Starbuck stands between Ahab and his demoniac goal; only Starbuck's disaffection can cause the crew to become "panic-stricken" and to "raise a half mutinous cry" (508). In Melville's legal parlance, the crew members are "Fast-Fish" while Starbuck remains a "Loose-Fish," "fair game for anybody who can soonest catch" his "coerced" but silently defiant will (396, 212).

The sequence of three chapters beginning with "The Quarter-Deck" (ch. 36) reveals the untenable position in which Starbuck finds himself, between a single-minded captain bent on maniac vengeance against "a dumb brute" and a "savage crew" incited to hunt the white whale in a ceremony in which all drink from "murderous chalices" to become "parties to this indissoluble league" of hunters (*MD* 163, 212, 166). In "The Quarter-Deck," Ahab, addressing all onboard, reveals that the crew has shipped to "chase that white whale . . . over all sides of earth, till he spouts black blood and rolls fin out" (163). Starbuck voices his disapproval, but Ahab silences him by pointing out that the crew are "one and all with Ahab" (164). He then emphasizes Starbuck's singular, isolated position aboard ship: "Stand up amid the general hurricane, thy one tost sapling cannot, Starbuck!" (164).

In "Sunset" (ch. 37), Ahab, alone in his cabin, reflects on the rallying of the crew to his purpose: "'Twas not so hard a task. I thought to find one stubborn, at the least but my one cogged circle fits into all their various wheels, and they revolve" (*MD* 167).[14] Ahab has created a "mobocratic spirit" aboard the *Pequod* in which the crew of "mongrel renegades, castaways, and cannibals" eagerly swear to supplant their contractual allegiance to Captains Bildad and Peleg by embracing Ahab's quest with "cries and maledictions against the white whale" (Lincoln 31; *MD* 186, 166).[15] By persuading the crew to adopt his lawless purpose, Ahab makes of the *Pequod* a vessel in which the seamen are mere interchangeable parts, revolving as "wheels" around the captain: "Ye are not other men, but my arms and legs; and so obey me" (*MD* 568). Ahab does not even acknowledge their humanity. For him, "the permanent condition of the manufactured man . . . is sordidness" (212). With a crew of such indistinguishable mongrel parts, Ahab is hastened to his "monomaniac revenge" (187). Ahab, crew, and vessel are one in an aberrant society fueled by single-minded mob frenzy.

Against this mob sensibility, Starbuck is "overmanned" (*MD* 169). Alone at the mainmast at "Dusk" (ch. 38), Starbuck ponders his insupportable position between a madman who "tows me with a cable I have no knife to cut" and a "heathen crew" that even now engages in "infernal orgies" in the forecastle below (169). Starbuck stands "alone here upon an open sea," unable to "frustrate" Ahab's purpose unless and until Ahab places the crew in present danger (515, 212). Even then, unsupported by the seamen, Starbuck's lawful resistance would fail, and so he "plainly see[s his] miserable office,—to obey, rebelling" (169). "[W]orse yet," he finds that he "hate[s] with a touch of pity" (169).

Starbuck's humanity both elevates him above the "heathen crew that have small touch of human mothers in them" and positions him as the sole reminder to Ahab of the civil society he left behind when he entered the "masoned, walled-town of a Captain's exclusiveness" (*MD* 169, 543). Shortly before the chase of Moby Dick begins, Ahab acknowledges that he has been "a forty years' fool" on the open sea. Then he commands Starbuck to draw near: "Close! stand close to me, Starbuck; let me look into a human eye; it is better than to gaze into sea or sky; better than to gaze upon God. By the green land; by the bright hearth-stone! this is the magic glass, man; I see my wife and my child in thine eye" (544).

The image Ahab sees reflected in Starbuck's eye is the familial representation of the community from which both men sprang. Ahab and Starbuck are natives of Nantucket and denizens of the island when ashore. In "purposely sail[ing]" with "the one and only and all-engrossing object of hunting the White Whale," Ahab has not only breached the contract made with the owners of the *Pequod,* he has violated the social compact made with the Nantucket Island dwellers—and fellow citizens—who comprise the investors in the vessel (*MD* 186). Although Captains Bildad and Peleg are the "largest owners" of the ship, a number of nameless Nantucket Islanders hold "shares" in the *Pequod:* "a crowd of old annuitants; widows, fatherless children, and chancery wards; each owning about the value of a timber head, or a foot of plank, or a nail or two in the ship" (73). The islanders have invested both their men's lives and their own fortunes—great and small—in the voyage, with the expectation of a "profitable" cruise "to be counted down in dollars from the mint" (186).

In purely contractual terms, Ahab's deviation from the purpose of the voyage violates positive law. Maritime law prohibits the master of a vessel from "deviat[ing] from the course of the voyage." A deviation for which the master is legally "answerable" is "any alteration of the risk insured against, without necessity or reasonable cause," including "departing from the regular and usual course of the voyage, or any unusual or unnecessary delay."[16] Ahab's intended abandonment of a voyage for profit for a voyage of revenge would be sufficient cause for "his old acquaintances on shore . . . to have wrenched the ship from such a fiendish man" if only they knew "what was lurking in him" (186).

In his violation of the positive law of society, Ahab violates the social contract of the community of which he feigns to be a part. Rousseau defines laws as "acts of the general will" to which we all are subject.[17] Laws are "the conditions of civil associations" determined by the citizens who have joined together as a "moral and collective body" (Rousseau 40). Under Rousseau's conception, Nantucket, like all civil states, is an association of individual members, each of whom "puts in common his person and his whole power under the supreme direction of the general will; and in return . . . receive[s] every member as an indivisible part of the whole" (18, 19). Within the social body, there must be "reciprocal" observation of the law, or the community sinks into anarchy (38). William Blackstone has described the "original contract of society" in much the same way as Rousseau, with mutual obligation as the necessary element for successful government: "the whole should protect all its parts, and . . . every part should pay obedience to the will of the whole, or, in other words, . . . the community should guard the rights of each individual member, and . . . (in return for this protection) each individual should submit to the laws of the community" (*Commentaries* 1:48). For Blackstone, only a system of laws could "maintain civil liberty" (*Commentaries* 1:126). Ahab's devil's pact made on the quarterdeck with his "heathen crew . . . [w]helped somewhere by the shark-ish sea" (*MD* 169) subverts both the social compact and the legal framework prescribed by society to assure its continued existence.

Ahab's purpose, to wreak "[v]engeance on a dumb brute . . . that simply smote [him] from blindest instinct" (*MD* 163), substitutes revenge for civic retribution, a reversal of the gradual development of the law "from barbarism to civilization" (*Common Law* 8). In *The Common Law*, Holmes traces the development of law from its early biblical, Greek, and Roman forms in which positive law was "grounded in vengeance" to a more advanced legal system formalizing liability (6). Holmes provides an early example of "vengeance on the immediate offender" in Exodus, in which the killing of a person by an animal requires the beast's death under law: "If an ox gore a man or a woman, that they die: then the ox shall be surely stoned, and his flesh shall not be eaten; but the owner of the ox shall be quit" (*Common Law* 10, 12; Exod. 21:28). The animal is subject to death, but the owner suffers no liability other than relinquishment of the beast, and vengeance is exacted against the dumb creature. Under Platonic law, Holmes offers up a similar example of the slave who kills a (free) man, thereby subjecting the slave to be "given up" to the family of the deceased for their own purposes (*Common Law* 10). Similarly, early Roman law provided for the surrender of an animal or slave causing damage (*Common Law* 10–11). Without reference to legal causation, early law enacted revenge against the animate "body doing the damage" (*Common Law* 13). For example, Roman law dictated surrender of the ox drawing a wagon under which a person was crushed, regardless of whether the driver was reckless or otherwise at fault (*Common Law* 15).

While revenge may be seen as a "legal prototype,"[18] modern legal systems, according to Holmes, substitute an external, objective standard of liability for the internal standard in which the object of vengeance is "actually and personally to blame" (*Common Law* 35). For example, under primitive law the ox driving the wagon in the example above is ultimately "to blame" and must "pay," not the owner or driver of the animal. In objectifying standards of liability and indemnity, modern law "channels rather than eliminates revenge" (Posner 58). Law retains a retributive purpose but emphasizes civic wrong (wrong against the state) rather than personal wrong justifying revenge. It represents a "refined development" of the "primitive form" of law practiced by early civilizations—and called for by Ahab as his right: "Moby Dick . . . brought me to this dead stump I stand on now. . . . Aye, aye! it was that accursed white whale that razeed me; made a poor pegging lubber of me for ever and a day!" (*MD* 163). Because he does not believe that any outside force can make him whole, Ahab demands his right to smite the creature that "dismasted" him.[19]

On the quarterdeck, Ahab makes clear his disdain for the "compensations" offered by adherence to the rules of civil society. When Starbuck voices his reluctance to hunt the whale for "my commander's vengeance," he asks his master, "How many barrels will thy vengeance yield thee even if thou gettest it, Captain Ahab? it will not fetch thee much in our Nantucket market" (*MD* 163). Ahab disparages Starbuck's appeal to monetary considerations, striking his chest and saying, "If money's to be the measurer, man, and the accountants have computed their great counting-house the globe, by girdling it with guineas, one to every three parts of an inch; then let me tell thee, that my vengeance will fetch a great premium *here!*" (163). Ahab, like a victim seeking redress in a primitive legal system, wants to lay blame, not gain monetary reimbursement to compensate for his bodily injury. The economic and civic ties binding Ahab to Nantucket (and Starbuck pointedly identifies their home base as "*our* Nantucket market") are overshadowed by his hatred of the animate being that is the "manifest cause" of his pain: "I will wreak that hate upon him" (*Common Law* 13; *MD* 164). Striking back against the perpetrator of an "undoubted deed" (*MD* 164) is a reflexive response, recognized and sanctioned under primitive law: "The hatred for anything giving us pain . . . wreaks itself on the manifest cause, and . . . leads even civilized man to kick a door when it pinches his finger" (*Common*

Law 13). But law in its "more refined development" exacts legal standards of conduct and liability and eschews the personal revenge contemplated by Ahab (*Common Law* 35).

That Ahab's insistence on the primitive "law" of revenge leads to the crew's acceptance of his deviant mission and their formation into a mob is predicted by Lincoln as an all-but-foregone outcome, fostered by Ahab's dismissal of societal rules and values. In his 1838 address, Lincoln foresaw the dangers Starbuck faces in the insular world of the ship. If the "lawless in spirit" become "lawless in practice" without restraint, civil society itself, the government of laws, is doomed (Lincoln 31). As it is in the larger community, so it is on-board ship: unrestrained lawlessness leads to the self-inflicted destruction of civil society. The danger, as contemplated by Lincoln, comes from within: "If destruction is our lot, we must ourselves be its author and finisher. As a nation of freemen, we must live through all time, or die by suicide" (29). So Starbuck cautions Ahab to beware of Ahab, the enemy within, the ruling authority aboard ship, who fosters "alienation" of the crew's "affections from the Government" of civil law for his own selfish purposes (32). As captain of the *Pequod*, Ahab "covenants that he will act honestly and with the best of his judgment" in "commencing and prosecuting the voyage" (Dana 185). While a captain has the "entire control of the navigation and working of the ship," including the discipline of the crew, his near-autocratic power shapes the tenor of the voyage:

> [U]pon the course of conduct he pursues, depend in a great measure the character of the ship and the conduct of both officers and men. He has a power and influence, both direct and indirect, which may be the means of much good or much evil. If he is profane, passionate, tyrannical, indecent, or intemperate, more or less of the same qualities will spread themselves or break out among officers and men.... [The captain] may make his ship almost anything he chooses, and may render the lives and duties of his officers and men pleasant and profitable to them, or may introduce disagreements, discontent, tyranny, and resistance, and, in fact, make the situation of all on board as uncomfortable as that in which any human being can be placed. (Dana 137–38).

As the ruling authority on board the *Pequod*, Ahab chooses to "continually despise and disregard" the laws under which he captains the vessel, and so breeds disaffection for law among the crew (Lincoln 32). Encouraging his "mongrel" crew to form an "indissoluble league" (*MD* 166) in search of Moby

Dick, Ahab creates an atmosphere onboard ship that Lincoln saw threatening the Union on land, a society in which the right of the people "to be secure in their persons and property, are held by no better tenure than the caprice of the mob" (Lincoln 32).

In the threatened, threatening society of the ship, Starbuck is the sole representative of moral authority. Starbuck, a native Nantucket Islander like Ahab, is a Quaker "by descent" (*MD* 115).[20] Among the Quaker characteristics noted by Crèvecoeur, an eighteenth-century visitor to the island, was "obedience to the laws, even to non-resistance."[21] Crèvecoeur found the inhabitants of Nantucket "unoppressed with any civil bondage . . . without governors, or any masters but the laws" (Crèvecoeur 136). The islanders' willing submission to the rules of civil conduct has created the kind of model society described by Blackstone, in which laws, "prudently framed, are by no means subversive, but rather introductive of liberty; for . . . where there is no law there is no freedom" (*Commentaries* 1:126). Crèvecoeur depicts the island society as one in which enforcement of the law is rarely necessary: "[W]ith all this apparatus of law, its coercive powers are seldom wanted or required. Seldom is it that any individual is amerced or punished; their jail conveys no terror; no man has lost his life judicially since the foundation of this town. . . . Solemn tribunals, public executions, humiliating punishments, are altogether unknown" (Crèvecoeur 105).

Son of the Nantucket community, Starbuck, a "staid, steadfast" man who is both "[u]ncommonly conscientious" and "humane," is assailed by Ahab for his deliberative and respectful temperament (*MD* 116, 358). When Starbuck quits the cabin after Ahab levels the musket at him but not before warning the captain to "beware of thyself," Ahab silently chides Starbuck for his "most careful bravery" (475). Moments later, Ahab ascends to the deck, where he tells the mate: "Thou art but too good a fellow" (475). Ahab means both to compliment Starbuck and to mark his exasperation with the chief mate for his adherence to conventions of law and morality Ahab himself purports to despise.

Although Ahab is deemed a "good" if sometimes "savage" man by Captain Peleg, he fits Holmes's formulation of a "bad man" in basing his conduct on avoidance of the detrimental consequences of the law rather than on a reverence for it (*MD* 79). Starbuck silently reminds a reluctant Ahab of "his humanities" (79). The chief mate's "honest eye" is always upon him and finally moves Ahab to relieve Starbuck of the duty to lower his whaleboat for Moby Dick: "That hazard shall not be thine" (166, 544). Ahab's gesture is both late and ineffectual. Ahab's irreverence for the laws he manipulates to his own selfish ends hazards and hastens the destruction of all aboard ship. In leading the *Pequod* to become a "hearse" whose "wood could only be American," Ahab fulfills Lincoln's fear of the "lawless in spirit" who, unrestrained by the "sound morality" of a Starbuck, orphan the community whose values they reject (*MD* 571; Lincoln 31, 36).

Notes

1. *Sampson v. Smith*, 15 Mass. 364, 369 (1819).

2. Charles Abbott, *A Treatise of the Law Relative to Merchant Ships and Seamen*, 2nd American ed. with annotations by Joseph Story (Newburyport, Mass.: Little & Co., 1810), 188.

3. *U.S. v. Givings*, 25 F. Cas. 1331, 1332 (1844). Hereafter cited as *Givings*. In *Givings*, the crew of the whaling ship *Hibernia* refused to go to sea in a vessel with rotten masts and of otherwise questionable seaworthiness. The court found that the crew had the right to defend themselves against the captain's violent attempts to force them to sail with the ship.

4. Positive law is the system of law enacted legislatively and enforced judicially by a political community. *Black's Law Dictionary*, ed. Bryan A. Garner (St. Paul, Minn.: West, 1999), 1182. Hereafter cited as *BLD*. Legal positivists find validity in a human system of law by virtue of its enactment by a political authority, not because of its consistency with a preexisting moral code (*BLD* 906).

5. Natural law is "a system of legal and moral principles purportedly deriving from a universalized conception of human nature or divine justice rather than from legislative or judicial action" (*BLD* 1049). Terms used synonymously with natural law include "higher law," "divine law," and "eternal law." Blackstone stated that the law of nature was "dictated by God himself" and "binding over all the globe, in all countries, and at all times." Sir William Blackstone, *Commentaries on the Laws of England*, vol. 1, ed. James DeWitt Andrews (Chicago: Callaghan & Company, 1899), 42. Hereafter cited as *Commentaries*. Natural-law proponents believe that higher-law principles of right and wrong form the basis for all human law.

6. Robert M. Cover, *Justice Accused: Antislavery and the Judicial Process* (New Haven, Conn.: Yale Univ. Press, 1975), 29. In *Justice Accused*, Robert Cover examines slavery through the "natural law idiom," in which the "disparity between law and morality" is represented by the divergence of "the law as it is" (positive law) and "the law as it ought to be" (law consonant with natural-law principles).

7. The chief mate's superstitious sense of doom is tempered by his hope that the ship will never encounter Moby Dick in the "round watery world" and that God may yet "wedge aside" Ahab's "heaven-insulting purpose" (*MD* 169).

8. W. Jeffrey Bolster, *Black Jacks: African American Seamen in the Age of Sail* (Cambridge, Mass.: Harvard Univ. Press, 1997), 70. Bolster likens the seaman's legal condition afloat to the condition of the slave, the distinction being that while the slave suffers from perpetual slavery, the seaman suffers from "situational 'slavery'" only for the period of time he is contracted to a ship.

9. Oliver Wendell Holmes, "The Path of the Law," *Harvard Law Review* 10 (1897): 457–78, 459.

10. Holmes perceived the confusion between moral and legal rights as arising from the "assump[tion] that the rights of man in a moral sense are equally rights in the sense of the Constitution and the law" ("Path" 460).

11. Abraham Lincoln, "Address to the Young Men's Lyceum of Springfield, Illinois, January 27, 1838. The Perpetuation of Our Political Institutions," in *Speeches and Writings 1832–1858* (New York: Library of America, 1989), 28–36, 29.

12. In his comments on bad law, Lincoln specifically referred to abolitionism and the necessity of resolving political disagreements by legislative enactment rather than resorting to "interposition of mob law," which is neither "necessary, justifiable, or excusable" (Lincoln 33).

13. Oliver Wendell Holmes, *The Common Law,* ed. Mark DeWolfe Howe (Boston: Little, Brown, 1963), 33.

14. The ease with which Ahab inspires the crew to adopt his quest is attributed in part to "the incompetence of mere unaided virtue or right-mindedness in Starbuck" (*MD* 186). In discussing the influence of *King Lear* on *Moby-Dick,* Charles Olson has dismissed Starbuck as having "the weak goodness of an Albany" (1997 ed., 49). For Olson, "the ambiguities do not resolve themselves by such 'right-mindedness'" as Albany's. He declares: "Albany is a Starbuck" (49). And in Ahab's dictatorial sway over Starbuck—"Look thou, underling! that thou obeyest [me]"—we do hear echoes of Goneril's ascendency over her husband, Albany: "—the laws are mine, not thine. Who can arraign me for't?" (5.3.159–60). William Shakespeare, *King Lear,* in *The Complete Pelican Shakespeare* (Baltimore: Penguin, 1969), 611. Yet Ahab's powers are not consonant with those of a monarch, and Ahab, unlike Goneril, is as cognizant as Starbuck of the bounds of the civil law outside of which Ahab, the self-styled "supreme lord and dictator" of the *Pequod*'s crew, must not stray (*MD* 122).

15. Lincoln warned that the "operation of this mobocratic spirit" would destroy the "bulwark" of the political community—the "*attachment* of the People" to the government of laws (31; emphasis in original).

16. Richard Henry Dana Jr., *The Seaman's Friend: A Treatise on Practical Seamanship* (Mineola, N.Y.: Dover Publications, Inc., 1997), 185, 186.

17. Jean-Jacques Rousseau, *The Social Contract and Discourse on the Origin of Inequality,* ed. Lester G. Crocker (New York: Washington Square Press, 1967), 40.

18. Richard A. Posner, *Law and Literature* (Cambridge, Mass.: Harvard Univ. Press, 1998), 49.

19. See Exodus 21:23–25: "[I]f injury ensues, you shall give life for life, eye for eye, tooth for tooth, hand for hand, foot for foot, burn for burn, wound for wound, stripe for stripe."

20. The Quakers, or Friends, were the "leading sect" on the island; Mary Starbuck, a convert and preacher, helped to establish the first Quaker Meeting early in the eighteenth century. Edwin P. Hoyt, *Nantucket: The Life of an Island* (Brattleboro, Vt.: Stephen Greene Press, 1987), 27, 28.

21. J. Hector St. John de Crèvecoeur, *Letters from an American Farmer,* ed. Susan Manning (New York: Oxford Univ. Press, 1997), 109.

Reading and Mapping

Morality and Rhetoric in *Moby-Dick*

MICHAEL KEARNS

In Chapter 128 of *Moby-Dick*, Captain Gardiner of the *Rachel* invokes the Golden Rule to try to melt Ahab's "iciness" and convince the latter to join the search for the missing whaleboat containing one of the captain's sons. "Do to me as you would have me do to you in the like case," Gardiner pleads. Standing "like an anvil," Ahab refuses: "God bless ye, man, and may I forgive myself, but I must go" (*MD* 532). Because the Golden Rule figures so prominently in this emotionally freighted scene, readers could easily take it as the novel's central moral principle. That interpretation would be supported by the Rule's mention much earlier in a crucial exchange between Ishmael and Queequeg and by its prominence in Western culture. However, to take this or any other single principle as the novel's most important lesson would not do justice to the novel's rhetoric. On the contrary, while the novel invites moral responses, it also reminds readers both that moral principles are contingent and that some rhetorical techniques prove highly effective in leading readers toward specific moral judgments. Of course *Moby-Dick* explicitly asserts human limitation and fallibility, but its moral work is furthered by formal features that carry rhetorical power and by Ishmael's ability to project an ethos of goodwill, good character, and high moral standing while demonstrating his moral agency. To experience the novel's rhetorical effect, however, a reader must accept the existence of a universal moral sense.

Ishmael writes that "any human thing supposed to be complete, must for that very reason infallibly be faulty" (*MD* 136). Ishmael's specific task at this point is to develop a "popular comprehensive classification" of whales, a task he has undertaken because he regards it as "almost indispensable to a thorough appreciative understanding of the more special leviathanic revelations and allusions of all sorts which are to follow" (134). This chapter concludes with the famous invocation: "God keep me from ever completing anything. This whole book is but a draught—nay, but the draught of a draught. Oh, Time, Strength, Cash, and Patience!" (145). Though explicit as it stands, this passage can carry even more rhetorical weight if a reader concludes that Melville is ventriloquizing his own immediate thoughts through Ishmael, and that both Melville and Ishmael hold that leaving incomplete a "cetological system" or "Cathedral of Cologne" is more in keeping with divine law than would be completing the job. The same explicit assertion of human limitation also occurs in Ishmael's thoughts on the composition of the whale's spout (ch. 85, "The Fountain"), and here too Melville may be taken as speaking through his narrator: "that down to this blessed minute (fifteen and a quarter minutes past one o'clock P.M. of this sixteenth day of December, A.D. 1850), it should still remain a problem, whether these spoutings are, after all, really water, or nothing but vapor—this is surely a noteworthy thing" (370). The problem assumes great importance because it has to do with Leviathan and because it would seem to be easily solved. But as Ishmael says, "I have ever found your plain things the knottiest of all" (373).

Given that even such apparently simple problems as the composition of the spout have remained insoluble for centuries (at least within Ishmael's frame of reference), and given that pragmatism and divine law concur that humans neither should nor can create perfect systems, how do we manage the thousands of situations about which we must make a judgment? According to Peter Levine, one way to negotiate life's contingent nature is by means of thickly described narrative. Levine's thesis in *Living without Philosophy* is that moral dilemmas can be settled without appeal to "*general normative principles or procedures that can be defended with arguments*"; the method he advocates is "more an art than a science, learned by experience rather than by the apprehension of principles or techniques."[1] The centerpiece of this method is "thick description" in narrative. This is a detailed and "value-laden" description of a particular situation, the purpose of which is rhetorical—to earn the assent of as many people as possible (Levine 5–6). Levine offers the following summary of an example from Gilbert Ryle: "If I say that someone's eyelids contracted, then I am offering a 'thin' description. But if I say that the person winked conspiratorially, then I have 'thickened' the description: I have depicted the contracting eyelid as something, by placing it in a narrative context. I have not just added more detail to my description; rather, I have offered additional facts that are morally *salient*" (31). Moral salience is established by the word "conspiratorially," by which a speaker signals to a hearer that the latter is being invited to assent to an evaluation. Levine fails to explain why adding the single adverb "conspiratorially" establishes a narrative context. A thorough treatment of the issue would take too long here, but in a nutshell, the adverb evokes "tellability" by implicating a tension that will be resolved in the telling of a story.[2]

Levine's approach shares much with that of Wayne Booth in *The Company We Keep,* but they differ in at least two ways. First, Booth does not treat the role of description in evoking a moral response but instead argues that simply to mention anything that might be termed an "achievement" is to imply value.[3] Levine goes further by asserting a correspondence between the amount of thick description and the likely effect of that description on a reader's moral response. Second, Booth emphasizes the public, communal, and comparative nature of the judging process, whereas Levine concentrates on individual interactions between audience and narrative. In this respect and in a consideration of ethos, Booth usefully complements Levine, as will be shown.

Levine likewise extends the argument for the moral efficacy of literature made by Martha Nussbaum. Writing on Henry James's *The Golden Bowl,* Nussbaum states that when texts speak in "universal terms" and assert "inviolable rules," as moral philosophy tends to do, they lose "the complexity, the indeterminacy, the sheer difficulty of moral choice."[4]

Nussbaum goes on to suggest that "the adventure of the reader of this novel . . . involves valuable aspects of human moral experience that are not tapped by traditional books of moral philosophy. . . . To work through these sentences and these chapters is to become involved in an activity of exploration and unraveling that uses abilities, especially abilities of emotion and imagination, rarely tapped by philosophical texts" (Nussbaum 143). To explain how moral decisions are made in a complex and contingent world, Nussbaum asserts the primary role of Aristotelian "perception," which she describes as "seeing a complex, concrete reality in a highly lucid and richly responsive way; it is taking in what is there, with imagination and feeling" (152). For Nussbaum, a literary text can foster this kind of perception by narrating "the experiences of beings committed to value" (149); to experience the moral salience of such a text, the reader must encounter the actual language and not a paraphrase of it. Comparing her paraphrase of a crucial scene in *The Golden Bowl* with James's actual language, she writes that the paraphrase, "not being a high work of literary art, [is] devoid of a richness of feeling and a rightness of tone and rhythm that characterize the original, whose cadences stamp themselves inexorably on the heart. A good action is not flat and toneless and lifeless like my paraphrase—whose use of the 'standing terms' of moral discourse, words like 'mutual sacrifice,' makes it too blunt for the highest value" (154–55). Furthermore, such terms do not carry with them instructions for their use; if they were "trusted for and in themselves" they would become "a recipe for obtuseness" (156).

By concentrating on the rhetorical function of thick description, Levine helps account for this difference between the original and a paraphrase. Nussbaum's use of phrases such as "high work of literary art" and "stamp themselves inexorably on the heart" unfortunately suggests a prescriptive elitism about both the literary text and how it is perceived. Of course some people respond more strongly than others to James's language, but Levine shows that certain terms are likely to connote evaluation, terms that carry, as he says, moral salience. In principle, a paraphrase could be as effective as the original if it simply substituted such terms with equivalents; it would be less effective if it were constructed as a brief abstract. "Conspiracy" connotes moral disapprobation; the "conspiratorial" wink differs qualitatively from, for example, the "slow" or "knowing" wink. The word "conspiratorial" has nothing inexorable, nothing transcendent about it but will have an effect for native speakers of English because of the way it is generally used.

Nussbaum's phrase "the experiences of beings committed to value" also requires clarification. In order for the narration of such experiences to carry the highest moral salience, the individuals must be portrayed as moral agents whose commitment is a matter of choice. Lynne Tirrell provides an excellent perspective on this requirement: "[T]he minimal necessary features of moral agency involve the capacities necessary for articulation" of one's actions.[5] Tirrell explains that a "moral agent is at least a minimally intentional being," must be a person (a distinguishable self with "historical and social" identity), and must have authority to act (Tirrell 116–17). This third criterion, the authority to act, is most important for Tirrell's discussion, because telling stories "develops and refines our agency"; the same is true of listening to them (117–18). Tirrell uses the example of Toni Morrison's novel *The Bluest Eye* to show how "a moral sensibility may emerge from a text even though no explicit invocations of rules or ideals, nor explicit final judgments of moral culpability are made by the narrator," as well as how such a sensibility can emerge "*in the telling of the story*" (120, Tirrell's emphasis). Tirrell concludes that "In telling stories one develops a sense of self, a sense of self in relation to others, and a capacity to justify one's decisions. These features are necessary for being a moral agent in the categorical sense. Telling stories may also increase our sophistication as agents" (125).

Tirrell does not say so, but the relationship between intentionality and moral salience has a rhetorical basis. Charles Altieri, although after different fish, makes this point. He writes, "One acts with an appeal to the approval of a community, not because the deed is rational but because it carries certain qualities of intentionality which an agent can project as deserving certain evaluations from *those who can be led to describe it as the agent does.*"[6] This principle helps explain the continuing value of such ideals as nobility and dignity, which are based not in theoretical judgment but in practical judgment. An action performed "in accord with theoretical reason . . . would only incidentally be my action, since the imperative is there in the methodology and the methodology is not in question. But when we make the kind of judgments that warrant speaking of a practical reason, the choice is deeply mine because my identity as a person depends on both the grounds of reasoning which I accept and the qualities that I exhibit in manifesting that acceptance. In practical reason I do not simply accept an established practice; rather, I treat the specific deed as establishing the kind of loyalties that give me distinctive claims to a public identity" (Altieri 137). These claims are intrinsically rhetorical, designed to win the assent of an audience, and they will probably be most successful if they incorporate thickly described narrative. Indeed, Levine would emphasize that a person faced with a moral judgment will most likely construct a narrative in order to understand the situation.

Two cautions are needed here: literary texts do not necessarily carry moral salience, although they may do so, and to read well is not necessarily to read morally. John Gardner's basic assertion in his widely known *On Moral Fiction* is appealing: "art is essentially and primarily moral—that is, life-giving—moral in its process of creation and moral in what it says."[7] But this leads him to the claim that "True art is *by its nature* moral" (19, Gardner's emphasis)—too sweeping a statement. Alexander Nehamas helps clarify the problem with such a claim when he questions one of Nussbaum's key points, that it is possible to abstract "general lessons from the situations depicted by literature, particularly by the literature Henry James composed."[8] The problem, he rightly points out, is that Nussbaum's acceptance of a mimetic theory of literature is somewhat at odds with her privileging of highly detailed, evocative descriptions; the situations described may be lifelike but almost certainly differ so much in their specifics from the life of any reader that the reader cannot read out of the story a lesson relevant to him or her (Nehamas 38). Nehamas fails adequately to deal with Nussbaum's emphasis on perception, a failure that leads him to attribute to her the simplistic proposition that "By reading properly we learn how to make better discriminations in life: the same, or very similar abilities, are involved in both; good readers are good people" (38). However, he correctly reminds us that "Sensitivity and obtuseness are in themselves neither good nor evil" (49). Being a "good reader" need not make someone a "good person"; "literature has much to teach us about life. But this is how to live, and that in turn is not the same as how to live morally" (51).

Narrative Rhetoric and Moral Effect

Moby-Dick offers both lessons, suggesting that obtuse reading endangers both physical and moral health and that reading all types of texts "in a highly lucid and richly responsive way" can be beneficial. These lessons are conveyed both overtly and rhetorically. As Axel Nissen shows by concentrating on Toni Morrison's novel *Sula*, a novel's narrative form implies an ethical stance: insofar as an author's choices (regarding perspective, focalization, representation of consciousness, balance of scene and summary, and other elements that can be subjected to narratological analysis) influence a reader's "attitude to the novel's characters and events, they are ethical choices."[9] According to Nissen, although Booth, Nussbaum, and others have insisted that the authorial ethos a reader infers from a text's formal elements necessarily invites readers to engage in ethical criticism, the work of these critics and philosophers has not sufficiently attended in a technical way to the formal elements (Nissen 263–64). Three of *Moby-Dick*'s formal elements can be understood as inviting a moral response and conveying moral authority: the rhythmical variation of verbal and rhetorical intensity, the occasional silences about matters that seem to invite judgment, and the stagelike presentation of some scenes. Supported by thick description, these features reinforce the local moral significance of certain events without contradicting Ishmael's explicit and Melville's implicit message that no absolutes can stand.

The rhythmical variation of intensity can be seen in Chapter 94, "A Squeeze of the Hand." Consistent with the morally neutral chapter title, the chapter begins with a thin description of the squeezing of spermaceti. Ishmael quickly adopts morally salient language suggesting that he regards this activity as conducive to an almost heavenly happiness. Of this "sweet and unctuous duty," Ishmael writes, "I bathed my hands among those soft, gentle globules" (*MD* 415). The description climaxes with a transcendent vision: "I saw long rows of angels in paradise, each with his hands in a jar of spermaceti" (416). After this climax, emphasized by a blank space and asterisks, Ishmael shifts back to a more mundane explanation of terms related to the process: "Now, while discoursing of sperm, it behooves to speak of other things akin to it, in the business of preparing the sperm whale for the try-works" (416). While at least in the narrative past Ishmael was definitely transported by this activity, the transport was temporary, a product of specific local conditions. The alternation between transcendence and business not only makes the novel much more readable than it might be if either mode dominated but also prevents a reader from determining that either of these attitudes has more authorial sanction.

Discussing the silences of a narrator who seems so verbose may seem strange, but a careful reader should notice how often Ishmael fails to provide a satisfying conclusion to rhetorically heightened passages. In the scene with the *Rachel*, after Ahab goes below, Gardiner returns to his own ship, which Ishmael says is continuing to search for the lost whaleboat. This would have been a prime opportunity for Ishmael to describe some character, for example Starbuck, rendering a moral judgment; such a description could clinch the implicit condemnation of Ahab. Instead, the reader must do so, if there is to be a judgment. The chapter concludes with Ishmael's metaphorical, nonjudgmental, yet emotionally heightened description of the final sight of the *Rachel*: "But by [the ship's] still halting course and winding, woful way, you plainly saw that this ship that so wept with spray, still remained without comfort. She was Rachel, weeping for her children, because they were not" (*MD* 533). Adding a moral to the end of the chapter, as would be done in a treatise on morals, could yield a sense of completion, but Ishmael definitely, and Melville almost certainly, understood the relative weakness of that technique for a narrative. Empathy may even comprise the novel's moral center, but by leaving this possibility unstated neither the author nor his narrator violates the other chief lesson, that mystery and uncertainty are inescapable.

The sequence of chapters from Chapter 36, "The Quarter-Deck," through Chapter 41, "Moby Dick," exemplifies how voices other than Ishmael's dramatize differing moral positions. As the "stage direction" following the chapter title "The Quarter-Deck" suggests, this chapter will be driven more by dialogue among the characters than by Ishmael's narrating voice. He does occasionally provide both commentary—"For with little external to constrain us, the innermost necessities in our being, these still drive us on" (165)—and thick description—"Stubb and Flask looked sideways from [Ahab]; the honest eye of Starbuck fell downright" (165–66). But the most morally salient feature of these chapters is the actual voicing of positions by the characters. Talking to Starbuck, Ahab by turns uses passion, reason, insult, social pressure, and finally flattery until he can see that he has forestalled any opposition: "Starbuck now is mine; cannot oppose me now, without rebellion" (164). Starbuck's murmured response, "God keep me!—keep us all!" (164), strengthens the dramatic tension, a tension that is further emphasized by Ishmael's description of such foreboding details as "the presaging vibrations of the winds in the cordage" and "the hollow flap of the sails against the mast" (164). The next two short chapters render a monologue from Ahab, concluding "Naught's an obstacle, naught's an angle to the iron way!" (168), and one from Starbuck, concluding "with the soft feeling of the human in me, yet will I try to fight ye, ye grim phantom futures! Stand by me, hold me, bind me, O ye blessed influences!" (170). No narrating voice intervenes to spell out this ethical debate between "iron" principle and "soft" humanity; Melville allows each of these characters to express his own moral compass at the climactic end of a chapter but leaves it up to individual readers to assess the relative merits of the two on the basis of the story's outcome and whatever other information seems relevant.

Ishmael's response to the quarterdeck scene only comes in Chapter 41 ("Moby Dick"): "I, Ishmael, was one of that crew; my shouts had gone up with the rest; my oath had been welded with theirs; and stronger I shouted, and more did I hammer and clinch my oath, because of the dread in my soul" (*MD* 179). He also attempts to explain at least by hypothesis Ahab's fascination for the white whale and his ability to excite his crew to join him in the hunt, but he admits in the final paragraph that "all this to explain, would be to dive deeper than Ishmael can go" (187). Of course the point isn't to explain but to describe, as Levine says, in ways designed to earn assent. By the time a reader encounters Ishmael's admission that "while yet all a-rush to encounter the whale, [I] could see naught in that brute but the deadliest ill" (187), the reader has already had plenty of opportunity to accept, if not to understand, the fascination exercised by both Ahab and the whale as well as the undoubted danger (to both body and soul) of that fascination.

Ishmael's silence in the face of some situations that strongly invite judgment, along with his stated inability to explain some troubling phenomena, may be regarded as resulting from his own recognition that respectful silence is sometimes the only appropriate response. One of the most explicit statements of this point comes at the conclusion of Chapter 104, "The Fossil Whale": "In this Afric Temple of the Whale I leave you, reader, and if you be a Nantucketer, and a whaleman, you will silently worship there" (*MD* 458). This statement expresses Ishmael's apparent belief that his task is to bring readers to the point of contemplation but not to direct them through that activity, although he also strongly implies that to attempt rationally to understand the whale by studying this fossil would be a mistake. Ishmael both recognizes that worshipful contemplation may be at times the only appropriate reaction and insists that confronting the fossil itself is important—Ishmael does not say that he is leaving his readers with the idea of the fossil but that he is leaving us actually there, in the "Afric Temple." Experience is essential for any valid assessment, whether that experience comes through the power of language, as in the Afric Temple passage, or is actually lived, as he emphasizes a few pages earlier in discussing a sperm whale skeleton: "How vain and foolish, then, thought I, for timid untravelled man to try to comprehend aright this wondrous whale, by merely poring over his dead attenuated skeleton, stretched in this peaceful wood. No. Only in the heart of quickest perils; only when within the eddyings of his angry flukes; only on the profound unbounded sea, can the fully invested whale be truly and livingly found out" (453–54). The parallel adverbs "truly and livingly" provide the key here: the most valuable lessons are gained by experience, not by measuring a skeleton or outline, and experience can influence reading. Ishmael's moments of withholding judgment, his technique of allowing characters to speak without his interference, and his variation of intensity create rhetorical spaces within which a reader can respond. That is, because Ishmael has chosen not to foreground his own narrative agency, a reader may experience a stronger invitation to exercise moral choice.

Ethos, Agency, and the Universal Moral Sense

Just as important to the moral efficacy of *Moby-Dick* is the reader's sense that Ishmael is a person of high morals, good character, and goodwill. This ethos is established in a variety of ways. As discussed above, he shows a consistent unwillingness to lay claim to complete understanding and to render moral judgments. Were he not a moral agent, this trait would have no significance. Much of *Moby-Dick* can be read as Ishmael's exploration of agency both in the narrative past (on the *Pequod*) and in the narrative present as he is composing his story. Agency is one of the novel's prominent themes. Ahab attaches both intentionality and agency to Moby Dick and wields over the crew both his absolute legal power as captain and a dominance by means of force of character; the mates, especially Stubb and Starbuck, have to confront the limits of their power during the voyage; the various prophecies underline the question of the relative prominence of "chance, free will, and necessity" (*MD* 215); Queequeg decides not to die of illness when he recollects "a little duty ashore, which he was leaving undone" and expresses the belief (Ishmael terms it a "conceit") that "if a man made up his mind to live, mere sickness could not kill him: nothing but a whale, or a gale, or some violent, ungovernable, unintelligent destroyer of that sort" (480). Both as a novice whaleman and as a common sailor, Ishmael is relatively powerless during the events of the story; like the rest of the crew he falls under Ahab's spell and "welds" with them his oath to hunt Moby Dick (179).

By Tirrell's criteria of intentionality, personhood, and authority, Ishmael the sailor may appear at best to be minimally sophisticated as an agent, if indeed he could even be called an agent in the "categorical" sense of affirmation or negation. At the beginning of his journey he possesses intentionality, but once he goes aboard the *Pequod* he seems to disappear as a distinguishable self and certainly does not present himself as having authority to act except insofar as his actions follow the orders of his captain and are swayed by the passions of the crew—apparently he only has enough authority to accede, opposition being out of the question. However, also by these criteria, Ishmael the narrator qualifies as a sophisticated agent, demonstrating a strong "sense of self" and "sense of self in relation to others." It would be impossible to determine how the act of telling his story might have contributed to Ishmael's development in these areas, but he definitely displays that development in the telling. In much of the novel's cetological center and in many other chapters as well (excellent examples being Chapter 24, "The Advocate," and Chapter 45, "The Affidavit"), Ishmael claims authority over his material; by whatever process, the novice whaleman has become a scholar of whales and whaling as well as at least a competent philosopher of epistemology and ontology.

Not only can Ishmael articulate his past actions in the contexts of the actions of those around him and of his personal history, he is also able to abstain from retrospective judgment of others. His silence about the relative morality of Ahab's decision to violate the Golden Rule is one of the more dramatic instances of this narrative-present restraint, but there are others: no comment on Starbuck's apparent weakness in the face of Ahab ("'God keep me!—keep us all!' murmured Starbuck" [164]), no comment on Flask's cruelty toward one old whale ("'A nice spot,' cried Flask; 'just let me prick him there once'" [357]), no comment on the racially motivated fight between Daggoo and the Manxman in the forecastle (177–78). By effacing himself from these scenes in the narrative past, Ishmael makes a space for readers to respond. This technique also enhances Ishmael's moral authority in the present. The epigraph to the epilogue, "And I only am escaped alone to tell thee" (573) from Job 1:19, strongly suggests that what matters most is telling, not evaluating or judging, and that the story is greater than its teller, a series of events to which silence is an appropriate response. Ishmael claims no special authority because he was the one who survived the wreck; his survival probably resulted from some mix of chance, fate, and his own agency, but it remains sufficiently mysterious in his eyes that he takes from it no right to judge others. One is tempted to infer that his restraint in this narrative situation constitutes yet another of Melville's implicit criticisms of the lingering Puritan tendency to read God's will out of natural phenomena.

Ishmael's apparent moral maturation either during the voyage or in the interval between being on the voyage and telling his story also contributes to his ethos and strengthens his personhood and authority. Summarizing a large body of research and theory, John Rich and Joseph DeVitis conclude that a key sign of moral and intellectual maturity (at least in Western culture) is regarding knowledge as "contextual and relativistic" and committing to well-thought-out responsibilities.[10] Early in the novel, Queequeg invites Ishmael to share his worship, and Ishmael reasons his way to an acceptance by deciding that it is "the will of God" that he join with this "wild idolator in worshipping his piece of wood" (*MD* 52): "What is worship? thought I. Do you suppose now, Ishmael, that the magnanimous God of heaven and earth—pagans and all included—can possibly be jealous of an insignificant bit of black wood? Impossible! But what is worship?—to do the will of God—*that* is worship. And what is the will of God?—to do to my fellow man what I would have my fellow man to do to me—*that* is the will of God. Now, Queequeg is my fellow man. And what do I wish that this Queequeg would do to me? Why, unite with me in my particular Presbyterian form of worship. Consequently, I must then unite with him in his; ergo, I must turn idolator" (52).

What motivates Ishmael in this direction to begin with? A cynic might say that he is working out a trade, having just accepted half of Queequeg's "thirty dollars in silver" as well as the cannibal's expressed willingness to die for his Christian friend. A more benign reading might say that Ishmael is practicing the Golden Rule of neighborly love: "Do unto others as you want others to do to you, as an expression of consideration and fairness among neighbors, where 'neighbor' means everyone."[11] However, Queequeg appears to be following a more admirable version of the Golden Rule, that of fatherly love: "Do unto others as you want others to do to you, imitating the divine paradigm" (Wattles 67). That paradigm is expressed thus, in the Sermon on the Mount: "If ye then, being evil, know how to give good gifts unto your children, how much more shall your Father which is in heaven give good things to them that ask him?" (Matt. 7:11). The novel does not hint at any motive to Queequeg's actions other than love, and surely Melville intended readers to notice that Ishmael has to reason his way beyond the strict proscription against idolatry while the "wild idolator" apparently without effort and without prompting decides to share his entire life with his new friend.

Melville probably wanted readers to applaud the final result of Ishmael's reasoning, but this early in his story Ishmael has to rely on that method and that it leaves him short of the cannibal's level.

In this scene, Ishmael's naive reliance on logic and his use of the phrases "wild idolator" and "will of God" suggest that he still functions fairly close to the moral level of dualism, at which decisions are characterized by either/or thinking. He does not seem willing to do away with the concept of idolatry or to see that the "magnanimous God of heaven and earth—pagans and all included" might actually be Yojo. By contrast, in the *Rachel* example not only does Ishmael keep silent about what he thought when the interaction between Gardiner and Ahab took place, he also renders no judgment from the narrative present. By focusing on the human anguish rather than on the selfishness of Ahab's decision, Ishmael may be showing an awareness that there are some situations in which empathy or even love is more admirable than moral judgment. Progressively in his actions, and especially in his present-tense commentary, Ishmael shows a commitment to empathy and a transcendence of the "drizzly November" of the soul that sent him on the voyage.

Additional evidence that Ishmael has developed morally comes in his explicit addresses to his readers. These addresses reveal a gradual development from categorizing his readers as outside of the fraternity of common sailors with which he aligns himself (for instance, he refers to "ye landsmen" and "ye shipowners of Nantucket" [108, 158]) to bringing his readers into this circle, as in the Afric Temple passage.[12] Bringing readers to an experiential space where a judgment can be made and then leaving them to render their own judgments, or just to stand silently and worship, counts as a recognition that judgments are "contextual and relativistic."

Booth's *The Company We Keep* shows how moral maturity can contribute to a reader's positive assessment of a text's ethos. Booth coins the term "coduction" to denote "what we do whenever we say to the world (or prepare ourselves to say): 'Of the works of this general kind that I have experienced, comparing my experience with other more or less qualified observers, this one seems to me among the better (or weaker) ones, or the best (or worst). Here are my reasons'" (Booth 72). Coduction differs from logical and scientific processes in that it can never be "apodeictic" and "can never be performed with confidence by one person alone" (73). Keeping constantly in mind both the universality of narrative in human experience and the resulting circularity of method, Booth says that a narrative works ethically by leading people "to *desire better desires*" (271, Booth's emphasis). He argues that someone who engages with a narrative in the context of an ethical system that is reflective, pluralistic, and subject to revision is also engaging more of the "whole self" than is someone who looks for "simple moral choices of the kinds that traditional codes are at least said to have provided" (271–72). The reflective person is able "to form a second-order desire" and to make a "judgment about the ethos-I-would-prefer-to-have-and-will-therefore-cultivate" (271). Thinking along these lines leads Booth to pose what he terms "the key question in the ethics of narration": "Is the pattern of life that this would-be friend [the implied author of the text] offers one that friends might well pursue together?" (222). Thus Booth values narratives that do something impossible for "discursive philosophy": they dramatize the complexity and difficulty of moral choice (288).

Booth explicitly connects narrative's ethical value to the recognition that "we must take responsibility for what we are to become" (Booth 271), that is, for the desires that we desire. We must do this even though we almost certainly have no "universal standards" for narrative, let alone "universal supreme goods" aside from such tautologies as "'It is good to live life well' or 'It is always good to improve one's soul'" (56). For this reason Booth (at least the ethos he displays in this book) qualifies as what theorists of moral development would term a "committed relativist": recognizing that moral choices are almost never simple and that there are no universally applicable rules, he still insists that choices matter, that we can become more or less admirable as humans depending on the desires we choose to desire, and that "the company a reader keeps" when reading shapes the ethos of that reader. Ishmael the narrator is able to function as "good company" because he demonstrates a position of committed relativism both by explicitly stating that no single principle can serve as a universal and by holding himself back from judging. This function is enhanced by the establishment within the text of a difference in moral level between Ishmael the narrator and his younger sailor self.

Finally, a universal moral sense binds together a reader and the ethos projected by a text. This claim contains two components: that all humans possess an attribute that can be termed a moral sense, and that this attribute enables a reader to respond to a rhetor's ethos. As to the first component, James Q. Wilson argues "that people have a natural moral sense, a sense that is formed out of the interaction of their innate dispositions with their earliest familial experiences. To different degrees among different people, but to some important degree in almost all people, that moral sense shapes human behavior and the judgments people make of the behavior of others."[13] This argument is based on research into the earliest signs of the moral sense, which arise before children have the linguistic ability to reason morally and which relate in a complex way to the child's "natural sociability" (Wilson 130, 147). Similarly, Colin McGinn bases his case for an innate moral faculty on some of the same grounds that justify the assumption of an innate language faculty:

"poverty of stimulus, richness of result, uniformity of basic principles."[14] Common sense, McGinn says, allows us to recognize that "there are many things that are obviously morally wrong—murder, torture, theft—and anyone who disagrees about these is either dishonest or confused" (49). McGinn does not claim that common sense is identical across all cultures or that such actions as betrayal are identically constructed regardless of culture, but that such actions exist in all cultures and are named by all languages in terms evoking disapprobation. As he says, "we know that stealing is wrong just by knowing what stealing is" (39).

In the twenty-first century it may be regarded as naive or even pernicious to assert the existence of a universal moral sense (although no difficulty is caused by considering as universal the needs for food, shelter, and companionship). It is frequently asserted that references to nonphysical human universals are nothing more than attempts to impose a specific ideology, attempts that are disparagingly labeled as "totalizing" or "essentialist." After all, if something is universal it is probably also immutable—universals inherently function to preserve the status quo. Terry Eagleton, however, reminds us that references to human nature need not constitute "totalizing" or reflect cultural hegemony.[15] According to Eagleton, "it is dogmatic of postmodernism to universalize its case against universals and conclude that concepts of a shared human nature are never important, not even, say, when it comes to the practice of torture" (Eagleton 49). He does not mention "moral sense" as one of the "concepts of a shared human nature," but it follows from his example of torture. Anyone who uses the word "torture" to describe what one person does to another is making a moral judgment and is expecting that judgment to be shared by those who hear the word. This basic transaction cannot happen unless the speaker and the audience share a preverbal agreement that some actions can be benevolent and others malevolent.

To claim the existence of a universal moral sense is not to claim that universal principles exist. According to Levine, no principle can generate "clear and reliable answers to all moral dilemmas," not even Kant's Categorical Imperative (Levine 3). Ishmael's transcendent vision of "long rows of angels in paradise, each with his hand in a jar of spermaceti" is fleeting; the chapter ends with the mundane statement that "Toes are scarce among veteran blubber-room men" (*MD* 418), reminding readers that human life isn't constructed so as to allow anyone to "keep squeezing that sperm for ever" as Ishmael wishes (416). That activity has its place, but so does the slicing of sheets of blubber, an activity that carries no moral weight as described here. Nor would it be appropriate to extract from this chapter the moral principle of giving up the self and blending into a universal "milk and sperm of kindness." To valorize this principle would be to deny the moral salience of other thick descriptions that can be read as advocating the preservation of individuality, such as those climaxing in references to the "universal cannibalism of the sea" and the "horrible vulturism of earth" (274, 308). Some other prominent phrases, images, and metaphors in the novel (such as "insular Tahiti" and "mutual, joint-stock world" [274, 62]) are also presented in highly charged, evocative language and climax narratives freighted with thick, morally salient description—in short, they are designed to earn readers' assent. Yet they remain only locally significant and never cohere into a system. As Levine says, "telling stories is a common way to thicken descriptions—and it is a morally effective one" (Levine 33). One of the important lessons of *Moby-Dick* is that moral effectiveness does not depend on whether or not a set of stories is self-consistent but does depend on readers reacting to words such as "horrible," "mutual," and "kindness" in ways that can be somewhat predicted, or at least shared, due to a shared and innate sense that goodwill, good character, and high moral standing are in fact desirable traits.

That assertion about how language works of course reflects the impossibility of proving, by appeal to logic or data, that an innate moral faculty exists. The fact that almost all humans make moral judgments could result from some emergent property of language as a social construction; it need have nothing to do with human nature. Ultimately all someone can say is "I believe that there is a universal moral sense." This apparent limitation also makes it impossible to prove, as one would like to do in a scholarly paper, the second component of my contention, that the existence of a universal moral sense makes possible the rhetorical appeal on the basis of ethos. Three lines of thinking point in this direction.

One line links the perception of ethos to our experience of language as intentional. According to Booth, the "ethical appraisal" of a text cannot be separated "from what looks like judgment of sheer craft," the basic premise being that the text "has been made intentionally" (Booth 92, 107). This premise seems to apply not only to the text's crafted quality but to its ethos. Readers do not self-consciously and logically assess the projected ethos in terms of good character, goodwill, and high moral standing, any more than we do this in our everyday encounters with each other; these categories can be objectively discussed, but they exist as part of our fundamental makeup as rhetorical and moral beings.

The second line is intersubjectivity as used by Adam Zachary Newton to discuss "narrative ethics."[16] "In the ethical dramas it rehearses—human separateness and the claims of recognition—every reading, we could say, stages a 'command performance,' the legislative power here belonging not to author or to text but to the critical and responsive act" (Newton 23). (Newton needlessly limits his argument's reach by equating narrative with fiction; his point about intersubjectivity holds as well for nonfictional narrative.) A narrative embodies acts of address, plea, trust, and so forth that can only be expressed and received when the entities involved share some fundamental assumptions, such as that benevolence is desirable and malevolence is not. Even if one entity is in large part created by the other, as may happen when a reader infers an "implied author" from a text, a common ground must be present. Even if two individuals totally disagree as to what is an admirable action (this is their subjectivity), they still share the concept "admirable action"; their sharing makes possible the interpenetration of subjectivities. As Christopher Clausen writes, "as long as the universe contains conscious beings whose willed actions cause themselves and each other many kinds and degrees of suffering and joy, moral questions will remain inescapably important."[17]

The third line originates in the Kantian notion of respect (*Achtung*). J. Hillis Miller argues that Kant's Categorical Imperative reveals the necessary "entanglement of narration and ethics": to act ethically is to act "at all times and places as if the private maxim according to which I choose to do or not to do were to be made the universal law for all mankind."[18] A person implements this imperative by using the imagination to create a "miniature novel" in order to assess the potential consequences of universalizing a given private maxim (Miller 28). A maxim that passes this test is worthy of respect: in Kant's words, "What I recognize directly as a law for myself . . . I recognize with respect, which means merely the consciousness of the submission of my will to a law without the intervention of other influences on my mind" (quoted by Miller 17). Respect, for Kant, is the only motivation not influenced by private or social motives (Miller 16). Ethos has strong private and especially social components, but those persons are generally agreed to be most deserving of respect who have done their best to transcend these components—that is, who have done their best to act in accordance with a potentially universal law.

As noted above, these lines of thinking are only suggestive. According to Miller, "Nothing is more urgently needed these days in humanistic study than the incorporation of the rhetorical study of literature into the study of the historical, social, and ideological dimensions of literature" (Miller 7). The "ethical moment" embodied in the encounter between a reader and a text "cannot . . . be accounted for by the social and historical forces that impinge upon it" (8). Putting this point slantwise, one could say that the rhetorical appeal on the basis of ethos also cannot be accounted for by such forces but that it must be grounded in a universal moral sense. *Moby-Dick* contains an invitation to "behave better," in Booth's phrasing, if one shares with Ishmael the belief that good and evil are valid categories, although we may disagree on what belongs in each. A reader may experience Ishmael as "good company" because of his ethos, not because he adheres to any single principle. Of the *Rachel,* Ishmael writes, "you plainly saw that this ship that so wept with spray, still remained without comfort" (*MD* 533). He is saying that any thoughtful, decent person would respond with compassion to the sight of the ship and the associated idea of Captain Gardiner still searching for his son. Ishmael could not write such a sentence—Melville could not have him write it—without the belief that readers share that basic compassion. It would be irrelevant that Ishmael comes across as a person of good character, high moral standing, and goodwill if there were no general understanding of what it means to have these traits or no general agreement that a person who has them is better than one who does not—better in the abstract and also better as someone with whom to share a bed, a whaling voyage, or a narrative. Ultimately, there must be some shared moral ground in order for a moral transaction to happen between text and reader. Ishmael's story reminds readers willing to listen (readers of goodwill) that no single principle can be universally privileged even if like the Golden Rule it is universally recognized. Simultaneously, as a component of the novel's rhetoric, this narrator who uses extremely thick, morally salient description, who carefully balances the transcendent and the mundane, and who admits limitations and weaknesses also creates a space within which such readers can come to their own conclusions about the story's main characters. Because we readers have a moral sense, we will do so.

Notes

1. Peter Levine, *Living without Philosophy: On Narrative, Rhetoric, and Morality* (Albany: State Univ. of New York Press, 1998), 4, Levine's emphasis.

2. See Michael Kearns, *Rhetorical Narratology* (Lincoln: Univ. of Nebraska Press, 1999), 41–42.

3. Wayne C. Booth, *The Company We Keep: An Ethics of Fiction* (Berkeley: Univ. of California Press, 1988), 93–97.

4. Martha C. Nussbaum, *Love's Knowledge: Essays on Philosophy and Literature* (New York: Oxford Univ. Press, 1990), 141–42.

5. Lynne Tirrell, "Storytelling and Moral Agency," *Journal of Aesthetics and Art Criticism* 48 (1990): 116.

6. Charles Altieri, "From Expressivist Aesthetics to Expressivist Ethics," in *Literature and the Question of Philosophy,* ed. Anthony J. Cascardi (Baltimore, Md.: Johns Hopkins Univ. Press, 1987), 137, my emphasis.

7. John Gardner, *On Moral Fiction* (New York: Harper Collins, 1978), 15.

8. Alexander Nehamas, "What Should We Expect from Reading? (There Are Only Aesthetic Values.)," *Salmagundi* 111 (Summer 1996): 37.

9. Axel Nissen, "Form Matters: Toni Morrison's *Sula* and the Ethics of Narrative," *Contemporary Literature* 40 (1999): 266.

10. John Martin Rich and Joseph L. DeVitis, *Theories of Moral Development* (Springfield, Ill.: Charles C. Thomas, 1985), 75.

11. Jeffrey Wattles, *The Golden Rule* (New York: Oxford Univ. Press, 1996), 67.

12. For an extended discussion of these passages, see Michael Kearns, "The Student and the Whale: Reading the Two *Moby-Dicks*," *Reader* 40 (Fall 1998): 1–27.

13. James Q. Wilson, *The Moral Sense* (New York: Free Press, 1993), 2.

14. Colin McGinn, *Ethics and Evil in Fiction* (Oxford, U.K.: Oxford Univ. Press, 1997), 45.

15. Terry Eagleton, *The Illusions of Postmodernism* (Oxford, U.K.: Blackwell, 1996), 26.

16. Adam Zachary Newton, *Narrative Ethics* (Cambridge, Mass.: Harvard Univ. Press, 1995), 23, 25.

17. Christopher Clausen, *The Moral Imagination: Essays on Literature and Ethics* (Iowa City: Univ. of Iowa Press, 1986), 5.

18. J. Hillis Miller, *The Ethics of Reading* (New York: Columbia Univ. Press, 1987), 25.

Moby-Dick's Lessons

or, How Reading Might Save One's Life

CAROL COLATRELLA

Moby-Dick incorporates a variety of generic conventions and narrative voices in celebrating the multicultural project of whaling and in focusing on issues of reading that link this story of a whale to other texts about whales and to contemporary narratives about literacy and moral rehabilitation.[1] The novel connects stories about Ishmael's development and survival, Ahab's bitter injury and revenge, and Moby Dick's mysterious and compelling behavior. Melville's interspersing of diverse subplots, generic styles, perspectives, and interpretations structurally and thematically highlights the difficulties of parsing texts and relating them to one another. Questioning reformist claims of literacy as empowerment, *Moby-Dick* suggests that reading and interpretation are multifarious processes with unpredictable consequences.

Readers have wondered about the narrative strategies exhibited in *Moby-Dick* since its initial publication in 1851. In an early review Evert Duyckinck argued that Melville created "an intellectual chowder." Over time, other readers have become more comfortable than Duyckinck with the heterogeneous nature of the narrative, recognizing the power of blending various genres—fiction, lyric, and drama—and various sorts of nonfictional prose, including etymology, travelogue, natural history, and philosophy.[2] The reader senses a distinct tension between chapters concerned with order and classification, as demonstrated in "Etymology," "Extracts," and various chapters on whales and whaling, and, on the other hand, those chapters exulting in the chaotic ambiguities of Ishmael's romantic meditations on the sea, mixed with socioeconomic analysis of those who serve it ("who ain't a slave?" he asks in the first chapter [*MD* 6]). Adding in Ahab's self-absorbed musings and wild ravings, other characters' meditations, and interpolated stories further complicates the reading process.

"Etymology" and "Extracts" collect definitions and illustrative passages concerning whales, suggesting the analogy that an author cuts and pastes words as whalers cut up whale blubber. Whaling is celebrated as a noble profession and described as tedious waiting alternating with heart-stopping whale hunting and gory processing of whale blubber. Humorously representing whales as books (ch. 32, "Cetology") and mates and harpooneers as "knights and squires" (chs. 26 and 27), Ishmael reveals his readerly obsessions: to classify the whale and to correct the record on whalers. It becomes difficult to distinguish between victims and villains: is the whale a magnificently divine creature or a monster? Are the whale hunters heroes or bloodthirsty, greedy men out for the kill? Complicating such decisions are injunctions overturning notions of human superiority: "for there is no folly of the beasts of the earth which is not infinitely outdone by the madness of men" (385).

The novel challenges readers to appreciate differences of politics, aesthetics, and culture, and to criticize hierarchical divisions of race, ethnicity, gender, religion, class, and sexual orientation as restricting social mobility and limiting moral understanding.[3] Stylistic heterogeneity assists political content, for both mode and message are linked. Reading diverse sources becomes a crucial human activity informing self-improvement and social progress.[4] *Moby-Dick* offers critical perspectives on philanthropic reforms in labor, education, and punishment; acknowledges socioeconomic constraints faced by sailors on the *Pequod;* and suggests that liberal tolerance is rarely achieved in the real world, although it is nurtured by wide-ranging reading.

Education is highlighted as a dynamic force in the narrative, one related to intrepretation. The question of how one learns to interpret and thus to learn from experience, including events related by others, becomes a focal point of the narrative. Diverse characters with different attitudes and outcomes demonstrate the unpredictability of reading. The novel represents the difficulty of parsing visual, written, and oral texts in showing how characters account for moral messages associated with objects, events, and stories. Chapters 36 and 99, concerning the doubloon and the various readings of the coin, provide the most celebrated consideration of the idiosyncratic nature of reading. Studying how various characters respond to this artifact, whale sightings, and the biographies and speeches of other characters, that is, considering the ways that characters interpret representations, helps readers recognize the novel's criticism of rehabilitative education.

Representations of reading and education—undertaken by characters, narrators, and readers—link issues of social justice with fears of death. *Moby-Dick* is a narrative largely told by an older Ishmael about his younger self, reflecting on his maturing character and on his ethnically diverse peers and superiors on the *Pequod*. Gams and interpolated stories stress outcomes for characters of different moral attitudes and serve as parables for both characters and readers. Thematic references to death and fate enable readers to formulate didactic lessons supplementing what characters and narrators understand.

Some secondary characters are developed via short biographies elaborating moral principles. Major characters, including the homodiegetic narrator, provide reactions to texts illustrating different capacities to understand narrative meanings and to apply its lessons to their lives. Ishmael is an exemplary reader who adjusts his outlook and behavior based on experiences and reflections, while Ahab represents a failed reader who cannot change his behavior even after confronting the disastrous outcomes seeing Moby Dick has had for other whaling crews.

Melville's imaging of the diverse prospects of reading counters theories promulgating the inevitable rehabilitative outcome of reading outlined by nineteenth-century reformers working with the poor and prisoners. Historical material, included in papers by reformers and in journal articles reviewing philanthropic and penal practices, offers a valuable context for understanding how Melville's narrative reconfigures popular nineteenth-century ideas concerning how education improves moral character. By incorporating diverse voices and describing the oppression of common sailors, Melville's novel can raise readers' attention to contemporary reform debates concerning immigration and acculturation that recommended literacy as a moral influence.[5]

The novel proposes several aspects of reading that counter the reform view of literacy improvement: the difficulty of developing stray references into a continuing narrative (such as Ishmael's inability to understand the references to death that haunt him before he enters the *Pequod*), the fragmented accounts of crew members offering a variety of perspectives, and the detailed process of understanding allusions and embedded narratives as opportunities for interpreting one's own circumstances.

Interwoven with the account of Ishmael's maturation as a result of his whaling experiences are textual references to insanity that reference Ahab's condition.[6] A number of articles appearing in penitentiary reform journals identify the limits of moral rehabilitation in representing the problem of pervasive criminality as insanity. Some interpolated stories and characters in *Moby-Dick* elaborate a more subtle connection between lunacy and transgression, particularly characterizations of Elijah, Ahab, Fedallah, Gabriel, and Pip, as demonstrated in Chapter 93 where the narrator tells of the abandoned Pip and argues that "man's insanity is heaven's sense" (414). If lunacy brings one closer to God than rationality, then the method of using reason and reading to rehabilitate souls and achieve economic stability, as prison reformers were wont to promote, becomes questionable.

Melville's narratives rewrite moral outcomes for reading identified by his contemporaries. In late eighteenth-century and early nineteenth-century New England, according to William J. Gilmore, "[l]iteracy was promoted . . . as a means of insuring individual salvation and a 'Bible Commonwealth' by the inculcation of enduring Christian values and behavior."[7] What one read and for what purposes were linked to political issues regarding individual rehabilitation and social reform.[8] Elizabeth Fry instituted a reading program for British female convicts. Captain Alexander Maconochie in the 1830s and 1840s promoted a system of prison discipline linking schools and prisons: "a penal establishment under this system should be one vast school, in which almost everything is made subservient to instruction in some shape or other, moral, religious, intellectual, or industrial."[9]

Like their British counterparts, U.S. reform institutions—schools and prisons—encouraged disciplinary measures to enhance moral character and economic prospects, including work, prayer, and reading, but American reformers differed regarding whether to employ force or encouragement in enacting them.[10] Journalist and social activist Lydia Maria Child argued that coercive aspects of rehabilitation for criminals reduced its effects. After an 1842 visit to Blackwell's Island, Child cited the prison superintendent's view "that ten years' experience had convinced him that the whole system tended to *increase* crime," confirming her claim "that coercion tended to rouse all the bad passions in man's nature, and if long continued, hardened the whole character."[11]

Penitentiary reformers generally disagreed with Child and instead promoted the benefits of lifetime imprisonment and physical punishment while debating which physical punishments (cold shower bath, flogging, and yoke) proved more effective than compensated work and directed reading.[12] Both the Auburn and Philadelphia systems offered "instruction . . . in trades, letters, morals, and religion," but contractors in New York penitentiaries pursued profits rather than education.[13] Eastern State's solitary confinement encouraged prisoners to read inspiring texts and to reflect on their own deviance, while congregate systems like Auburn's used reading as a privilege that could be suspended for resistant prisoners.

Prison reformers linked illiteracy in English to social problems associated with immigrants, especially juveniles, who were perceived to be more instinctively inclined to corruption and crime than native-born citizens. An article entitled "How Shall the Convict-Army Be Reduced?" and appearing in an 1852 issue of the *Pennsylvania Journal of Prison Discipline* argues for the establishment of penal schools. The article links an overwhelming increase in crimes of theft, vagrancy, and prostitution committed by juveniles in New York to increasing numbers of immigrants.[14]

Philanthropists identifying education as a primary force in social acculturation and moral rehabilitation promoted teaching poor children and illiterate adults to read, recognizing reading as the ability to recognize and pronounce words in texts. Over time, the comprehension of topics also became an important component of reading. Reading instruction in U.S. schools in the 1840s promoted "intelligent citizenship" by emphasizing the imparting of democratic models to students.[15] Citizenship depended upon docility, for education reformers advocated that children be taught "conformity, silence, and obedience" because "initiative and curiosity were not the goals of the public school curriculum for poor children."[16] Forming appropriate taste in reading was a significant component of moral education for children and adults. The tendency to regard reading as both a pragmatic skill for individuals and an idealistic social project persisted through the early and mid-nineteenth century as reformers reflected on the power of reading to transform individual lives and fortunes.

Representing the multicultural communities of whaling documented by cultural historians,[17] *Moby-Dick* houses diverse points of view highlighting religious, ethnic, and national differences. Readers are privy to voiced and unvoiced thoughts of an astonishing number of individuals in addition to Ahab and Ishmael—Starbuck, Stubb, Flask, Fleece, Pip, Dough-Boy, Father Mapple, Elijah, and Fedallah—as a means of understanding how different people read and understand, and sometimes fail to understand, texts. The novel blends the voices of the *Pequod* crew and represents them as bound by Ahab's cause, symbolized by the gold doubloon. Acceptance into the community means agreeing to kill Moby Dick, whatever the price paid. Chapter 40, "Forecastle, Midnight," is entirely composed of the dialogue and songs of anonymous sailors designated by ethnic or regional affiliation—they are Dutch, French, Manx, Icelandic, Maltese, Sicilian, Chinese, English, Danish, Tahitian, Portuguese, and come from the Azores, Belfast, St. Jago's, Long Island, and Nantucket.

In *Moby-Dick* temperaments interact in a small arena dominated by Ishmael's meditative capacity to both fear and condone Ahab's vengeful scheme, a capacity that is shared by the other crew members forced either to accept Ahab's plan or to mutiny. Ishmael relates "A wild, mystical, sympathetical feeling was in me; Ahab's quenchless feud seemed mine" (*MD* 179). Democracy's dangers include the possibility that individuals might accept an irresponsible leader. Sailors and readers are riveted by Ahab's presence, captivated by his performance, and disciplined in their relations with him.[18] For example, Chapter 34, "The Cabin Table," demonstrates Ahab's authority as leader, showing the charismatic and dramatic force of his personality.[19]

The different sections of the novel are held together by our interest in Ishmael as reader and as survivor, or perhaps more appropriately, as the surviving reader who can tell us the outcome of Ahab's rage against the great White Whale. After sharing narrative perspectives of the captain and various *Pequod* crew members, the novel ends with Ishmael's necessary return as witness testifying to the demise of the ship's crew. He has privileged status as primary narrator. By choosing Ishmael as survivor yet blending narrative voices into what could have strictly been Ishmael's story, the author adds a political dimension to the novel. Melville cedes narrative authority to ordinary sailors and officers who have risen from the ranks, men whose voices represent diverse cultural experiences.

Ishmael's attitude toward cultural difference provides a sympathetic model for readers as he acknowledges his shift from ethnocentrism in anticipating monstrousness of a "primitive" Queequeg (ch. 3) to celebrating his friend as model worshipper in the First Congregational Church of humanity (ch. 18). As in *Typee, Omoo,* and *Mardi,* South Seas islands appear a locus of natural virtue and of peculiar customs; however, whereas Melville's early narrators never resolve the paradox between these, Ishmael comes down firmly on the side of Queequeg.

Ishmael resolves his anxieties about Queequeg by arguing, "Better sleep with a sober cannibal than a drunken Christian" (*MD* 24), but other crew members are less kind to those who appear different. Stubb complains that the devil-like Fedallah's mysterious practices bode no good; he wants to throw the Parsee overboard (ch. 73). Furthermore, he berates the black cook Fleece by stereotyping him as lazy, incompetent, and rebellious (ch. 64).[20] Stubb's desire to destroy what he does not understand increases readers' sympathy for Ishmael's tolerance. *Moby-Dick* demonstrates that ethnicity does not signify character in any reliable way, although one's attitude toward ethnic difference may indicate a character's own moral value.

Allusions to whaling's dangers provide evidence for readers forming moral interpretations. Offering information while omitting interpretive conclusions challenges and engages readers, as the novel forces readers to develop the meaning that a work has for them by remembering one episode and linking it to another. This interpretive process reveals the ambiguities of reading, for connecting one's understanding of separate episodes and collating them into a synthetic understanding can be complicated. The novel's construction as a narrative composed of diverse perspectives exemplifies such interpretive limits in that captains and crews represent different capacities to derive meaning from experience, revealing that how one reads in part defines and determines one's character. "Ourselves are Fate," writes Melville in *White-Jacket* (321), claiming that character, action, and destiny are bound together.

Moby-Dick connects reading ability with open-mindedness regarding diversity in unsystematic ways. Queequeg's characterization belies stereotypes about cannibalistic behavior because he has astute interpretive abilities that enable him to develop a sophisticated understanding of how humans and whales behave. Starbuck's reverential attitude toward nature and his acceptance of his captain's authority mark his passivity as a reader whose personal values are subsumed by Ahab's desires. Ishmael is an exemplary reader, adjusting outlook and behavior based on experience and meditation, while Ahab represents a monomaniacal reader, driven by vindictive rage to destroy Moby Dick despite evidence of the whale's capacity to harm any ship crossing its path.

While prison philanthropists envisioned literacy as enabling individuals to climb the socioeconomic ladder, *Moby-Dick* describes the continued captivity of the *Pequod*'s sailors whether they are literate or not. That many Melvillean protagonists—Tommo, Typee, Taji, Redburn, White-Jacket, and Ishmael come to mind—are more literate and literary than their shipboard counterparts counts for nothing in terms of shipboard hierarchies, and as Ishmael's dreamy revery at the try-works demonstrates, thoughtful meditations work against the efficient operation of the whaling ship. The broad understanding of the world that reading brings to individuals, according to reformers emphasizing its rehabilitative powers, means nothing to sailors like Bulkington, who signs up for voyage after voyage without any intermission between trips (*MD* 23).

Characters' diverse approaches to reading emerge in chapters that sketch different views of Ahab, the doubloon, and whales. The interpretive skills of mates and harpooneers connote past success at whaling and likely future success in finding Moby Dick. The opportunity to reinterpret observation and experience and properly apply this knowledge becomes a trope related to the crew's recognition of Ahab's authority. Chapter 36, "The Quarter-Deck," details Ahab's offering a gold doubloon to the first man who sights Moby Dick. Only Starbuck appears disinterested in Ahab's bribe, and the first mate reminds the captain of his duty to shareholders, an issue that resurfaces when the ship is leaky near Japan. Ahab refuses to follow Starbuck's suggestion to stop for repairs that would protect the investors' capital: "the only real owner of anything is its commander; and hark ye, my conscience is in this ship's keel" (*MD* 474). Ahab's unquenchable rage, revealed in his thoughts on the doubloon in Chapter 99, suggests he cannot see beyond his own interest in finding and destroying the White Whale.

The doubloon posted on the mast seemingly permits an egalitarian set of relationships endorsing secular commercialism above all else: each individual reinterprets the significance of the doubloon he might earn for sighting Moby Dick. Ahab's nailing of the coin confirms his authority while encouraging the ambitions of others, for "the meaning of the coin—and the meaning of the white whale—depends on the subject, on the one who does the looking."[21] Because Melville draws on structural conventions of dramatic monologue and staged dialogue, he supplies "inside" views of characters representing their experiences. In "The Doubloon," Ahab pauses before the coin and thinks that its represented images (flame, tower, cock) are versions of him: "all are Ahab" (*MD* 431). Starbuck's reverential reading emphasizes the dark valleys between heavenly peaks, seeing that "God girds us round" (432). The matter-of-fact Stubb relies on a book to interpret the signs of the zodiac, and his explanation gives way to observation of how others approach the coin. All observers sense significance, but their interpretive accounts differ substantially and offer more information about temperaments and interpretive strategies of men who read it than about the coin's message.

Melville finishes the doubloon chapter with a description of one who avoids interpreting the symbolic significance of the gold piece. Speaking immediately after Ahab nailed up the gold piece, Pip, in fear and trembling, asked God to "have mercy on this small black boy down here: preserve him from all men that have no bowels to feel fear!" (*MD* 178). Near the end of the *Pequod*'s journey, Pip is reduced to observing "I look, you look, he looks; we look, ye look, they look" (434), a formulation that subverts particular interpretation and aptly conjugates the novel's multiple focalization.[22]

As the focal symbol of Ahab's revenge, the doubloon signifies greedy, gory aspects of whale hunting and Ahab's coercion of his crew. Accepting his blasphemous plot to fight against nature, to pursue the White Whale until its death, the sailors are attracted by Ahab's magnetism to unite for his cause. Fear of flogging exhibited by Redburn and White-Jacket becomes a more subtle form of persuasion and intimidation on the *Pequod*.[23]

Moby-Dick's criticism of nineteenth-century theories of rehabilitation through reading contributes to its criticism of social inequality by questioning the means and ends of rhetorical persuasion in appealing to ideas of social justice. Ahab's tyrannical authority and the power of officers over crew mark the ship as a penal school in which immigrants provide the brawn and are acculturated to shipboard society. The intellectual Ishmael characterizes the whaling ship as his university, but the ship that keeps seamen in thrall to

Ahab can easily be identified with penitentiaries that transformed illiterate immigrants into captive laborers and American citizens.

In reports printed in penitentiary reform journals, particularly the *Pennsylvania Journal of Prison Discipline* and the New York Prison Association annual reports, reformers indicated how public institutions ought to encourage moral instruction through reading and working to contain an overwhelming increase in urban crime. Moral reformers illustrated the inevitable outcomes for criminals in works such as *Scenes Where the Tempter Has Triumphed* (published by Harper Brothers in 1844), which demonstrates that transgressions are always punished. The stories in the volume reinforce the theme of crime resulting from a sense of impunity by noting that the overconfidence of criminals predicts their downfall, that circumstances before and after a crime can provide the "truth" of innocence or guilt, and that reading stories about criminals discourages transgression.

Similar didactic tales about moral error and punishment appear in various parts of *Moby-Dick*. By considering the belief systems and philosophical attitudes exhibited by the *Pequod*'s crew and captain, readers can recognize that one's ability to learn from one's own experiences as well as from events related in oral and written texts becomes a focal point of a narrative in which whaling is celebrated and feared as a unique and an exemplary human profession. "Etymology," "Extracts," and the accounts of Ishmael's initiation into whaling and his meeting with Queequeg refer to deathly aspects of whaling, culminating in Father Mapple's sermon about Jonah and the whale. Numerous allusions to fate and death haunt Ishmael's time in New Bedford and Nantucket and shadow his introduction to the *Pequod* in Chapter 15: "It's ominous, thinks I. A Coffin my Innkeeper upon landing in my first whaling port; tombstones staring at me in the whalemen's chapel; and here a gallows! and a pair of prodigious black pots too! Are these last throwing out oblique hints touching Tophet?" (*MD* 66). Ishmael relates signs of death to his audience, who could assume that the fate of any whaler could be destruction, even though Ishmael does not connect early references to any narrative outcome. At the end of the novel, Ahab similarly meditates on his life, fortune, and fate in Chapters 134 and 135 as he thinks about his choice to go to sea for forty of his fifty years. Various superstitions and portents of death revealed piecemeal throughout the narrative coalesce in Ishmael's narration about Ahab's character, where the prophecies act dynamically rather than as a static determinant of his morality and behavior.

Melville designates Ishmael to tell the story of Ahab and the whale within a narrative full of deathly references and allusions to Bible stories, Shakespeare's plays, and texts about whaling. The embedded biblical story about Jonah focuses on failures of interpretation and powers of faith, heightening readers' attention to moral decisions made in times of crisis. Ishmael's descriptions of New Bedford and Nantucket foreshadow Ahab's quest for Moby Dick: becoming prepared for danger and death and having one's deeds memorialized in secular pictures and in sermons indicating how one should behave. The "boggy, soggy, squitchy picture" Ishmael observes in the Spouter-Inn ambiguously attributes consciousness to the whale: "The picture represents a Cape-Horner in a great hurricane . . . an exasperated whale, purposing to spring clean over the craft, is in the enormous act of impaling himself upon the three mast-heads" (*MD* 12, 13). Although Ishmael characterizes his "theory" about the painting as a consensus influenced by conversations with peers, it is questionable whether the collision was deliberate or accidental.

The church's memorial tablets confirm that some sailors die, while others survive to remember their relatives and friends. The risks of whaling are apparent in adventures ending in violent death for many who earn their livelihoods by searching the seas for whales to be chopped up for oil. Meditating on the tablets causes Ishmael to reflect that his body serves as only a transitory location for his soul. In the chapter in which he paraphrases three tablets in the whaleman's chapel, where he hears Father Mapple's sermon, Ishmael asserts his faith that his soul might live on even after "a stove boat and a stove body" (*MD* 37). The sermon offers a two-stranded lesson on Jonah, for the listener and the teller are assumed by Father Mapple to derive different information. Listeners are absorbed in Jonah's tale of a man who impossibly hopes to escape his calling to divine God's word, but the minister interprets the moral as resignation to God's will. One wonders if Ishmael can resign himself to the will of God with more equanimity than Jonah did. Led by Father Mapple to think about the roles of audiences, readers speculate about how, why, and in what way Ishmael's reading skills might enhance or constrain his understanding of Jonah's fate and of Mapple's message.

Other meditations and unvoiced thoughts also reveal fears of death and risks of whale hunting. In Chapter 24, "The Advocate," which sets forth the aesthetic grandeur of whaling, Ishmael lists reasons why whaling should be respected and admired, claiming it as a scholarly pursuit: "for a whale-ship was my Yale College and my Harvard" (*MD* 112). Mindful of death, Ahab sees the cabin as a "tomb" (127), but his meditation offers little hope for his survival nor does he envision grandeur in dying. His thoughts reveal only that his inevitable end approaches soon, one he will share with almost all members of his crew.

Some chapters forecast the *Pequod*'s destruction by Moby Dick. "The Grand Armada" (ch. 87) imagines the ship's end, as Ishmael describes when Queequeg attacks the great parade of whales, "as the swift monster drags you deeper and deeper into the frantic shoal" (385). In "The Castaway" (ch.

93) the narrator hints at the novel's outcome: "a most significant event befell the most insignificant of the Pequod's crew; an event most lamentable; and which ended in providing the sometimes madly merry and predestinated craft with a living and ever accompanying prophecy of whatever shattered sequel might prove her own" (411). Many whale skeletons described in Chapters 102 through 105 remind us that a battle with Moby Dick could result in the death for the creature or for the *Pequod* crew.

Material references to Queequeg's death also invest Ahab's project with supernatural significance. Ahab's prosthetic leg is crafted of ivory from the jaw of the whale by the carpenter who makes Queequeg's coffin. Chapter 110 describes how even the preeminent Queequeg catches a chill and gets a deadly fever, inspiring "awe" in onlookers: "the drawing near of Death, which alike levels all, alike impresses all with a last revelation, which only an author from the dead could adequately tell" (*MD* 477). Queequeg and Pip speak ancient tongues, which Starbuck says serves as a sign of closeness to heaven (479). Queequeg's body and coffin bear duplicate hieroglyphics: the ship relies on the coffin as a life buoy, associating the *Pequod* with supernatural forces, whether it be the devilishness claimed by Fedallah and Ahab or the reverence for God demonstrated by Starbuck, and portending its approaching destruction.

Moby-Dick's interpolated stories draw attention to issues of reading, interpretation, and normed behavior. Gams prepare readers for the *Pequod*'s demise, while stories concerning the moral characters of specific crew members and captains warn readers of how moral failings determine one's destiny. The account of the blacksmith's life as favored until his encounter with demon alcohol is an exemplary narrative revealing transgression, outcome, and punishment. Everyone "now knew the shameful story of his wretched fate": Perth the blacksmith's intemperance led to "the loss of the extremities of both feet," his economic ruin, and the deaths of his wife and children (*MD* 484, 485). Perth's short biography precedes his dialogue with Ahab near the forge (ch. 113), a conversation that notes how the captain's determination to battle Moby Dick outweighs any sense of familial responsibility, social propriety, or reverence for God. Perth creates a harpoon that Ahab claims is baptized by the devil. Perth's own life story presses readers to shudder at Ahab's hubris and determination to confront death.

While criminal reformers used didactic tales about failed criminals to discourage transgressions, Melville's narrative resists reductive interpetation in making Ahab appear both more heroic for taking fate in his hands, damning devil and God, and more foolish for ignoring what many readers predict as a reasonable outcome of his revenge. Each sighting of a whale offers an opportunity for reflection on the possible fate of the *Pequod*'s crew. Just as the blacksmith's story becomes a backdrop for Ahab's tragedy, each gam becomes a text, what Walter Bezanson calls "a scroll which the narrator unrolls," for the *Pequod*'s sailors, especially Ishmael, and *Moby-Dick*'s readers ("Work of Art" 54). Yet Ahab's resistance to learning from his or others' experiences makes him an obdurate reader, one incapable of flexibly incorporating new information or synthesizing new ideas.

Information from the gams is sketchy but ominous. In Chapter 52 the *Pequod* encounters the *Albatross,* "long absent from home" and homeward bound. Ishmael observes this whaler as having "a spectral appearance" with its "long channels of rust" and "spars and rigging . . . furred over with hoar-frost" (*MD* 236). Its crew is "long-bearded" and appears dressed in "the skins of beasts." Responding to Ahab's question of whether they have seen the White Whale, the *Albatross*'s captain loses his trumpet, a gesture seen as an omen by the narrator and other sailors, since it is "the first mere mention of the White Whale's name to another ship" (237).

Later in Chapter 54, the *Town-Ho,* also homeward bound, provides "strong news of Moby Dick" in the form of a story, "which seemed obscurely to involve with the whale a certain wondrous, inverted visitation of one of those so called judgments of God which at times are said to overtake some men" (*MD* 242). The voyage of the *Town-Ho* would have ended in port without "the least fatality, had it not been for the brutal overbearing of the mate Radney, a Nantucketer, and the bitterly provoked vengeance of Steelkilt, a Lakeman and desperado from Buffalo" (243–44), characters whose confrontation highlights issues about legal and moral authority that also appear in the contrast drawn between Ahab and Starbuck.

The feud on the *Town-Ho* stems from what the narrator describes as a natural conflict initiated when a man in authority, acting out of "dislike and bitterness," wants to destroy a subaltern who seems superior (*MD* 246). Radney grazes the disobedient Steelkilt with his hammer and suffers a debilitating blow in return. The altercation nearly becomes a mutiny when Steelkilt's supporters among the crew enter the fight, until the captain intervenes. Along with nine others, Steelkilt chooses the brig over mutiny. His followers eventually desert Steelkilt's cause, and he is almost executed for refusing to follow orders until the captain relents (254). Steelkilt tries to avenge Radney's insult by murdering the mate but fails (255). Although the crew agreed to ignore any whales to shorten the voyage, one crew member sights Moby Dick. Radney's boat, with Steelkilt as bowsman, is the first out, quickly striking the whale and "spilling out the . . . mate" (256). The whale "seized [Radney] . . . between his jaws; and rearing high up with him, plunged headlong again, and went down" (257). That Steelkilt survives to desert the ship and to escape retribution marks the interpolated story of the *Town-Ho* as a didactic tale: the innocent man is vindicated and the guilty one punished, albeit by a whale.

Lessons about fanatical behavior and punishment also appear in other gams. In Chapter 71 the *Pequod* speaks the *Jeroboam*, also out of Nantucket. Although Captains Mayhew and Ahab are limited to communicating from a distance as the *Jeroboam* has an epidemic on board, they manage to converse with only minor interruptions from the sea and the so-called prophet Gabriel. Stubb and others on the *Pequod*, although not Ahab, have already been informed by the *Town-Ho*'s crew that a young "scaramouch . . . had gained a wonderful ascendancy over almost everybody in the Jeroboam" (*MD* 314). Gabriel's insanity gives him power over many superstitious crew members, especially after a plague strikes them. Mayhew tells Ahab during the gam that the *Jeroboam* has seen Moby Dick and that chief mate Macey and five others who ignored Gabriel's injunction to set out against the whale were quickly destroyed. Gabriel's influence on the *Jeroboam* increases after Macey's death, and he warns Ahab that to go after Moby Dick is to blaspheme. Ahab turns away from the prophet, telling Captain Mayhew that the *Pequod* has mail for a *Jeroboam* sailor, coincidentally the dead Macey. Gabriel's response that Ahab ought to deliver Macey's letter himself makes a dramatic impression on the crew of the *Pequod* and readers of the novel who recognize that both Gabriel and Ahab are madmen keeping others in thrall to their manias.

The *Pequod*'s fortunes do not always seem to dim as a result of the gams. Chapter 81 describes the exploits of the *Virgin* (a German ship), suggesting that perhaps the competent *Pequod* crew can find and destroy Moby Dick. The German captain asks for and receives oil from the *Pequod*, but the appearance of whales incites a competition between the American and German crews. Flask and Stubb task the *Pequod*'s crew to chase an aging, one-finned, blind, intestinally ill whale, while Starbuck inveighs Flask not to prick the poor creature. The *Pequod*'s crew gains this whale, revealing their violent competence, while the *Virgin* takes after a finback whale, called "uncapturable" by Ishmael (*MD* 360). In Chapter 91, readers also observe Stubbs's clever diddling of the *Rosebud*'s French captain, who releases the blasted whales after Stubb predicts an epidemic. The French mate who colludes in the diddling detests the smell of the whales, while Stubb covets the ambergris. The *Pequod* only briefly prospers from such transgressions.

Ahab risks all in chasing the White Whale, while others who are thereby harmed behave more moderately, as demonstrated in Chapter 100 where the *Samuel Enderby*, an English ship, gams with the *Pequod*. After Moby Dick attacks Captain Boomer, this sage captain does not seek another meeting with the White Whale because he has already lost one arm to amputation and is not eager to give up the other. The surgeon Bunger's explanation that the whale cannot digest an arm and therefore does not act out of malice conflicts with Boomer's and Ahab's views of Moby Dick, but Boomer avoids what he knows will be an injurious and possibly fatal encounter. Ahab admits dangerous aspects of Moby Dick but takes a different course: "he will still be hunted, for all that. What is best let alone, that accursed thing is not always what least allures. He's all a magnet" (*MD* 441).

Gams with the next three ships (*Bachelor, Rachel,* and *Delight*) show how the magnet is deadly by outlining the cause-and-effect relationship of encountering the whale. These meetings show that any ship confronting the whale finds trouble, while those ships not meeting with it are fine. In Chapter 115 the *Pequod* gams with the *Bachelor,* another Nantucket ship that can be seen as its antithesis, for the *Bachelor* is near the end of a successful voyage: they have not sighted Moby Dick, but they have filled every container with oil, bartered for more casks, and welcome future prosperity. Ahab muses that the *Bachelor* is full and homeward bound, while the *Pequod* is empty and outward bound (495). Yet for many of his crew this encounter with the *Bachelor* seems to bring good luck to the *Pequod,* as they slay four whales the next day.

In Chapter 128, the *Rachel* asks for help in looking for sailors, including the captain's twelve-year-old son, lost during a battle with the whale. Undeterred from his mission, Ahab refuses help and sets off to find Moby Dick. Emphasizing that encountering Moby Dick will bring only ill fortune, Chapter 131 tells of the *Delight,* a ship shattered by the whale, its captain insisting "The harpoon is not yet forged that will ever" kill the White Whale (*MD* 540). Even Ahab begins to wonder after this meeting whether forty years of whaling have been worth sacrificing home, comfort, and family, until he glimpses Moby Dick, first appearing lovely and peaceful (548–49) before turning to attack the boat. After Starbuck asks him to reconsider the plan to kill Moby Dick (561), Ahab cannot be swayed from seeing himself as "the Fates' lieutenant" (561). He regrets, but does not alter, his choices, his fate, and his destiny. The *Pequod* is destroyed and all hands are lost, save Ishmael, picked up by the *Rachel,* searching for its orphans but finding the sole survivor of the *Pequod.*

Moby-Dick's allusions to the powers of reading impute multivalence to the processes of reading employed by different individuals. Ishmael collects references to death that indicate likely destruction associated with whaling. In conversations with Starbuck, Perth the blacksmith, and other captains, Ahab recognizes that his quest to kill Moby Dick might result in his own and others' deaths, but he cannot be dissuaded. Starbuck's adherence to disciplinary codes makes him unable to intercede on behalf of shareholders, himself, the crew, or their families. Readers follow allusions and meditations, but it remains impossible to connect overlapping, yet sometimes contradictory, visions into a monolithic moral. Keeping Moby Dick an absent presence for much of the story about Ishmael's maturation and Ahab's dangerous quest, the novel resists the urge to become a coherent narrative and retreats from asserting a specific moral message about literacy as empowerment, rather suggesting that redemption is unpredictable.

Deliberately seeking to create a reputation as an American original, Melville incorporated diverse points of view both for structural and aesthetic reasons—to write a tragedy in novel form, and for philosophical and political reasons—to advocate on behalf of the downtrodden who are often denied the possibility of speaking.[24] Ahab's anger causes the demise of the *Pequod*'s crew, with the notable exception of Ishmael, whose survival shows that democracy's project of diversity remains vulnerable to individual desires and luck.[25] Although Ahab's project to destroy Moby Dick dooms his crew, Queequeg's convictions impel him to protect his passage into the afterlife by demanding a coffin. Both men, one actively and one passively, manage their destinies, but only Ishmael, whose willingness to adapt his understanding with regard to other cultural practices, survives these attempts, benefiting from his friend Queequeg's foresight and generosity in asking for a coffin to be built and in later donating it as a life buoy. *Moby-Dick*'s readers have been understandably wary of assigning specific material or supernatural meaning to the fates of different characters. Like interpreters of the doubloon, critics have agreed to disagree in seeing how various interpretations remain possible, recognizing the power of reading as an unpredictable force for individual and social development, a position diametrically opposed to theories of literacy promoted by prison reformers in Melville's time.

Notes

1. This essay is adapted from material previously published in Carol Colatrella, *Literature and Moral Reform: Melville and the Discipline of Reading* and appears with the permission of the University Press of Florida. See also Colatrella, "'I Hear America Singing': Multiple Voices in Melville's *Moby-Dick*," 50–61; I am grateful to Magdalena Zaborowska for helping me consider multiculturalism in Melville's works.

2. As William Ellery Sedgwick pointed out, "A cosmopolite, it is not to be pinned down by easy definitions." See *The Tragedy of Mind* (New York: Russel, 1944).

3. Elizabeth Schultz analyzes illustrations of the novel in relation to its ethnic representations in "Visualizing Race."

4. James Justus, "*Redburn* and *White-Jacket*: Society and Sexuality in the Narrators of 1849," in *Herman Melville: Reassessments*, 65.

5. Priscilla Wald elaborates a fundamental connection between literature and culture in

Constituting Americans: Cultural Anxieties and Narrative Form (Durham, N.C.: Duke Univ. Press, 1995), 13.

6. For a particularly cogent formulation of the connection between literacy and social empowerment, see T. R. Townsend's report in New York State Inspectors of the State Prison at Auburn, *Annual Report* (Albany, N.Y., 1843): 74–79. Examples in the *Pennsylvania Journal of Prison Discipline* include essays and notices in its January 1845 issue (article 7: "Religious and Moral Instruction in Philadelphia County Prison"), January ("Pauperism—Its Cause and Cure"), and April 1853 (article 1) that connect illiteracy and deviancy.

7. William J. Gilmore, *Reading Becomes a Necessity of Life: Material and Cultural Life in Rural New England, 1780–1835* (Knoxville: Univ. of Tennessee Press, 1989), 34–35.

8. Jennifer Monagha and Wendy Saul, "The Reader, the Scribe, the Thinker: A Critical Look at Reading and Writing Instruction," in *The Formation of School Subjects: The Struggle for Creating an American Institution.* ed. Thomas S. Popkewitz (New York: The Falmer Press, 1987), 85–122.

9. Maconochie, *General Views Regarding the Social System* (Hobart Town, 1839), quoted in Janet Fyfe, *Books behind Bars: The Role of Books, Reading, and Libraries in Brititsh Prison Reform, 1701–1911* (Westport, Conn.: Greenwood Press, 1992), 133.

10. Robert Levine connects slavery and ships at sea with "the new asylums, prisons, and other self-contained reform institutions" in "Fiction and Reform I," *The Columbia History of the American Novel,* ed. Emory Elliott (New York: Columbia Univ. Press, 1991), 148.

11. Child, Letter XXIX, *Letters from New York* [1845] (Freeport: Books for Libraries, 1970), 204

12. By the late 1850s, critics of corporal punishment were more vocal. See "Torture and Homicide in an American State Prison," about the various measures used at Auburn State, *Harper's Weekly,* Dec. 18, 1858, 808–09 and "Influence of Penal Laws," *United States Magazine and Democratic Review* 22 (Mar. 1848): 233–40. Also see the Report of the Committee Appointed by the Legislature of New York in the *Pennsylvania Journal of Prison Discipline* 7.2 (Apr. 1852): 56–75.

13. "First Report of the Prison Association of New York, December 1844," *Pennsylvania Journal of Prison Discipline and Philanthropy* 1.1 (Jan. 1845): 39. The sixth report of the Prison Association of New York (1851) notes problems at Auburn State and Sing Sing impeding the educational program related to the few copies of books available for prisoners, the lack of time in their schedules for reading, and the lack of light in their cells; the report is included in the *Pennsylvania Journal for Prison Discipline and Philanthropy* 6.3 (July 1851): 143–64. As one inspector indicated, "I greatly question whether one in ten of the most intelligent and best men in society could be subjected to such a course of treatment without its greatly debilitating his intellect and corrupting his morals" (161).

14. "How Shall the Convict Army Be Reduced?" *Pennsylvania Journal of Prison Discipline* 7 (Oct. 1852): 146.

15. Nila Banton Smith, *American Reading Instruction* (Newark, Del.: International Reading Association, 1965), 76.

16. Marianne Bloch, "Becoming Scientific and Professional," in *The Formation of School Subjects,* 31.

17. Lisa Norling, *Captain Ahab Had a Wife: New England Women and the Whalefishery, 1720–1870* (Chapel Hill: Univ. of North Carolina Press, 2000), 96–97.

18. Etsuko Taketani argued this point in a talk on the theatrical mob in *Moby-Dick* at the 1996 meeting of the Society for the Study of Narrative Literature in Columbus, Ohio.

19. I have been aided in my interpretation by the commentary on Michel Foucault's *Discipline and Punish* in Frank Lentricchia, *Ariel and the Police* (Madison: Univ. of Wisconsin Press, 1988):

"In the theater of terror what is produced, or so the sovereign-playwright desires, is a single message: I can pursue without fear a policy of terror because my force is invincible" (42).

20. See historical descriptions of such stereotyping in Ronald Takaki, *A Different Mirror: A History of Multicultural America,* ch. 5 (New York: Little, Brown, 1993).

21. R. E. Watters, "The Meanings of the White Whale," *University of Toronto Quarterly* 20 (Jan. 1953): 157. See also Paul Royster, "Melville's Economy of Language," in *Ideology and Classic American Literature,* 313–36.

22. Conversations on focalization with Robert F. Denton have clarified this point.

23. Norling, *Captain Ahab Had a Wife,* 23 and 120.

24. See C. L. R. James, *Mariners, Renegades, and Castaways,* 18–19, and Donald Pease, "National Narratives, Postnational Narration," *MFS: Modern Fiction Studies* 43 (Spring 1990): 1–37.

25. David Reynolds notes that "*Moby-Dick* is the literary culmination of the radical egalitarianism that had its roots in Jacksonian democracy and that had taken on paradoxical, devilish intensity in the working-class fiction of the 1840s." *Beneath the American Renaissance,* 289.

Mapping and Measurement
in *Moby-Dick*

ANNE BAKER

The marked differences between Ishmael and Ahab have sometimes been seen as creating a contrapuntal effect in the narrative of *Moby-Dick*. Whereas Ahab's intense desire to take revenge on the white whale drives the plot of the novel toward its violent conclusion, Ishmael's reveries and reflections on the nature of the whale slow it down, forcing the reader to pause rather than recklessly follow Ahab to his quest's denouement.[1] A careful look at the novel, however, reveals that the two characters overlap in at least one crucial respect: both map and measure in ways that enable Melville to explore the increasingly important role that scientific exploration played in the nineteenth-century United States. Ishmael's measurement of a whale skeleton temple in "A Bower in the Arsacides" (ch. 102) and Ahab's mapping of the migration routes of sperm whales in "The Chart" (ch. 44) both echo episodes from Charles Wilkes's *Narrative of the U.S. Exploring Expedition* (1845), which Melville owned.[2] But to see that text as a source for *Moby-Dick* is to see only part of the picture. For the real significance of Ishmael's act of measurement lies not simply in its connection to Wilkes's narrative, but in Melville's curious juxtaposition of sources in that episode. By linking the Wilkes expedition to biblical apocalypses, Melville points to a major shift in thinking about American geography and in ways of rationalizing the incorporation of new territory into the national sphere. Similarly, the full significance of Ahab's mapping arises not solely from the parallels between "The Chart" and Wilkes's own pet project of mapping sperm whale migration routes, but from Ahab's later abandonment of the very scientific methods of knowing the world and locating oneself in it that the Wilkes expedition practiced and even represented in the popular imagination.

The most famous exploring expedition in U.S. history was undoubtedly the Lewis and Clark Expedition, which has achieved a prominence in popular culture unrivaled by its many successors. No other government-sponsored exploring expedition has been the subject of a Ken Burns documentary or the inspiration for a new coin (the Sacajawea dollar). In terms of historical significance, however, the Wilkes expedition was every bit as important as its famous predecessor.

The idea for a naval expedition that would circumnavigate the globe making maps and collecting scientific specimens arose as early as the 1820s. Its staunchest advocate was Jeremiah Reynolds, a writer and exploration enthusiast, who is best known today for his impact on his literary contemporaries. (He wrote "Mocha Dick or the White Whale of the Pacific"—one source for *Moby-Dick*—and was a passionate proponent of John Symmes's theory that the earth was hollow and that there were entrances at the poles. It was Reynolds's articulation of Symmes's theory that inspired Poe's *The Narrative of Arthur Gordon Pym.*) Reynolds's ardent campaigning finally bore fruit in 1836, when Congress appropriated $300,000 for the voyage. Under the command of Wilkes, the expedition left Washington, D.C., in 1838 amid great fanfare and public acclaim. On board were a philologist, two naturalists, a conchologist, a mineralogist, a botanist, and a horticulturalist.[3] Researches in "hydrography and geography" were to occupy the "special attention" of the naval officers, along with inquiries related to astronomy, terrestrial magnetism, and meteorology (Wilkes xxix). Over the course of the next four years and 87,000 miles, this unprecedented collection of scientists would assemble enough scientific data and specimens to warrant the founding of the Smithsonian Museum, while the naval officers mapped regions—most notably the South Pacific and the Pacific Northwest coast—that would prove invaluable to the nation's military and commercial interests.

Critics have discovered a number of parallels between characters in Wilkes's narrative and in *Moby-Dick*. Wilkes himself, for example, "apparently behaved as autocratically as Ahab in many respects."[4] Queequeg and Fedallah also very likely owe something to characters that Wilkes encountered in New Zealand and the Philippines.[5] While the recognition of these characterological parallels has provided important insight into Melville's composition of *Moby-Dick*, they are not my primary focus here. Instead, my interest in the expedition lies in what might be called its national and imperial flavor. In order to understand what this phrase means, one needs, first, to understand the nationalist sentiment that fueled the expedition and, second, to know something about recent scholarship on the role of European mapping and surveying in Asia and Latin America.

From the very beginning of his campaign to launch the U.S. Exploring Expedition, Jeremiah Reynolds saw the project in nationalistic terms. While he certainly recognized the commercial and scientific benefits to be gained from it, he saw it above all as a means of increasing "national dignity and honor."[6] His most persuasive argument for the launching of such an expedition was that the time had come for the United States to take its place alongside the European world powers who had already sponsored scientific exploring expeditions. Similarly nationalistic arguments were invoked by the secretary of the navy, who immediately prior to the expedition's launch reminded its officers that "the undertaking which they are assisting to accomplish, is one that necessarily attracts the attention of the civilized world," adding that "the honour and interests of their country" were at stake.[7] The publishers of Wilkes's narrative attempted to increase their sales by declaring the work "a great and truly national one," assuring readers that all aspects of the book were "strictly American" and proclaiming it "a book worthy of the country."[8] And Wilkes himself begins the introduction to his narrative by reminding readers that the expedition was "the first, and is still the only one fitted out by national munificence for scientific objects that has ever left our shores" (Wilkes xiii).

The most overt aim of the expedition, then, was to enable the United States to make a name for itself as a nation to be reckoned with. This was not, however, the expedition's sole function. For just as the *Pequod* has been read as a ship of state in pursuit of additional territory to annex, so too the Wilkes expedition was clearly intended to incorporate—through a series of largely symbolic gestures—certain previously uncharted regions into the United States' sphere of influence. Among the most important of these gestures were measurement and mapping.

Mary Louise Pratt points to the mid-eighteenth century as the date of a fundamental shift in the way European elites thought about the world, and she cites as the chief manifestation of this shift the emergence of the "totalizing, classificatory project" of natural history, nothing less than the "systematizing of nature" and the production of order out of chaos. Whereas older European representations of the world had "constru[ed] the planet above all in navigational terms," the newer "representations or categories [of natural history] constituted a 'mapping' not just of coastlines or rivers, but of every visible surface."[9] A variety of apparatuses, in Pratt's account, made this classificatory project possible—Linnaeus's classification system for *all* plants, even those yet unknown, for example. But the standardization of European units of measurement is the most important for my purposes here.[10]

This new emphasis on measurement and quantification, along with the invention of the chronometer, a device for accurately figuring longitude, made possible modern cartography, and with it the rise of modern geography. The planetary latitude-longitude grid that developed at this point functioned as "a general matrix for measurement,"[11] and the measurements taken and the mathematical calculations done by the explorers and navigators of the eighteenth and nineteenth centuries filled in the blank areas on that matrix.

The emergence of modern cartographic conventions, in turn, had far-reaching political consequences. Thongchai Winichakul has argued that the displacement of indigenous conceptions of space by new conceptions associated with modern geography contributed significantly to the emergence of the nation-state. With its emphasis on precise boundaries, the modern map, in Winichakul's view, constituted a "prime technology" of nationhood. While Winichakul is primarily interested in the way Western conceptions of space interacted with premodern Siamese notions of space, many of his ideas can usefully be applied to the early national United States. For without a doubt the Wilkes expedition's directive to map the Pacific Northwest coast was designed to help crystallize the new nation's sense of itself by establishing a more coherent picture of what was imagined by many (correctly, it turned out) to be its future Western boundary.

Considerable scholarly attention has also been paid recently to the relationship between cartography and empire. Matthew Edney and Graham Burnett, for example, have both shown that surveys played a decisive role in the history of British imperialism by turning "terra incognita into a mapped and bounded colony" and by consolidating the colonizers' sense of themselves as possessors of scientific knowledge and so as justifiable rulers of less "civilized" peoples.[12] Even leaving aside the agency of particular European practitioners of cartographic surveying, however, there is also the basic fact that by its very nature "a map appropriates a spatial object by its own method of abstraction into a new sign system" (Winichakul 55).

The Wilkes expedition can be seen as the naval equivalent of the various surveying expeditions that Edney and Burnett examine. For despite the fact that the South Pacific was not, strictly speaking, a colony of the United States in quite the same way that India, for example, was a colony of Britain, the Wilkes expedition was intended to secure the continued success of the United States in the whaling industry there and ensure the nation a place in the race among European nations to dominate various non-European parts of the globe.[13] Melville was aware of the national and imperial functions served by measurement and mapping, and he dramatizes those functions by weaving references to the Wilkes expedition into the fabric of *Moby-Dick*.

"A Bower in the Arsacides," the chapter in which Ishmael surreptitiously measures a whale-skeleton temple on a South Sea island, is an intriguing combination of slapstick humor, lyrical intensity, and metaphysical inquiry, as well as a tour de force of Melville's exuberant literary style. At first glance, however, it seems to bear little structural relation to the novel as a whole. And unlike other digressive chapters such as "The *Town-Ho*'s Story," which has been shown to have thematic ties to the novel's central plot, it has received relatively little scholarly attention. In fact, the basic question—what it means for Ishmael, at this point in the novel, to measure the whale-skeleton temple and tattoo the measurements on his body—has remained uninvestigated.[14]

"A Bower in the Arsacides" begins as yet another of Ishmael's meditations on the nature of the whale, a phenomenon quite familiar to readers from the earlier cetology chapters. Having "chiefly dwelt upon the marvels of his outer aspect," he observes, "it behoves [*sic*] me now to unbutton him still further" and to "set him before you in his unconditional skeleton" (*MD* 448). He then briefly recounts his dissection of a "small cub Sperm Whale"—an act that foreshadows the invasive nature of his measurement of the temple—before moving on to the primary action of the chapter. Ishmael recalls that "years ago," while on the island of Tranque, ruled by Tranquo, he encountered a vast whale skeleton that had been turned into a temple. He describes the temple in a passage that is characteristically Melvillean in both its language and metaphysical preoccupations. After first establishing the exotic appearance of this South Sea island temple ("The ribs were hung with trophies; the vertebrae were carved with Arsacidean annals, in strange hieroglyphics"), he turns his description of the temple in its verdant, natural setting into an elaborate simile: "the industrious earth beneath [the temple] was as a weaver's loom, with a gorgeous carpet on it, whereof the ground-vine tendrils formed the warp and woof, and the living flowers the figures" (449). The simile, in turn, prompts an impassioned plea for clues to some underlying meaning or purpose in the world. This plea suggests that if Ishmael's mad captain sees the physical world as a mask to be broken through, Ishmael himself sees it as a machine whose operator refuses to explain it: "Oh busy weaver! unseen weaver!—pause!—one word! whither flows the fabric? . . . wherefore all these ceaseless toilings?"

Since the "weaver-god" refuses to speak, Ishmael is left to his own empirical devices as he attempts to navigate between the marvel of a king who regards the chapel—a sacred space—as merely "an object of vertù" and that of priests who swear that the whale's "smoky jet" (created by a continuous flame burning in its skull) is "genuine." First Ishmael breaks through the ribs of the skeleton and wanders with a ball of twine, like Theseus in the labyrinth, through the temple's "many winding, shaded colonnades and arbors." His line soon runs out, however, and he emerges from the skeleton-temple having seen "no living thing within." He then cuts "a green measuring rod" and once more enters the temple (450).

It is not particularly surprising to find Ishmael measuring a whale skeleton. After all, he has from the very beginning of his narrative displayed an intense desire to know the true nature of the whale. And as we have already seen, measurement in the eighteenth and nineteenth centuries was increasingly regarded as an effective and important part of the acquisition of knowledge about the world. That Ishmael measures a whale-skeleton *temple,* however, is both more unexpected and more significant. For his measurement recalls episodes in three apocalyptic texts of the Old and New Testaments, all three of which suggest that the measurement of the temple of Jerusalem is a crucial prerequisite for the reestablishment of the kingdom of the Israelites, which is or will be fallen due to the sins of its people.[15]

In the book of Ezekiel, the eponymous prophet addresses the Israelites, who are captive in Babylon, and describes a vision, sent to him by God, which details the steps to be taken if they wish to be restored to their freedom and their homeland. In the vision, Ezekiel is carried to the land of Israel, where he encounters a temple and a man "whose appearance shone like bronze" and who carries a linen cord and a measuring rod in his hand. He is then told to look and listen attentively, for he has been brought there that he might "declare" all he sees "to the house of Israel." The next two chapters consist of a detailed account of the man's measurement of every part of the temple, after which the prophet is instructed to "describe the temple to the house of Israel, and let them measure the pattern, . . . and write it down in their sight, so that they may observe and follow the entire plan and all its ordinances." The book of Zechariah, which consists of the prophet Zechariah's visions of what will be necessary to restore Israel to its previous strength and purity also portrays "a man with a measuring line in his hand," whose declared purpose is "[t]o measure Jerusalem."

In the book of Revelation, the visionary himself does the measuring. John of Patmos, the author of this particular apocalyptic text, writes, "Then I was given a measuring rod like a staff, and I was told, 'Come and measure the temple of God and the altar of those who worship there.'" Here, as in the earlier books of the Hebrew scriptures, measurements are taken with an eventual restoration of the sacred temple in mind. Revelation differs from Ezekiel and Zechariah, however, in that the reestablishment of the temple is intended to occur after the end of the world and the second coming of Christ.

If, as seems likely given the extent of his biblical allusions elsewhere in *Moby-Dick,* Melville was indeed echoing the motif of temple measurement in biblical prophecy, then the significance of the parallel can easily be interpreted.[16] *Moby-Dick* has often been read as a political allegory in which the white whale represents Western territory. Just as annexation of Western territory will cause the debate over slavery to erupt into Civil War, so too Ahab's sacrilegious determination to destroy the white whale leads to the destruction of the *Pequod,* an event that has clear eschatological overtones. By alluding to biblical prophets as the *Pequod* nears its doom, Melville turns Ishmael into a prophet for America, whose measurement of the temple can provide the blueprints for his nation's restoration.[17]

Identifying Melville's references to biblical prophecy, however, reveals only part of the meaning of "A Bower in the Arsacides," for this episode, like Ahab's doubloon, can have various meanings depending upon which source or allusion one chooses to focus on. Melville dangles before his readers the possibility of a simple allegorical reading in which Ishmael's actions have a single biblical referent. Such a simple, clear-cut reading becomes untenable, however, when we consider that Ishmael's measurement of a temple on an idyllic South Sea island also bears a significant resemblance to an episode from the Wilkes narrative. In Chapter 1, volume 5 of his narrative, Wilkes describes the discovery of a South Pacific island previously unknown to Americans or Europeans, which he gives the unromantic name "Bowditch Island." Eager to survey the island, Wilkes dispatches a group of officers and sailors to shore, where they encounter natives who manifest a strong "desire that our people should depart" (Wilkes 14). Determined, despite this opposition, to remain on the island in order to collect specimens and to catalog its people and their customs, the crew makes every effort to calm the natives, though Wilkes notes that "nearly an hour elapsed before they were tranquillized."

His use of the word "tranquillized" deserves further attention in light of Melville's language in "A Bower in the Arsacides." A close reader of Wilkes can easily hear verbal echoes in *Moby-Dick*. When Melville describes the "devious zig-zag world circle of the *Pequod*'s circumnavigating wake" (*MD* 201), for example, it recalls Wilkes's description of the "devious and extensive cruise" (Wilkes 457) of his own world circumnavigation. In thinking about connections between "Bower" and Wilkes's narration of the "Bowditch Island" episode, one should also consider that Melville's naming of "Tranquo," ruler of "Tranque," may well be a similar echo of the exploring expedition's "tranquillized" natives. A verbal link here would not only reinforce a connection between the two places but would also highlight Melville's interest in the relationship between Americans and natives in "Bower."

After calming the natives and looking around, the Wilkes crew members find that "[t]he most remarkable building was that which they [the natives] said was their 'tui-tokelau' (house of their god)." It is a large building with a thatched roof, a not terribly unusual example of Polynesian architecture (unlike the fantastic skeleton-temple of "A Bower in the Arsacides"). But its simplicity and setting make it "one of the most beautiful and pleasant spots," and a drawing of it included in the published narrative makes it seem lovely and idyllic indeed. Like Ishmael on "Tranque," the officers among the party are determined to see the inside of the temple, and they do so in spite of religious injunctions against their presence. "[The natives] were at first unwilling that the officers should enter; but upon the explanation that what was taboo for them, would not be so for the Papalangis [white men], they were admitted by an old priest, but not without reluctance" (14). And like Ishmael, they make measurement a top priority. They measure the gods themselves, which are actually located outside the temple ("The largest of these was fourteen feet high and eighteen inches in diameter. . . . The smaller idol was of stone and four feet high"), as well as the tables or benches where the gods are supposed to sit ("four feet long by three broad and the same in height" [15]). Wilkes's straightforward, unremarkable narration of the episode seems a far cry from the lyricism and humor of "A Bower in the Arsacides"; Melville has made the episode uniquely his own. But the similarity between that chapter and the island temple episode in the Wilkes narrative shows Melville's awareness, born out of his interest in cross-cultural encounters in the South Pacific, that measurement can be a means of defining or laying claim to what one sees.

Melville reinforces this connection between measurement and ownership as he concludes the episode. After Ishmael takes the whale's measurement, the priests shout, "How now! . . . Dar'st thou measure this our god!" Ishmael's story then moves into slapstick comedy mode, with a scene that would not be out of place in a *Three Stooges* episode. Ishmael wryly asks, "Ay, priests—well, how long do ye make him, then?" Then, "a fierce contest rose among them, concerning feet and inches; they cracked each other's sconces with their yardsticks" (*MD* 450–51). To measure, in this story, means to define or lay claim to, and the priests' disagreement over the whale's measurements—and their use of yardsticks as weapons—clearly represents the disagreements of various sects over religious doctrine. At stake is the question, "Who shall define God?"

The issue then shifts abruptly, becoming not religious doctrine (what one might call figurative "ownership" of God), but more literal property ownership. Again, however, possession and measurement are complementary processes. After noting that other whale skeletons are owned and on display in England and the United States, Ishmael observes that the two known proprietors of sperm whale skeletons both claimed their specimens "upon similar grounds": King Tranquo seizing his because he wanted it; and Sir Clifford, because he was "lord of the seignories of those parts" (451). But this comic exposure of the arbitrary nature of property ownership conventions serves to point out that "there are skeleton authorities" we (the readers) "can refer to, to test [Ishmael's] accuracy." Other whales are owned, and other whales have therefore been measured.

If "A Bower in the Arsacides" does indeed echo apocalyptic books of the Bible as well as the Bowditch Island episode of the Wilkes narrative, what, then, are we to make of Melville's juxtaposition of sources in this chapter? His awareness of the relationship between biblical rhetoric and national expansion is certainly not unique to "A Bower in the Arsacides." (Think, for example, of "Brother Jonathan, that apostolic lancer," who regards Texas as a "loose fish" [*MD* 398].) So to identify Melville's biblical allusions in that chapter simply adds another chapter to an old story. But his creation of an episode of measurement that is both a pastiche of the biblical prophets as well as a parody of an episode of Wilkes's narrative shows us Melville's creative imagination responding to a major cultural shift. Religion provided the primary framework for thinking about national expansion from the nation's beginnings through the Mexican War. "Manifest Destiny"—the notion that the United States was divinely ordained to spread across the North American continent—is the most well-known manifestation of religion's influence on conceptions of American space. But in fact, Manifest Destiny should be thought of as only one part of a larger phenomenon known as "geographical predestination."[18] Immediately after the Revolution Americans both for and against expansion began to designate successive geographical barriers (the Alleghanies, the Mississippi, the Rockies, and finally the Pacific) as the natural, God-given boundaries of the nation.

While there's no doubt that religion continued to be an important element in American nationalism, by the 1840s science—as practiced by exploring expeditions like that of Wilkes—had begun to play an increasingly important role in shaping public opinion about the territory that the United States was in the process of incorporating.[19] By inviting readers of "A Bower in the Arsacides" to hear echoes of both biblical prophecy *and* Wilkes's scientific expedition, Melville expresses his misgivings about U.S. imperialism in two ways: one rooted in the Bible and focused on the consequences of expansion; the other based in a keen awareness of the new processes by which modern nations assimilated new territory and made space national.

But the dual echoes in the chapter also analogize the two methods of figuratively assimilating geographical space (the religious and the scientific) and in doing so reveal that neither can justify its claims to absolute authority. A reference to biblical prophecy alone, for example, might suggest that Melville is simply following in the footsteps of various Puritan authors who identified America with Israel. But while Melville by no means rejects the possibility of an analogy between the two peoples and their histories, his juxtaposition of religious and scientific contexts for measurement calls into question the absoluteness of each context. The Bible, this chapter suggests, is only one tool, among many, for interpreting historical events.

Likewise a parodic allusion to the Wilkes expedition's visit to Bowditch Island, taken by itself, could reveal simply the comic undertones in a transgressive cross-cultural encounter. Alongside the prophetic associations of measurement in the chapter, however, the reference to the expedition's predilection for measuring—and its underlying assumption that numbers capture some essential reality of a place—becomes an exploration of what Matthew Edney has called "the empiricist delusion" (Edney 30). According to Edney: "[T]he empiricism of the later Enlightenment posited a direct, visual link between an entity in the world, the individual's mental perception of that entity, and the individual's inscription of that perception on paper. The inscription could involve any combination of numbers, written statements, or graphic sketches but, regardless of its form, it was assumed to be an 'essential' and literal copy of the original entity" (40). Edney's exploration of this delusion, as carried out by British surveys of India, involves highlighting the "conditions of observation" and "the subjective condition of the observer." Melville's, on the other hand, involves noting that, like the biblical interpretation of history, measurement requires that some external template (in this case instruments of measurement) be brought to bear on an object in ways that may ignore, or even diminish, the object's local, contextual meaning (in this case its religious significance within the local culture).

At the end of "A Bower in the Arsacides," Ishmael describes having the measurements he has taken tattooed on his arm, observing that "at that period, there was no other secure way of preserving such valuable statistics" (*MD* 451). How are we to read the phrase "such valuable statistics" given the multiple allusions of the chapter in which it occurs? With considerable irony, surely. For if Ishmael's measurement invoked biblical apocalypses alone, the statistics in question might indeed be valuable, if only as symbols for a destroyed ideal. But in the context of the Wilkes expedition's visit to Bowditch Island and the comical measuring proclivities of the priests, we are clearly intended to question their value. While statistics that lead to better maps are valuable because they enable successful commercial ventures, statistics like Ishmael's measurement of the whale skeleton or the Wilkes crew's measurement of the gods of Bowditch Island are *not*—except insofar as they provide the measurer with a sense of mastery.

Where Melville's invocation of biblical prophecy and the Wilkes expedition in "Bower" analogizes religion and science in order to question their representations of themselves as uniquely effective interpretive tools, his portrayal of Ahab mapping and measuring focuses more exclusively on the claims of science. As in "Bower," the Wilkes expedition is a key ingredient in Melville's exploration of the role science, quantification, and the collection of numerical data played in Western assimilation of global territory during the eighteenth and nineteenth centuries. Ahab's mapping of sperm whale migration routes recalls Wilkes's own pet project, carried out during the expedition he commanded.[20] But Ahab's gradual movement away from navigational practices based on numerical data as he draws closer to the white whale suggests science's shortcomings as a means of achieving Ahab's more daring goal. Whether one reads that goal in philosophical or political terms—as retribution for the world's injustice or as hubristic territorial annexation—is immaterial. For in either case, the quantifying gestures of the U.S. Exploring Expedition prove inadequate in Ahab's eyes.

Charles Wilkes ends his five-volume account of that expedition with a chapter called "Currents and Whaling." Noting that "It may at first sight appear singular that subjects apparently so dissimilar . . . should be united to form the subject of one chapter," he goes on to make a persuasive argument that his charting of ocean currents (which carry with them "the proper food" of whales) will enable whaling captains to determine "not only the places to which they [whales] are in the habit of resorting, but the seasons at which they are to be found frequenting them" (Wilkes 457). Wilkes has discovered, in other words, the very scientific method of whale finding (observing currents, observing whales, finding correlations between the two sets of observations) that Ahab practices in "The Chart" as he "thread[s] a maze of currents and eddies": "Ahab, who knew the sets of all tides and currents; and thereby calculating the driftings of the sperm whale's food; and, also, calling to mind the regular, ascertained seasons for hunting him in particular latitudes; could arrive at reasonable surmises, almost approaching to certainties, concerning the timeliest day to be upon this or that ground in search of his prey" (*MD* 199).[21] The resemblance stops, however, at that methodological similarity. For while Wilkes merely carries out his straightforwardly commercial goals with characteristic zeal, Ahab's devotion to "that monomaniac thought of his soul" clearly betrays his madness (199).

A related difference between this final chapter of Wilkes's *Narrative* and "The Chart" is that whereas Wilkes is utterly uninterested in the phenomenon of his own mind making the observations and drawing the conclusions that he reports, Melville is fascinated by Ahab's mental processes. As Ahab works at his "large, wrinkled roll of yellowish sea charts," a lamp throws "shifting gleams and shadows of lines upon his wrinkled brow, till it almost seemed that while he himself was marking out lines and courses of the wrinkled charts, some invisible pencil was also tracing lines and courses upon the deeply marked chart of his forehead" (*MD* 198). The most obvious reading of this passage is that Ahab's obsession with finding Moby Dick is "marking" his mind, or driving him insane. But it is important to note also that both Ahab and his tools for finding the whale (the charts) take on the whale's distinguishing characteristics. Just as Moby Dick is known for his vast wrinkled brow, the charts are "large" and "wrinkled"; and just as Ahab himself marks the charts, "some invisible pencil" also inscribes similar marks upon his own brow.

In addition to depicting Ahab's madness, then, the passage can also be seen as an examination of the relationship between observer and observed. In representing Ahab's mental processes, Melville has been influenced by two models of vision that overlapped in the first part of the nineteenth century. The first, dominant during the Enlightenment but common in scientific circles for much longer, took the camera obscura—essentially a walk-in pinhole camera—as the model for human vision. The presupposition was that just as the camera obscura separated the viewer from the world (the viewer would be inside a darkened box looking at an image of the outside world thrown on a rear wall), so too in the everyday world vision was a mechanistic activity in which the viewer was entirely separate from an objective, exterior world, which his reason (like an element of the camera obscura) then shaped into a coherent picture. Ahab, far from remaining a detached and impartial observer—as Wilkes's "scientifics" and the imperial surveyors that Edney and Burnett have studied imagined themselves to be—merges with his object of scrutiny. In doing so, he already takes his first step away from the scientific gaze.

The "heavy pewter lamp suspended in chains over his head" under which Ahab works as he "ponder[s] over his charts" also highlights the workings of his mind but suggests an alternative, newly emergent model of vision. As M. H. Abrams has demonstrated, during the Romantic period the lamp replaced the mirror as the vehicle of choice for metaphors of the mind, the change reflecting a fundamental shift in popular views of the mind's role in perception. While the mirror analogy conveyed a view of the minds as "passive receiver," the lamp analogy suggests an active mind that in perceiving "discovers what it has itself partly made."[22] In "The Chart," then, the lamp above Ahab's head represents his powerful intellect and creative imagination.

That the lamp is "suspended in chains," however, hints at both a kind of captivity to his diabolical purpose and the consequences of his Promethean overreaching. But as Ahab draws closer to Moby Dick, he not only defies divine authority (as Prometheus did) but also rejects the technology for locating oneself according to the modern cartographic grid. In "The Quadrant" (ch. 118), Ahab uses the quadrant to measure the distance of the sun from the horizon and then, "with his pencil upon his ivory leg," he "calculate[s] what his latitude must be at that precise instant" (*MD* 501). Angered, however, by the tool's inability to locate the white whale, he smashes it, after delivering the following diatribe: "Foolish toy! babies' plaything of haughty Admirals, and Commodores, and Captains; the world brags of thee, of thy cunning and might; but what after all canst thou do, but tell the poor, pitiful point, where thou thyself happenest to be on this wide planet, and the hand that holds thee: no! not one jot more! Thou canst not tell where one drop of water or one grain of sand will be to-morrow noon; and yet with thy impotence thou insultest the sun! Science! Curse thee" (501). Ahab's condemnation of science's inability to provide answers to the questions that drive him reveals the shortcomings of the worldview that was the foundation of the Wilkes expedition and signals his final rejection of Enlightenment epistemology. That Ahab then turns to the occult knowledge of Fedallah as an alternative to the quadrant also suggests that his smashing of the quadrant is a form of blasphemy. Enlightenment epistemology, in other words, has acquired the status of religious doctrine.

The question of whether Ahab's frustration with science—like his hunt for the white whale—is insane, peculiarly admirable, or some combination of both these attributes, remains for individual readers to decide. But rethinking some of Ahab and Ishmael's actions in the context of the Wilkes expedition does allow us to see Melville as an astute observer of his own culture. Whereas most Americans saw in the Wilkes expedition merely a way to enhance the prestige of their own country in the eyes of the world or to facilitate whaling, Melville accurately saw in it the embodiment of a relatively new geographical worldview that would enable Europeans and Americans to dominate the globe. That his two main characters both, in the beginning at least, act on the basis of that worldview suggests, perhaps, its pervasiveness. That Ahab rejects this worldview so shortly before his final encounter with Moby Dick may well suggest that to see beyond its orthodoxy required a deeply transgressive mind.

1. See, for example, Robert P. Caserio, *Plot, Story, and the Novel* (Princeton, N.J.: Princeton Univ. Press, 1979), 133–66.

2. Charles Wilkes, *Narrative of the U.S. Exploring Expedition during the Years 1838, 1839, 1840, 1841, 1842 in Five Volumes and an Atlas* (Philadelphia: Lea & Blanchard, 1845).

3. Daniel C. Haskell, *The United States Exploring Expedition 1838–1842 and Its Publications 1844–1874* (n.p., ca. 1942), 94–96.

4. Kathleen E. Kier, *A Melville Encyclopedia*, 2:1103. Also, "A more thorough-going model [for Ahab] was Charles Wilkes, naval officer and author of *Narrative of the of the U.S. Exploring Expedition*. . . . Both Wilkes and Ahab may be described as dangerous, eccentric, and mysterious, and both as dauntless, flawed by insolence and pride, persistent, seawise and soul-sick, and wrathful. Parallels exist in the lives of both, and their voyages were parallel at times and included similar gams" (Robert L. Gale, *Herman Melville Encyclopedia*).

5. "Queequeg's background, appearance, artifacts, character, and behavior may owe something to the detailed comments on an amiable New Zealand chief named Ko-towatowa, of Kororarika, by Charles Wilkes in his *Narrative* . . ." (Gale 375). "Fedallah's garb may be partly based on descriptions by Charles Wilkes in his *Narrative of the U.S. Exploring Expedition During the Years 1838, 1839, 1840, 1841, 1842* (5 vols. and an atlas, 1845) of natives and mestizos in Manila . . . , while Fedallah's perfidious nature may owe something to Wilkes's comments on Sulus, especially the Sultan and his son, also in the Philippines" (Gale 136).

6. Donald Dale Jackson, "Around the World in 1,392 Days with the Navy's Wilkes—and His Scientifics," *Smithsonian* 16.8 (1985): 50.

7. Secretary of the Navy James K. Paulding's instructions to Wilkes are included in Wilkes's narrative. Wilkes xxxi.

8. Prospectus with specimen pages, for *Narrative of the U.S. Exploring Expedition* . . . (Philadelphia, 1844), title page.

9. Mary Louise Pratt, *Imperial Eyes: Travel Writing and Transculturation* (London and New York: Routledge, 1992), 28–30.

10. Other scholars suggest that measurement became more prominent after 1800. Jonathan Crary, for example, argues that "Measurement takes on a primary role in a broad range of the physical sciences between 1800 and 1850, the key date being 1840 according to Thomas Kuhn." Jonathan Crary, *Techniques of the Observer: On Vision and Modernity in the Nineteenth Century* (Cambridge, Mass.: MIT Press, 1992), 17. He adds that "Kuhn is supported by Ian Hacking: 'After 1800 or so there is an avalanche of numbers, most notably in the social sciences. . . . Perhaps a turning point was signalled in 1832, the year that Charles Babbage, inventor of the digital computer, published his brief pamphlet urging publication of all the constant numbers known in the sciences and arts.'"

11. Thongchai Winichakul, *Siam Mapped: A History of the Geo-Body of a Nation* (Honolulu: Univ. of Hawaii Press, 1994), 54.

12. The quotation is from D. Graham Burnett, *Masters of All They Surveyed: Exploration, Geography, and a British El Dorado* (Chicago: Univ. of Chicago Press, 2000), 3. Edney provides the most penetrating discussion of the way science shaped the self-image of imperial Britain.

13. The founding of the "National Institute" (now the Smithsonian Museum) in 1840 in order to house the specimens collected by Wilkes's "scientifics" suggests that the expedition was intended to put the United States on an imperial map as well. For a discussion of the relationship between imperialism and colonial archeology, see Benedict Anderson, *Imagined Communities*, revised edition (London: Verso, 1991), 178–85.

14. Two readings of "A Bower in the Arsacides" that do not take into account the allusiveness of this chapter can be found in Henry Nash Smith, "The Image of Society in *Moby-Dick*" and Shawn Thomson, *The Romantic Architecture of Herman Melville's* Moby-Dick. Nash focuses on the loom simile as evidence that "industrialism and technology had made a deep impression on Melville" (62). Thomson does briefly note that in the measurement episode "Ishmael's creative imagination takes ownership . . . of the skeleton" (195). His ultimate goal, however, is quite different: to link Ishmael—the novel's "center of consciousness"—to Romantic ideology.

15. In the writings of the Old Testament prophets, the temple referred to is the temple of Solomon, which was destroyed by the Babylonians when the Israelites were taken into captivity. In the New Testament book of Revelation, the temple is the "second temple," which was built to replace Solomon's temple after the Israelites regained their freedom.

16. The most complete catalog of Melville's biblical allusions remains Nathalia Wright, *Melville's Use of the Bible*. Wright does discuss apocalyptic imagery but does not address the measurement motif in the biblical apocalypses or in "A Bower in the Arsacides."

17. The seminal work on *Moby-Dick* as political allegory is Alan Heimert, "*Moby-Dick* and American Political Symbolism." For a more recent study of the novel as political allegory, see the chapter called "Nationalism and Providence in Ishmael's White World" in James Duban, *Melville's Major Fiction.*

18. Albert K. Weinberg, *Manifest Destiny: A Study of Nationalist Expansionism in American History* (Baltimore: Johns Hopkins Univ. Press, 1935), 2.

19. The overland expeditions of John C. Fremont in the 1840s (the first to the Rocky Mountains, the second to Northern California) were particularly important in this regard. Fremont's very popular narratives of his expeditions portrayed the gathering of scientific data in heroic terms and in so doing portrayed Western territory as assimilable, despite the obstacles it presented.

20. Daniel Henderson, *The Hidden Coasts* (New York: William Sloane Associates Publishers, 1953), 115.

21. Before publishing *Moby-Dick* in October 1851, Melville added a footnote to his account of Ahab's method, in which he informs readers that an official circular was issued in April of that year by Lt. Maury of the National Observatory. That circular, he notes, announces that a chart correlating whale sightings with ocean currents "is in the course of completion" (199).

22. M. H. Abrams, *The Mirror and the Lamp: Romantic Theory and the Critical Tradition* (Oxford: Oxford Univ. Press, 1953), 57–58. As in the lines from Wordsworth's *Prelude,* in which he describes his early creative powers: "An auxiliar light / Came from my mind which on the setting sun / Bestow'd new splendor," quoted in Abrams (60).

Flood-Gates of the Wonder World:
Race and the Americas

"In This Simple Savage Old Rules Would Not Apply"

Cetology and the Subject of Race in *Moby-Dick*

MARK K. BURNS

"We comprehend the universe only as filtered through the categories which are constitutive element of our subjectivity."
—Kant[1]

Michel Foucault begins his preface to *The Order of Things* by citing a humorous passage from Jorge Luis Borges, one supposedly taken from "a certain Chinese encyclopedia" in which all animals are divided into the following classifications: "(a) belonging to the Emperor, (b) embalmed, (c) tame, (d) sucking pigs, (e) sirens, (f) fabulous, (g) stray dogs, (h) included in the present classification, (i) frenzied, (j) innumerable, (k) drawn with a very fine camel hair brush, (l) *et cetera,* (m) having just broken the water pitcher, (n) that from a long way off look like flies."[2] This passage's odd, whimsical groupings make us laugh, of course, but not without a certain unease: Borges not only makes light of scholars and others who feel compelled to put things in categories even at the cost of conceptual coherence,[3] but also indirectly implies an important though easily obscured fact—that objects never present themselves in some natural, self-evident system of classification, in other words, that they never manifest to us the means by which they should be grouped or catalogued. Things may fall apart, as Yeats wrote, but they don't just fall together into groups, and because there is no magic attraction or magnetic pull between disparate objects in the real world, categories and classifications need to be chosen and imposed from the outside, leaving open the possibility for alternate, competing ways to organize and order the infinity of objects in the universe. Even a relatively concrete project such as the classification of animals, then, presupposes assumptions about the characteristics that constitute similarity and difference within that realm, criteria that are themselves the result of subjective choice.[4]

Coincidentally, the narrator of Herman Melville's *Moby-Dick* at one point engages in a project remarkably similar to the ironic attempts at animal classification described by Borges—that of the Linnaeus-like categorization of the world's whales. Chapter 32 narrates Ishmael's extended, convoluted attempt to tackle this challenging task, and his ordering system for whales proves to be less whimsical but no less troubling than Borges's description. Throughout the rest of the novel, Ishmael and many of *Moby-Dick*'s other characters undertake a different, ongoing project of classification that has far more important ramifications than the academic concerns of cetology do—that is, the process of racial differentiation and stereotyping. Though they are seemingly unrelated issues, *Moby-Dick* links these discussions of cetology and race in several subtle though unmistakable ways throughout the novel. As its chapter on cetological classification challenges the very nature of classification itself, Melville implies that broad classifications of the world's races are every bit as problematic and vexed as Ishmael's erratic attempt to organize and systematize the world's whales.

"Cetology" and the Challenge of Classification

Chapter 32 of *Moby-Dick*, entitled "Cetology,"[5] comprises Ishmael's attempt to think through and present a "systematized exhibition" of the world's whales—necessary background information for the reader, he believes, before the narrative proceeds further (*MD* 134).[6] Ishmael's first hint that his attempt to establish a biological classification of all whales is a difficult undertaking is implicit in his warning at the beginning of "Cetology." He immediately stresses in this warning the difficulty of his undertaking and emphasizes that this is no cut-and-dried task because nothing readily distinguishes one species from another. In fact, he informs his readers, "The classification of the constituents of a chaos, nothing less is here essayed." Ishmael also quotes others who have attempted the same frustrating assignment before him: "Utter confusion exists among the historians of this animal," says one; "[there exists an] impenetrable veil covering our knowledge of the cetacea," says another; "A field strewn with thorns" (134) another cetologist labels this field.

Ishmael's warning and his subsequent listing of these failed attempts at classifying whales emphasizes from the start the uselessness of the supposed authorities of cetology—"those lights of zoology and anatomy" (*MD* 135)—when it comes to this most fundamental task of their profession. These opening gestures serve to immediately question what the reader would suppose to be the objective nature of cetological categorization and act as a prelude for Ishmael's later undercutting of his own status as a reliable source of information on whale classification.

Ishmael next makes an important point in reference to all these attempts at classifying whales: although experts stress the difficulty of categorizing them, that does not keep many others from putting forth their opinion on the matter. As Ishmael tells us, "though of real knowledge there be little, yet of books there are a plenty; and so in some small degree, with cetology, or the science of whales" (*MD* 135). The mere mass of information on cetology, in other words, does not necessarily imply humans know a great deal about whales. He adds ironically that of a long list of those who have written about whales, only a few have actually seen whales and only one is a professional whaleman. Thus, of all the many writings about whales, "there are only two books in being which at all pretend to put the living sperm whale before you, and at the same time, in the remotest degree succeed in the attempt" (135). So, supposedly valid authority is not necessarily reliable in the process of classification that Ishmael is about to embark on; of those who have tried it before him, the experts could not do it and the nonexperts should not have tried. As well, the authority that seemingly validates the various classifications is primarily a text-based authority—it is grounded not so much in the physical body of the whale as it is in the canon of perceptions of amateur cetologists that have chosen to comment on the whale.

After these remarks in the first few pages of "Cetology"—remarks that have already established the very real possibility that his project is doomed to at least partial failure—Ishmael finally does begin to lay out a possible classification system. Immediately, however, he runs into a fundamental problem that retards his progress just as he is getting underway: it is still not clear in cetology if whales are fish or not. Rather than offering some resolution to this problem, Ishmael instead cedes to tradition and invokes a pseudoauthority as so many others left with no other recourse have done before him: "I take the good old fashioned ground that the whale is a fish, and call upon holy Jonah to back me" (*MD* 136). He then refines his classification of whales even more by distinguishing them from other fish by their "obvious externals" (137)—concrete appearance, he reminds the reader, always being the first basis of classification.

Once this issue of whether or not the whale is a fish has been settled, Ishmael decides on external appearance as the basis for distinguishing different types of whales. The arbitrary nature of Ishmael's initial criteria for his system of classification is underscored by the fact that he tellingly chooses to label his categories with the names of different types of books, with chapters as in a book being used for the subdivisions within each category. The literariness of these categories stresses the constructed, artificial, even fictive nature of the divisions that Ishmael will establish: he is forced to borrow a classification system from a completely different field because there is no system inherent within the body of the whale itself.

Even within the "literary" categories for whales that he thus finally establishes, there exists, as Ishmael tells the reader, no firm basis for determining one distinct subcategory from another. For example, Ishmael's first category of whales includes the sperm whale, an important category because, of course, Moby Dick is himself a sperm whale. After cataloguing many of the names by which this type of whale is known—the variety of names itself implying a certain indeterminacy of identification—Ishmael remarks with regard to the sperm whale's name that "Philologically considered, it is absurd" (*MD* 138), and this absurdity originates in past uncertainties over the whale's identification.

In the next category—that of the right whale—he once more records the indefiniteness of the category, saying that "There is a deal of obscurity concerning the identity of the species thus multitudinously baptized" (*MD* 138). Ishmael next describes of the finback whale and seems at first to at least have this category well defined because of the finback's prominent and distinctive fin. But after investigating the finback more thoroughly, he concludes that all categories based on external characteristics such as the fin are actually suspect:

> It is in vain to attempt a clear classification of the Leviathan, founded upon either his baleen, or hump, or fin, or teeth; notwithstanding that those marked parts or features very obviously seem better adapted to afford the basis for a regular system of Cetology than any other detached bodily distinctions, which the whale, in his kinds, presents. . . . [T]hese are things whose peculiarities are indiscriminately dispersed among all sorts of whales, without any regard to what may be the nature of their structure in other and more essential particulars. (140)

These external characteristics—even those as singular as a fin on the back of a whale—lack the consistency that they at first appear to have and thus "they form such irregular combinations . . . as utterly to defy all general methodization formed upon such a basis" (140). So in spite of earlier indications in the chapter, Ishmael finally rejects external appearance as a reliable basis for the classification of whales.

He next considers a classification based "in the internal parts of the whale, in his anatomy" because "there, at least, we shall be able to hit the right classification." But he must quickly admit that not even internal characteristics can be used to establish clear-cut distinctions between whales. Finally, Ishmael concedes that he can proceed to classify whales only on the basis of size because this method of categorization is "the only one that can possibly succeed, for it alone is practicable" (*MD* 140).

With this finally determined, Ishmael proceeds over the next few pages to categorize several different types of whales by size. An insidious subjectivity undercuts once again this seemingly objective description, however, when Ishmael adds one more section to the chapter. In this he mentions a "rabble of uncertain, fugitive, half-fabulous whales, which, as an American whaleman, I know by reputation, but not personally" (*MD* 144). This last admission makes Ishmael's whole schema seem tentative. These uncertain, fugitive whales will always lurk beneath the surface of the whole categorization, and the reader can only suppose that Ishmael's detailed system would need to be revised yet again if one of these other whales were to emerge. The possibility of this occurrence seems open given Ishmael's last comment in the chapter. He says that all he has laid out in "Cetology" is unfinished and will remain so: it is, along with all of *Moby-Dick,* "but a draught—nay, but the draught of a draught" (145).

This long, detailed account in "Cetology" of cetological methodology seems, even by Melvillean standards, well drawn out. Since the narrator, even after pages of this methodological wrangling, reaches no exact conclusions and succeeds only in undermining his own legitimacy as a cetologist, one is led to consider the chapter as above all else a self-referential event—one that calls attention to the rules of its own making via its striking surface texture. Literally, the chapter attempts to establish a system of classification for whales; rhetorically, however, it ends up primarily establishing the futility of the whole process of establishing a system of classification. Its implicit message seems clear: the process of categorization—of making sense of any set of natural data—becomes an artificial, arbitrary, subjective exercise in hopelessness. One can still try it, of course—Ishmael and hundreds of others before him are testimony to that—but the fact remains that establishing an accurate, objective, meaningful order among things is always a necessarily flawed enterprise.

Ishmael, then, uses the same basic data as the other cetologists that have gone before him but arrives (if one can call it that) at a different classification of whales than they have—a different interpretation, that is, of the data that the whole cetological community shares. The discrepancy between Ishmael's results and those of his cobiologists results from a lack of innate "meaning" in whale data that would automatically organize itself a certain way or congeal into its own categories—no *a priori* classification that Ishmael need merely discover or read. As Melville expresses it in *Pierre*, "Say what some poets will, Nature is not so much her own ever-sweet interpreter, as the mere supplier of that cunning alphabet, whereby selecting and combining as he pleases, each man reads his own peculiar lesson according to his own peculiar mind and mood" (*Pierre* 342). When whale data does somehow get organized into categories though—as it does in the "Cetology" chapter—then this happens as a result of choices made by some erratic, fallible, organizing agent. Ishmael's attempt to classify whales in "Cetology," then, thematizes the slipperiness of the project of classification, showing any categorization of objective data to be a product of human intervention rather than nature.

THE THEMATIZATION OF RACIAL ISSUES IN *MOBY-DICK*

"Cetology" posits the extreme difficulty of establishing firm systems of classification; the rest of *Moby-Dick* demonstrates how that lesson relates to human as well as leviathan society—in particular, to the project of racial differentiation and stereotyping. If, as "Cetology" demonstrates, the classification of whales is a nonobjective process in spite of whales' external or anatomical differences and similarities, then surely—*Moby-Dick* implies—the classification of human beings into races proves equally problematic and nonexact in spite of our own apparent differences and similarities.

Recent critical work on the concept of race in literature has reinforced the idea that what we think of as "race" is actually, in a biological sense, an artificial, arbitrary classification. Henry Louis Gates Jr., for instance, writes that the idea of "race" as it is generally used is—despite its pretensions to objective classification—in fact a dangerous trope, no more than a figure of speech or metaphor that substitutes for characteristics that we choose to apply to a certain person or group of people.[7] Anthony Appiah approaches this issue in part from the biological perspective and details how modern scientists have concluded that, in scientific terms, no such thing as "race" actually exists, and that the word refers to nothing that science recognizes as meaningful or real.[8] The problem, however, as he acknowledges, is that theories of race continue to hold sway in our culture independent of their lack of validity from a scientific perspective, and that these still-accepted ideas of race presuppose the still-continuing fact of racism.[9]

In *Moby-Dick* itself, Ishmael's gradual realization that Queequeg and the other dark-skinned harpooners on the *Pequod* are noble human beings demonstrates both this social fact of racial prejudice and its potential instability as an intellectual concept. Ishmael, in other words, comes to learn empirically the truths about racial categorizations that he demonstrates in his chapter on cetology and that contemporary research now reinforces: that social differentiations based on ideas about race are relatively arbitrary, and that in reality human beings who happen to differ in skin color still possess far more similarities between them than dissimilarities.

Ishmael first encounters one of these foreign whalers when he is assigned early on in the novel to bunk with Queequeg at the Spouter Inn. Even before he meets his roommate for the night, Ishmael admits that "I could not help it, but I began to feel suspicious of this 'dark-complexioned' harpooneer" (*MD* 15). This confession to the reader is sincere, but seems tinged with racism, especially given the typographical emphasis on Queequeg's skin color.

Ishmael's first impressions when Queequeg enters the room at night are no less negative. Though he attempts to remind himself when he spies his roommate's tattoos that "It's only his outside; a man can be honest in any sort of skin" (*MD* 21), fear and prejudice soon overtake him once more. He quickly decides that "It was now quite plain that he must be some abominable savage or other," and Queequeg's nightly religious ritual further convinces him that this stranger "must indeed be a heathen" (22). Ishmael, for all his best intentions, appears near the beginning of *Moby-Dick* to be a prejudiced man with very well-defined notions of race based both on external physical characteristics and religious background.

Despite his initial prejudice, however, Ishmael gradually begins to see Queequeg as an equal and to realize that his previously biased classification of him was unfounded. Though at first he makes little progress toward this end—"For all his tattooings he was on the whole a clean, comely looking cannibal," he remarks—Ishmael starts to give Queequeg and his friends the benefit of the doubt after he comes to know them better, although his crescendoing compliments do sound patronizing at times. His direct contact with these harpooners convinces him, for instance, that "these savages have an innate sense of delicacy, say what you will," and that "it is marvellous how essentially polite they are" (*MD* 27).

Ishmael's first step toward erasing the racism and racialism he unwittingly prescribes to occurs when he begins to look past the color of Queequeg's skin to his other physical features. He observes after watching Queeugueg for a time that "Savage though he was, and hideously marred about the face . . . his countenance yet had a something in it which was by no means disagreeable" (*MD* 49). Though his initial praise seems only indirect, Ishmael imputes other positive characteristics to more of Queequeg's features: "Through all his unearthly tattooings, I thought I saw the traces of a simple honest heart; and in his large, deep eyes, fiery black and bold, there seemed tokens of a spirit that would dare a thousand devils" (49–50). Ishmael's most generous (though strained) comparison relates to the shape of Queequeg's "phrenologically excellent" head: "Queequeg was George Washington cannibalistically developed" (50).

In these comparisons, Ishmael assumes that certain physical characteristics connote related internal characteristics—assumptions not based on anything other than his own romantic imaginings. More importantly, however, as a result of his direct experience with Queequeg, he begins to move away from race-based assessments in his judgment of him. In fact, on the passage across to Nantucket, Ishmael is smugly amused by the other passengers who see him and Queequeg together and "who marvelled that two fellow beings should be so companionable; as though a white man were anything more dignified than a whitewashed negro" (*MD* 60). The comparison itself is somewhat odd, but Ishmael seems to subscribe now to a true equality between himself and his new friend, and discounts skin color as a valid or meaningful way of distinguishing between them.

Several other scenes in *Moby-Dick* show the bonds between Ishmael and Queequeg being strengthened and Ishmael moving closer to discounting race as a valid classification between human beings. One occurs in Chapter 72 where Ishmael describes his feelings when Queequeg was lowered to work on a captured whale. The two of them were tied by a "monkey rope"—a sort of umbilical cord connecting Queequeg to Ishmael and assuring Queequeg's safety as he worked. Ishmael comments on the arrangement that "for better or for worse, we two, for the time, were wedded," and then experiences a moment of intimate companionship with his friend: "while earnestly watching his motions, I seemed distinctly to perceive that my own individuality was now merged in a joint stock company of two." Here Ishmael extrapolates from this particular friendship to an awareness of the bonds that unite all humans independent of race: "every mortal . . . has this Siamese connexion with a plurality of other mortals" (*MD* 320).

The crew members attain the same universal companionship as they near the final chase at the close of *Moby-Dick*. Ishmael writes that "They were one man, not thirty. For as the one ship that held them all; though it was put together of all contrasting things—oak, and maple, and pine wood; iron, and pitch, and hemp—yet all these ran into each other in the one concrete hull" (*MD* 557). These shipbuilding materials act as metaphors for the wide racial diversity of men found on the *Pequod*, and the trope stresses the uniting in a common purpose of the ship's disparate personalities. Ishmael completes the comparison, however, not by indicating that the metaphor refers to the different races of men found on the boat. Instead, he bases his classification of the different sailors on their different personality types independent of race: "all the individualities of the crew, this man's valor, that man's fear; guilt and guiltlessness, all varieties were welded into oneness, and were all directed to that fatal goal which Ahab their one lord and keel did point to" (557).

By the climax of the novel, then, Ishmael has shunned the prejudiced, classification of humanity based on skin color that characterized his thoughts and feelings during his first encounter with Queequeg. He has learned onboard the *Pequod* that the dark-skinned harpooners that had once disgusted and alienated him are human beings similar to himself, and that classifications based on race are vulnerable to change when one is forced to live, work, and fight for survival with others from different nations or cultures. Ishmael's attempt to classify whales in "Cetology" was doomed from the start; hopefully, the racism that presupposes classifications of human beings by race will likewise be doomed as we all work and live together on our own personal *Pequod*s.

Notes

1. Cited in Lloyd Spencer and Andrzej Krauze, *Introducing Hegel* (New York: Totem Books, 1996), 31.

2. Cited in Michel Foucault, *The Order of Things: An Archeology of the Human Sciences* (New York: Vintage Books, 1970), xv.

3. Carl Rollyson and Lisa Paddock note that Melville also pokes fun at pedants in his two satirical opening sections "Etymology" and "Extracts" at the beginning of *Moby-Dick*. *Herman Melville A to Z: The Essential Reference to His Life and Work* (New York: Checkmark Books, 2001), 125.

4. Foucault admittedly employs this Borges citation to introduce a more crucial point—that no "space" exists in which all of these categories can be juxtaposed, or that in each age a certain set of underlying ideological conditions make some thoughts and ideas possible and others not possible. He writes in this regard that "The monstrous quality that runs through Borges's enumeration consists . . . in the fact that the common ground on which such meetings are possible has itself been destroyed. What is impossible is not the propinquity of the things listed, but the very site on which their propinquity would be possible. . . . He does away with the *site*, the mute ground upon which it is possible for entities to be juxtaposed" (xvii).

5. This particular chapter is just one of several digressive, cetology-based chapters that collectively comprise much of the middle section of the novel. When scholars refer to these sections as "Cetology," they generally group all these chapters together and not just Chapter 32 of the novel. Elizabeth Duquette notes that this cetology section of the novel has received a great deal of critical attention of late and is the basis for a kind of philosophy of digression employed by Melville in the novel ("Speculative Cetology"). Lawrence Buell also discusses the novel's cetology chapters and describes how this section repeatedly moves from factual material about whales and whaling into more metaphorical and mythological subjects ("*Moby-Dick* as Sacred Text").

6. Ishmael's lighthearted introduction to cetological classification in this chapter indirectly signals to the reader that the chapter should be read with an eye to the subtle, sophisticated

irony that Melville often employs when addressing issues above and beyond the text's literal meaning. For a complete discussion of Melville's use of humor within the broader context of nineteenth-century American comic writing in general, see John Bryant, *Melville and Repose*.

7. Henry Louis Gates Jr., intro., in *"Race," Writing, and Difference*, ed. Henry Louis Gates Jr. (Chicago: Univ. of Chicago Press, 1986), 5–6.

8. Anthony Appiah, "The Uncompleted Argument: DuBois and the Illusion of Race," in *"Race," Writing, and Difference*, 21–37. See also Anthony Appiah, "Race," in *Critical Terms for Literary Study*, ed. Frank Lentricchia and Thomas McLaughlin (Chicago: Univ. of Chicago Press, 1990), 277.

9. Anthony Appiah, *In My Father's House: Africa in the Philosophy of Culture* (New York: Oxford Univ. Press, 1992), 19.

"Kings of the Upside-Down World"

Challenging White Hegemony in *Moby-Dick*

SUSAN GARBARINI FANNING

A lthough "Benito Cereno" is recognized by Melville scholars as Melville's first portrayal of black revolt against white oppression, the author's earlier fiction displays an increasing boldness in its representation of nonwhite characters. Not surprisingly, this boldness corresponds to the rising antislavery sentiment in American society. As more Americans began to question the institution of slavery and theories of racial difference, Melville's depiction of nonwhites became more brazen, developing from the relatively nonthreatening Polynesians found in *Typee* to the deceptive and menacing figure of Babo in "Benito Cereno."

Melville's view of blacks has long been a subject of debate among critics. Arnold Rampersad has noted how Melville's inconsistency in his writing and indirect, muted approach to his themes have posed a special challenge for scholars attempting to pinpoint his attitudes on race. Harry Levin, commenting upon Melville's inclination to support "brotherhood between the races," notes that in "Benito Cereno" the author "seems ready to concede that life is a blood-feud," underscoring a separation that exists between blacks and whites (190). In contrast, Milton Stern, writing of Melville's depictions of Polynesians and Europeans in *Mardi*, argues that the author does not differentiate between the two: "The Polynesian and European are distinct faces of the same being" (108). Some scholars take a more cautious approach to Melville's views on race. For example, Priscilla Allen Zirker writes that there is an "ambivalence" in Melville's representation of Negro characters in *White-Jacket* (written two years prior to *Moby-Dick*) and in "the final qualifications of the egalitarian theme of the narrative." She argues that Melville's "implicitly apologist stance grew out of his fear of the delicate question of slavery," and that his ambivalence "was not a conscious effect that he recognized and recreated with artistic detachment as it was when he wrote 'Benito Cereno' in 1856, but the symptom of an ideological contradiction which he had yet to resolve" (482, 485–86). Edward S. Grejda writes that throughout his fiction, Melville appears to condone rebellion, whether by whites or nonwhites, when the individual's natural rights have been denied. He admits, however, that Melville's depictions are "neither overt nor entirely consistent"; rather, they reflect the author's "growing social and cultural awareness, a movement from misconception to awakening consciousness to realistic judgment," and emerge from Melville's evolving awareness "of the fundamental sameness of all human kind" (10, 11).

Melville's representations of nonwhites throughout his fiction reflect his conscious career-long effort to decenter national prejudice regarding race difference. This idea expands upon an earlier contention made by Carolyn Karcher in *Shadow over the Promised Land: Slavery, Race and Violence in Melville's America* that slavery and race are themes of vital importance in Melville's fiction (xi). Melville's "decentering" of racial prejudice appears to reach subvolcanic intensity in *Moby-Dick*. By manipulating the satiric device of the "symposium," or feast, and usurping the linguistic consciousnesses of black Fleece and Pip, Melville exposes the tenuous foundation of a hegemonic structure based on race domination. He also reveals the threat posed by revolution should America fail to emancipate and embrace her bondsmen. Through the use of irony, parody, grotesque material, bodily imagery, and what Mikhail Bakhtin terms the "inappropriate word" (cursing abuse), Melville challenges "official truths," allowing conflicting viewpoints to surface in the text. This loosening of the gag on black speech mimics America's democratization. In a series of subtle "crownings" and "uncrownings" in *Moby-Dick,* the slave is often installed as the master, symbolically reversing the hegemonic structure.

DINNER IS SERVED

Melville uses the satiric device of the feast to level hierarchy—a tactic he may have learned from observing African American commemorative celebrations such as the Pinkster Festival during his childhood days in Manhattan and Albany. Sterling Stuckey suggests the likelihood that Melville witnessed many of these colorful displays, including the Emancipation Day Parade in New York City on July 5, 1827, noted for its jubilant spirit of celebration and license among African Americans marching in the procession and applauding it from the sidewalks (39). Melville's extensive reading of Rabelais prior to writing *Moby-Dick* would have apprised him of the aesthetic possibilities that use of the feast convention afforded an author. According to Bakhtin, in classical and medieval periods, official feasts were (as they usually still are) serious in nature: they reinforced a society's established hierarchy. Although these feasts emphasized stability, where points of crisis were relegated to the past, an author could subvert that stability, using the feast scene to invert hierarchy often by repositioning himself in the role of feast giver within the narrative framework. In the free banquet atmosphere, the lowest characters are thrust within elbow's range of the most exalted ones, stripping away normal codes of etiquette, in doing so suspending the entire notion of hierarchical rank. As a result, "comic crownings and uncrownings occur" and an uninhibited truth can be spoken.[1]

While his narrator Ishmael does not physically preside over the "feasts" described in *Moby-Dick,* Melville has other surrogates at his disposal. The first "official" feast occurs in "The Cabin Table" (ch. 34) and is attended exclusively by whites, where the curious dinner ritual of the *Pequod's* officers is described. The white steward Dough-Boy announces dinner to his "lord and master" (Ahab). After a moment's inattention, Ahab calls out, "Dinner, Mr. Starbuck." Starbuck deferentially lingers on deck until Ahab disappears, then calls to Stubb (identified here as the "second Emir") before he, too, disappears. Stubb, also waiting a respectful interval, calls out to Flask. However, as Flask waits for Stubb to descend, the restraint of this "third Emir" evaporates, preparing the reader for a more raucous scene to follow. Flask "winks" at the crew, performs a silent "hornpipe right over the Grand Turk's head" and descends, "reversing all other processions, by bringing up the rear with music." Only at the cabin threshold does clownish Flask don his ceremonial mask, and he "enters King Ahab's presence, in the character of Abjectus, or the Slave." The meal itself is highly ceremonial and ritualistic: "Ahab presided like a mute, maned sea-lion on the white coral beach, surrounded by his war-like but still deferential cubs." The narrator wryly remarks, "For, like the Coronation banquet at Frankfort, where the German Emperor profoundly dines with the Seven Imperial Electors, so these cabin meals were somehow solemn meals, eaten in awful silence" (*MD* 149–51). Speech is gagged and no threat of revolution can arise, for Ahab presides over his table as portentously as a king or slaveholder. The officers seated at Ahab's table participate in a hierarchy; each accepts his rank without protest, consuming his portion of the spoils, however small it might be. Flask's portion is quite small, like that of Sancho Panza in *Don Quixote,* who as "governor" of a feast also goes hungry, as Howard Vincent has pointed out (143).

Sharply contrasted with this official feast is the "care-free license and ease, the almost frantic democracy of those inferior fellows the harpooneers" (*MD* 152) displayed at the same table after Ahab and his officers have withdrawn. In *Moby-Dick,* these men appear to be successors to the Maori harpooneer Bembo Melville depicts in *Omoo,* who as disfranchised figure is described as a "dark, moody savage," one noted for his ferocious disposition (71). Such figures held a fearful place in the white imagination during the antebellum period, for they conjured associations of free black seamen who sailed aboard maritime vessels and roamed the port cities. Such individuals were regarded with suspicion by Southerners in particular, for they conversed freely with slaves and were believed to be responsible for inciting the latter to run away or rebel.[2] The turbulent feasting of the harpooneers in *Moby-Dick* parodies Ahab's silent, austere banquet. These dark-skinned men are also described as "lords," but of a savage variety. They eat with gusto, "chew[ing] their food with such a relish that there was a report to it." Queequeg's lip-smacking terrifies pale Dough-Boy, the only white present, who waits on their table as he did the others' (152, 153).

Hierarchy is in this manner turned upside down, for a white servant now serves dark masters. When the harpooneers grow impatient with Dough-Boy's sluggish service, Tashtego pricks him in the back with a fork. The narrator recounts that Daggoo once lifted the steward over a trencher while the knife-wielding Tashtego made mock preparations to scalp him. The Gay Head Indian, also as a joke, threatens to pick Dough-Boy's bones, terrorizing the white steward and foreshadowing a more grisly shipboard scene that Melville would later depict in "Benito Cereno." Whereas in the latter story the image of Don Aranda's exposed skeleton evokes horror, events in this cabin scene are more restrained; a sense of comedy diffuses the violent undercurrent of Dough-Boy's mock uncrowning. Also, here it is not a black menacing the white with weapons, but a Native American. Melville seems to use extreme caution in testing his audience. Hierarchy may be overturned in the second cabin scene, but this is done subtly, perhaps because Melville sensed that his American readers would reject outright the image of blacks ascendant over whites.

Melville more boldly repositions himself as "feast-giver" in "Stubb's Supper" (ch. 64). By blurring material bodily images of the masticating Stubb with those of the ravenous sharks eating the whale, and by usurping the linguistic consciousness of the black cook Fleece, Melville decenters the white hegemonic structure, showing the steep price to be paid for the society's regeneration. Fleece is the last in a line of black ship cooks in Melville's novels. Richard Chase, F. O. Matthiessen, Eleanor Simpson, and Edward Stone have viewed Stubb's scenes with Fleece as humorous.[3] This seems a natural reaction, since the old cook seems no different from the stereotypical butts of humor in the burlesque black minstrel show, a popular type of entertainment during Melville's youth. However, despite the cook's comical, minstrel-like entry on deck, with a "shambling," "shuffling and limping" gait caused by "his knee-pans, which he did not keep well scoured like his other pans" (*MD* 294), Fleece differs greatly from his cook predecessors in Melville's fiction. As Grejda has noted, Fleece's "sulking and occasional balking at Stubb's commands set him apart from the completely docile Baltimore" in *Omoo;* "his swearing distinguishes him from the pious Mr. Thompson" in *Redburn;* "and he lacks . . . the jolly good spirits of Old Coffee's assistants" in *White-Jacket.* Fleece also has a more serious function than do the other cooks, Grejda asserts, which is to indict white racism (105–06).

Melville goes to great lengths to disguise his satire. Marsha Vick writes that Fleece's sermon is presented as "a type of riddle," and that Melville throws the reader off balance by staging the sermon on the deck of a whale ship instead of in a church, by infusing the black cook's speech with profanity, and by having him deliver his address to a shoal of sharks instead of humans (335). As Stuart Woodruff and Howard Vincent both have noted, Melville establishes with the image of the feasting sharks a man-shark analogy, and Melville's anger appears to be directed against the cannibalism of the slave system.[4] Significantly, the individual who appears to be the object of attack in the scene (Fleece) actually functions as the agent of attack against the true object of Melville's satire (Stubb and white society's viciousness toward blacks).

Clearly, Fleece is Melville's first full-blooded black character to openly express rancor against white oppression. Stubb asks Fleece where he was born, and the cook testily replies, "Hind de hatchway, in ferry-boat, goin' ober de Roanoke" (*MD* 296). Fleece's birth in "Roanoke country," not far from Southampton County, Virginia, site of the Nat Turner slave insurrection, links him with the cradle of black rebellion in America. Fleece's birth in a ferryboat further associates him with the theme of rebellion, for Charon, the ferryman of Hades, is a stock figure of Menippean satire. Charon, along with interlocutors such as Menippus and Diogenes, engages in dialogues with proud and often royal deceased personages, and as a result of these encounters hierarchy is overturned, with kings and noblemen being reduced to the level of slaves—a grim irony of existence in the "democracy of death." Fleece's language, despite its occasional piety, violates accepted norms of speech, and this points to its similarity with Menippean satire. His invective, what Bakhtin terms the "inappropriate word," liberates the black cook from all constraints of normal manners of speech that would mask a corruption as something acceptable. Fleece's sermon may appear to teach the lesson of *caritas,* but at heart, it emerges as a malediction against white Americans for their depraved treatment of blacks.

In spite of—or perhaps because of—his degradation by Stubb, Fleece attains power through speech. Leaning out over the whale carcass, he resembles the black minister or "black Angel of Doom" Ishmael recounts seeing in the black church in New Bedford in "The Carpet-Bag" (ch. 2). However, instead of presiding over a "great Black Parliament sitting in Tophet" like the minister in that church, who presumably was exhorting his congregation to improve their morals while awaiting deliverance from bondage, Fleece addresses the congregation of tail-smacking, flesh-tearing sharks. His sermon reflects a black evangelical rather than a white evangelical Christian outlook, for as C. C. Goen explains, the black evangelical Christianity of the antebellum period was sharply distinguished from white evangelical Christianity by the former's absence of "naïve assumptions about the goodness and perfectability of human nature." Black ministers not only condemned individual immorality, but also prophesied God's punishment of those who oppressed and exploited the weak. To black ministers, "Slavery was 'the work of Satan,' destined to be overcome as decisively and dramatically as God had delivered the Hebrews from Egyptian bondage."[5] Fleece similarly harbors no innocent assumptions about the goodness and perfectibility of human nature. Curbing curse words that rise to his tongue, Fleece exhorts the sharks to display charity toward their brethren: "Don't be tearin' de blubber out your neighbour's mout. . . . Is not one shark good right as toder to dat whale?" He forgives them for their "wicked natur," something that "can't be helped," yet exhorts them to display temperance, for their lack of self-control bars them from attaining perfection: "You is sharks, sartin; but if you gobern de shark in you, why den you be angel; for all angel is not'ing more dan de shark well goberned" (*MD* 295). Through this animal metaphor, Melville raises the dilemma that for post-Adamite man, government is an evil necessity.

The implication of Fleece's sermon is illustrated in the image of Queequeg striking at the sharks with his whaling spade in "The Shark Massacre" (ch. 66), which immediately follows. This bloody scene reveals the consequence of humanity's lack of self-government. Frenzied by the whale's spilled blood, the sharks "viciously snapped, not only at each other's disembowelments, but like flexible bows, bent round, and bit their own; till those entrails seemed swallowed over and over and over again by the same mouth, to be oppositely voided by the gaping wound" (*MD* 302). Queequeg's action with the spade, combined with Fleece's words, reveals the delicate balance between power and liberty, hinting that the restoration of moral right often necessitates the use of violence. Melville's illustrative parallel may have been inspired by similar examples found in political writings of the Revolutionary era. For example, in Hector St. John de Crèvecoeur's *Letters from an American Farmer,* the author illustrates government's role in harnessing humanity's passion and greed through the image of James verbally warning and occasionally striking quail on his farm who quarrel over food. In another more startling episode from the work, pacifist James shoots a king-bird who steals honey from a bee hive, Crèvecoeur's allegory for the conflict created by the Revolution: the king-bird symbolizes the English tyrant attempting to steal from the colonist (bee) the fruits of his labor (honey). Crèvecoeur's animal metaphors vividly illustrate the dilemma that civil war created for peace-loving colonists who wished to steer clear of partisan conflict. James's actions with his stick and gun suggest that in certain instances, brute strength is required to preserve one's liberty and natural rights. Black abolitionist leaders gradually came to embrace the same view as the American Civil War loomed closer. According to Geneviève Fabre, by the 1850s, African American orators and ministers had shifted their emphasis in speeches and sermons from a focus on self-improvement of their race in anticipation of citizenhood to a reverence for "new symbols" related to power—"black warriors here, rebels or fugitives there"—thus stressing not the weakness of blacks but their roles as "diligent historical actors."[6]

The horrific image of the flesh-tearing sharks also recalls similar images in Rabelais relating to the lower bodily stratum. In a famous scene in *Gargantua and Pantagruel,* Gargamelle, after eating too much tripe following the slaughter of 367,014 oxen, suffers the falling out of her own right intestine. Bakhtin writes of this image, "The limits between animal flesh and the consuming human flesh are dimmed, very nearly erased. The bodies are interwoven and begin to be fused in one grotesque image of a devoured and devouring world. One dense bodily atmosphere is created, the atmosphere of the great belly" (*Rabelais and His World* 221). In the case of Rabelais, however, these images of material bodily effluence possess a regenerative force (as indicated by Gargantua's birth immediately following his mother's mishap). Such grotesque imagery is multivalent, for the lower region of the body connotes both death and regeneration. While oaths and gestures could degrade an object, banishing it downward "to the absolute bodily lower stratum . . . to be destroyed," abuses and mocking gestures could also serve a regenerative function, for they allow new forms of language—and life—to rise in their place (*Rabelais and His World* 28). This imagery is ultimately positive, for it is associated with rebirth and the future.

Melville's use of such material images in *Moby-Dick* is more ambivalent, for it focuses on the destructive, death-creating aspect of the shark's action. Fleece's anger has the intensity of a black abolitionist preacher who excoriates the larger white society for its wickedness in oppressing its weaker black members. His final "benediction" dims any hope of the goodness and perfectibility of human nature: "Cussed fellow-critters! Kick up de damndest row as ever you can; fill your dam' bellies 'till dey bust—and den die" (*MD* 295). Fleece's invective may find a precedent in conversion legends, for as Janez Stanonik has noted, various Franciscan stories show St. Francis of Assisi cursing animals for their voracious, violent propensities (56). However, Fleece's shifting back and forth between respectful language and praise of the sharks and cursing abuse as he is baited by Stubb has a comical effect and seems more typical of the billingsgate abuse found in Rabelais, the kind of rhetoric Bakhtin terms "a two-faced Janus . . . ironic and ambivalent" (*Rabelais and His World* 164–65). Such abusive expression, found in popular-festive carnival speech, reflects "the struggle against cosmic terror and every other kind of fear of superior powers" and is "precisely directed against the superior powers of the sun, the earth, the king, the military leader" (*Rabelais and His World* 352). Despite Fleece's billingsgate idiom, one can hardly detect any glint of regeneration in the image of the self-devouring sharks. His final malediction toward the white mate Stubb, whom he refers to as "Massa"—"Wish, by gor! whale eat him, 'stead of him eat whale. I'm bressed if he ain't more of shark dan Massa Shark hisself" (*MD* 297)—reinforces the connection between the sermon's underlying message and slavery, as Vick has noted (336–37).

Fleece's name further reinforces this association, for in medieval writings the behavior of animals was invested with an allegorical significance: lambs were equated with Christ, and predators such as wolves were equated with rapacious men (Stanonik 57). Melville appears to play with this medieval convention, for the predatory sharks serve as appropriate analogues for man's murderous nature and Fleece's name associates him with the lamb, a symbol of Christ. Therefore, while Fleece's alternating praise and abuse of the murdering and murdered sharks and his hope that Stubb's meal (a whale) will eventually ingest Stubb himself could potentially be charged with a generative force, heralding a past that gives birth to the future, it emphasizes the destruction and death that must accompany such a historical cataclysm. A few may survive, but countless will fall as casualties, and no progeny will follow. Melville illustrates, through grotesque material bodily imagery and use of the "inappropriate word," that liberty and natural right cannot be taken for granted. Should humanity fail to restrain its own base impulses, revolution and perhaps extinction for all will result.

Ironically, the diminutive black ship-keeper, Pip, the lowest of the low in the *Pequod*'s hierarchy, makes some of the most searing pronouncements on race and revolution. Described by one critic as playing "Fool to Ahab's Lear" (Eleanor Simpson 30), the "gloomy-jolly" Pip exemplifies Melville's use of the ancient clown figure to overturn existing hierarchy. Depicted with his jangling tambourine, Pip of Alabama seems as much a minstrel stereotype as Rose-Water, May-Day, or Sunshine of *White-Jacket*. Yet Pip's isolated and lowly position as black shipkeeper gives him an ideal vantage point from which Melville can denounce the corruption of a hegemonic structure built upon race. Interacting with what are presumed to be superior intelligences aboard the *Pequod*, Pip reveals the false basis of an ideology of whiteness and obliquely prophesies the catastrophe that awaits America for the victimization of his race. Further, Pip's encounters with Ahab symbolically invert the master-slave relationship, signifying a historical uncrowning.

In "The Castaway" (ch. 93), Pip contrasts with a white counterpart: Dough-Boy, the steward. Dough-Boy has a politically loaded name, for the term "dough-face" referred to a Northern politician opposed to the Wilmot Proviso—in short, a defender of slavery.[7] In contrasting the black shipkeeper with the white steward, Melville delivers a blow to this ideology: "In outer aspect, Pip and Dough-Boy made a match, like a black pony and a white one. . . . But while hapless Dough-Boy was by nature dull and torpid in his intellects, Pip, though over tender-hearted, was at bottom very bright" (*MD* 411). The reader concludes that Dough-Boy is dim, Pip is intelligent, and contemporary theories of race and intelligence are thus shattered with one stroke. Melville's narrator crab-steps, however, quickly diluting his praise of Pip's intelligence. The boy's brightness was "that pleasant, genial, jolly brightness peculiar to his tribe; a tribe, which ever enjoy all holidays and festivities with finer, freer relish than any other race. For blacks, the year's calendar should show naught but three hundred and sixty-five Fourth of Julys and New Year's Days" (411–12). Yet, the narrator emphasizes his earlier point: "Nor smile so, while I write that this little black was brilliant, for even blackness has its brilliancy" (412).

Melville has exposed the black boy's brilliance and adroitly disguised it behind the stereotypical "jolly brightness" a nineteenth-century reader might reflexively ascribe to the dark race; and while the narrator's mention of the black's love of holiday spirit should not stir alarm, the two holidays he identifies—the Fourth of July and New Year's Day—had special importance to African Americans, as they were associated with black emancipation. July

4 celebrations stirred particular controversy in the black community, since the tenets of the Declaration did not include the slave population. After 1827, July 5 emerged as a day of "counterceremony" for blacks in New York and other cities, because on that day the 1799 and 1817 gradual emancipation laws went into effect and slavery was abolished.

New Year's Day also carried great importance for African Americans, since it commemorated the abolition of the slave trade on January 1, 1808, and became an occasion of great feasting and speeches made for emancipation. The Pinkster Festival, with its procession, music, dancing, and freedom banners, was closely linked with rituals of January 1 (Fabre 79). Melville was familiar with the carnival spirit associated with Pinkster, and his narrator's remark in *Moby-Dick* that blacks should be granted riotous license every day of the year may actually be a covert sanction of revolution. The horrific image later described of Pip entangled in the whale-line after jumping from a whale boat serves as a grim pantomime of the black race's tenuous position in human history. Like a newborn fetus nearly strangled by its umbilical cord, Pip's predicament illustrates the "stillbirth" of American blacks, their abandonment by the society. Pip's idiocy following this accident serves as an indictment of White America. As Louise K. Barnett writes, "Cut off from all community when a society that places little value on his life abandons him, Pip dramatizes the connection between membership with a group and speech by his inability to speak thereafter in a recognizable idiom"(141).

Yet a close study of Pip's seemingly unintelligible speech reveals Melville's satiric purpose. Pip's brightness, as lurid as Ahab's insanity, "in the end was destined to be vividly illumined by strange wild fires, that fictitiously showed him off to ten times the natural lustre" with which he previously shone (412). Pip, in his abnormal psychological state, looms as a clown or fool, the ancient stock figure of satiric literature. The fool is an ambivalent figure, what Bakhtin defines as king of the upside-down world, the satirist's key agent in challenging official ideology.[8] As Rabelais, Shakespeare, and other Renaissance authors were aware, the clown or fool figure is not mad or dim-witted; on the contrary, his "stupidity" is a tactic used to expose falsehood, often in the supposedly superior intelligence of his interlocutor. This stock figure can be found in ancient literature of all cultures and appears in the Roman Saturnalia in the form of various servants or slaves who serve as comic doubles to the ruler or master.[9] The fool exposes the sordid aspect of human life, and his object of attack is usually a society's feudal structure, for such a structure transcends limitations of time: hierarchy exists in human relations in all historical periods. The fool derives his privilege partly from his connection with the common people. Straddling a barrier between two realms, he is "in life, but not of it, life's perpetual spy and reflector." The fool figure therefore allows for the "repositioning of the author," enabling the latter to assume the disguise of a peasant, slave, minstrel, or jester and to cry out against falsehood with abandon ("From the Prehistory" 161–62, 160, 159).

Acquainted with the fool-device from his reading of ancient and modern satire, Melville uses Pip's voice, along with Fleece's, to project his own authorial intentions. Melville's stratified discourse serves as a battleground for conflicting points of view expressed within the text. "The Forge" (ch. 113) emphasizes Pip's connection with the fool: the narrator exclaims, "Oh, Pip! thy wretched laugh, thy idle but unresting eye; all thy strange mummeries not unmeaningly blended with the black tragedy of the melancholy ship, and mocked it" (MD 490). Melville's pun—"black tragedy"—reveals the true object of Pip's attack: a social hierarchy built upon race domination.

In "The Doubloon" (ch. 99), Pip's intelligence flares more brightly in his torrent of seemingly unintelligible speech. Ahab has nailed the gold doubloon to the mainmast, a reward for the man who first raises Moby Dick. On the doubloon is engraved the name "Republica Del Equador: Quito" and the image of three peaks: one bearing a flame, another a tower, and the third a crowing cock. The signs of the zodiac are also visible, "with the keystone sun entering the equinoctial point at Libra" (MD 431). Kathleen E. Kier has pointed out that no such South American coin exists, and she speculates that Melville modeled this doubloon on the "onza" (ounce) of Ecuador (see Kier, entry for "Doubloon"). Yet, Ahab remarks that "this round gold is but the image of the rounder globe, which like a magician's glass, to each and every man in turn but mirrors back his own mysterious self" (431). An American reader, therefore, might regard the doubloon as a symbol of the American republic. As Ishmael explains, this coin has been minted in "a country planted in the middle of the world, and beneath the equator" and "midway up the Andes, in the unwaning climate that knows no autumn." Inverting this geographical reference, the reader might envision the United States in place of Ecuador. The image of the sun hovering over Libra suggests to Ahab, at least, that they are entering the period of storms; however, the orb's alignment with Libra's scales of justice suggests that some divine judgment is to be made. Ahab believes that the "firm tower," the "volcano," and the "victorious fowl" symbolize himself. However, to black Pip, reduced to the level of a slave, the tower serves as apt symbol of the proud slave republic that holds him prisoner; the fire the volcanic rebellion that is about to burst; and the crowing cock the birth of a new day, a new nation.

But a new nation for whom?

Stubb eavesdrops on the various crew members who peer at the gold piece, each articulating his own interpretation of its significance. When the speechless Queequeg steps forth, Stubb lampoons what he guesses to be the harpooneer's interpretation. Like a complacent slaveholder, he miscalculates the implication of Queequeg's comparison of the sun on the doubloon with the tattoo on his thigh. The Polynesian's remark is a highly symbolic gesture, for by comparing the sun with his thigh (groin) area, Queequeg has invested himself with the power of regeneration. Yet, even the unfearing, disrespectful Stubb is unnerved by the "half horrible" sight of Pip's "unearthly idiot face" as the latter speaks: "I look, you look, he looks; we look, ye look, they look . . . And I, you, and he; and we, ye, and they, are all bats; and I'm a crow, especially when I stand a'top of this pine tree here. Caw! caw! caw! caw! caw! caw! Ain't I a crow? And where's the scare-crow? There he stands; two bones stuck into a pair of old trousers, and two more poked into the sleeves of an old jacket" (*MD* 434–35). It is unclear whether Pip detects the second mate's presence nearby. Melville, however, makes his satiric thrust: in a reversal of power, the "crow" (black Pip) chases away the "scare-crow" (white Stubb), the latter mumbling that Pip is "too crazy-witty for [his] sanity" (435). This leaves Pip alone on deck facing the doubloon. The fact that this diminutive black boy is granted the final speech in the scene suggests that Pip's interpretation of the coin's symbolism has ascendance over all other interpretations. Pip's "muttering," as Stubb terms it, reveals apocalyptic flashes of black liberation ideology:

> Here's the ship's navel, this doubloon here, and they are all on fire to unscrew it. But, unscrew your navel, and what's the consequence? Then again, if it stays here, that is ugly, too, for when aught's nailed to the mast it's a sign that things grow desperate. Ha, ha! old Ahab! the White Whale; he'll nail ye! This is a pine tree. My father, in old Tolland county, cut down a pine tree once, and found a silver ring grown over in it; some old darkey's wedding ring. How did it get there? And so they'll say in the resurrection, when they come to fish up this old mast, and find a doubloon lodged in it, with bedded oysters for the shaggy bark. Oh, the gold! the precious, precious gold!—the green miser 'll hoard ye soon! Hish! hish! God goes 'mong the world blackberrying. Cook! ho, Cook! and cook us! Jenny! hey, hey, hey, hey, hey, Jenny, Jenny! and get your hoe-cake done! (435)

Pip's description of the men "all on fire to unscrew it" may be Melville's allusion to a joke that if you unscrew your navel your bottom will fall off.

However, in terms of the bodily grotesque, this image illustrates the desperate attempts made by the nation's leadership, as represented by the *Pequod*'s officers, to reverse the historical cycle that has brought them to this impasse.

Pip wonders how can one "unscrew" a "navel," yet he concludes that leaving an ulcerous scab, as symbolized by the doubloon, seems equally unthinkable. The black boy's insistence that the White Whale will "nail" Ahab hints that the nation's captains will be crucified for the national sin. Pip's cryptic description of the old darky's wedding ring embedded in the trunk of a tree looms as a metaphor for the Founding Fathers' aborted pledge to America's black population. The image of the ring and tree may be derived from Tom Paine's important symbol in *Common Sense:* Paine warned that in "the seed-time of Continental union," any fracture among the colonists would be "like a name engraved with the point of a pin on the tender rind of a young oak; the wound will enlarge with the tree, and posterity read it in full grown characters."[10] The fact that Pip's father was from "old Tolland County" in Connecticut and Pip comes from Alabama, both states where slavery was legal, suggests that successive generations of the black race are regressing further into slavery, despite their hopes for emancipation. Like this silver ring, America's covenant with all her citizens—black included—has been buried in the living wood of the growing republic. The gold coin nailed to the *Pequod*'s mast represents a false covenant, one based on greed, profit, and the cannibalization of the black race. However, it is a doomed covenant, as suggested by Pip's prediction that "the green miser" (green moss) will soon "hoard" (hide) the gold when it lies fathoms below in the sea on Judgment Day. In the meantime, America's blacks will continue to suffer, as Pip's pun, "God goes 'mong the world blackberrying," would indicate. A new political order eventually will emerge, but black lives will be sacrificed in the process.

For all his seeming pessimism, Melville does leave glints of hope in *Moby-Dick* that regeneration is possible. Much (and many) will be sacrificed if the black race is to gain its proper place in the society, but this sacrifice is necessary and inevitable. In "The Log and Line" (ch. 125), the Manxman foreshadows this impending upheaval with his remark that "the skewer seems loosening out of the middle of the world" (*MD* 521), and for Ahab this proves true. When Ahab rebukes the Manxman for his rejection of black Pip and offers his hand to the black boy, saying, "Here, boy; Ahab's cabin shall be Pip's home henceforth, while Ahab lives. Thou touchest my inmost centre, boy; thou art tied to me by cords woven of my heart-strings. Come, let's down" (522), Pip's response contains both praise and abuse. His query while examining Ahab's hand—"What's this? here's velvet shark-skin"—jolts the reader back to the sinister reality of their relationship. Ahab's words to Pip as he leads the boy down to his cabin,

"Come! I feel prouder leading thee by thy black hand, than though I grasped an Emperor's!" (522) have a deep irony, for they herald Ahab's own uncrowning and the mock crowning of black Pip. In "The Cabin" (ch. 129), Ahab tells Pip that "[t]he hour is coming when Ahab would not scare thee from him, yet would not have thee by him. . . . Do thou abide below here, where they shall serve thee, as if thou wert the captain. Aye, lad, thou shalt sit here in my own screwed chair; another screw to it, thou must be" (534–35). Melville's symbolism clearly conveys his point: in a mock ritual imitating the uncrowning of a ruler, Ahab, the deposed king, has installed his servant as the new ruler. Black Pip is left sitting on Ahab's throne, imagining himself a great admiral hosting a feast for "white men with gold lace upon their coats" (535).

Melville's views toward slavery, as they surface in *Moby-Dick*, seem far more pronounced than critics have previously noticed. The supposition that Melville harbored an ambivalence toward the darker race can be called into question; Zirker's contention that Melville's representations of blacks was "implicitly apologist," originating from his reluctance to offend slavery's defenders and "an ideological confusion which he had yet to resolve," is unconvincing (485). Similarly, Grejda's attribution of Melville's shifting portrayal of nonwhite characters throughout his fiction—from the "noble savage" and "jolly minstrel" stereotypes to more complex individuals—to the author's own evolving awareness of the humanity of blacks is also hard to accept. On the contrary, careful study of Melville's rather crafty portrayal of blacks in *Moby-Dick* suggests that he was acutely aware of what he was doing and calls for a closer scrutiny of the nonwhite characters who appear in his earlier fiction as well. Melville's exposure to African American culture and emancipation celebrations during his boyhood and his interaction with black seamen aboard maritime vessels as a young adult would have apprised him of blacks' humanity, intelligence, and desire for equality, if not supremacy. If Melville's portrayal of blacks and nonwhites in *Moby-Dick* or elsewhere in his fiction seems ambivalent, it may be less the symptom of a psychological or ideological confusion on his part than a sign of his conscious and cautious testing of his American readers—what they were and were not yet prepared to contemplate in the figure of the black. As notions of innate white supremacy were increasingly questioned by Americans, Melville's representation of the restless darker race grows more audacious, and the subtle uncrownings and liberation of black speech in *Moby-Dick* clear the way for the terrifying image of the hatchet-wielding Ashantee who finally looms forth in "Benito Cereno."

Notes

1. Mikhail Bakhtin, *Rabelais and His World*, trans. Hélène Iswolsky (Bloomington: Indiana Univ. Press, 1984), 9–11, 285.

2. W. Jeffrey Bolster, *Black Jacks: African American Seamen in the Age of Sail* (Cambridge, Mass.: Harvard Univ. Press, 1997), ch. 7; and Philip Hamer, "Great Britain, the United States, and the Negro Seamen Acts, 1822–1848," *Journal of Southern History* 1 (Feb. 1935): 3–28.

3. Chase, *Herman Melville*, 85; Matthiessen, *American Renaissance*, 431–32; Simpson, "Melville and the Negro"; and Stone, "The Other Sermon," 217, 220–21.

4. Woodruff, "Stubb's Supper," 46, and Vincent, *Trying Out*, 233.

5. C. C. Goen, *Broken Churches, Broken Nation: Denominational Schism and the Coming of the Civil War* (Macon, Ga.: Mercer Univ. Press, 1985), 162.

6. Geneviève Fabre, "African-American Commemorative Celebrations in the Nineteenth Century," in *History and Memory in African-American Culture*, ed. Fabre and Robert O'Meally (New York: Oxford Univ. Press, 1994), 87.

7. Louis Filler, *The Crusade against Slavery, 1830–1860* (New York: Harper and Brothers, 1960), 95; and Herbert D. A. Donovan, *The Barnburners* (New York: New York Univ. Press, 1925), 100.

8. Bakhtin, *Rabelais and His World*, 81–84; and "From the Prehistory of Novelistic Discourse," in *The Dialogic Imagination: Four Essays by M. M. Bakhtin*, ed. Michael Holquist (Austin: Univ. of Texas Press, 1992), 58.

9. Bakhtin, "Forms of Time and Chronotope in the Novel," in *Dialogic Imagination*, 159.

10. Thomas Paine, *Common Sense: On the Origin and Design of Government in General, with Concise Remarks on the English Constitution in Writings of Thomas Paine*, ed. Moncure Daniel Conway (New York: Burt Franklin, 1969), 1:85.

"So Spanishly Poetic"

Moby-Dick's Doubloon and Latin America

Rodrigo J. Lazo

n much of Melville's fiction, from *White-Jacket* (1850) to "Benito Cereno" (1855), narrators write about Latin America's terrain, people, and history. At times, allusions push readers to excavate either their own knowledge or consult reference books for grounding in the geography and history of the area. Such is the case in *The Confidence-Man* when the embarking and disembarking of passengers on the *Fidèle* is likened to the "Rio Janeiro fountain, fed from the Corcovado mountains, which is ever overflowing with strange waters, but never with the same strange particles in every part" (*CM* 8). In *The Encantadas, or Enchanted Isles,* the pseudonymous Salvator R. Tarnmoor is fascinated by the Galápagos Islands, their topography, animals, legends, and visitors, and he luxuriates in his own enchanting point of view. Melville's references begin to explain why Gabriel García Márquez, one of numerous Latin American writers who have expressed interest in Melville, dropped him into a scene in the historical novel *The General in His Labyrinth.*[1] As Simón Bolívar's mistress, Manuela Sáenz, waits out the end of her life in the whaling port of Payta, Peru, she takes consolation in a visit from Melville, "who was wandering the oceans of the world gathering information for *Moby-Dick.*"[2] The incident, Hershel Parker argues, is fictional (1:203). Melville's interest in Latin America, however, is real. His texts repeatedly touch on places and people along South America's Pacific coast.

But his narrators do not offer facile representations. More often, they refuse readers a mimetic sense of the locales in question. Instead, they tease out multiple meanings offered by Latin American contexts and depict the inability of Latin America's visitors to move beyond subjective interpretations and limitations in perspective. Readers are often pushed in the direction of Amasa Delano, who cannot make sense of Benito Cereno and thus figures, "to the Spaniard's black-letter text, it was best, for awhile, to leave open margin" (*PT* 65). Such uncertainties connect Melville's epistemological concerns to nineteenth-century U.S. efforts to understand the southern Americas, which held remarkable material resources for U.S. investors. Melville questions a person's ability to make sense of territories to the south of the United States in light of stereotypes about Latin Americans that circulate in U.S. society. The doubloon scene in *Moby-Dick* underscores the challenges of interpreting Latin America.

Melville composed most of his fiction during a period when Latin America occupied a central place in U.S. political debates and foreign policy questions. The U.S.-Mexico War and Treaty of Guadalupe Hidalgo placed Mexico and its people on the front pages of newspapers on a daily basis. In the wake of that war, debates raged in the U.S. Congress over moves to annex Cuba as a state. And the limits of expansionism became a topic of discussion in periodicals when filibusters such as William Walker attempted to seize territories to the south of the United States.[3] These events were accompanied by the publication of numerous histories, ethnographies, and travel accounts of the region. In *Moby-Dick,* Ishmael does not attempt to elude the discursive constructions of Latin America circulating in the mid-nineteenth century. Instead, his discussions of Latin America raise questions about representations of the region, a process exemplified in the chapter "The Doubloon." Ishmael, like other narrators in much of Melville's fiction, is concerned about cultural difference, if not as reality, definitely as a discursive formation that has real effects on the way people view the world and relate to one another.

The first section of this essay proposes that many of Melville's narrators complicate the assumptions of difference (as in racial difference, for example) by replicating stereotypical assumptions and then questioning them. Melville's work can be considered alongside and against Charles Wilkes's narrative of an exploration expedition funded by the U.S. government, a multivolume work that Melville used as a source. The essay then moves toward a reading of the doubloon in relation to Latin America by focusing on the coin's imagery and the responses of those aboard the *Pequod* who react to it. In this manner Melville calls on those who read Latin America in the nineteenth-century United States to resist facile conclusions about the region. This call continues to be relevant today, and thus the essay concludes by relating "The Doubloon" to contemporary efforts to complicate a North-South binary in the study of Latin America.

Moby-Dick approaches difference by playing with stereotypes and raising questions about them. On the one hand, Don Pedro and Don Sebastian can come off as clownish mechanisms for the telling of "The *Town-Ho*'s Story." "Nay, Señor; hereabouts in this dull, warm, most lazy, and hereditary land, we know but little of your vigorous North," Pedro replies to Ishmael's explanation of the word "Canaller" (*MD* 248). But even as Melville's fiction ridicules Catholicism and some inhabitants of Latin America, it does not begin to approximate the downright offensive descriptions in Richard Henry Dana's imperialist manuals *Two Years Before the Mast* (1840) and *To Cuba and Back: A Vacation Voyage* (1859). If anything, Don Pedro returns to close the initial assertion of a gap between the conventions and mores of North and South, proclaiming, "The world's one Lima. I had thought, now, that at your temperate North the generations were cold and holy as the hills" (250). Pedro questions two depictions circulating in the mid-nineteenth century United States: one that associates Spaniards with Catholic corruption and another that connects weather in southern regions to physical dispositions. For example, on his visit to Havana, William Cullen Bryant writes, "That there is something in a tropical climate which indisposes one to vigorous exertion I can well believe, from what I experience in myself, and what I see around me."[4] By proclaiming the world one Lima, Pedro calls attention to his earlier irony in describing people of the region as lazy. This demonstrates a classic strategy of Melville's narrators—to set up the stereotype, and then force the narrator and/or reader to recognize the problems of his or her own Delano-like acceptance of those views.

The doubloon scene exemplifies the way Melville replicates stereotypes but turns away from the fixed descriptions and language of management that are so much a part of travel writing, exploration narratives, and scientific descriptions of Latin America. Eric Wertheimer has argued that Melville's treatment of Darwin in *The Encantadas, or Enchanted Isles* calls attention to the gap between the imperial gaze of scientific study and representative history on the one hand and objective reality on the other. Wertheimer writes, "Melville opposes the objective 'realness' of racial inferiority and, in so doing, refuses the nostalgic position in historical progress, and declines as well a condescending faith in the virtues of romantic savageness and imperial mapmaking."[5] More intriguing, though, Melville's narrators embrace something like "romantic savageness" and other such traps. "Benito Cereno" contains many racial stereotypes and characterizations of the Latin American world. The ironic discovery at the end puts Amasa Delano's perspective in check. But the story's antiessentialist conclusion, its calling into question Delano's bias, does not eliminate the circulation of those perspectives. A lack of objective reality, the story tells us, does not make the perceived differences of terrain and people less real. Therefore in Latin American contexts, Melville's narrators show enthusiasm about and even take pleasure in their own illusions and delusions, even when they are reluctant to claim certainty in what they see. How else can one explain the proposition that the doubloon's South American engravings bring "added preciousness and enhancing glories" (*MD* 431)?

Melville's narrators simultaneously embrace and reject stereotypical representations of Latin American people and territory circulating in the 1840s and 1850s. Melville was familiar with and used as a source an imposing apparatus of representation, Charles Wilkes's five-volume *Narrative of the United States Exploring Expedition during the Years 1838, 1839, 1840, 1841, 1842* (1845), which came with an atlas in a sixth volume. In 1847 Melville bought a twenty-one-dollar copy of this impressive set of octavo-sized volumes that included plates and drawings (Sealts 102). Mary K. Bercaw lists Wilkes as a source for numerous texts, including *Moby-Dick* and *The Confidence-Man* (130). The expedition was a remarkable assemblage of six ships and more than 650 men, some of whom were picked up along the way, and included a botanist, mineralogist, taxidermist, naturalist, philologist, and artist. It departed from Norfolk and rounded South America, stopping at Rio de Janeiro, the Antarctic area, Valparaiso, and Lima, then moved to the South Pacific via the Fiji Islands and Hawaii before journeying back to California and out again to Japan. The expedition was commissioned and paid for by the U.S. Congress, "having in view the important interests of our commerce embarked in the whale-fisheries." The letter to Wilkes instructed him to "determine the existence of all doubtful islands and shoals, [so] as to discover and accurately fix the position of those which lie in or near the track of our vessels in that quarter, and may have escaped the observation of scientific navigators."[6]

Wilkes's *Narrative* provides an example of what Melville, in addition to his own observations during travel, was working with and against in his library. Wilkes's expedition narrative provides extensive descriptions of various parts of the globe. Opening with the letter of commission and a list of all the expedition participants, the set of books presents the material collected in a methodical and thorough manner. The narrative exemplifies the nexus of the political, commercial, and scientific interests of the United States in the regions visited. In addition to geographic details, the narrative includes drawings of "natives," descriptions of local customs, and discussions of flora and fauna. At times, it even shifts into historical narrative, as when it discusses post-independence political events in South America under a chapter heading titled "Self-aggrandizement the Object of Rulers" (1:283). "In the beginning of the year 1827," the book tells us, "the Peruvians, through their intrigues, effected a revolt among the Colombian troops, who made prisoners of their officers, put an end to the authority of the Dictator Bolivar, and freed Peru from the presence, as well as the expense, of foreign troops" (1:285–86). Such passages create a view of governmental processes in Chile and Peru as torn by the individual-political interests of generals. One could say that Wilkes's narrative seeks to "discover and accurately fix" not only geographical details but also people, whether in government leadership positions or living in rural communities, who come under the gaze of the expedition party.

Melville's complex presentations of Latin American scenarios prevent a facile equation of literary text with expedition account or travel article. In other words, an analogy between Melville's texts and Wilkes's *Narrative of the United States Exploring Expedition* within a discursive field proves inadequate for considering the workings of either text. Similarly, Amasa Delano's *A Narrative of Voyages and Travels in the Northern and Southern Hemisphere* (1817) served as a source for "Benito Cereno," but it differs radically in terms of tone and narrative conventions from Melville's work. Without delving into the way different genres offer different perspectives, we can see that Melville's narrators do not possess the certainty of Wilkes, and Wilkes does not display the humor of Melville's narrators. Nor does Melville offer up Latin American places and people as objects that can be easily known. "Ask me not, Señor," Hunilla repeats twice. The metaphysical anxieties of the chola widow remain unknown; as the narrator of *The Encantadas, or Enchanted Isles* concludes, "The half shall here remain untold" (*PT* 157). Instead of offering certainties, Melville uses references to Latin America to develop the questions of his fiction. Nevertheless, neither he nor anyone in the nineteenth-century United States can escape representations like those that appear in Wilkes's books.

Melville's narrators run directly into such representations. For example, Melville appears to draw from Wilkes for his reference to the *saya y manta* in "Benito Cereno." Wilkes offers an extended discussion of the saya y manta during the expedition's visit to Lima, saying, "however fitted it may be to cover intrigue, [it] is not, certainly, adapted to the display of beauty" (1:237). He goes on: "Intrigues of all kinds are said to be carried on under it" and "In this dress, it is said, a wife will pass her own husband when she may be walking with her lover, and the husband may make love to his wife, without being aware it is she" (1:238). Only after expressing this gendered anxiety about women's ability to move clandestinely in public does Wilkes offer a description of the actual articles of clothing, the manta being a "kind of cloak . . . brought over the head and shoulders from behind, concealing every thing but one eye" (1:238). The earlier proposition that what goes on behind that outfit is difficult to decipher is overwritten at the end of the section by a sentence that purports to manage gender through clear-cut description: "The walk of the Lima ladies is graceful and pretty, and they usually have small feet and hands" (1:238).

When Melville picks up on the saya y manta as a metaphor in "Benito Cereno" he does so in the context of Captain Delano's limited vision. As the *San Dominick* enters the harbor at the island of Santa Maria, "a small, desert, uninhabited island toward the southern extremity of the long coast of Chili" (*PT* 46), the ship, breaking through low-creeping clouds on the horizon, "showed not unlike a Lima intriguante's one sinister eye peering across the Plaza from the Indian loop-hole of her dusk *saya-y-manta*" (*PT* 47). Although he might have seen such a sight during his visit to Lima, Melville's use of the word "intriguante" appears to pick echo Wilkes's repetition of "intrigue" to describe the wearing of this outfit. But while Wilkes offers description and ultimately a judgment of the women under the saya y manta, Melville marshals the outfit as foreshadowing that even as Delano reads Benito, Babo is reading Delano. There's no telling who is behind the saya y manta. Ultimately, the sense of distrust that Wilkes associates with the person within the saya y manta is turned on the reader himself, who must distrust his or her own vision of events in the story. "Benito Cereno" also reminds us to distrust Wilkes, for he might well be missing the point of who, if anyone, can be rightly described as sinister.

The process of looking and being looked at, reading and being read, in a Latin American context is a central concern in "The Doubloon." This chapter has drawn the attention of Melville critics interested in the question of interpretation. Samuel Otter has discussed "The Doubloon" scene in relation to ethnographical encounters and the nineteenth-century quest to make sense of racial difference (168–71). Otter emphasizes Ishmael's investment in the physical features of the coin and subsequent readings into the self that prevent access to the meanings of those features. The presence of Pip, Fedallah, Queequeg, and Ahab, among others, indeed brings forth race and ethnicity as dimensions of this reading encounter. But the doubloon highlights another kind of difference, one between regions, both territorial and cultural. The doubloon, whatever it ends up being, starts out as an object of Quito. Even before the engravings on the coin are described, the gold is characterized as coming out of "the heart of gorgeous hills" (*MD* 431), and even within the rustiness of the *Pequod,* the coin preserves its "Quito glow." In other words, the coin retains not only its glow but the ways Quito has marked that glow. Precisely that Quito glow "set[s] apart" the coin from the temporal specificities of the *Pequod,* the ruthless hands and the passing from dark to light. Time changes the *Pequod* and its crew, but not the doubloon, at least not before the sinking of the ship. Every sunrise sees the coin where it was left before, as if the crew is unwilling or unable to touch it.

The doubloon's distinctness is elaborated in the paragraph on "fancy mints," which exemplifies the way Melville's fictions can offer a broad and stereotypical vision of the southern Americas: "Now those noble golden coins of South America are as medals of the sun and tropic token-pieces. Here palms, alpacas, and volcanoes; sun's disks and stars; ecliptics, horns-of-plenty, and rich banners waving, are in luxuriant profusion stamped; so that the precious gold seems almost to derive an added preciousness and enhancing glories, by passing through those fancy mints, so Spanishly poetic" (*MD* 431). In this paragraph the doubloon is placed within a continental context, part of South American production tied to the sun and tropics. "Here" can refer to the southern hemisphere, for the palms could be Caribbean as well as South American, while alpacas and volcanoes tie the coins to the Andes or, more generally, volcanic chains that stretch northward into Mexico. In this case, the engravings, the various signs of the southern Americas, create a luxuriant profusion. The gold, then, is infused with an added preciousness, the result of a kind of colorful view that emerges in banners and horns filled with goods. The mints are not just utilitarian but "fancy," for they stamp a value on ornate engravings as well as the monetary value of the coin. The process of commodity production unites raw material and labor to give the mints an added preciousness. To Ishmael, at least at first, those enhancing glories are the effect of the poetic style of Spanish America.

"Spanishly poetic" has numerous connotations. On the one hand, Spanish America is an operative term for the region in the mid-nineteenth century, so "Spanishly" can be taken as a regional reference. Melville's texts sometimes interchange the more generic "Spanish" or "Spaniard" for a specific place or national affiliation. But "Spanish" has cultural connotations, and thus the doubloon can be read as a cultural object. "Poetic" could refer to the poetry or poetic sounds of the Spanish language, for Melville read both Spanish and Portuguese. His editions of the Spanish dramatist Pedro Calderón de la Barca and the Portuguese poet Luis de Camões contain marked passages in both English and Spanish (Sealts 46–47). Saying that something is Spanishly poetic after referring to palm trees, alpacas, and other southern markers imbues the doubloon with an exotic sense. For readers in New England in the 1850s, a palm tree is an exotic plant. "[T]he royal palm looks so intensely and exclusively tropical!" writes Dana in *To Cuba and Back.*[7] This tropical sense of the exotic, tied to regional and cultural difference, gives value to the doubloon in Ishmael's initial reading.

In terms of narrative sequence, Ishmael is the first to take a stab at the doubloon. The doubloon begins to change even before we move to the second reader. While Ishmael ties it to South America and Spanish culture, he complicates that link quickly by introducing a particularity of place. The doubloon is, he tells us, more specifically a coin from the "Republica Del Ecuador: Quito" (*MD* 431). The inclusion of these capitalized words emphasizes the coin's national connection. And here the term "Spanish" breaks down in the face of wars of liberation that have partitioned the continent into republics. In a book-length, Spanish-language study, *Melville y el mundo Hispánico* (Melville and the Hispanic World, 1974), José De Onís argues that a series of objects in *Moby-Dick,* including the doubloon and the white whale, create an allegory of the U.S. pursuit of the Spanish Empire. Analyzing Melville's treatment of Spanish-language literature such as *Don Quixote,* De Onís frames his study in the broad strokes of the concept "Hispanic world." But Melville's fiction questions the very designation of the Hispanic, or Spanish-American, world as a unitary entity. While Melville's texts use designators such as "Spaniard" or "Spanish," they also call attention to places and people as discrete entities in particular historical circumstances and geographic locations. Melville seems all too aware of the anticolonial dimensions of these national projects, and thus the "Quito glow" of just two paragraphs before now takes on another dimension, that of Quito, the capital of a country, Ecuador, and this in turn brings forth a more specific location than that in the phrase "noble golden coins of South America."

Stubb continues to challenge a regional association of the doubloon when he contemplates it in relation to coins from other countries. He differentiates between coins of "old Spain," a preindependence realm, and those of Chile and Peru. The *Pequod*'s doubloon differs from those of other countries, Stubb argues, thus further destabilizing the earlier association of the doubloon with South America. Ishmael is aware of the differences between old Spain and new; in the chapter "The Advocate," he notes that whalemen affected the liberation of Latin American countries from Spain and the "establishment of the eternal democracy in those parts" (*MD* 110). Stubb moves the reading outside the markers of culture and region into a more abstract realm of "signs and wonders." And furthermore, he breaks down the North-South difference by emphasizing that it is a "doubloon of the Equator." Here Stubb returns to Ishmael's point that "this bright coin came from a country planted in the middle of the world, and beneath the great equator, and named after it" (431). The repetition of "equator" echoes "Ecuador" on the coin's engravings.

In *Moby-Dick* and other Melville fiction, at the equator the constant weather affects how people view and read objects. In Chapter 29 the *Pequod* goes "rolling through the bright Quito spring, which, at sea, almost perpetually reigns on the threshold of the eternal August of the Tropic" (*MD* 126). Thus the equator connotes warmth and lack of change. The word "unwaning" reappears in the doubloon chapter when Ishmael says that the coin "had been cast midway up the Andes, in the unwaning clime that knows no autumn" (431). Such weather leads to effusive responses from those in the area. Ishmael, for one, perceives that "warmly cool, clear, ringing, perfumed, overflowing, redundant days, were as crystal goblets of Persian sherbet" (126). That flight of fancy recalls another equatorial location in Melville's fiction, the Galápagos Islands, where, Salvator Tarnmoor tell us, change never comes but enchantment does. And just as Tarnmoor is driven to extravagance in the telling of his excursion to the Galápagos, Ishmael finds that the constant weather the *Pequod* encounters at the equator lends "new spells and potencies to the outward world" (126). Thus Melville implies that the unchanging weather creates an atmosphere in which objects appear more enchanting than they would in a place where the weather changes. In the end, the *Pequod* holds "her path towards the Equator" and ends up in "Equatorial fishing-ground" (523) in search of the whale. Ahab suffers from an inability to resist the traps of the equator; he does not heed Ishmael's warning to "Be cool at the equator" (307).

Why the tension between equatorial calm and the perceptions of those who respond strongly in this latitude? This provides a key to Melville's reading of Latin America and, more generally, difference. The equator is a place between difference, between North and South. It is also a hot place because of its relative proximity to the sun, and thus it calls on people to remain calm and collected, to "retain, O man! In all seasons a temperature of thine own" (*MD* 307). To keep your cool can be read as a caution in the face of difference and change. But, as Ishmael points out, it is "hopeless to teach these fine things." Ahab is among those who cannot keep calm. When Starbuck makes a final appeal to return and enjoy summertime, equatorial-like "mild blue days" (544) in Nantucket, Ahab associates the mild wind and sky with the Andes: "they have been making hay somewhere under the slopes of the Andes, Starbuck, and the mowers are sleeping among the new-mown hay" (545). The Andes figure prominently in Ahab's mind because, per the doubloon, they lead back to himself.

The unchanging weather associates the Andes (like the Galápagos) with a temporal backwardness at odds with the progress of science. If change never comes to these places, then Darwinian science would have been interested in them because they have not been affected by "civilization." For nineteenth-century visitors to South America, the Andes offered sights both sublime and conquerable. Deborah Poole, among others, has pointed out that the Andes drew the attention of scientific explorers such as Alexander von Humboldt, historians such as William Hickling Prescott, and landscape painters such as Frederic Edwin Church. Church's painting *Heart of the Andes* (1859) was seen by twelve thousand people during the first three weeks of its exhibition in New York.[8] Poole associates the vision of Church's painting with Emersonian transcendental communion that grants a privilege to the seer and thus constitutes what she calls an "imperial subject." Certainly Church's painting, like much of the work of the Hudson River School, offers viewers an all-consuming perspective. *Heart of the Andes* presents a panorama that is simultaneously Amazonian, with dense vegetation at the front of the vista, and Andean, with snow-capped highlands in the back. The canvas, roughly six feet by twelve feet, offers a waterfall, majestic trees, a town next to a lake, local people praying at a cross, a house with a smoking chimney in the distance, and, behind it all, a white and icy mountain. Church used a common optical technique by painting the picture in a series of receding parallel planes (Poole 114–15). Moreover, the narrative of Wilkes's expedition contains textual portrayals of the Andes that include plates displaying the mountains and its people. Wilkes's first volume offered a comparable perspective to *Heart of the Andes:* the highest (white) peak in the background rises above darker mountains in the foreground that cross in a V-shape. The drawing of LaVienda Mountain in Peru by Alfred T. Agate positions the viewer along a road that appears to lead up to the seemingly unreachable snowy peak (Wilkes 1:257).

Moby-Dick, interestingly enough, alters the terms of such views by turning the gaze on the viewer or reader of the Andes. Given the source books at his disposal, Melville could have provided more developed description of Andean scenery. But unlike scientists and painters, Melville offers through the doubloon a double removal, a representation of a representation: "the *likeness* of three Andes' summits" (*MD* 431; emphasis added). The front cover of the collection *Moby-Dick as Doubloon* features a photo of an 1843 Ecuadorean eight-escudo piece that resembles Ishmael's description of the *Pequod*'s doubloon. That piece offers no realistic representation of the Andes, nor does it provide the receding planes (one mountain behind another) that appear both in Wilkes's book and in the Church painting. Ishmael's initial passage gives more attention to the three objects on top—a flame, a cock, and a tower—than to the mountains themselves. Ahab reads nothing but himself into those summits. Most importantly, *Moby-Dick* makes no particular pretense to capturing the Andes.

Ultimately, Melville presents the reader not Latin America but readings of an object, the doubloon, that could represent Quito. Keeping Latin America in mind, we could read the readings in this way. Ahab looks at the Andean peaks on the doubloon and sees the grandiosity of all "mountain-tops" a part of him within all (*MD* 431). He says nothing about Latin America and thus offers a perspective so truncated as to call attention to the limits of imperial vision. Starbuck looks at the Latin American scene but returns to a prior text, the Bible, and clothes the doubloon in the language of religion and metaphysics. His vision, like those of many Melville narrators, is affected by intertextual musings. Stubb severs the doubloon's connection to South America as a region, comparing it to coins of other nations, then pulls away from an association of the doubloon with nation to a more abstract sense of "signs." For him, the doubloon says more about the zodiac than anything else. Flask could well be the budding imperialist investor, who compares this object of Latin America to products that have exchange value. He sees the doubloon as a commodity that can be exchanged for cigars (possibly from Cuba). Thus Flask points toward a history developing in the mid-nineteenth century, that of U.S. and English exploitation of Latin America's resources. Queequeg draws a connection between himself and the doubloon; the relationship resides in a cultural and regional difference. Others would read him as they read the people and places of Latin America. Or so Stubb would have us believe. We never hear from Queequeg on this point. He is either a silent reader, or Stubb cannot hear him. The same goes for Fedallah, for all we get is Stubb's reading of him as a "fire worshipper" bowing to the sun on the doubloon. (The other fire worshipper is, of course, Ahab, whose inability to keep his cool under the equatorial sun will get him killed.) Queequeg's and Fedallah's readings remind us of the sad fact of imperial conquest and missed cultural connections, which come with readings unknown and readings imposed.

Pip, of course, complicates the entire process of reading the doubloon by calling into question all of the readings, and even all future readings. Like the crowing cock on the Andean summit, he becomes a harbinger of another time, another dawn when the doubloon will be raised from the bottom of the ocean. What will be left? "Oh, the gold! the precious, precious gold!" (*MD* 435). Does that mean the markings that add their own form of preciousness will be erased? Is the doubloon's regional association with Latin America a temporal engraving that in time will be washed away under the depths of the ocean? Pip implies that only the substance of the coin remains, so that an interpretation is always contingent on a reader in time. When we fall for the spell of the doubloon, we tease out meaning, but that meaning cannot remain static. One of the doubloon's lessons is that those who read representations of the people and places of Latin America will encounter uncertainty at the end of an interpretive process.

The reader of the doubloon ends up in a comparable position to the reader of the *The Encantadas*, for those who take Tarnmoor's enchanted narrative at face value end up in the inscrutability of a rock. And just as *The Encantadas* lead nowhere but to the clinker, Melville's references to people, objects, and places in Latin America often take the reader to an epistemological stopping point. The reader of Latin America gets caught in the trap of imposing meaning on the region only to find that the meaning is contingent on a particular moment. The message for those who engage with Latin America is that you will look, but meaning will be intertwined with a variety of circumstances. If we take Pip seriously, then we can no longer talk about Latin America but must begin to question this thing we call Latin America, and consider how we impose meanings.

"The Doubloon" serves as a fine introduction for reading (readings of) Latin America in the nineteenth century as well as today. Melville's doubloon, like his inscription of Latin America in general, is relevant to a growing critique of regional representation in the fields of area studies. What kinds of assumptions influence people to view a part of the world as a region, and what are the implications of such a perspective in terms of power relations? Melville calls attention to the limits of documents published about Latin America in the nineteenth century and how they offered ideological representations circulating in their day. And Melville can also tell us much about how representation and the attendant ideologies of difference (sometimes marked in terms of superiority) circulate in the nineteenth century and today. In recent years, area studies have come under scrutiny in part because they support a view of the world based on self and other. In the case of U.S.-based Latin American studies, books and articles about the region are intricately tied to questions of domination and information management. Latin American studies as a field grew tremendously during the cold war and particularly after the Cuban Revolution of 1959. Given the early history of U.S. imperialism in Latin America, of which Melville is all too aware, what is the effect of developing a regional view of a part of the hemisphere? These discussions can proceed without Melville, and they do as scholars debate what Alberto Moreiras has called "Latinamericanism," which he characterizes "as the set or the sum total of engaged representations providing a viable knowledge of the Latin American object of enunciation."[9] Latinamericanism fixes the meaning of objects, identities, and places in order to exert control over cultural difference and integrates them into a global capitalist order. Melville offers a historically contingent call for resisting that type of epistemic homogenization. But his call simultaneously reminds us that debunking the terms of difference will not make them go away. If anything, as the U.S. Latino population grows, the types of difference based on stereotypes and assumptions, which Melville encountered and countered in his fiction, will most likely become more abundant. The highly complex questions thereby raised are tied to contemporary debates over identity and who represents groups.

Integrating a Melvillean perspective into discussions of Latin America, particularly as they emerge in nineteenth-century texts, can help begin to break down the binary of the United States and Latin America, which gives rise to a view of the latter as a homogenous region that stands in contrast to a superpower. For a start, Melville's fiction prompts a reconsideration of the words we use to describe places in other parts of the world. "The Doubloon" chapter prompts us viewers of this place called Latin America to question our own assumptions, to interrogate how our own subjective experiences influence the way we infuse meaning into the world, and to note that the object at which we look can change depending on who is doing the looking. If *Moby-Dick*'s doubloon prompts us to consider the Andean region and its sociopolitical history, it also points to the epistemological constraints of reading difference.

Notes

I thank scholars who attended the panel on ethnicity and race at the "*Moby-Dick* 2001" conference for their comments and questions.

1. Another allusion to Melville occurs in Reinaldo Arenas's novel *El Mundo Halucinante,* when the protagonist is thrown overboard from a ship only to find himself on a whale "of the whitest color imaginable." Reinaldo Arenas, *The Ill-Fated Peregrinations of Fray Servando,* trans. Andrew Hurley (New York: Penguin, 1994), 49 (trans. of *El Mundo Halucinante*). See also Jorge Luis Borges's poem "Herman Melville," in *Selected Poems*, ed. Alexander Coleman (New York: Penguin, 2000), 376–77.

2. Gabriel García Márquez, *The General in His Labyrinth,* trans. Edith Grossman (New York: Knopf, 1990), 261.

3. In her biography of Melville, Laurie Robertson-Lorant offers an interesting connection between the filibuster William Walker, who tried to take over Nicaragua in the mid-1850s, and "slick operators" like the one in *The Confidence-Man* (362).

4. William Cullen Bryant, *Letters of a Traveller; or, Notes of Things Seen in Europe and America,* (New York: George P. Putnam, 1850), 358.

5. Eric Wertheimer, *Imagined Empires: Incas, Aztecs, and the New World of American Literature, 1771–1876* (New York: Cambridge Univ. Press, 1999), 138.

6. The instruction letter from the Navy, written by J. K. Paulding, was included among the opening documents of the *Narrative's* first volume. Charles Wilkes, *Narrative of the United States Exploring Expedition during the Years 1838, 1839, 1840, 1841, 1842,* 5 vols. (Philadelphia, Pa.: Lea & Blanchard, 1845).

7. Richard Henry Dana Jr., *To Cuba and Back,* ed. C. Harvey Gardiner (Carbondale: Southern Illinois Univ. Press, 1966), 47.

8. Deborah Poole, "Landscape and the Imperial Subject: U.S. Images of the Andes, 1859–1930," in *Close Encounters of Empire,* ed. Gilbert M. Joseph, Catherine C. LeGrand, and Ricardo D. Salvatore (Durham, N.C.: Duke Univ. Press, 1998), 108.

9. Alberto Moreiras, "Global Fragments: A Second Latinamericanism," in *The Cultures of Globalization,* ed. Fredric Jameson and Masao Miyoshi (Durham, N.C.: Duke Univ. Press, 1998), 86.

Dreaming a Dream of Interracial Bonds

From *Hope Leslie* to *Moby-Dick*

YUKIKO OSHIMA

Melville scholars consider it a common fact that the literary gathering in the Berkshire Mountains on August 5, 1850, was Herman Melville's first personal encounter with Nathaniel Hawthorne. I would like to propose that Melville's encounter the same day with Catharine Maria Sedgwick's novel *Hope Leslie* (1827) should be recognized as another important event.

Sedgwick was highly celebrated in the mid-nineteenth-century literary world, and her sentimental historical romance *Hope Leslie* was one of her best-selling works. The story takes place in Massachusetts in the aftermath of the 1636–1637 Pequot War. The Pequot were a tribe with a fearsome reputation. In *Moby-Dick*, Melville calls the Pequot "celebrated" (*MD* 69); in *Hope Leslie*, Sedgick writes: "the Pequod race, a name at which, but a few years before, all within the bounds of the New England colonies, English and Indians, 'grew pale.'"[1] With the help of the Pequots' Indian rivals, the British waged a preemptive attack on Mystic Fort, the tribe's major village-fort. The British and their Indian allies surrounded and set fire to the fort in a predawn surprise attack. Most of the Pequots—the number varies from four to eight hundred depending on the historian—died within an hour; the British, in contrast, lost only two men out of eighty. This was not an attack but a massacre.[2] The devastation of their major fortified village brought victory in subsequent battles to the British and official "extinction" to the Pequot.[3] As Sedgwick depicts in *Hope Leslie*, the survivors were systematically hunted down by hostile tribes and by the British, either to be killed or sold as slaves to other tribes or to the West Indies (*HL* 55).[4]

One of the heroines of *Hope Leslie* is a fifteen-year-old Pequot survivor named Magawisca. Her sachem father Mononotto, who was absent during the Mystic Fort attack, survives the war in shame. With other surviving warriors, he seeks shelter with the Mohawks; all except Mononotto are killed. Magawisca and her younger brother Oneco miraculously survive the Mystic Fort attack by hiding themselves beneath a rock with their mother. After the war, they are "given for a spoil to the soldiers" (*HL* 21) and live as servants with a white family, the Fletchers, in Boston. Such survival becomes possible under the instruction of Massachusetts governor John Winthrop, whose special mercy toward Magawisca and Oneco stems from the pro-white stance their father had taken even in opposition to other prominent sachem. Magawisca eventually comes to love the white boy Everell Fletcher.

Meanwhile, a strong feeling of sisterhood develops between the lively heroines of the novel, Pequot Magawisca and British Hope Leslie. Each girl willingly risks her life for the other, whereas most of the people around them harbor racist sentiments. Later Magawisca joins her father in the wilderness. He has failed to persuade the other tribes to unite and drive the British from American soil.

Catharine Sedgwick had many affinities with the literary group gathered together on August 5, 1850. In the afternoon, Melville, Nathaniel Hawthorne, Evert A. Duyckinck, Cornelius Mathews, Henry Sedgwick, Oliver Wendell Holmes, James T. Fields, Joel Tyler Headley, and others were led through Stockbridge's "Ice Glen," one of the settings in Sedgwick's first novel, *A New-England Tale* (1822). Earlier in the day some of the group had climbed up the hill to "Sacrifice Rock," the setting for a famous episode in *Hope Leslie*.[5]

Duyckinck wrote to his wife about afternoon tea, when the group, including Melville, was invited to the Sedgwicks' home, where a cross-examination on *Hope Leslie* took place. Duyckinck wrote: "Talk and tea and a tall Miss Sedgwick and a cross examination which I did not stand very well on Hope Leslie and Magawisca" (Leyda 385). Regardless of whether "stand" meant to understand or to endure, that this was a cross-examination that even Duyckinck did not "stand very well" suggests the depth of the argument. Melville must have felt a strong interest in this topic of cross-racial sisterhood in *Hope Leslie,* especially because of his creation of the Ishmael-Queequeg bond in his work-in-progress, *Moby-Dick.* Even if Melville had not yet read Sedgwick's novel, he probably read it soon after. At the very least, Melville had some knowledge of *Hope Leslie* while he was working on *Moby-Dick* from listening to this cross-examination.

Among critics, only Laurie Robertson-Lorant has touched on the possible connection between the two novels. The relationship of Ishmael and

Queequeg, Robertson-Lorant writes, "probably owes more of a literary debt to the blood sisterhood of Hope Leslie and Magawisca than to the stilted friendships between Indians and settlers in James Fenimore Cooper's novels of the frontier" (246–47).

Duyckinck reported to his brother on August 7, 1850, that "Melville has a new book mostly done" (Leyda 385), yet *Moby-Dick* was not finished for almost a year after that. Scholars have suggested various reasons for Melville's rewriting of his almost-complete work, such as his meeting and subsequent discussions with Hawthorne and his rereading of Shakespeare. In this essay I propose another: the possible influence of *Hope Leslie* on *Moby-Dick*. First, Magawisca's Pequot sachem father, Mononotto, possibly influenced the creation of the revengeful Captain Ahab; and second, the sisterhood between Hope and Magawisca may have been incorporated into the symbolic marriage between Ishmael and Queequeg.

From *Hope Leslie*

The preface to *Hope Leslie* purports to understand the Native American trait of choosing death rather than servitude as "high-souled courage and patriotism" (*HL* 4). This seems a radical revision of American history; nonetheless, the third-person narration in the main body of the novel maintains a white perspective. Magawisca does not appear in the novel until after the novel's Puritan perspective has been established in the first two chapters.

When Magawisca tells Everell Fletcher of the Mystic Fort attack, she begins, "It was such a night as this—so bright and still, when your English came upon our quiet homes" (*HL* 48). Her eloquence evokes images in her listener of the predawn attack, in which most people were killed by fire. Fire at that time was a totally unprecedented weapon for Native Americans, which made the massacre all the more devastating. Everell cannot help feeling "sympathy and admiration of her heroic and suffering people" (*HL* 56) who fought the losing battle bravely. Yet this sort of feeling toward the Pequot is repeatedly nullified by what follows: a raid on the Fletchers by "the ruthless, vengeful savage" (*HL* 75) led by Magawisca's father. The description of the raid is accompanied by praise of how "the noble pilgrims lived and endured for us" (*HL* 75). At another point, the idea of evolution posited by the third-person narration prohibits the "reasonable instructed" reader from sympathizing with "the vanishing race": "Imagination may be indulged in lingering for a moment in those dusky regions of the past; but it is not permitted to reasonable instructed man, to admire or regret tribes of human beings, who lived and died, leaving scarcely a more enduring memorial, than the forsaken nest that vanishes before one winter's storms" (*HL* 86). This comment implies that savages who could leave no "enduring memorial" deserve to be vanquished not only from the earth but also from national "history."

In *Hope Leslie,* the bond between Hope and Magawisca cannot sustain itself at crucial moments regarding marriage and religion. For instance, when Hope comes to know that her long-lost sister Faith, who has been held captive for seven years, has married Magawisca's brother Oneco and "gone native," Hope initially reacts with despair: "My sister married to an Indian!" To this Magawisca exclaims, "An Indian!" recoiling "with a look of proud contempt" (*HL* 196). Hope desperately begs Faith to come back. The couple hurriedly returns to the wilderness without uttering more than a few words of greeting, although bilingual Magawisca is willing to interpret for Faith, who has forgotten her English. According to Louise K. Barnett in *The Ignoble Savage: American Literary Racism, 1790–1890,* the marriage between Faith and Oneco is "the only rare interracial marriage that ends with a happy ending in early American Literature."[6] However, by depriving the couple of their voices and thus the ability to talk about the alternative happiness they have found, even Sedgwick, who depicts a happy interracial marriage, ultimately negates it.

Magawisca, too, positions the narrative on the side of civilized whites. Sedgwick presents Magawisca's peace-loving and self-sacrificing stance as a possible solution to race wars. For instance, Magawisca tries to persuade her father to give up revenge on the whites. She also expresses her willingness to risk her life to protect the Fletchers. She puts herself at great risk in a failed attempt to save Everell's mother during a raid on the Fletchers by a party led by her father. Magawisca "sunk down at her father's feet, and clasping her hands, 'save them—save them,' she cried" (*HL* 65). In a parallel situation, when Everell, whom she loves dearly, is about to be beheaded by her father at Sacrifice Rock, Magawisca jumps out and eventually loses her arm: "Magawisca, springing from the precipitous side of the rock, screamed—'Forebear' and interposed her arm. . . . The stroke aimed at Everell's neck, severed his defender's arm, and left him unharmed. . . . The lopped quivering member dropped over the precipice" (*HL* 97). This scene shows similarities to the legend of Pocahontas and Captain John Smith in Virginia. As noted earlier, on August 5, 1850, Melville visited "Sacrifice Rock." There he might have wryly contemplated on the meaning of Native American self-sacrifice.

Near the close of the novel, Magawisca is forced to choose between as-similating herself into the Puritan society or leaving. She leaves, risking her life. She says, as if to sum up the whole novel, "the law of vengeance is written on our heart . . . the Indian and the white man can no more mingle, and become one, than day and night" (*HL* 349). Later she joins her father in the wilderness, and the two of them disappear as fugitives into invisibility, out of American "history": "That which remains untold of their story, is lost in the deep, voiceless obscurity of those unknown regions" (*HL* 359).

Though underestimated by feminist critics writing about *Hope Leslie*, who tend to emphasize Magawisca's resistance to her father, Magawisca comes to understand her father's sentiments. Moreover, Magawisca has already warned Everell of these sentiments when she begins her account of the Mystic massacre: "Then listen to me; and when the hour of vengeance comes, if it should come, remember it was provoked [by the British]" (*HL* 48).

Sedgwick creates a vivid character in Magawisca—she is "the only Indian woman in early American fiction invested with substance and strength"[7]— and gives her a rare voice to criticize the whites. The author, however, basically remains within a white Christian framework: Sedgwick neither fully sympathizes with Native Americans nor fully condemns the Puritans, and she accepts the impossibility of the coexistence of the two races. At one point, the narration contrasts "the ruthless, vengeful savage" and the "noble" Pilgrims who "came forth in the dignity of the chosen servants of the Lord, to open the forests to the sun-beam, and to the light of the Sun of Righteousness" (*HL* 75). Nina Baym, Mary Kelley, Lucy Maddox, Philip Gould, and Michelle Burnham, among other critics, note that in spite of her forward-thinking liberal views, Sedgwick retains an ethnocentric side as well.[8]

Hope Leslie was published in 1827; the 1820s were the decade of Indian novels, reflecting the debate over Indian removal, which was enacted from 1830 onward (Baym 154–86). Though white philanthropists meant well for Native Americans and took pains for what they believed to be their well-being, the majority of Native Americans regarded Americanization as their death. The conclusion reached by philanthropists, including Sedgwick as expressed in *Hope Leslie*, was that the value systems of the two races were incompatible. This conclusion, drawn by those who presumably knew much about Native Americans, enabled the general public to blame the victim: "the vanishing race," which was too adamant to convert.[9]

Hope Leslie was celebrated because its ideology did not challenge but conformed to the dominant society's preference for Native American assimilation. On that August 5, *Hope Leslie* could have given Melville food for thought not only about the possibility of and limitations of interracial bonds but also about tribes like the Pequot, who were too proud to submit to the strong.

The creation of the revengeful Captain Ahab seems to be influenced by Magawisca's father Mononotto. This connection, however, is hard to discern. Logan, a war leader of the Mingo tribe, seems to play an intermediary role between the two leaders of the Pequot/*Pequod*. Logan seems to be bracketed with Ahab in *Moby-Dick* in a passage that explains how Ahab is alien to Christendom. The narrator compares Ahab not only to the last "Grisly Bear" on the frontier but also to the Native American Logan: "[Ahab] lived in the world, as the last of the Grisly Bears lived in settled Missouri. And as when Spring and Summer had departed, that wild Logan of the woods, burying himself in the hollow of a tree, lived out the winter there, sucking his own paws; so, in his inclement, howling old age, Ahab's soul, shut up in the caved trunk of his body, there fed upon the sullen paws of its gloom!" (*MD* 153). It was well known in the nineteenth century that Logan had been friendly to the whites, yet he was betrayed by the Virginians when his family and relatives were brutally killed after an invitation from a white family in 1774.[10] Logan then became "a deeply disturbed man who believed himself pursued by evil manitous" (White 361) and recruited a war party, only to be defeated.

Presumably Melville understood that the Pequot were wronged by the British. In *Israel Potter,* the narrator suddenly compares the protagonist Israel in the enemy's land, England, to an "amazed runaway steer, or trespassing Pequod Indian, impounded on the shores of Narragansett Bay, long ago" (*IP* 164). Melville must have known that, while officially being put into extinction, about eighty Pequot survivors were taken as slaves by the rival tribe, the Narragansett, who joined the British in the attack on the Pequot.[11]

A passage near the end of *Hope Leslie* urges one to posit a link between the leaders of the Pequot/*Pequod*. Magawisca is imprisoned for helping Hope meet her long-lost sister Faith. Later as Hope attempts to take Magawisca out of prison, Hope makes her tutor Cradock, who loves her, disguise himself as Magawisca and stay in prison instead of her. Against this, Cradock scolds his student by saying, however mistakenly,[12] "Was not Jehoshaphat reproved of Micaiah the prophet, for going down to the help of Ahab?" (*HL* 328). This abrupt comparison in time and place of the Pequot Magawisca with the wicked Old Testament king links the Pequot with another wicked Old Testament king, Ahab. To presume this passage might have tickled Melville's fancy can explain the missing link between the name of the whaler and the name of its captain. To demonize the Pequot with wickedness in general was prevalent. For instance, *Clarel* contains a brief reference to the Puritans' view of the Pequot as "pestilent to God" (*Clarel* 63). However, to connect the tribe specifically with the Hebrew King Ahab was unusual.

In *Moby-Dick,* Mononotto could have been transformed into the captain of the *Pequod,* following Master Cradock's hint of the connection between the two symbols of wickedness for Christians, the wicked tribe, the Pequot, and the wicked king, Ahab. Mononotto's surroundings reverberate with Captain Ahab's words. When Magawisca entreats her father to renounce monomaniacal vengeance and spend his remaining years in peace, he replies, "Speak not to me of happiness, Magawisca; it has vanished with the smoke of our home. . . . It is in vain—my purpose is fixed" (*HL* 87). In this scene, Mononotto self-absorbedly meditates on a solitary pine that stands blasted in the beautiful spring landscape. Like Captain Ahab, Mononotto is damned in the midst of paradise: "The old chief fixed his melancholy eye on a solitary pine, scathed and blasted by tempests. . . . That leafless tree was truly, as it appeared to the eye of Mononotto, a fit emblem of the chieftain of a ruined tribe" (*HL* 87). This tree image partly overlaps with Ishmael's first impression of Ahab. As he stands on the quarter-deck, Ahab "looked like a man cut away from the stake, when the fire has overrunningly wasted all the limbs without consuming them. . . . It resembled that perpendicular seam sometimes made in the straight, lofty trunk of a great tree, when the upper lightning tearingly darts down it, and without wrenching a single twig, peels and grooves out the bark from top to bottom" (*MD* 123). The difference between the two images, between Ahab's tree that still retains some green and Mononotto's dead tree, could be attributed to the prospect of materializing their revenge. These three otherwise peace-loving men—Mononotto, Logan, and Captain Ahab—transform themselves into vengeful monomaniacs against the whites or whiteness only when provoked, and they do so in a curious way.

In contrast to Sedgwick's sachem of the Pequot who fails in gathering together a pan–Native American league, Melville's captain succeeds in compelling crew members from different backgrounds to become involved in his quest. Melville gives Ahab great eloquence against the whiteness embodied by the white whale. At the same time, Melville presents an alternative to Ahab's destructive course by his novel's subplot that celebrates interracial bonding.

INTERRACIAL "MARRIAGE" UNDER THE SHADOW OF YOJO

Through a curious overlap between Queequeg of the South Seas and the Native Americans, Melville insinuates into *Moby-Dick* his dream of happy interracial marriage as an alternative to race wars. This seemingly far-reaching or impossible dream is embodied in the two Ishmael-Queequeg embraces.

In the first embrace, Ishmael finds himself in Queequeg's "bridegroom clasp" (*MD* 26) when he wakes at the Spouter-Inn. Ishmael recalls a similar circumstance during the sixteen-hour confinement in his bed as a punishment by his severe stepmother: "My arm hung over the counterpane, and the nameless, unimaginable, silent form or phantom, to which the [supernatural] hand belonged, seemed closely seated by my bedside" (26). Wakening within the embrace of Queequeg's arm, whose tattoos blend with the hues and checkered patterns of the patchwork-quilt counterpane, finally exorcises Ishmael's childhood trauma.

In the scene that follows Ishmael's awakening, Queequeg embodies several Native American elements. As Carolyn L. Karcher and a few others have noted, Melville deliberately blurs racial lines in his portrayal of Queequeg.[13] Karcher writes: "The scene that follows evokes the historical encounter between white settlers and American Indians. . . . Queequeg responds warmly to Ishmael's overtures, and the two seal their friendship over that hoary Indian symbol, the peace pipe" (*Shadow* 72). Though Queequeg is an amalgam of various races, his African element is limited to the comparison of the color of his God Yojo to that of "a three days' old Congo baby" (*MD* 22). But Polynesian Queequeg's double image as a Native American proves stronger than what has thus far been pointed out by critics. The landlord of the inn assuages Ishmael's fear of his as-yet-unknown bedfellow, who is out peddling human heads, by saying, "Queequeg here wouldn't harm a hair of your head" (23), on the surface negating and yet projecting Native American scalping unto Queequeg. Among the three nonwhite harpooneers, Queequeg is depicted closer to Native American Tashtego than to African Daggoo in terms of their eating and in their professional abilities. Daggoo "was wonderfully abstemious, not to say dainty" (152) compared with the voracious eating habits of the other two harpooneers. Moreover, Daggoo seems less capable than the other two: he mistakes a giant squid for Moby Dick in Chapter 59 while Tashtego later sights the white whale. In Chapter 87, while Daggoo can do nothing but watch as Tashtego sinks into the ocean trapped in a whale's head, Queequeg immediately saves Tashtego.

In *White-Jacket* (1850), Melville created a model for Queequeg in the figure of a Sioux in a pioneering village on the western bank of the Mississippi peddling human hands. This Sioux is "a gigantic red-man, erect as a pine, with his glittering tomahawk, big as a broad-ax, folded in martial repose across his chest . . . striding like a king on the stage . . . exhibiting on the back of his blanket a crowd of human hands, rudely delineated in red; one of them seemed recently drawn" (*WJ* 266). For the reader of *Moby-Dick,* Queequeg seems to emerge from this striking picture. Melville very likely witnessed such a Native American, perhaps in July of 1840 when he visited his uncle in Illinois (Parker 1:178). Therefore, Melville might have combined Native American and Polynesian elements in Queequeg.

Melville might have had a strong reservation about having Ishmael choose a full-blooded Native American like Tashtego for his bosom friend, much less for his "marriage" partner.[14] Instead, by explaining that Queequeg's homeland cannot be located—it is "not down in any map; true places never are" (*MD* 55)—Melville has made Queequeg into an imaginary amalgam of nonwhite races. Thus, the author has found a way to insinuate his prayer for interracial marriage, especially between whites and Native Americans, into the background of Ishmael's and Queequeg's hilarious "marriage" at the inn. Ishmael describes the scene that introduces their "hearts' honeymoon" (52) when Queequeg "pressed his forehead against mine, clasped me round the waist, and said that henceforth we were married" (51).

Under a similar comic guise, Melville gives one more twist to the novel's non-Christian value system, through the life buoy that was originally a coffin made for Queequeg. Queequeg's God Yojo, introduced as a "curious little deformed image with a hunch on its back" (*MD* 22) or "insignificant bit of black wood" (52), can be interpreted as having more saving power than critics have allowed.[15] In hindsight, Queequeg's strange sickness and his even more mysterious abrupt recovery from it loom as Yojo's preparation for the future rescue of Ishmael. The coffin completed, dying Queequeg lies inside it to check the fit and crosses his arms on his breast with Yojo between in a quasi-ceremonial manner (478). Later, when the frenzied hunt for Moby Dick embarks on its final stage, all the hands become so immersed in it that they decide to "leave the ship's stern not provided with a buoy when by certain strange signs and innuendoes Queequeg hinted a hint concerning his coffin" (525). Queequeg adamantly has his unnecessary coffin caulked and put at the stern as a life buoy, leaving his fellow crewmen stunned.

The reader should recall that Ishmael has pleased Yojo, by worshipping the idol as Queequeg recommended and by going alone to choose the whaleship on which he and Queequeg would sail under Yojo's instruction. In other words, however strange it might seem to nonbelievers, Yojo might have his own divine reasons to embrace Ishmael. Yojo's agent to save Ishmael is the coffin (used as a life buoy) with Queequeg's tattoo pattern carved on the lid. The shape of the buoy undergoes a symbolic change: the original one lost during the voyage had grips attached to it as usual whereas this new one has lifelines. These lifelines can be read as Queequeg's arms. Thus, Ishmael, who has already been saved spiritually in Queequeg's clasping arm in the warm bed, is once more saved by Queequeg's arm, this time physically.

Yojo's protection points a challenge to the Judeo-Christian God. After the *Pequod* is sucked into the whirlpool, "the coffin life-buoy shot lengthwise from the sea, fell over, and floated by my side" (*MD*, 573), as if the buoy has approached Ishmael by its own free will. Clinging to it, Ishmael floats safe from imminent dangers: "The unharming sharks, they glided by as if with padlocks on their mouths; the savage sea-hawks sailed with sheathed beaks" (573). Remaining silent about this supernatural survival, the usually garrulous Ishmael challenges the reader to grasp the meaning. He has no words of gratitude for the Judeo-Christian God. Instead, he identifies himself with the biblical Ishmael, the outcast man of the wilderness. The name Ishmael means "whom God hears." However, when Melville's Ishmael presumably prays to God for help after the shipwreck in the Pacific, the God who hears his voice could be Yojo. Though the importance of Christianity to Melville is undeniable, Melville's theology sometimes moves beyond orthodoxy and approaches a sort of world religion.[16] Religion formed the fatal touchstone in Anglo-American discourse that gave sanction to exclude Native Americans. Had she not been forced to convert, Magawisca could have stayed in white society; she had learned English from a white captive to such an extent as to make *The Faerie Queene* her favorite book, and she can deeply love white people and be loved by them in return.

Melville may have reacted to *Hope Leslie*, especially in writing the two metaphorical embraces of Ishmael and Queequeg, the first of which started and the last of which consummated their bond. Queequeg's embraces contrast with Magawisca's lopped-off arm at Sacrifice Rock, which dropped over the cliff still quivering. The gap between the two closings naturally reflects the author's view.

His Exhilarating X Mark

Melville did not have Ishmael and Queequeg survive hand in hand. This, however, need not be read as the author's cowardly evasion but rather as a calculation. Melville's critical book review of Francis Parkman's racial nonfiction, *The California and Oregon Trail,* appeared in the *Literary World* in March 1849. For his review, Melville wrote a letter of apology to the editor Duyckinck: "I shall never do it again" (*Cor* 149). Accordingly, when he wrote *Moby-Dick,* he could easily predict unfavorable reader response to heresy should he make the survival of flesh-and-blood Queequeg possible while all the others, including righteous Starbuck, are lost. Melville probably judged that Queequeg's symbolic body in the form of the life buoy would enhance the sense of Queequeg's absence and make the reader miss him. This ending would be more profound in its moral implication than a simple happy ending in which both Ishmael and Queequeg survive.

In *Hope Leslie*, as in Fenimore Cooper's *The Last of the Mohicans* published in the previous year, the reader can easily accept the disappearance of the Native American protagonists, understanding that they have no place in America. At the end of *Hope Leslie*, Hope is too immersed in joy that she, not her rival Esther, can marry Everell to miss Magawisca or to worry about Magawisca's survival—at least Sedgwick gives no description of such feelings of concern for Magawisca by Hope. In terms of love, Hope's bridal joy also contrasts with Magawisca's suffering: they have both loved the same man, and now Magawisca has to ask Hope for Everell's miniature as a memento.

The reader's impression after reading *Moby-Dick* is different from the treatment of the disappearance of the Native American in the closure of *Hope Leslie*. Ishmael in a way keeps living with his deceased counterpart, whereas Hope obliterates Magawisca as one lost in darkness. Far from distancing himself from his nonwhite friend, Ishmael makes himself similar to Queequeg by having nearly his whole body tattooed. In particular, Ishmael's tattoo on his arm of the "skeletal dimensions" of a stranded whale (*MD* 451) resembles Queequeg's grand tattoo all over his body, not in degree but in kind: Ishmael's is also "a mystical treatise on the art of attaining truth" (480). One could argue that "[b]y making Ishmael physically akin to Queequeg, whose tattooing makes him 'a wondrous work in one volume,' Melville deepens the parallel between the two and further obscures their racial difference."[17] That Ishmael has his arm tattooed while staying with his "royal friend Tranquo, king of Tranque, one of the Arsacides" (449) in the southwest Pacific suggests Ishmael's ongoing affection toward the South Seas natives. Moreover, the way Ishmael narrates "The *Town-Ho*'s Story" in Lima in an ironic fashion "challenges . . . imperial power from below."[18] In short, Ishmael has not gone native but is still free from racism, and he still misses Queequeg.

Around the time he completed *Moby-Dick*, Melville's letters to Nathaniel Hawthorne are marked by an exalted tone of voice. Melville, for instance, was proud of himself for "my ruthless democracy on all sides" (*Cor* 190) and similarly for his "unconditional democracy in all things" (191). Melville closed his first letter to Hawthorne after the completion of *Moby-Dick* with "his X mark" (200). Since this is a signature mark used by illiterate Queequeg to sign his contract with the *Pequod*, Melville jokingly identified himself with Queequeg.

This mark also invites us to read not the hopelessly incompatible coexistence of the races as in *Hope Leslie* but the felicity in interracial bonds in *Moby-Dick.* Though Sedgwick also envisioned an interracial bond, it is a bond predicated on Native Americans' acceptance of assimilation and even on self-sacrifice, while the happy interracial marriage in Native American culture—that of Oneco and Faith—was hurriedly pushed into the work's background.

Melville's Sedgwick-related experiences—the visit to "Sacrifice Rock" and the following "cross examination" on Magawisca and Hope—could have provoked Melville to react to Sedgwick's best-selling novel, *Hope Leslie,* and contributed to enrich his overcoming an understanding of race relationships that assumes Native American sacrifice is a prerequisite to coexistence. If this reading is right, August 5, 1850, which has so far been famous in American literary history predominantly as Melville's encounter with Hawthorne, bears further significance.

First, the creation of Captain Ahab reverberates with the words of Mononon-onotto. Ahab and Mononotto transform themselves into revengeful mono-maniacs only when they feel wrong has been done to them. Second, Ahab's whaler is named after the "wicked" tribe connected with Mononotto. A hint for the connection could have been given by Master Cradock's words in *Hope Leslie* that haphazardly connect the tribe and King Ahab both as symbols of wickedness for Christendom. In order to transcend Captain Ahab's vengeance plot, an alternative is offered by the Ishmael-Queequeg bond. Melville's plot humorously amends the limitations of the Hope-Magawisca bond, which failed because the whites forced religious conversion on Native Americans. As if to give voice to the supposedly felicitous marriage between Faith and Oneco, Melville allows Ishmael to speak humorously of his happy interracial "marriage," marked by religious inclusiveness. Yojo could have seen Ishmael not just as Queequeg's "marriage" partner but also as a welcome convert. The heresy here is overwhelming. Melville rebels in a peculiar way: rather than exerting power in Captain Ahab's fashion to challenge the Judeo-Christian God, all one has to do is to relax and accept nonwhite values without even losing one's own identity, religious or otherwise. This might be the biggest joke embedded in *Moby-Dick,* a didactic joke that reveals Melville's distance from conventional readings. Along with Ishmael's and Melville's affinity to Queequeg, this bonding may stem from Melville's ruthless democracy. Yojo's inscrutable power over Ishmael's miraculous survival, a giveaway sort of generosity, gives the reader food for thought. The more strongly the reader feels the sense of unfairness in not seeing Queequeg survive with Ishmael, the more strongly Melville undermines the reader's assumptions about the incompatibility of the races. Furthermore, in view of Queequeg's affinity to

Native Americans, there is room to consider whether Melville has slipped his dream of interracial bonds, especially between Native Americans and whites, into *Moby-Dick*.

NOTES

1. Catharine Maria Sedgwick, *Hope Leslie; or, Early Times in the Massachusetts* (New York: Penguin, 1998), 359. Hereafter cited as *HL*.

2. In the 1990s, the federal government allowed the Pequot to operate the billion-dollar-a-year Foxwoods Resort and Casino, which is a virtually tax-free casino immune from personal injury suits and state labor laws. Kim Isaac Eisler, in *Revenge of the Pequots: How a Small Native American Tribe Created the World's Most Profitable Casino* (New York: Simon & Schuster, 2001), 37, maintains that this privilege attests to the official recognition that the Fort Mystic attack was a massacre.

3. In a postwar treaty in 1638, the English terminated Pequot sovereignty and outlawed use of the tribal name, putting the tribe into official "extinction." Later, however, the name Pequot came to be used again. There were quite a number of Pequot survivors: a study shows that at the close of the Pequot War "several bands of Pequots were scattered throughout southern New England. It is difficult to know their precise numbers, but an estimate of 2,000 to 2,500 Pequots remaining at the close of the war is not unreasonable. The postwar Treaty of Hartford, made in September 1638, between the colonists and their Indian allies, mentions "200 Pequot males to be divided equally between the Mohegans and Narragansetts," Kevin A. McBride, "The Historical Archaeology of the Mashantucket Pequots, 1637–1900: A Preliminary Analysis," in *The Pequots in Southern New England: The Fall and Rise of an American Indian Nation*, ed. Laurence M. Hauptman and James D. Wherry (Norman: Univ. of Oklahoma Press, 1990), 104–5.

4. Alfred A. Cave, *The Pequot War* (Amherst: Univ. of Massachusetts Press, 1996), 158–63.

5. Edward Halsey Foster, *Catharine Maria Sedgwick* (New York: Twayne, 1974), 37; Leyda 384–85.

6. Louise K. Barnett, *The Ignoble Savage: American Literary Racism, 1790–1890* (Westport, Conn.: Greenwood Press, 1975), 119.

7. Mary Kelley, "Explanatory Notes," in *Hope Leslie; or, Early Times in the Massachusetts* (New Brunswick, N.J.: Rutgers Univ. Press, 1993), xxvi.

8. Nina Baym, *American Women Writers and the Work of History, 1790–1860* (New Brunswick, N.J.: Rutgers Univ. Press, 1995), 156–59; Kelley xxxiv; Lucy Maddox, *Removals: Nineteenth-Century American Literature and the Politics of Indian Affairs* (New York: Oxford Univ. Press, 1991), 103–11; Philip Gould, "Catharine Sedgwick's 'Recital' of the Pequot War," *American Literature* 66 (1994): 641–62; Michelle Burnham, *Captivity and Sentiment: Cultural Exchange in American Literature, 1682–1861* (Hanover, N.H.: Univ. Press of New England, 1997), 116.

9. Francis Paul Prucha, *The Indians in American Society: From the Revolutionary War to the Present* (Berkeley: Univ. of California Press, 1985), 19–23, 55; Dimock 115–39; Maria Karafilis, "Catharine Sedgwick's *Hope Leslie*: The Crisis Between Ethical Political Action and U.S. Literary Nationalism in the New Republic," *ATQ* 12 (1998): 327–44.

10. Richard White, *The Middle Ground: Indians, Empires, and Republics in the Great Lakes Region, 1650–1815* (New York: Cambridge Univ. Press, 1991), 358–62, 394.

11. It is only in the past three decades that "the assumption of the Pequot culpability has been challenged by revisionist scholars who have found the war's origins not in Pequot malevolence but in Puritan greed, prejudice, and bigotry" (Cave 4). Melville's overlapping of Israel Potter with the Pequot, thus, is unique.

12. Here Sedgwick seems a little confused. Carolyn L. Karcher explains, "Jehoshaphat receives no warning not to assist [King] Ahab. Perhaps relevant here, however, is that Ahab tries to escape his fate by exchanging clothes with Jehoshaphat," Carolyn L. Karcher, "Explanatory Notes," in *Hope Leslie; or, Early Times in the Massachusetts* (New York: Penguin, 1998), 396.

13. Carolyn L. Karcher, *Shadow over the Promised Land*, 66, 72; Robert K. Martin, *Hero, Captain, and Stranger: Male Friendship, Social Critique, and Literary Form in the Sea Novels of Herman Melville* (Chapel Hill: Univ. of North Carolina Press, 1986), 23, 79; Timothy B. Powell, *Ruthless Democracy: A Multicultural Interpretation of the American Renaissance* (Princeton, N.J.: Princeton Univ. Press, 2000), 160–61.

14. Nonwhite harpooners Tashtego and Queequeg are differentiated. As Queequeg's insistence on turning his coffin into a life buoy indicates, Queequeg is not so involved in Ahab's frenzy after his recovery from sickness. It is Tashtego, and not the first harpooner and the main character Queequeg, who deserves to nail the captain's red flag to the mast, and, as the last man, goes down with the *Pequod*, whose namesake is the tribe put into "extinction."

15. Timothy Marr is an exception. He notes Yojo's inscrutability in relation to ethnicity: "Melville's new use of ethnic agency placed ethnic bodies not as mouthpieces of texts, but rather—like the black idol Yojo—as underwriters of his own literary plotting, as inscrutable icons of the active will to create," Timothy Marr, "Melville's Ethnic Conscriptions," *Leviathan* 3 (Mar. 2001): 22.

16. In *Mardi*, the island Serenia where Babbalanjaa finally decides to stay presents something akin to a world religion, a mixture of Brami, Manco, and Alma. Though God had made his last revelation as Alma (Christ), "[Alma] had appeared to the Mardians under the different titles of Brami, Manko [i.e., Manco Capac, an Inca demigod-figure] and Alma. [Alma's] maxims, which as Brami he had taught, seemed similar to those inculcated by Manko" (*M* 348–49).

17. Valerie Babb, *Whiteness Visible: The Meaning of Whiteness in American Literature and Culture* (New York: New York Univ. Press, 1998), 116.

18. Wyn Kelley, "The Style of Lima: Colonialism, Urban Form, and 'The Town-Ho's Story,'" in *Melville "Among the Nations": Proceedings of an International Conference; Volos, Greece, July 2–6, 1997*, ed. Sanford E. Marovitz and A. C. Christodoulou (Kent, Ohio: Kent State Univ. Press, 2001), 61–70.

Very Like a Whale:
Moby-Dick in Translation

§§

"There's another rendering now"

On Translating *Moby-Dick* into German

DANIEL GÖSKE

"Let us not be pedantical, for all love."
—Stephen Maturin

L iterary translation is a peculiar form of creative criticism that requires more than time, patience, strength, and cash. Serious translators of a book like Melville's momentous masterpiece must be particularly well versed in at least two languages, literatures, and cultures. Moreover, they must be playful and inventive as well as disciplined and subservient. Yet even a seriously playful translation of *Moby-Dick* that utilizes all the philological, electronic, and critical resources now available will always stand unfinished, like the "great Cathedral" of Ishmael's cetological system (*MD* 145). This essay on the history of *Moby-Dick* in German is even less complete. However, as the editor of a new translation, published by the Hanser Verlag in 2001, I would like to offer some observations on the problems and pleasures of rendering and reading *Moby-Dick* in other languages.[1]

"LOOMINGS": MAJOR PROBLEMS IN TRANSLATING *MOBY-DICK*

Reading Melville's disorderly but all-the-more-exciting novel poses a particularly formidable task since it is "a book in love with language" (Brodhead 6). Translators, however, face an even more challenging task than readers of the original. They must always be, as it were, of at least two minds while working on Melville's novel. Their job does not consist solely of getting the nautical or cetological terminology right or rendering characteristic speech patterns in their own language. They must also pay attention to a host of cultural associations and literary allusions inscribed in Melville's text, and they must try to match them, as best as possible, to those of the target culture. At the same time serious translators must attempt to find effective equivalents to the sounds and rhythms of the words, phrases, and sentences in this truly polyphonic novel. I see them now: ever dusting their old lexicons and grammars, straining their ears, and racking their brains in order to create a kindred sense of the book's stylistic variety and exuberance in their own language, literature, and culture.

In contrast to the critic, who can focus on selected passages or aspects of a text, the serious translator has to function as the author's mouthpiece all the way through. In the case of *Moby-Dick,* both translator and editor must come to grips not only with Melville's neologisms and puns but also with his extraordinarily volatile rhetoric and, as John Bryant says, its "alternating periods of tension and repose"—and with numerous idiosyncrasies or discrepancies in terms of plot, syntax, diction, punctuation, and even spelling (*Melville and Repose* 186). True, the fact that Melville's often bold and nervous language was not polished and corrected by a literary counselor or an astute editor makes *Moby-Dick* all the more attractive, but it also raises countless problems for translators. How are they to deal with, for instance, his densely packed metaphors, which are often, at least on the surface, illogical collocations? How about the "frigid inscriptions" on the marble tablets in the chapel or the "shivering frost" of the sea's spray or Ahab's "inclement, howling old age" (*MD* 36, 104, 153)? How do you render, in another language, the "little lower layer" (164) that Ahab thinks Starbuck seems to require? What precisely does Ishmael mean when he talks about the "hidden handful of the Divine Inert" (148)? And in what sense does the grog the sailors are quaffing "fork out at the serpent-snapping eye" (165)? Clearly, the question is not *whether* a translation ought to recreate an author's idiosyncratic use of language but *how* he or she should attempt to do it.

Melville's parodistic use of language also becomes a problem. The text of *Moby-Dick* is packed not only with artful quotations and (sometimes rather bawdy) allusions but also with involuntary echoes. In an annotated edition, some of them can be explained in the appendix. But how about classic intertexts that inform a whole literature and culture? The vocabulary and even the inflections of Melville's language in *Moby-Dick* are deeply colored by, first and foremost, the King James Version of the Bible, but also by Shakespeare's plays and by the works of John Milton, Sir Thomas Browne, Robert Burton, Thomas Carlyle, and many other Anglophone classics. This poses even more difficulties for seriously playful translators who attempt to recreate Melville's novel in all its intertextual richness. The German translator finds himself, in this respect, in a rather fortunate situation. Even though Martin Luther's Bible (completed 1545) is often simpler and more vernacular than the learned King James Version (1611), its cultural significance equals that of the "Authorized Version" for the Anglophone world because it formed the bedrock of modern German language and literature. Moreover, the relations between the English- and the German-speaking cultures have traditionally been strong, and translators can draw on the famous rendering of Shakespeare by the Romantics (August Wilhelm Schlegel, Wolf Graf Baudissin, Wilhelm and Dorothea Tieck) as well as on several historical, though not classic, translations of Milton, Byron, or Carlyle. Yet the translator of *Moby-Dick* must carefully compare and collate the English and German Bibles, the English and German Shakespeare, and the like, to catch the nuances of Melville's style and meaning and to find approximate versions in the target language. This poses a formidable challenge that, in my view, none of the earlier translators has sufficiently met.

"*MOBY-DICK* HISTORICALLY REGARDED": A SURVEY OF EARLIER TRANSLATIONS

Melville's foreign reputation reflects the history of his critical reception in the Anglophone world. Outside of academic circles and apart from popular film versions, his international reputation as a writer is of course largely based on translations, as Leland Phelps's admirable research guide proves.[2] The situation in the German-speaking countries proves exceptional insofar as complete translations of *Typee, Omoo,* and *Redburn* were already published in 1847, 1848, and 1851, respectively. Moreover, a considerable interest in Melville's exotic, ethnological early romances can be gleaned from numerous articles in journals or handbooks throughout the nineteenth and early twentieth centuries. The only early German version of *Moby-Dick* I have been able to locate so far, however, is a six-page adaptation of Emile Forgues's French plot summary in the *Revue des Deux Mondes* of 1853, which appeared two years later in a Viennese journal.[3] Melville's mature works remained untranslated and therefore largely unknown in continental Europe before the Melville Revival of the 1920s. The first book translation of *Moby-Dick* into any language appeared in 1927 in Berlin, together with new translations of

Typee, Omoo, and a lot of non-German adventure fiction, in the "Romane der Welt" series edited by Thomas Mann. Wilhelm Strüver's German text, however, is an abridged version, like the first Finnish (1928), French (1928), Polish (1929), or Portuguese (1935) editions. Fewer than three hundred pages long, it concentrates on Ahab's revenge plot, lacks most of Ishmael's more reflective passages, and can thus be seen as a forerunner of the numerous adaptations for young readers that began to appear in the 1950s.[4]

The decade between 1929 and 1939 saw several complete translations of *Moby-Dick* into Dutch, Hungarian, Czech, and other European languages. Most influential were the Italian version by Cesare Pavese (1932) and a joint venture by Lucien Jacques, Joan Smith, and the French novelist Jean Giono (1939), which sparked off an intense critical reception of Melville as a modern writer *avant la lettre.*[5] Various projects by German publishers, however, were severely hampered by the turmoil of the Nazi period, the Second World War, and the postwar decade. The German reception of Melville's mature works began with his major novellas, and in view of the restrictive nationalism of the German book market in the Third Reich, it seems surprising that Richard Kraushaar's *Benito Cereno* and Richard Möring's *Billy Budd,* both published in 1938 and often reprinted, received a fair amount of attention in the German press and in private circles.[6] A complete translation of *Moby-Dick,* however, which had already been planned for the late 1930s, had to be shelved. While the first Italian and French translations remained unrivaled for many years, five full German versions appeared between 1942 and 1956 in Switzerland, West Germany, and East Germany.[7]

The first German *Moby-Dick* was published in 1942 by the Büchergilde Gutenberg, the trade union's publishing house, which had been forced into Swiss exile.[8] The book, lavishly illustrated by the surrealist painter Otto Tschumi, has never been reprinted and remains a rare collector's item. Maybe this was for the best: Möckli von Seggern's translation is rather faulty and uninspired. Moreover, it is clearly indebted to Jean Giono's French text and was soon superseded by Fritz Güttinger's version of 1944, published by the prestigious Manesse Verlag in Zurich and the first of the five full German versions of *Moby-Dick* still in print. Güttinger had worked on the translation for two years while living in New York City. He clearly tried to produce a readable, even racy German text for contemporary readers. Scrupulously avoiding Melville's highly rhetorical structures as well as his more lyrical passages, Güttinger toned down Ahab's Shakespearean pathos and reduced the stylistic variety of Ishmael's narrative voice. Indeed, he even felt free to omit many obscure or awkward phrases, and by introducing many phrases and terms from German literature and philosophy, he consistently followed a strategy of linguistic naturalization ("Eindeutschung") and modernization of the original. Thus Ishmael's "metaphysical professor" in "Loomings" becomes a quintessentially German "Dichter und Denker" (poet and thinker), and even rather innocuous English words like "life" or "meditation" are rendered as "Dasein" or "Wesensschau," key terms from Heidegger's or Husserl's philosophical thought (Güttinger 24–26).

Thesi Mutzenbecher's version, revised by the sailor-novelist Ernst Schnabel, appeared only two years later in Hamburg, the first volume of a complete edition, later aborted, of Melville's works. The two translators went even further than Güttinger in presenting *Moby-Dick* as a decidedly contemporary novel—at least in the matter of diction. By transforming Melville's polyphonic mélange of many styles into a fairly uniform and colloquial idiom, their text clearly conforms to the unadorned, prosy parlance that was to become the dominant feature of early postwar German fiction. Moreover, the translators seem to have interpreted Melville's novel along the lines of a Christian humanism that many German readers in the immediate postwar years must have found particularly comforting. Toward the end of Ishmael's meditation in "The Matmaker," it is not "chance" that "rules . . . necessity" and "free will" (*MD* 215) but man's free will ("Wille") that rules necessity and chance (Mutzenbecher 203). And whereas Ishmael puts himself in an implied contrast to his readers who "live under the blessed light of the evangelical land" (*MD* 223), his German counterpart remains in the congregation of the pious by blithely confessing: "*Wir* sind Christen" (Mutzenbecher 210).

One can easily point out numerous errors and interesting deviations from the original in these early and, comparatively speaking, rather loose translations. But a note of caution seems in order here. Like their colleagues in other European countries, the translators of the 1940s could not yet draw on annotated editions and other helpful material from the fast-growing Melville industry in the United States and elsewhere. Hence they often silently omitted what they did not understand, and many of their renderings of obscure words or difficult phrases were clearly wild guesses. The translators of the midfifties found themselves in a better position, and they had the additional benefit of taking their cue from their predecessors. Richard Mummendey's *Moby-Dick* of 1954, for instance, shows a clear debt to the 1944 and 1946 versions, yet this text stays much closer to the original, at least in terms of meaning and syntax. Mummendey's obvious desire to produce a complete and reliable text, however, was not matched by literary skills, and his rather plodding prose often reads like an interlinear version of a minor Victorian novel. Incidentally, his translation is a curious case since it was only commissioned to provide a text for more than a hundred remarkably realistic illustrations by Herbert Pridöhl. All in all, Hans and Alice Seiffert's translation of 1956 is probably the most reliable and readable German text of the period. Part of an edition of Melville's works for readers in the German Democratic Republic, it was often reprinted in both East and West Germany. For all their reliance on the versions of 1946 and 1954 (and despite numerous lapses and a tendency to "correct" obvious errors and minor discrepancies in the original), the Seifferts did a much better job in at least occasionally reproducing the stylistic variety of Melville's often highly poetic prose. Theirs turned out to be the most useful of all the earlier translations that Matthias Jendis consulted when he created his text.

For a brief comparison of major translations from Pavese (1932) and Giono (1939) to Seiffert (1956) and Jendis (2001), let me cite a few examples that show that many of the earlier translators were especially uncomfortable with Melville's idiosyncrasies. Take Ahab's soliloquy on manhood's pondering repose "of If," his view of men as "Ifs eternally" (*MD* 492). Giono, von Seggern, Güttinger, and Mummendey simply omitted this important phrase, and all the others avoided the unusual plural form, unlike Jendis, who even emphasized man's "Grübeln über das *große* Wenn" ("the *big* If," Jendis 751). Or take the philosophical histrionics of Ahab's Fire Sermon in "The Candles": "In the midst of the personified impersonal, a personality stands here" (*MD* 507). While Güttinger eliminated the whole sentence altogether, Giono, Mutzenbecher, and Seiffert took the edge off Ahab's oxymoronic outburst and altered its meaning.[9]

Finally, let us look at Melville's memorable coda in the last chapter: "Now small fowls flew screaming over the yet yawning gulf; a sullen white surf beat against its steep sides; then all collapsed, and the great shroud of the sea rolled on as it rolled five thousand years ago" (*MD* 572). The power of this passage owes itself to an inspired mix of expressive imagery (the "sullen" surf, the "shroud" of the sea), alliteration and assonance ("Now small fowls flew"), and cadence: the ponderous monosyllables of the first two clauses, the arrested movement of the phrase "then all collapsed" (so eerily suggestive even before the pictures of 9/11), and then the more expansive, rolling rhythm with its allusion to the biblical Flood that, according to the Septuagint chronology to which Melville alludes, would indeed have happened five millennia before 1850. The older translations of this passage show significant differences. Pavese's Italian text may not sound as darkly suggestive as the original but it follows its syntax and meaning closely. Not so the first French and German versions, which also reduce the idea of total collapse to a mere leveling out ("s'égalisa") or closing ("schloß") of the "open" (instead of "yawning") gulf:

Piccoli uccelli volarono ora, strillando, sull'abisso ancora aperto; un tetro frangente bianco si sbatté contro gli orli in pendio; poi tutto ricadde, e il gran sudario del mare tornò a stendersi come si stendeva cinquemila anni fa. (Pavese 587)

Maintenant, les petits oiseaux voletaient en criant sur le gouffre encore ouvert. Une écume blanche et morne battit contre ses riodes parois; puis tout s'égalisa; et le grand linceul de la mer se mit à rouler comme il roulait il y a cinq mille ans. (Giono 547)

Andere kleinere Vögel kreisten kreischend über dem offenen Abgrund, gegen dessen Wände weißer Schaum schlug. Dann schloß er sich, und das Meer, ein weites Leichentuch, rollte wieder dahin, wie es schon vor fünftausend Jahren gerollt war. (von Seggern 453)

Güttinger clearly aimed for a more sonorous rhythm but recoiled from Melville's expressive metaphors: the "sullen" surf is only "lackluster" ("glanzlos"), the "great shroud" merely a "dark sheet" ("das dunkle Laken"): "Kleine Vögel schossen kreischend über dem noch klaffenden Abgrund hin und her; glanzloser Gischt brandete gegen die steilen Wogenhänge, dann stürzte alles ein, und das dunkle Laken des Meeres wogte weiter, wie es vor fünftausend Jahren gewogt" (Güttinger 911).

Mutzenbecher was at once more specific (the "small fowls" are turned into "seagulls") and less rhetorical. And like the two translators from the fifties, she missed Melville's allusion to the Flood. Their versions focus not on that mythical catastrophe "five thousand years ago" but on the duration of the waves' continuous rolling "for" ("seit") five millennia.[10] Jendis deviated from all his predecessors in several respects. He paid much closer attention to the haunting rhythm and other sound effects, reproduced the bold, anthropomorphic imagery, and emphasized the biblical allusion with a ponderous reference to the Flood "five millennia" ago: "Nun flogen kleine Vögel kreischend über dem noch gähnenden Abgrund; mürrische weiße Wellen schlugen gegen seine steilen Wände; dann brach alles ein, und das große Leichentuch des Meeres wogte weiter wie vor fünf Jahrtausenden" (Jendis 864). It seems fair to say that Jendis tried to recreate the stylistic variety, polyphonic texture, and "careful disorderliness" (MD 361) of Melville's novel more consistently than any of his predecessors. We must not forget, however, that they worked under less auspicious circumstances.

The Hanser edition, the first complete German *Moby-Dick* to appear in almost fifty years, is the first that is based on clear editorial and translational principles and on the full and close cooperation of translator and (external) editor while the translation was in progress. Only after this unusual form of teamwork was completed did the text go to the publisher's editorial department. Like other enterprises of this scale and significance, the Hanser edition has a long and somewhat tortuous history that cannot be discussed here. Suffice it to say that the project started out in the early 1990s with Friedhelm Rathjen's intriguing but highly idiosyncratic version, which he withdrew when the editor and publisher suggested numerous changes.[11] Then we asked Matthias Jendis to take over. With a master's degree in English and history at Göttingen University and numerous translations of serious fiction and nonfiction to his credit, he was well suited for this task, and this all the more so since he is also an experienced mariner of sorts, having served for two years in the German navy. This has stood him in good stead as a translator of Patrick O'Brian's maritime novels and other naval fiction. *Moby-Dick* posed quite a different challenge that, however, Jendis has met, as the acclaim he received suggests. Yet neither the translator nor his editor would assert, in the language of blurbs and puffs, that this new translation was entirely faithful. This can be dismissed as an empty and meaningless claim unless one states clearly "in what faithfulness consists," as Matthew Arnold wrote in *On Translating Homer*, a book Melville studied intensely as his numerous marginalia testify.[12] How should translators keep their faith? Faith in whom? In what? In the holy original? The letter killeth, says one of Melville's favorite authors, and what if (as in the case of *Moby-Dick*) we do not have an "original," authorized version so that it is often tantalizingly unclear what precisely the author's intentions were? How can one be faithful to what the author might have meant but did not make clear because he lacked "Time, Strength, Cash, and Patience" (*MD* 145)?

Hence our editorial policy, outlined in a three-page note, was to present the modern German reader with a text that is as energetic, unconventional, sometimes contradictory, and essentially "unfinished" as Melville's own "draught of a draught" (*MD* 145). In other words, Jendis did not make smooth the rugged path where its ruggedness works, where it has an aesthetic purpose. But his translation represents a new venture in more than this respect. It is the first ever to be based on the critical text of the Northwestern-Newberry edition, and we followed that edition in *not* emending even Melville's obvious lapses, whereas most earlier translators, understandably, did. In order not to modernize the original Jendis tried to recreate the hidden sources of Melville's style by consulting concordances of key texts like the Bible, Shakespeare, and Milton as well as historical dictionaries like the *Oxford English Dictionary* and its German cousin, the thirty-three volumes of the *Deutsches Wörterbuch,* started by the brothers Grimm, as well as bilingual dictionaries of Melville's time. Moreover, we drew on annotated editions of *Moby-Dick* and consulted earlier translations into various languages. Numerous works of Melville criticism, preferably of the text-based sort, recent studies on the American whaling industry, and helpful tools like Eugene Irey's *Concordance to* Moby-Dick also came in handy.[13] The latter proved particularly helpful since it alerted us not only to the intricate texture of verbal patterns and leitmotifs but also to some discrepancies that could not—and cannot—be explained by Melville's method of "careful disorderliness."

Ishmael's and Ahab's inconsistent use of the philosophical difference between "agent" and "instrument" or "principal" presents an important case in point. At first "agent" refers to an unreasoning substitute or vehicle: Ahab wants to wreak his hate upon Moby Dick, "be the white whale agent, or be the white whale principal" (*MD* 164), and Ishmael calls the whale "an unintelligent agent" (184). Two pages later, however, he effectively reverses the earlier distinction when he says this about Ahab's intellect: "That before living *agent,* now became the living *instrument*" (185, emphasis added). Still later, the same terms appear in both, and obviously contradictory, meanings (see 202). How does one deal with this apparent (and apparently unintended or at least dysfunctional) discrepancy—and with rendering Ahab's final word in this matter? In Chapter 135 he declares: "all the things that . . . outrage mortal man . . . are bodiless, but only bodiless as objects, not as *agents*" (564). Jendis decided to activate the two meanings of the English word "agent," which does not have a similarly ambiguous equivalent in German, by using different terms in his translation ("Werkzeug" or "Wirkungskraft" as opposed to "Urheber" or "Ursache"). He could do so because a note in the appendix alerts the reader to the apparent inconsistency in the source text (Jendis 963).

This symbiosis of translation and scholarly apparatus is one of the many benefits of a fully annotated, edited translation of a classic text. Most publishing houses, regrettably, do not want to invest cash, time, strength, and patience in such a project, and we are deeply grateful that the Hanser people were willing to make this investment. Despite its 1,041 pages (on Bible leaves!), our edition has turned out a compact and attractive little bedfellow. Peter-Andreas Hassiepen has provided a beautiful cover with photographic variations of the sea surface and, hence, its eerie emphasis on the problem of perception. The publisher granted us plenty of sea room in which to maneuver. Apart from a long afterword, a chronology of Melville's life, and a glossary of nautical terms, the edition features 120 pages of explanatory notes on cultural and literary history as well as on textual variants and problems of interpretation and translation. This enabled us to alert our readers to some of the "pains and penalties" (*MD* 8) but also to the pleasures of translating *Moby-Dick*.

Let me begin with the pain. A close reading of Melville's novel makes clear that the original text would have benefited enormously from an eagle-eyed yet sympathetic editor. It includes not a few passages of painfully awkward prose when Melville (or, technically, Ishmael) is awash and awallow in a sea of abstractions, ponderous noun phrases, and cumbersome constructions (unbearable even for Germans!) that do not serve any recognizable purpose such as satire or pastiche. Sometimes the temptation is overwhelming to disentangle Melville's often unnecessarily convoluted syntax, correct his dangling participles, and flesh out incomplete clauses. Jendis occasionally did so without, however, converting, as many translators have done, his often thumping rhetoric into something bland and prosy. Similarly, he carefully reproduced Melville's almost Homeric epithets like "dark Ahab," "moody Ahab," or the "ivory Pequod" as well as many other repetitive phrases even though they may put off most readers of German prose, for whom the principle of elegant variation usually obtains.

Melville's often highly compressed (and sometimes almost bathetic) metaphors are another ticklish matter. How does one render a "spasmodic gunwale" (*MD* 285) of a boat or the "unnamable imminglings" of the "dark Hindoo half of nature" (497)? How do you reproduce Ahab's "earthquake life" (507), his voice crying out "in his walrus way" (437), without resorting to lame, lukewarm, or ludicrous circumlocutions? One can easily understand why most of the earlier translators shied away from Melville's bold imagery. Let me cite just one famous example. In Chapter 28 "moody stricken Ahab" suddenly enters the stage "with a crucifixion in his face" (124). In the London edition of 1851, however, his face expresses only "an apparently eternal anguish" (936). Similarly, most German translators presented Ahab's face as merely "tormented" or expressing a "holy sorrow."[14] In contrast, Jendis felt that this bold image must not be watered down and, like his eminent predecessors Pavese and Giono, he rendered it accordingly: "Der schwermütige, geschlagene Ahab stand vor ihnen *mit einer Kreuzigung* im Gesicht" (Jendis 214, emphasis added). Another example concerns the "Portuguese vengeance" with which, Ishmael implies, God's flood "had whelmed a whole world" (*MD* 273). Few critics have ventured a comment on this mysterious (blasphemous and racist?) remark, and early translators were clearly baffled. Pavese, in 1932, stuck fairly close to the original: "con vendetta degna di un portoghese aveva sommerso tutto un mondo" (Pavese 304). The French translators of 1939, however, converted Jehovah's "Portuguese vengeance," by way of a sly reference to Napoleon, into "un raffinement de vengeance *corse*" (Giono 276), and most of their German colleagues evaded the problem by substituting something like "incomparable" or "wild" vengeance. Jendis could keep Ishmael's enigmatic slur on the "Portuguese" because a note in the appendix discusses the issue and mentions Melville's observations on the violent but also much maligned "'Gees" from the Cape Verde Islands (Jendis 984–85).

Translating a vast and multifaceted novel like *Moby-Dick* entails many frustrating losses, yet it also provides ample opportunities for creative gains. To compensate for numerous untranslatable elements of the original Jendis occasionally used what semantic leeway he had to make Melville's text a little more resonant to a German audience. Two examples, bawdy the first and gloomy the second, must suffice here.

Ishmael's fun with the whale's phallus, never directly named as such, in Chapter 95 is a ticklish matter, mainly because Melville's verbal wit operates here, as elsewhere, on various levels, running the gamut from a low "locker-room leer" to, maybe, "sardonic black humor" (Dillingham 48–49). The chapter's title ("The Cassock") as well as the pun on the "archbishoprick" at its end poke fun at the "robed investiture" (*MD* 117), the hieratic hierarchy of both the Roman Catholic and Anglican or Episcopalian churches, the latter probably being the immediate target of Melville's satire. Translators whose target language has no synonym for "cassock" that could evoke these cultural associations and, at the same time, suggest the close-fitting garment alluded to here are forced to deviate from the original. Pavese, rendering the title as "La sottana" (Pavese 443), referred unambiguously to the tight-fitting undergarment used by the Catholic clergy, and later French translations followed suit ("La Soutane" or "La Chasuble").[15] Giono and his collaborators, however, cut the allusion to clerical hierarchy altogether since "La Capote" (Giono 406) denotes a loose raincoat or a soldier's hooded cloak. The German translations reflect a similar variety of options. While von Seggern took her cue from Giono with an obsolete word for an unspecific "Leibrock" or "coat" (von Seggern 331), her immediate rival suggested the flowing robe or "Amtstracht" worn by any public official (Güttinger 685). The other translators sided with either of the two major denominations in Germany, referring to the loose "Talar" or cloak of Protestant pastors (Mutzenbecher 371, Mummendey 509) or the "Soutane" (Seiffert 478) worn by Catholic clergy. Jendis's suggestive solution avoids the denominational and sartorial dilemma altogether by slyly foreshadowing Melville's mischievous and, alas, untranslatable pun in the chapter's final sentence. "Der Überzieher" (Jendis 651) is a slightly outmoded word for a gentleman's overcoat. In modern German slang, however, it is also a synonym for a jonny, a rubber, a condom—in a sense, a fitting "candidate for an archbishoprick" indeed (*MD* 420). Jendis's bold double entendre in the chapter's title may be more explicit than the author himself could afford to be. Many of his Victorian (and modern) readers may not have realized what the "very strange, enigmatical object," that "unaccountable cone," signifies, which the illiterate sailors call, in perfect Latin, the whale's "grandissimus" (*MD* 419). Yet while Melville's anti-Victorian doublespeak about sex *more hominum* depended on nuance and indirection, we felt that our German readers should be made aware, both in the translation proper and in the annotations to this chapter, of his extraordinary dexterity in telling his tale in both locker- and drawing-room fashion.

My second example has more serious implications. When discussed at some length, it will illustrate the complex interplay of careful recreation (on various levels) and cautious innovation in which a seriously playful, linguistically nimble translator of *Moby-Dick* must engage. Immediately after the Rabelaisian humor of "The Cassock" comes the lurid scene at "The Try-Works" where the narrator's tone shifts abruptly from light banter to dark prophecy. Ishmael, standing at the helm, witnesses an infernal scene that combines elements of pagan worship, a perverted Pentecostal meeting, a Hindoo funeral, and a Hieronymus Bosch version of "the left wing of the day of judgment" (*MD* 422). In a long, magnificent, increasingly agitated period Melville moves from the crew to the harpooneers and the raging elements only to zoom in on the *Pequod*, which, in the culminating cadence, appears like the embodiment of her captain's madness:

> As they narrated to each other their unholy adventures, their tales of terror told in words of mirth; as their uncivilized laughter forked upwards out of them, like the flames from the furnace; as to and fro, in their front, the harpooneers wildly gesticulated with their huge pronged forks and dippers; as the wind howled on, and the sea leaped, and the ship groaned and dived, and yet steadfastly shot her red hell further and further into the blackness of the sea and night, and scornfully champed the white bone in her mouth, and viciously spat round her on all sides; then the rushing Pequod, freighted with savages, and laden with fire, and burning a corpse, and plunging into that blackness of darkness, seemed the material counterpart of her monomaniac commander's soul. (*MD* 423)

This is poetry in the grand manner. Yet Giono, von Seggern, Güttinger, Mutzenbecher, and many other translators who apparently wanted to present a more modern text cut this magnificent passage up into several shorter sentences. Here and elsewhere they tended to eliminate those oratorical figures of speech (alliteration, anaphora, assonance, parallelism, polysyndeton) that give this novel its unmistakable flavor and power. Jendis, however, followed Pavese or Seiffert in carefully recreating Melville's ringing rhetoric. Indeed, he went even further, taking advantage of the fact that the morphology and stress patterns of the German often resemble those of the English language. If you read his version aloud, you will notice how the rhythmical phrases begin to pile up, wavelike, in varying iambs, spondees, and dactyls. In the final sentence, moreover, Jendis topped the whole passage off with a particularly ominous synonym for "commander" that all of his German predecessors had avoided:

> Wie sie einander ihre verruchten Abenteuer erzählten, Geschichten des Grauens, in launige Worte gefaßt; wie ihr rohes Lachen aus ihnen emporzüngelte wie die Flammen aus ihren Öfen; wie vor ihnen die wilden Harpuniere mit ihren gewaltigen Gabeln und Kellen herumhantierten; wie der Wind heulte und die See wogte und das Schiff ächzte und stampfte und doch stetig seine rote Hölle weiter und weiter in die Schwärze der See und der Nacht warf und trotzig den weißlichen Knochen in ihrem Maule zerbiß und wütend die Gischt nach allen Seiten spie, befrachtet mit Wilden, beladen mit Feuer, mit einem brennenden Leichnam an Bord auf dem Weg in die schwärzeste Finsternis—da stürmte die Pequod dahin wie das stoffliche Abbild der Seele ihres besessenen Führers. (Jendis 656)

Owing to the perversion of true leadership under the "Führer" Adolf Hitler, native speakers of German are still uncomfortable with this tainted term unless it appears in compound words like "Schiffsführer" (captain of a ship) or "Führerschein" (driver's licence). Significantly, Jendis's predecessors all resorted to a harmless "Kapitän" (Mummendey 514 and Seiffert 483), a mere "Schiffer" or "skipper" (Mutzenbecher 374), or the naval rank, inappropriate for a whaler, of "Befehlshaber" (von Seggern 336) and "Kommandeur" (Güttinger 691). All things considered, however, we thought that the association with the darkest years of Germany's recent past should not be shunned and was, in this context at least, even apt. The critical response to Melville's prophetic novel in the wake of September 11 and, indeed, in the context of the recent wars in Afghanistan and Iraq, proved, moreover, that Ahab's quest in *Moby-Dick* lends itself to more than one political reading (see below).

Fortunately, Melville's masterpiece is a book for all seasons and many uses, especially for those happy few who approach it from an intercultural perspective. One of the happiest and most rewarding aspects of literary translation is that one gains many insights that most native readers of the original might not be aware of. "Call me Ishmael"—the very first words of the first chapter—is a case in point. For the translator into German (and many other languages), it is highly ambiguous. First, it does not specify the addressee in terms of number. Does Ishmael address the single "gentle reader" of conventional Victorian fiction or does he speak to a number of listeners? Neither does the English imperative qualify the degree of familiarity whereas German or French speakers can and must distinguish between informal, intimate "du" or "tu" and a more formal "Sie" or "vous." Hence Ishmael's ominous opening sentence can be rendered in several ways, each impinging on the impression we get of a recurring speech situation in *Moby-Dick*—its often distinctly oral rather than literary or writerly quality. In most German and many other foreign versions we encounter four essentially different op-tions, with additional variations. In the first (incomplete) version of 1927, the whole opening passage was simply omitted. In 1942 von Seggern adopted the second option. Here Ishmael addresses a single reader or listener, and he does so in intimate terms, roughly equivalent to the English "thou": "*Nenne* mich Ismael" (von Seggern 7). Two years later Güttinger chose yet another strategy. He used the indefinite pronoun, thus avoiding direct address but creating a stand-offish, rather bookish tone from the very beginning: "*Man nenne* mich Ismael" (Güttinger 22). The majority of translators into various languages, however, seem to have followed Pavese's example ("Chiamatemi Ismaele"), as did Jendis: "*Nennt* mich Ismael."[16] Still implying informal familiarity, Ishmael now introduces himself to a number of addressees. This option, it seems, fits the narrator's ambiguous tone of "genial despair" (Bryant 204) best.

Ishmael's blunt opening provides only one of many examples in which a translator, in contrast to the reader or critic of the original, has to take a plunge because the system of the target language forces him to do so. Take, for instance, Melville's deft use of the "stately dramatic thee and thou of the Quaker idiom" (*MD* 73), a culturally specific feature of the English language that has no equivalent in other languages, including German. The translator must resort to other means of recreating the quaintly theatrical otherworldli-ness and the archaic flavor of Bildad's, Peleg's, or Ahab's speech, and Jendis did so by resorting to the equally dated but dramatic diction of Luther's Bible. The English way of addressing people by the indeterminate pronoun "you" poses a standard problem in translating fiction or dubbing movies. Take the standard situation when boy meets girl, or rather, man meets woman. When are they, in the foreign language versions, supposed to switch from the formal "Sie" or "vous" to the intimate "du" or "tu"? After the first beer?

After the first kiss? Or should they start out on an informal basis? Then they would never experience the thrill of becoming linguistically intimate that is such a titillating feature of communication in these languages.[17]

There are many other systemic differences even between source and target languages that are as closely related as English and German. Certain grammatical features and syntactical structures can have a direct bearing on interpretive options or aesthetic effects. Significantly enough, the last word of Ishmael's narrative, at the end of the epilogue, is "orphan" (*MD* 573). In contrast to English, French, Spanish, and Italian usage, however, the rules of German syntax require that the concluding relative clause end with the verb "fand" ("found"). Indeed, all six of our German predecessors have opted for this obvious but less ominous solution. Jendis, however, deviated from Melville's syntax by composing two independent main clauses. The result is a carefully cadenced conclusion that culminates in the German word for "orphan" ("Waise") and rings almost as true as the original: "Es war die umherirrende Rachel; auf der Suche nach ihren verschollenen Kindern fand sie nur eine weitere Waise" (Jendis 866). Many other passages, even apart from Ahab's speeches in blank verse and Ishmael's meditations in poetic prose, require this kind of tinkering with sound and sense. That Jendis has paid particular attention to this task is probably not the least of his achievements.

"Epilogue": The Critical Reception of the New German *Moby-Dick*

Judging by the critical and even commercial success of Jendis's translation in Austria, Germany, and Switzerland, *Moby-Dick* is no longer seen as a romance of adventure (or a screenplay for popular movie adaptations) but as a highly suggestive novel "in love with language." When our edition appeared in September 2001, it received wide attention in the German-language papers. Many reviewers praised the stylistic "virtuosity" of Jendis's version, and some saw *Moby-Dick* as a precursor of Joyce's *Ulysses:* a "formal and linguistic experiment of whale-like proportions."[18] Of course, the 150th anniversary of the novel's original publication (and the controversy arising from Rathjen's excerpts) created additional interest. The fact, moreover, that our edition appeared just two weeks after the terrorist attacks on the World Trade Center had an unforeseeable impact on how the new *Moby-Dick* was received. One of the most circumspect reviews, published in the widely respected Hamburg weekly *Die Zeit,* placed Melville's monomaniac commander in the context of other deluded fanatics who are prepared to sacrifice many lives for their own revengeful campaign or crusade: "Adolf Atta Ahab." In view of Ishmael's and even Starbuck's admiration for Ahab's driven and "noble soul" (*MD* 544), however, the critic read *Moby-Dick* as an "ambiguous meta-parable on the dubiousness of Manichaean demoniza-tion."[19] Another saw Melville's novel as a study of the "psychopathology of terrorism," with Ahab as a former "sleeper" who embarks on his final voyage to destroy "(imagined) devils and demons."[20] Yet another review, published in Zurich in February 2002 and titled "Captain Bush and Moby Bin Laden," saw in Ahab's quest a suggestive analogy to America's global war on terrorism.[21] That these readings from Old Europe were not completely off the mark is shown by a number of comparable responses in the United States that were published later, especially in view of the war in Iraq.[22]

Moby-Dick, while susceptible to these and other topical readings, will outlast any "*Grand Contested Election for the Presidency of the United States,*" any "Bloody Battle in Affghanistan" (*MD* 7) as long as publishers around the world provide adequate editions of a book that reminds us that, as E. L. Doctorow so beautifully put it, "we are never in one place alone at any given minute, but in two—in the present that is the past, or on the land that is the sea, or in the sea that is the soul, or in the novel that is God's ineffable realm."[23] Despite the numerous jeremiads about the widespread loss of literacy in this age of the screen, the happy few who let themselves be fascinated by Melville's exuberant, inspired art range in the thousands. This is certainly true for the German-language audience. With well over fifteen thousand copies sold to date, the Hanser edition has found many new readers. Moreover, Melville's masterpiece has also reached thousands of listeners, and this is perhaps pe-culiarly appropriate since the test of genius, Ishmael suggests, lies as much in rousing oratory as in effective writing: "Has the Sperm Whale ever written a book, spoken a speech?" (*MD* 346). Jendis had made it a rule to try out his translation by reading it aloud. Only if a given passage passed this test was it allowed to stand. This strategy was essential for rhetorical set-pieces like Ahab's speeches or Ishmael's rhapsodies, but it even applied to the quieter, more lyrical passages of the book. As a result, Jendis's translation received various prestigious prizes. Moreover, it was used in a thirty-hour reading marathon at the Literaturhaus in Cologne and adapted for a highly praised radio play by Klaus Buhlert, commissioned and aired by Bavarian Public Radio in the winter of 2002 and available on CD and MC.[24]

"There's another rendering now; but still one text," says stoic Stubb at the end of "The Doubloon" (*MD* 434). To render a text that is as much in love with language and speculation as *Moby-Dick* entails many "pains and penal-ties" (8) but also peculiar profits and pleasures. Comparison is the mother of knowledge. I hope to have indicated that much is to be learned from reading various renderings side by side with their source text, not least because we are constantly forced to negotiate the spaces between two (and more) languages, literatures, and cultures. While Jendis's *Moby-Dick* offers the most reliable, resonant, and readable rendering in German to date, our annotated edition makes clear that it is but a "draught of a draught." And this is all for the good. As the examples of the Bible, or Dante, or Shakespeare prove, each generation should produce new renderings and hence new readings of the truly great works of world literature.

NOTES

1. Herman Melville, *Moby-Dick oder Der Wal,* ed. Daniel Göske, trans. Matthias Jendis (Munich: Hanser, 2001). This is the first volume of a new, annotated edition of Melville's works and was followed by Christa Schuenke's version of *Pierre* in 2002 and the translation of Melville's letters and journals (with biographical interchapters) by Werner Schmitz and Daniel Göske in 2004. Among numerous Melville aficionados I benefited from, I want to thank Paul Ingendaay, Wolfgang Matz, John Logan, Gordon Poole, and Mary K. Bercaw Edwards for many helpful suggestions.

2. For a survey of Melville's international reputation see Sanford E. Marovitz, "Herman Melville: A Writer for the World," in Bryant, *Companion,* 741–80.

3. Daniel Göske, "Melville's Early Reception in German Translation and Criticism," *Amerikastudien / American Studies* 36.2 (1991): 209–26, 223–24.

4. Herman Melville, *Moby Dick oder der weiße Wal,* trans. and adapt. Wilhelm Strüver (Berlin: Knaur, 1927).

5. *Moby Dick o la Balena,* trans. Cesare Pavese (1932; Milan: Adelphi, 2001); *Moby Dick,* trans. Lucien Jacques, Joan Smith, and Jean Giono (1939; Paris: Gallimard, 1941).

6. In occupied Paris of 1941, Carl Schmitt, Ernst Jünger, and a select group of conservative opponents of the Nazi regime discussed *Benito Cereno* as a paradigm of their country's fate, with the moody Spanish captain as a symbolic type of the powerless intellectual in Nazi Germany. Möring's fine but rather loose version of *Billy Budd,* which is partly based on Pierre Leyris's French translation of 1935, was reprinted, despite the paper shortage of Germany's war economy, as late as 1942, probably to boost the morale of the troops. Möring, a poet of exquisitely formal verse under his pen name Peter Gan, had become *persona non grata* and was forced to escape to Paris in November 1938 while the reviewers back home interpreted his *Billy Budd* in the contexts of martial law, political theory, theology, and German literature. Many of these and later responses may have been self-serving or forced, and the status of Melville's ambiguous testament seemed secured only in 1956, when Thomas Mann extolled *Billy Budd* as the most moving, masterly, and "modern" story in a two-volume anthology of world literature. See Daniel Göske, *Herman Melville in deutscher Sprache* (Frankfurt: Lang, 1990), 100–105 and 263–68.

7. *Moby Dick oder der weiße Wal,* trans. Margarete Möckli von Seggern, illus. Otto Tschumi (Zurich: Büchergilde Gutenberg, 1942). All the other full translations predating Jendis's new version are still in print: *Moby Dick,* trans. Fritz Güttinger (Zürich: Manesse, 1944), *Moby-Dick,* trans. Thesi Mutzenbecher and Ernst Schnabel (Hamburg: Claassen & Goverts, 1946), *Moby*

Dick oder der weiße Wal, trans. Richard Mummendey, illus. Herbert Pridöhl (1954; Darmstadt: Wissenschaftliche Buchgesellschaft, 1966), and *Moby Dick oder der Wal,* trans. Alice and Hans Seiffert (1956; Berlin: Aufbau, 1982). My back translations from these and other German sources are indicated by quotation marks.

8. For a more detailed survey see Daniel Göske, "'Writing a Book, Speaking a Speech': Narrator, Fictive Audience, and Narrative Mode in Melville's *Moby-Dick* and Its German Translations," *Literatur in Wissenschaft und Unterricht* 21.1 (1988): 38–51.

9. "Au milieu de l'impersonnalité générale, ici se tient quelqu'un" (Giono 485). "In der Masse der Menschen steh ich allein, ein Mensch" (Mutzenbecher 441). "Inmitten des gestaltgewordenen Wesenlosen steht hier ein Mann" (Seiffert 570).

10. "Kreischend schwirrten die Möven über dem gähnenden Schlund; gegen seine steilen Wände brandete brausend der weiße Gischt. Dann stürzte alles in sich zusammen, und das weite Leichentuch des Meeres wallte fort wie seit fünftausend Jahren" (Mutzenbecher 497; see Mummendey 682 or Seiffert 643).

11. Extracts of Rathjen's version were later published in *Schreibheft* 57 (2001): 11–125; the journal also features his disarmingly frank (and alarmingly confusing) "confessions of a self-righteous translator" (127–37). The essay reappears in the recent collector's edition of Rathjen's complete translation, with Rockwell Kent's stark illustrations: *Moby-Dick; oder: Der Wal* (Frankfurt: Zweitausendeins, 2004), 947–58. Rathjen's version of an uncompromisingly "faithful" rendering of *Moby-Dick* depends on his view of Melville's masterpiece as "an absolute impossibility ['Unding'], a monstrosity, a bastard" (951), indeed, "the epitome of literary chaos"—"literarische Wirrnis schlechthin" (958). I disagree entirely with this sweeping verdict; whether it fits Rathjen's translation, however, may be left to the wise to determine. For critical comments see Wolfgang Matz, "Willensverwirrung verwickelter Worte: Einige Anmerkungen zu Friedhelm Rathjens *Moby-Dick* und zum Übersetzen überhaupt," *Neue Rundschau* 115.4 (2004): 200–207.

12. Matthew Arnold, *On Translating Homer* (1865; London: Smith, Elder & Co., 1896), 3. "In literary translation," observes Louis Kelly, "fidelity follows intangibles, rather than units of the text." Modern critics and translators like Hilaire Belloc or Ezra Pound knew that fidelity "was the obligation of deciding what was important, and the choice of how this was to be reproduced or represented in the target text. Much depends on the insight the translator brings to his text, on the balance perceived between meaning, sound and form." Louis Kelly, *The True Interpreter: A History of Translation Theory and Practise in the West* (Oxford, U.K.: Oxford Univ. Press, 1979), 210–11.

13. Eugene F. Irey, *A Concordance to Herman Melville's Moby-Dick* (New York: Garland, 1982).

14. See Güttinger 219, Mutzenbecher 129, Mummendey 168, Seiffert 154. Even Rathjen's allegedly "faithful" translation of 2004 presents Ahab only with "Marterspuren" ("traces of torment") in his face (Rathjen 175).

15. *Moby Dick,* trans. Armel Guerne (1954; n.p.: Presses Pocket, 1981), 480, and *Moby Dick,* trans. Henriette Guex-Rolle (Paris: Flammarion, 1989), 431.

16. Pavese 37 and Jendis 33. See also the first Spanish version: "Llámenme Ismael." *Moby Dick: La ballena blanca,* trans. Guillermo Guerrero Estrella, Hugo E. Ricart, and Alejandro Rosa (Buenos Aires: Emecé, 1944; Mexico: Unam, 1960), 27. There are still other variations. The first French and a recent Italian translation skirt the issue, avoiding any form of address: "Je m'appelle Ishmaël" (Giono 25) or, more elaborately, "Diciamo che mi chiamo Ismaele." *Moby Dick o la balena,* trans. Bernardo Draghi (Milan: Frasinelli, 2001). Two German translations also use the second option but add a note of grudging assent, as if the narrator was merely

reacting to being called Ishmael: "Nennt mich meinethalben Ismael" (Mutzenbecher 23) or "So nennt mich denn Ismael" (Mummendey 25). No German translator picked the modern, formal address known from many twentieth-century novels ("Nennen Sie mich Ismael").

17. For a related issue see Milton M. Azevedo, "Shadows of a Literary Dialect: *For Whom the Bell Tolls* in Five Languages," *Hemingway Review* 20.1 (2000): 30–48.

18. See Thomas Linden, "Ewiger Kampf zwischen Meer und Mensch," *Kölnische Rundschau,* Oct. 27, 2001, and Georg Patzer, "Einfach mörderisch," *Mannheimer Morgen,* Nov. 29, 2001.

19. Dieter E. Zimmer, "Adolf Atta Ahab," *Die Zeit* (Literaturbeilage), Nov. 2001, 4.

20. Jens Voss, "Dämonischer Kämpfer an Bord," *Rheinische Post,* Dec. 24, 2001.

21. Klaus Modick, "Kapitän Bush und Moby Bin Laden," *Tages-Anzeiger,* Feb. 5, 2002.

22. See, for instance, Jason Epstein, "Leviathan," *New York Review of Books,* May 1, 2003, 13–14, or David Ignatius's comment with the programmatic title "Bush must steer clear of Ahab's error," first published in the *Washington Post* but also available in old Europe thanks to the reprint in the *Guardian Weekly,* Feb. 20–26, 27.

23. E. L. Doctorow, "Composing *Moby-Dick:* What Might Have Happened," *Leviathan: A Journal of Melville Studies* 5.1 (2003): 5–14, 5. Rpt. in *"Ungraspable Phantom"*; see p. 15.

24. Herman Melville, *Moby-Dick,* adapt. Klaus Buhlert (Munich: Hörverlag, 2002). Numerous well-known actors participated in the production, which lasts almost ten hours and includes wonderful music and highly suggestive sound effects.

The Brazilian Whale

IRENE HIRSCH

M*oby-Dick* is undoubtely the most popular of Herman Melville's works in Brazil, considering the number of translations and adaptations that are available. Other works like *Bartleby, Billy Budd, Typee,* and some tales have also been translated, but *Mardi, Redburn, Pierre, White-Jacket,* and *Israel Potter,* not to mention his poetry and other prose pieces, are virtually unknown to a Brazilian public dependent on translations into Portuguese.

Translation has always assumed great importance in Brazilian literature, and scholars have recently studied the impact of translation on national literary production. Some of this research focuses on the reception of the translated work, analyzing the various kinds of transformations the original went through and identifying the reasons for those changes. Political as well as moral censorship has been responsible for major alterations of classic novels. Nevertheless, the economic factor has had a determining role in many of these alterations as well. The Brazilian market is perceived as having a demand for mainly three different kinds of translations, as defined by John Milton in "The Translation of Classic Novels in Brazil."[1] *Moby-Dick* belongs in all three categories.

The first kind of translation aims at a demanding adult public who requires an integral and faithful version of the text. Two translations of *Moby-Dick* fall into this category, one by Berenice Xavier (Editora José Olympio, 1950) and another by Péricles Eugênio da Silva Ramos (Editora Abril, 1972). Both publishing houses demonstrate concern for creating books of high quality (with minor translation problems). Editora José Olympio, besides purchasing

Rockwell Kent's rights to reproduce his illustrations, hired another graphic artist, Poty, the illustrator of the books by Guimarães Rosa, to give his Brazilian visual interpretation of the narrative.

The second kind of translation aims at a less affluent adult public and transforms the original severely. Milton calls these "covert" translations because omissions and suppressions are not made clear to the reader and frequently are hidden under the euphemism "special translation." This is the case of the first edition of *Moby-Dick* in Brazil published by Companhia Editora Nacional in 1935. Two translators worked on it: Monteiro Lobato, an influential Brazilian writer and one of the founders of the company, and Adalberto Rochsteiner. This edition reduced the original 135 chapters to only 55 condensed chapters. The resultant work differs radically from Melville's.

José Maria Machado produced another covert translation in 1957. Printed on cheap paper without illustrations, the translation was shaped to fit the format of the books of the Clube do Livro. This enormously successful book club published monthly volumes and distributed them by post. *Moby-Dick* was printed in two different volumes of about 180 pages each and launched in consecutive months. The original underwent a different process of transformation: although whole chapters as well as passages were suppressed, condensation of the remaining chapters did not play an important role.

The third kind of market—and the largest—consists of illustrated adaptations for children. There are twelve different versions of *Moby-Dick* with varied editorial treatment. The variety ranges from a visual narrative with balloons to a retold text by Carlos Heitor Cony, one of Brazil's best-known living writers.

A "FAITHFUL" TRANSLATION

Fidelity in translation has been intensively discussed in this field of studies, so the use of quotation marks in the phrase "faithful" translations indicates the copying of an original in another language. Inevitably, changes occur in every translation. Nevertheless, Berenice Xavier's translation of *Moby-Dick* aims at being a copy of the original.

In his study of "Conjoint Phrases as Translational Solutions," Gideon Toury describes the kinds of shifts found in Berenice Xavier's translation, like the use of near-synonyms instead of source text single lexical items.[2] This shift can be illustrated with the passage in which Stubb tells Flask about his dream. The repetition of the word "says" is replaced in translation with three different terms in Portuguese ("disse," "respondeu"/"respondi," and "tornou"):

But I had only just lifted my foot for it, when he roared out, "Stop that kicking!" "Halloa," *says I*, "what's the matter now, old fellow?" "Look ye here," *says he*; "let's argue the insult. Captain Ahab kicked ye, didn't he?" "Yes, he did" *says I*—"right here it was." "Very good," *says he*—"he used his ivory leg, didn't he?" "Yes, he did," *says I.* (*MD* 132; emphasis added)

Porém mal havia erguido o pé, quando êle rugiu: "Detém êste pontapé!" "Olá," *disse eu*, "que é isso agora, meu velho?" "Ouve," *respondeu êle*, "vamos discutir êste insulto. O Capitão Acab te bateu, não foi?" "Sim," *disse eu*, "bem aqui!" "Muito bem," *tornou êle*, "bateu com a perna de marfim, não foi?" "Sim," *respondi.*[3]

This fragment illustrates another kind of shift observed by Antoine Berman: embellishment (*l'ennoblissment*).[4] The translation follows the classic model of translation whereby the translator attempts a "better" ("plus belle") book than the original. Stubb's misuse of English grammar is changed into correct Portuguese, thus changing his character and presenting the reader with an educated character. Another passage that illustrates such "embellishment" more clearly is Fleece's sermon to the sharks, where the dialect lost through "correction" can be easily traced. Here is the original:

Your woraciousness, fellow-critters, I don't blame ye so much for; dat is natur, and can't be helped; but to gobern dat wicked natur, dat is de pint. You is sharks, sartin; but if you gobern de shark in you, why den you be angel; for all angel is not'ing more dan de shark well goberned. Now, look here, bred'ren, just try wonst to be cibil, a helping yourselbs from dat whale. Don't be tearin' de blubber out your neighbour's mout, I say. Is not one shark good right as toder to dat whale? And, by Gor, none on you has de right to dat whale; dat whale belong to some one else. (*MD* 295)

This becomes "pure" Portuguese:

Vocês são vorazes, irmãos em Deus, e não os culpo muito disso. Está na sua natureza e não se pode dar jeito. Porém é preciso dominar esta natureza, é o que é. Vocês são tubarões, é certo, mas se conseguissem dominar o tubarão que trazem dentro de si, então seriam anjos, porque um anjo não é mais do que um tubarão que se domina. Escutem, irmãos, procurem ser educados uma vez na vida, ao comer essa baleia. Não tirem o espermacete da bôca de seu vizinho. Por acaso não têm os outros tanto direito a essa baleia como vocês, tubarões? E por Deus, nenhum de vocês, a falar a verdade, tem direito a ela, que é propriedade de outros. (Xavier 447)

Which translates back to:

You are voracious, brethren in God, and I do not blame you for it. It is in your nature and it cannot be helped. But it is necessary to dominate this nature, this is it. You are all sharks, that is right, but if you could dominate the shark that you bring inside yourselves then you would be angels, because an angel is nothing but a shark that can control itself. Listen, brethren, try to be polite for once in life when you eat this whale. Do not take the sperm [sic] out of your neighbour's mouth. Don't you think the others have the same right to this whale as you, sharks? And by God, none of you, to tell the truth, has the right to it, because it is someone else's property.

Another excess of zeal in Xavier's translation that proved inappropriate is the addition of another extract to "Extracts." After Melville's "Whale Song" the editor inserted a footnote explaining the deliberate inclusion of an extract of a Brazilian writer, Frei Manuel de Santa Maria (1704–1768), which reads as follows,

Monstro do mar, gigante do profundo,
Uma tôrre nas ondas soçobrada,
Que parece em todo o âmbito rotundo;
Jamais bêsta tão grande foi criada:
Os mares despedaça furibundo
Co'a barbatana às vezes levantada:
Cujos membros tetérrimos e broncos
Fazem a Tétis dar gemidos roncos.
Baleia vulgarmente lhe chamamos . . . (Xavier 38)

My translation:

*Monster of the sea, giant of the depths,
A shipwrecked tower on the waves,
Which appears in all rotund circuits,
Never before was such a beast created:
Furious breaks the seas.*

With a sometimes lifted fin
Whose somber and coarse limbs
Makes Tetis roar thunders.
Ordinarily called Whale . . .

So-called faithful translations such as Xavier's can flatten ambiguities. Words, expressions, or sentences with more than one meaning do not always find an easy equivalent in the other language, and they are usually translated into just one of the many possibilities. Melville's controversial beginning "Call me Ishmael," understood as an informal invitation to the reader to take part in the adventure, is lost in Xavier's translation "Chamai-me Ismael." The option to use the formal treatment, the second person plural ("Cham*ai*-me") instead of the second person singular ("Cham*a*-me"), seems more in accord with the reading that understands "Call me Ishmael" as being a formal invitation implicit in the use of a biblical name rather than an informal one because of Ishmael's more informal tone. This option proves decisive as it determines the relationship between Ishmael and the reader throughout the narrative.

Melville's irony challenges the skills of many "faithful" translators. Some passages of *Moby-Dick* force translators to make use of explanatory footnotes, where they often avow the difficulty of translation. Such is the case when the old Manx sailor delivers his "sexy" speech in "Forecastle—Midnight": "Well, well; belike the whole world's one ball, as your scholars have it; and so 'tis right to make one ball-room of it. Dance on, lads, you're young; I was once" (*MD* 175). The word "ball" has more than one meaning here: it could refer to a solid round sphere or to a social gathering for dancing, or it could have a sexual connotation, referring to intercourse. Xavier opts for the sphere, creating a sentence because it is nonsensical: "Bem, bem, consideremos o mundo como uma bola como a dos colegiais; assim é direito fazer dêle um salão de baile. Continuem a dançar, rapazes, vocês são jovens. Eu também já fui" (Xavier 301). Which translates back to: "*Well, well; let's consider the world's one sphere like a student's; and so it is right to make one ball-room of it. Dance on, lads, you're young; I was once.*"

Another passage that poses difficulties for translators is that in which Ishmael and Queequeg arrive at the Try Pots Inn on Nantucket. Their dialogue with Mrs. Hussey has multiple meanings, impossible for the translators to render into another language without some losses:

"Clam or Cod?"
"What's that about Cods, ma'am?" said I, with much politeness.
"Clam or Cod?" she repeated.

"A clam for supper? a cold clam; is *that* what you mean, Mrs. Hussey?" says I; but that is a rather cold and clammy reception in the winter time, ain't it, Mrs. Hussey?" (*MD* 66)

The intended pun on "clam" and "clammy" is lost when Xavier uses two different words to translate: "mexilhões" for "clam" and "pobre" for "clammy":

—*Mexilhões* ou bacalhau?
Mexilhões para a ceia, Mrs. Hussey?—disse eu muito cortesmente.—
Mas não acha que é uma recepção muito fria e *pobre* para uma noite de inverno? (Xavier 134)

Back translation:

"Mollusk or Cod?"
"A mollusk for supper? A cold mollusk; is that what you mean, Mrs Hussey?" I said politely; but isn't that a rather cold and poor reception for a winter night?"

In "The Log and the Line," the dialogue between the Manxman and Ahab is another text worth examining:

"I know not, sir, but I was born there."
"In the Isle of *Man*, hey? Well, the other way, it's good. Here's a *man* from *Man*; a *man* born in once independent *Man*, and now *unmanned* of *Man*; which is sucked in—by what?" (*MD* 521; emphasis added)

Melville deliberately employs the word "man" seven times with different meanings, thus creating a puzzle for the translator. Xavier chooses to use three words—"homem" for the human male, "Man" for the geographic location, and "desarraigado" for "unmanned"—instead of one. Because the repetition cannot be reproduced, the ironic effect of the passage is lost to the reader:

—Não sei, senhor, porém foi lá que nasci.
—Na ilha do *Man*, hein? Bem, não está mal. Temos aqui um *homem* do *Man*, um *homem* nascido no *Man*, outrora independente, agora *desarraigado* do *Man*, absorvido . . . Porquê? (Xavier 810)

Another shift of translations observed by Antoine Berman occurs when idiomatic expressions are destroyed (Berman 79). The expression "a rolling stone gathers no moss" finds no equivalent in Portuguese and is therefore eliminated from Ishmael's description of the carpenter.

> Was it that this old carpenter had been a life-long wanderer, whose much rolling, to and fro, not only had gathered no moss; but what is more, had rubbed off whatever small outward clingings might have originally pertained to him? (*MD* 467–68)

> Por acaso esse velho carpinteiro teria sido durante toda a sua vida um vagabundo, que à força de rolar de um lado para outro não somente havia criado môfo como também conseguira desembaraçar-se de todas as aderências externas que lhe pudessem ter pertencido anteriormente? (Xavier 726)

> *By chance this old carpenter had been a life-long wanderer, whose much rolling from one side to the other, not only had gathered no mold, but had rubbed off all outward clingings that might have originally pertained to him?* (back translation)

Punctuation is another matter worthy of consideration: how faithful can a translator be to Melville's endless semicolons? But perhaps the most dramatic alteration in this translated text of *Moby-Dick* is a question of gender, performed not by the translators nor the publishers, but by language constraint: in Portuguese—as may well be the case in other languages—the whale is referred to as female. Because *Moby-Dick*'s universe is predominantly peopled by men, it seems quite bizarre that all those seamen, mariners, whalemen, harpooners, and sailors should chase a creature of the opposite sex, a female. Of course this could lead to a completely different understanding of Melville's narrative, besides making the whole Chapter 95, "The Cassock," nonsensical.

Although these shifts may change Melville's original writing, they are not unique to Xavier's translation of *Moby-Dick* to Portuguese. Xavier's text illustrates some common translation problems. Despite the authorial presence of the translator in Melville's text, Xavier's translation, along with the translation of Péricles Eugênio da Silva Ramos, expand the popularity of Melville significantly in Brazil.

Berenice Xavier's translation was first published in 1950 by Editora José Olympio, n° 96 in the series Fogos Cruzados (Crossed Fires), with a preface by well-known novelist Rachel de Queiroz. After the Hollywood film was released in 1956, this translation received a more luxurious edition, with Rockwell Kent's illustrations as well as Poty's visual interpretation. José Olympio then sold the rights of this translation to different publishers: in 1967, Editora Ediouro published it in paperback, followed by Editora Francisco Alves, and in 1998, Publifolha also reprinted it. The Publifolha edition was the largest reprint: 24,000 copies, which were distributed with one of the major Brazilian newspapers, *Folha de São Paulo,* at a promotional price (less than U.S. $2).

Péricles Eugênio da Silva Ramos's translation resembles Xavier's in many ways, as it also presents an integral and faithful version of the text aimed at a more demanding public. It was published by Editora Abril in 1972, with a red cover, the title printed in gold letters, and it was accompanied by a twenty-page illustrated pamphlet. For the new edition, released in 1980, the cover was changed and the book was printed in two volumes.

COVERT TRANSLATIONS

As already mentioned "covert translations," of which there are two examples of *Moby-Dick* in Brazil, transform the original without informing the reader of the change. Besides reducing production costs, such textual suppression also "domesticates" Melville's voluminous work. What may have seemed "too complicated" or "too long" is simplified for the public, thus giving the public the illusion of accessible (and cheap) erudition. Not revealing the technique of suppression also forms part of the marketing strategy.

Besides reducing the number of chapters, suppression can take more insidious forms. For example, both editions leave out Stubb's dream along with its "Queen Mab" chapter, as well as Fleece's sermon. In fact, Fleece is cut from the novel altogether, revealing yet another form of suppression: the removal of minor characters from the narrative, at the cost of penalizing stylistic registers.

Suppression is not restricted to chapters or characters: sometimes a paragraph is only partially translated or a metaphor is excised. The description of Ahab's scar in Machado's translation can be taken as a case in point. The sections that have been cut out are italicized.

> It resembled that perpendicular seam sometimes made in the straight, lofty trunk *of a great tree,* when the upper lightning tearingly darts down it, *and without wrenching a single twig,* peels and grooves out the bark from top to bottom, *ere running off into the soil, leaving the tree still greenly alive, but branded.* (MD 123)

> Lembrava essa marca perpendicular que, às vêzes, perdura nos troncos direitos e altos xxxxxx, fulminados por coriscos xxxxxxxx

xxxxxxxxxxxxxxxxxxxxxxxxxxxx que os descascam de alto a baixo *xxxxxx xxxxxxx xxxxxxxxxxxxxxx xxxxxxxx xxxxxxxxxx xxx x xxxxxxxxxxxx xxxxx.*[5]

However; while Machado's work mainly involves suppression, Lobato and Rochsteiner prefer condensation. Rather than cut, they summarize the narrative, reducing the passage quoted above into:

—lembrando certos lanhos que os coriscos deixam nas árvores fulminadas e que as marcam para sempre de alto a baixo.[6]

Which is translated back into English as:

—resembling certain slashes lightning leaves on struck down trees and brands them forever from top to bottom.

The criteria used for deciding what stays and what should be deleted is not always the same for both "translations." While Machado's cuts seem to be aimed mainly at reducing costs, Lobato's translation resembles in many aspects the adaptations for children, where the emphasis is placed on the linear narrative of Ahab's quest, at the expense of Melville's subtler, more ambiguous universe. Characters are simplified and their exotic characteristics highlighted, giving the reader stereotyped individuals. Thus, Daggoo becomes a dignified black savage with big earrings, whose description reads:

O terceiro arpoador chamava-se Daggoo, um negralhão prêto como pixe e de andar imponente. Trazia nas orelhas argolas de ouro de demarcadas dimensões. Muito moço ainda embarcara num navio baleeiro que fizera escala em sua terra natal—e nunca mais mudara de profissão. Daggoo conservava tôdas as características da selvageria primitiva, e era de vê-lo atravessar o convés com seus dois metros e cinco de altura—imponentíssimo.

Detalhe curioso: este negro agigantado fizera-se escudeiro do homem de menor estatura do Pequod—Flask, o qual, ao seu lado, lembrava um peão de xadrez rente ao rei. (Lobato 61)

Which in English would be translated as:

The third harpooner was called Daggoo, a negro as black as pitch with an imposing step. He had two very large golden hoops on his ears. Still very young he embarked on a whaler which called at his native land—and never again did he change profession. Daggoo retained all his barbaric virtues and to see him move about the deck with his six feet eight inches—very pompous.

A curious detail: this gigantic black was the squire of the shortest man on the Pequod—Flask, who looked like a chess-man next to the king when beside him.

Compare the English back translation to Melville's original:

Third among the harpooners was Daggoo, a gigantic, coal-black negro-savage, with a lion-like tread—an Ahasuerus to behold. Suspended from his ears were two golden hoops, so large that the sailors called them ring-bolts, and would talk of securing the top-sail halyards to them. In his youth Daggoo had voluntarily shipped on board of a whaler, lying in a lonely bay on his native coast. And never having been anywhere in the world but in Africa, Nantucket, and the pagan harbors most frequented by whalemen; and having now led for many years the bold life of the fishery in the ships of owners uncommonly heedful of what manner of men they shipped; Daggoo retained all his barbaric virtues, and erect as a giraffe, moved about the decks in all the pomp of six feet five in his socks. There was a corporeal humility in looking up at him; and a white man standing before him seemed a white flag come to beg truce of a fortress. Curious to tell, this imperial negro, Ahasuerus Daggoo, was the Squire of little Flask, who looked like a chess-man beside him. (*MD* 120)

Along with all the metaphors, Daggoo's origins are absent from Lobato's description. The comparison with Ahasuerus receives no mention, nor does Africa, nor Nantucket, nor the "pagan harbors most frequented by whalemen."

Nevertheless, Monteiro Lobato was a pioneering figure on the Brazilian publishing and literary scene, and the period in which his translation was launched, between 1930 and 1940, saw considerable growth in the book industry and in the number of translations in Brazil. Because translated literature, especially of American works, thrived at that time, publishers hired a number of well-known Brazilian writers to translate classic works. Therefore, Lobato's translation of *Moby-Dick* in 1935, despite not being an integral and faithful version, can be considered innovative, as it suited the interests of an emerging reading public.

Similar in many aspects to both kinds of translation previously examined, children's adaptations nevertheless give a clearer indication to readers of what they can expect from the book. The use of expressions like "retold by" or "adaptation of" on the front cover or title page reflects more respect toward both the public and the author.

Although these versions emphasize the linear events of the adventure with few references to Melville's symbolic universe, they are to a large extent responsible—along with John Huston's 1956 film—for Melville's popularity in Brazil. Indeed, the influence of Hollywood can clearly be seen in these editions. After the film's debut, several children's editions were published in Brazil, some with illustrations of a Captain Ahab resembling Gregory Peck.

According to André Lefevere's theory of refracted literature, translation plays an important part in disseminating the work of writers. Refracted texts are works that have been revised for certain audiences, children for example, or adapted to a certain poetics or ideology. Lefevere claims that, before reading a classic, readers have already perceived it for many years as a series of refractions, from the comic strip through the extract in school anthologies to films, television serials, plot summaries, and even critical articles. He stresses the importance of these rewritings, drawing parallels with the popularity of the Bible, which relatively few people have had the opportunity to read in the original. He illustrates his point of view with historic examples demonstrating that William Blake owes much of his permanence to Swinbourne's and Yeats's refractions, and John Donne and the metaphysical poets owe much to T. S. Eliot's.[7]

In October 1948 the first children's edition of *Moby-Dick* was published in Brazil by Editora Ebal. It was a translation of the 1942 *Classic Comics,* illustrated by Louis Zansky. The next children's editions of *Moby-Dick* were published simultaneously in 1962 by two different publishing houses, Editora Melhoramentos and Editora Record, each consisting mainly of verbal text with black-and-white pictures. The former, Maria Teresa Giacomo's adaptation with its ten editions, became the most popular. Its forty-nine condensed chapters resemble Lobato's "translation": however, the translator adapts lexical items to children's vocabulary. Indirect speech is changed into direct speech, fragmenting the text into simplified dialogues. Melville's long paragraphs are shortened to five to eight lines each, and nautical and cetological information is reduced to a few references. Characters are stereotyped, and in this version we have the following for Daggoo:

Daggoo, o terceiro arpoador—era um negro retinto, imponente como um leão selvagem. Trazia penduradas nas orelhas argolas de ouro tão pesadas que se podia pensar em prender nelas as cordas da gávea. Engajara-se muito môço, mas conservava todo o seu aspecto de selvageria. Agora passeava no convés com seus dois metros de altura, olhando do alto o resto da tripulação.

Por ironia, era ajudante do pequeno Flask que, ao seu lado, parecia uma grotesca peça de xadrez.[8]

Back translation:

Daggoo, the third harpooner—was a jetblack negro, imposing like a wild lion. Hanging from his ears there were two golden hoops, so heavy that you could consider tying the top-sail halyards to them. He had joined when he was very young but kept all his wild appearance. Now he walked about the deck, six feet five tall, looking down at the rest of the crew.

Ironically he was the assistant of little Flask who looked like a grotesque chess-piece when beside him.[9]

Francisco da Silva Ramos's adaptation, published by Record in the same year, offers a more severely reduced version. It occupies number seventeen of a series called Livros para a Juventude (Books for Youth). The same author translated other installments in this collection.

Other Portuguese versions of *Moby-Dick* have followed, and Francisco Manuel da Rocha's adaptation, first published by Editora Bruguera, was better manufactured by Editora Abril in 1972 in the series called Clássicos da Literatura Juvenil (Classics of Juvenile Literature). It includes both text and impressive illustrations made by pop graphic artist Luis Trimano, who updated the visual information of the work. Trimano's fifteen pictures show a strong influence from the cinema, though not the cinema of Hollywood. The presence of German expressionism and Soviet cinematography can be seen in the technique of montage that is used in the black-and-white images employed by the artist. This rendition stresses not the linear adventure but the epic dimension of the work; it aims at translating Melville's complex narrative strategy.

The 1970s also brought a verbal update: Editora Ediouro hired well-known writer Carlos Heitor Cony to retell the story, and the result was a high-quality text with few pictures in a cheap edition. Award-winning Cony, who continues to enjoy celebrity in the late 1990s, was already famous then. At the very start of the book, before beginning his version, he warns the reader that *Moby-Dick* can be read in two different ways; one is scholarly, the reading of the original, and the other he calls popular, which stresses the episodic aspect of the book. The twenty-six renamed chapters are written in a fluent text with simplified vocabulary. Says Cony:

> In a very rigorous list of the ten biggest books of all times, one would include without hesitations the great novel of Herman Melville, *Moby-Dick*. Therefore, it is a key work of universal literature. It is placed with *Gulliver, Tom Jones, D. Quijote* and other literary monuments.
> Like the above mentioned *Moby-Dick* allows for two readings: the scholarly, which does not dispense with the reading of the original; and the popular, which only uses its episodic aspect.[10]

Moby-Dick underwent more radical changes too. The text was fragmented into speech bubbles with a picture narrative in the Editora Hemus edition in which Captain Ahab resembles Gregory Peck. This undated adaptation with a new format is a Brazilian version from the American Pendulum Press edition by Irwin Shapiro with a new cover by a Brazilian artist, Décio Guedes. Another translated adaptation is Yone Quartim's from a Spanish edition, printed in Colombia and distributed by Editora Tempo Cultural in 1989.

A popular children's version of *Moby-Dick* is Editora Scipione's, which has had more than five editions since it appeared in 1985. Besides modernizing the text and the visual aspect, it thematically "updates" the novel as well. Werner Zotz tells the reader of a more psychologically complex captain than the bloody, revengeful one of the previous versions. The chapter suggestively called "Amor, ternura, conflitos íntimos" ("Love, tenderness and private conflicts") offers an adaptation of "The Symphony," previously cut out from other adaptations. Although Ahab's soliloquy is reduced to "Escuta: sou um homem marcado pelo destino" (Listen: I am a man marked by fate), this version keeps his dialogue with Starbuck along with his hesitation.

In 1990, Editora Abril invested for the third time in *Moby-Dick*. After having published one version for adults (Péricles Eugênio da Silva Ramos's translation) and one for children (Francisco Manuel da Rocha's adaptation), the famous Brazilian publishing house chose to publish a comic. It is a translation of the adaptation of *Classics Illustrated* by Bill Sienkiewicz and Dan Chichester, and it is the first book of a series with the same name.

In 1996 Editora Verbo published Maria Guerne's adaptation, and in 1997 Editora Melhoramentos published Luiz Antonio Aguiar's adaptation, with colored illustrations. A recent Brazilian adaptation of *Moby-Dick* came out in 1998, another comic rendition: fashionable Editora Companhia das Letras hired Carlos Sussekind to translate Will Eisner's adaptation and presented the juvenile public with a third comic version of the story.

Important Brazilian artists worked on Melville's text, as mentioned above, creating a visual register with local color. Napoleon Potyguara Lazzarotto (1924–1998) was an important Brazilian graphic artist. Besides being an illustrator of books by significant Brazilian writers such as Jorge Amado, Graciliano Ramos, Euclides da Cunha, and Machado de Assis, Poty was also a painter, designer, and engraver. Poty's twelve *Moby-Dick* plates were published together with Rockwell Kent's by Editora José Olympio in 1957, and the former's focus is on the chase of the whale. The sea dominates Poty's narrative, and he created sequences of pictures that suggest movement, for example, the boat and the tail of a whale, the boat and the head of a whale, and the boat and the body of a whale. His plates constitute an independent narrative that does not coincide with the events in the text. Poty does not depict the urban landscape and he disregards most characters: even Ishmael has a secondary role in his black-and-white pictures.

Other artists like Oswaldo Storni, Luis Trimano, Lee, and Maria Cecília Marra also interpreted Melville's fiction with drawings. As their work was published in children's editions, they tended to concentrate on characters and events. However, Storni's fifty-two black-and-white pictures of different sizes suggest a better understanding of the several possibilities offered by the narrative.

There have also been a large number of stage adaptations of *Moby-Dick* in Brazil recently. In 1997, Centro Cultural de São Paulo put on an adaptation directed by Cintia Alves that was aimed at a teenage public. The script by Cintia Alves and Wagner Santana was awarded the Coca-Cola Prize for Plays for Young Audiences. A musical staged in a circus ring, it had ten actors interpreting the main characters: Ahab and Ishmael; the mates Starbuck, Stubb, and Flask; the harpooners Queequeg, Tashtego, and Daggoo; the cook Fleece; and the prophet Elijah. The adventure formed the main thread of the narrative.

Another Brazilian staging was the free adaptation of the group Circo Mínimo presented in 1999, also at Centro Cultural São Paulo. The group, set up by Rodrigo Matheus in 1988, mixed circus techniques with dramatic language. Cristiane Paoli-Quito directed the play, which was awarded two prizes, including the Shell Theater Prize, for Rodrigo Matheus's set and Wagner Freire's illumination. It was written for two actors and performed with them spending most of the time aloft, hanging from ropes. They did not interpret a specific character but simulated tempests, fights, shipwrecks, and hunts using illumination and sound track as basic components of the script in a fifty- to sixty-minute spectacle.

The presence of Melville's work in Brazil encompasses a wider range nonetheless, not restricted to these works. Besides boosting the number of publications and the sales of books, the impact of John Huston's film has shaped the imagination of many readers for whom Captain Ahab *is* Gregory Peck. Other references can be found in television cartoons, in children's games, in lyrics, or even in films. Although the cultural industry has not produced as many goods as in the United States, quite a few have appeared in Brazil.

The examples of the different versions of *Moby-Dick* in Portuguese here discussed give a sample of some transformations the original went through on its arrival in Brazil. Each of these works was adapted to the needs of a specific public, which includes readers from various ages and backgrounds. The large number of rewritings shows the influential presence of Melville in Brazil; now, more than sixty years after the first publication, the figures show an increasing interest within the Brazilian public for *Moby-Dick* in particular and for Melville's works in general.

Notes

1. John Milton, "A tradução dos romances clássicos do inglês para o português no Brasil," *Cadernos de Lingüística Aplicada* 24 (1995): 66.

2. Gideon Toury, *In Search of a Theory of Translation* (Tel Aviv: Porter Institute for Poetics and Semiotics, 1980), 111.

3. Herman Melville, Moby-Dick *ou A Baleia,* trans. Berenice Xavier (Rio de Janeiro: Editora José Olympio, 1957).

4. Antoine Berman, *Les Tours de Babel* (Mauvezin: Trans-Europ-Repress, 1985), 72.

5. Herman Melville, *Moby-Dick,* trans. José Maria Machado (São Paulo: Clube do Livro, 1957), 97.

6. Herman Melville, *A fera do mar,* trans. Monteiro Lobato (São Paulo: Companhia Editora Nacional, 1935), 63.

7. Andre Lefevere, "Literary Theory and Translated Literature," *Dispositio* 8 (1982): 19–20.

8. Herman Melville, *Moby-Dick,* adaptation by Maria Thereza Cunha de Giacomo (São Paulo: Editora Melhoramentos, 1962), 62.

9. To compare with the original see previous page.

10. Herman Melville, *A Baleia Branca,* adaptation by Carlos Heitor Cony (São Paulo: Ediouro, 1970), 10.

Modern Breachings:
Moby-Dick on Stage and Web

Leviathanic Revelations

Laurie Anderson's, Rinde Eckert's, and John Barrymore's *Moby-Dick*s

SAMUEL OTTER

In both Laurie Anderson's *Songs and Stories from Moby Dick* (1999) and Rinde Eckert's *And God Created Great Whales* (2000), Captain Ahab dances. In Anderson's multimedia spectacle, Ahab announces that he has seen the white whale and leaps on and over his crutches at the end of his first speech. In Eckert's chamber opera, while the protagonist Nathan and his Muse discuss Ahab, who feels the itch of "phantom limbs" and seeks his "missing parts," Nathan does not move with the stiffened right leg that characterized his first portrayal of Ahab. Instead, while the crew dances above deck, he bounces on the tips of his feet. These scenes evoke the memory of John Barrymore's once-famous Warner Brothers Ahab, with Barrymore as the star of both silent (1926) and sound (1930) film versions of Melville's book. At the start of both films, Ahab is shown capering in the ship's ropes long before his encounter with Moby Dick; later, after the excruciating loss of his leg and the struggle to use his prosthetic limb, and after he kills Moby Dick, he once more becomes an acrobat in the rigging.[1]

These nimble Ahabs surprise us. Like so much else in these representations of Melville's text, they help us to see the book anew. They are gestures that diverge from the text but also return us to it with renewed understanding. The dancing Ahabs remind us of the agility of Melville's one-legged captain, and of the ways in which his psychic loss far exceeds the physical one. Although Anderson in one of her monologues makes fun of the 1926 Barrymore film—the plot twists and new characters such as Ahab's love interest Esther and his conniving half brother Derek—she herself revels in such interventions. Anderson reorders, combines, and creates passages. She introduces songs and juxtaposes words, sounds, music, and images. She eliminates and augments characters. Both Anderson and Eckert absorb Melville into their own work. They manipulate, illuminate, and transform.

Thus they treat Melville as he treats his own sources. They respond, as so many artists have in the twentieth century, to the narrator's invitation at the end of "The Prairie" chapter in *Moby-Dick:* "Read it if you can" (*MD* 347). Melville repeatedly raises questions of translation, adaptation, and representation in "Etymology," "Extracts," the three chapters on whale pictures, and the cetology chapters. Artists who adapt *Moby-Dick* continue the sequence of draughts that Melville's narrator theatrically laments at the end of "Cetology." Anderson and Eckert's *Moby-Dicks* raise questions not only about their individual perspectives on Melville's work but also about artistic creation. Like Ishmael drawn to Ahab, they are confronted with the lure of immersion and the challenge of self-definition.

Anderson and Eckert imaginatively tack and veer. The most straightforward responses to *Moby-Dick,* such as John Huston and Ray Bradbury's 1956 film, also prove the least interesting. In the preface to a 1926 photoplay edition of *Moby-Dick,* published by Grosset and Dunlap to capitalize on the success of *The Sea Beast,* S. R. Buchman of Warner Brothers defends the screenwriter's changes in character and plot. Rather than signifying "a profanely wanton alteration" or "an unprincipled desire for melodramatic heightening," the changes, Buchman contends, were dictated by the transfer from page to film and the demands of a different medium. While one might argue that the happy endings—Moby Dick dead and Ahab and Esther in each other's arms (as Buchman puts it, "Ahab had suffered enough to be granted expiation and its rewards")—represent a classic Hollywood compromise rather than artistic necessity, it is harder to dismiss the screenwriter Bess Meredyth's pursuit of Melville's hint about a wife. Like Anderson and Eckert, and like Sena Jeter Naslund in her novel *Ahab's Wife* (1999), Meredyth extracts a feminine presence from *Moby-Dick.* All these artists meditate on the text and critically transform it. Despite—or maybe because of—its discrepancies, the 1926 *The Sea Beast* offers the most powerful portrayal of Ahab's anguish and grace in any of the four films made to date. Refracting *Moby-Dick* through stage and song, Anderson and Eckert call attention to "missing parts" and "phantom limbs" in Melville's text. They engage a dialectic between the absent and the present and the part and the whole, and this lends an ache and an exhilaration to their performances.[2]

In a radio interview with the BBC, Laurie Anderson described *Songs and Stories from Moby Dick* as "my homage to him [Melville] in terms of his style and his questions." As several reviewers have observed, Anderson responds in Melville to the kinds of storytelling she herself has practiced in such performances as *United States Live* and *The Nerve Bible:* associative, imagistic, self-conscious, experimental in form and point of view. Anderson is accompanied by four male actor-singers and a bass player. She is backed with prerecorded music and sound effects and makes use on stage of huge screens and floating spheres on which images are projected. *Songs and Stories* alludes to the plot of *Moby-Dick:* the departure of the *Pequod*, Ahab's entrance, the loss and recovery of Pip, the quest for one white whale, the cataclysm, and Ishmael's sole survival. Yet plot, for both Melville and Anderson, does not tell the whole story.[3]

Sampling Melville's text, Anderson moves from "Loomings" to the cetology chapters to "The Carpenter," "The Doubloon," "The Grand Armada," "A Bower in the Arsacides," "The Fossil Whale," "The Tail," "Ahab and the Carpenter," "Stubb's Supper," "Fast-Fish and Loose-Fish," the "Epilogue," and then back to "Loomings" and finally to "The Albatross." She sets scenes to music. The precarious reveries in "The Mast-Head" become the lyrical concerns of a sailor who imagines that if he slipped he would fall "through a hole in the world," in the song "The Last Man." Pip's glimpse of God's foot upon the treadle of the loom is transformed into Anderson's plangent "Boy Overboard." She digresses about Melville's letter to Sarah Morewood warning that his book is woven of rough ropes and chains, about modern groups who try to make contact with whales by dressing up in squid costumes ("sort of suicidal"), about the 1926 *Sea Beast*, and about whales who have become disoriented by the technological clamor that fills modern oceans. She finds visual and aural analogues for Melville's obsessions: lapping waves, haunting strings, creaking boards, chains that scrape, passages from *Moby-Dick* scrolling or tumbling on screen, the mesh of industrial gears, things that are white, whispers, gasps, an insistent bass, the tapping of typewriter keys, the chime of a carriage return.

"Pieces and Parts" is Anderson's signature song. In it, she reflects on the vulnerability and partiality of knowledge. Anderson crafts the song from the chapters "The Fossil Whale" and "The Tail" and also "Loomings" and "The Fountain." She emphasizes the poetry in Melville's prose, using as her pivot the final image from "The Fossil Whale" about the discovery of prodigious relics: "But by far the most wonderful of all cetacean relics was the almost complete vast skeleton of an extinct monster, found in the year 1842, on the plantation of Judge Creagh, in Alabama. The awe-stricken credulous slaves in the vicinity took it for the bones of one of the fallen angels" (*MD* 457). As Melville's narrator explains, these bones were identified by Alabama doctors as those of a giant reptile and by the English paleontologist Richard Owen as belonging to a whale of an extinct species. Thus the find is "A significant illustration of the fact, again and again repeated in this book, that the skeleton of the whale furnishes but little clue to the shape of his fully invested body" (457). In *The Trying-Out of Moby-Dick,* Howard Vincent tells us that a gentleman named Albert Koch in 1845 manufactured a huge skeleton from several wagonloads of the Alabama bones and exhibited it to audiences at a great profit.[4]

In Melville's anecdote, Anderson unearths a lesson about his themes and methods and also her own. Joining the passage in "The Fossil Whale" with the acknowledgment at the end of "The Tail" that the narrator cannot discern either the back or front parts of the whale ("Dissect him how I may, then, I but go skin deep" [*MD* 379]), Anderson, like Melville, suggests that credulity and credibility cannot be easily separated, that knowledge can be obtained only in parts, and that these parts do not signify the whole. For Melville and for Anderson, the objects of knowledge include not only whales but also works of art. In interviews, Anderson talks about her inability to stage Melville's book and her strategy of fragments.[5]

The lyrics of the song take up these ideas: "We see him only in parts / The flash of a tail, his beating heart. / He's in pieces and parts . . . We see him only in parts / A fountain, fins, a speck on the horizon / Giant teeth, and open mouth / Look out, look out, look out, look out." Look out, Anderson counsels: be aware and beware. Using Melville's analogy between the tails of whales and the trunks of elephants from "The Tail" and alluding to the sanguine descriptions in "Stubb Kills a Whale," Anderson shifts attention from the object to the vulnerable subject: "Hit an elephant with a dart / He just reaches around and pulls it out with his trunk / But hit a whale in the heart / And the ocean turns red. It turns red . . . Get hit in the head/ And there may be a few things you can't recall / But get hit in your heart / And you're in pieces. In parts. / Pieces and parts." The song points forward to a monologue by Anderson about the composition of *Moby-Dick.* In this monologue, she voices her main concern in *Songs and Stories*—desire and how it fragments both objects and subjects: "Hundreds of pages had gone by, and still no one had seen Moby Dick. Sometimes they thought they had, but it always turned out to be just another big cresting wave, or a giant squid, or a squall in the distance. But desire is a funny thing. When you really want something, bits of it start to appear in everything that you see."[6]

"Pieces and Parts" also points backward to Price Waldman's monologue, in which he catalogs the features of the whale: tail, mouth, brow, facelessness, and head. Anderson is fascinated by the cetology chapters. Often slighted in film and stage responses to *Moby-Dick* (and in many literary critical accounts), cetology is on prominent display in *Songs and Stories.* Anderson announces that "I've finally decided that what *Moby-Dick* is really about is enormous heads," and she says that her favorite story in the book is Queequeg's delivery of Tashtego from the whale's head (from "Cistern and Buckets"). Pictures of whales and whale parts are projected on large screens. Tom Nellis, in a skeleton costume, sings about the "bones of Leviathan," with lines taken from "A Bower in the Arsacides." He seizes upon and repeats a phrase from the end of the chapter, when Ishmael describes how he did not trouble himself with "the odd inch" while transcribing the measurements of the whale skeleton to his right arm (*MD* 451). Like Melville, Anderson delights in the "odd inch": the telling detail, the unsettling phrase, the curious juxtaposition. Rather than dramatizing the usual set pieces from the book—Mapple's sermon, Ahab's quarter-deck speech, the final cataclysm—she focuses on words, bones, images, and digressions. She makes the text strange again.[7]

And not only the idea of the "odd inch" intrigues Anderson, but its *sound*. Nellis savors and repeats the phrase. On Anderson's stage, we hear the music in Melville's words: the spondee of the "odd inch," the trochees of a "fallen angel," the anapests in "but the draught of a draught," the anaphora and antistrophe in the chapter "Fast-Fish and Loose-Fish." In her essay in the *Stagebill* for *Songs and Stories,* Anderson explains that, after several readings, she "began to hear [*Moby-Dick*] as music. The rambling, rolling sentences, the lapses into iambic pentameter, the lyrical poems all mixed in with the thee's and thou's of another time. . . . *Moby-Dick* is a curiously silent book. . . . the music is all in the words and the way they riff and trip, skip and lumber." Anderson emphasizes the rhythms of Melville's prose, thus suggesting a deeper continuity between the verbal experiments in the earlier and later parts of his career than literary critics have acknowledged.[8]

Anderson mistrusts Melville's narrative lures in *Moby-Dick*. In essays and interviews, she has described "Call me Ishmael" as "among the strangest [words] in the book," "the three most deceptive words in the whole book," and "the biggest phony bait in the whole book." She insists that the narrator is "hundreds of different voices." The *Stagebill* for *Songs and Stories* contains no listing for the role of "Ishmael." Anderson offers a caution for literary critics, who have treated Ishmael as the narrative focus since Sedgwick (1944), Vincent (1949), and especially Bezanson (1953). In our desire for a narrator, she suggests, bits of him may start to appear in everything we see.[9]

Although the program for *Songs and Stories* lists Anderson in the roles of Pip, the Whale, and a Reader, the show itself confounds the idea of a bill that can assign a predictable relation between performer and character. Anderson does not exactly play the black cabin boy Pip. Instead, she narrates his plight and sings a song about him. She does indeed perform the whale in at least two senses. A rather small mammal, she substitutes on stage for the largest of all mammals, and she gives the whale a haunting melody on the strings of her acoustically enhanced violin. *Songs and Stories* opens with the vivid image of Anderson in silhouette, her back turned toward the audience, playing her whale song before a vast screen of surging waves. As the Reader, she acts as orator, bibliophile, interpreter, and manipulator.

Anderson stages this ebb and flow of roles. Against a backdrop of fluid images, accompanied by splashes and sloshes, performers step in and out of different characters, and they comment on the action. Tom Nellis's Ahab announces "I never read the book!" Lines from *Moby-Dick* are mixed and tangled. Nellis's first line is "Call me the Captain," and later in the show he is given Ishmael's Ahab-like speech from "The Whiteness of the Whale" about how the "palsied universe lies before us a leper" (*MD* 195). Ishmael's words are dispersed among several speakers. Near the end of the production, after delivering lines from the epilogue, Anderson speaks the first words of the narrative—"Call me Ishmael." This is the first time she names herself as the character. At Anderson's end, even more than at Melville's beginning, the "Call me" calls into question the character's singularity. In *Songs and Stories,* voices are electronically altered. Nellis, as Noah, speaks in liquid tones, as though from the bottom of the sea. Anderson produces low masculine and high-pitched childish voices that are familiar to those who have experienced her other stage shows. Faces are projected on floating spheres. Figures withdraw from the stage and emerge at different levels.

This ebb and flow of character forms one of the rhythms of Melville's *Moby-Dick,* too. Ishmael is eclipsed as narrator in the dramatic chapters that follow Ahab's speech in "The Quarter-Deck," and he must make a new entrance five chapters later. He often seems absorbed into the objects of his contemplation. Characters such as Bulkington are featured prominently and then vanish—and then reappear, if we accept Harrison Hayford's theory in "Unnecessary Duplicates" that Melville's characters "hide out" and then return in other forms. At the end of the book, Ishmael narrates himself as the "third man" in Ahab's whaleboat. He watches himself fall into the ocean.[10]

Yet the distance between perception and experience, subject and object, first and third person, cannot be maintained. In the epilogue, Ishmael tells his readers that he had been pulled in by the suction of the whirlpool that had swallowed the ship. He was drawn from the margin to the center and revolved ever more tightly toward "the button-like black bubble at the axis" (*MD* 573), at the last minute sustained by Queequeg's coffin. These final pages tell a story, on the level of point of view and figure, about the vulnerability of the observer's body and about the dilation, contraction, and dilation of the I and the eye. Anderson conveys such fluctuations through story, song, space, and sound. She invokes Melville's formal experiments, his heterogeneous materials and perspectives, and his complex irony in which the observer risks becoming lost or goes so far inside that he or she is outside—aspects that also have characterized her own performances. Anderson's encounter with Melville and *Moby-Dick* thus dramatizes the concerns and practices of both artists—and also amplifies the risks.

Anderson seems to have found the artistic vortex difficult to navigate. *Songs and Stories from Moby Dick* signaled a departure for her. It was the first time she had based her performance on a source text with a set of characters and a preexisting narrative and the first time she had performed with other actors and singers. In interviews, she has described the technological difficulties in mounting such an elaborate show and the psychological obstacles of being tied to someone else's text and being unable to find an anger within herself commensurate with Ahab's. She has acknowledged the inevitable failure of any attempt to represent *Moby-Dick* on stage (thus echoing Ishmael's own paean to failure in "Cetology"), the discomfort of dwelling in the past ("I can't be in the 19th century another second!"), and her own constitutional inability to complete anything (again in sympathy with Melville's narrator). *Songs and Stories* culminates a series of allusions to Melville during Anderson's career, including *DEARREADER, United States, Strange Angels,* and *The Nerve Bible.* Preparing for *Songs and Stories,* she read *Moby-Dick* six times (five of the readings in a row). Enticed by the language, the music, the peculiarity, the beauty, and the obsessive reflectiveness of the book, Anderson ultimately may have found the encounter too intimate. Whatever the reasons, after repeated attempts to record *Songs and Stories* for commercial release, she abandoned the effort. The first three tracks of her CD *Life on a String*—"One White Whale," "The Island Where I Come From," and "Pieces and Parts"—survive alone to tell the story of her production.[11]

While Anderson selects idiosyncratic parts of *Moby-Dick* for her multimedia, high-technology collage, Rinde Eckert performs the set pieces on an austere stage in his two-person chamber opera *And God Created Great Whales.* Eckert gives his audience Ishmael and Queequeg's first encounter at night in the Spouter Inn, Father Mapple's sermon in the Whalemen's Chapel, Ahab on the quarterdeck, and the final battle with Moby Dick. Yet these set pieces are framed and sequenced in remarkable ways. Like Orson Welles, who had an acting company perform in his *Moby Dick—Rehearsed* (1955), Eckert places sections of his opera in the context of an effort to represent Melville's book. Eckert plays Nathan, a piano tuner composing an opera based on *Moby-Dick.* Both Welles and Eckert reflect an artistic process, offering draughts of draughts.[12]

The "piece" is a key structural device in Eckert's opera, as it is in Anderson's *Songs and Stories,* but with a difference. Nathan is suffering from an unnamed degenerative neural disease. He struggles to finish his opera before he completely loses his memory: "In the end you will appear to remember nothing at all," the experts have informed him. "Eventually you will forget how to breathe. One might say you will drown in your own ignorance" (1). In an attempt to counter the effects of his disease, Nathan has hung a tape recorder around his neck and bound it to his waist. He listens to audiotapes he has made to remind himself of his progress and to guide him toward completion. Eckert renders Ahab's scar—"that perpendicular seam" running from the top of his head down his face and inside his clothing (123)—horizontal. Nathan is held together with gray duct tape wound around his waist. He is goaded by an African American Muse, a "product of your imagination" as he tells himself (1). This Muse has been created in the shape of Olivia, an opera singer whose piano Nathan had tuned and with whom he had discussed his magnum opus. While Nathan continues to write and, with his Muse, perform fragments of his opera, he becomes caught up in the character and quest of Ahab. He desires to feel in control again and he dreams of transcendence. While Nathan labors to compose and to recall, he progressively forgets and regresses. The further his tape unwinds, the more he has lost his mental faculties. Nathan struggles to remember the pieces and to complete his opera before his mind disintegrates. In script, music, and performance, Eckert makes visible and audible a sense of time and its costs. Both Eckert and Anderson invoke Ishmael's celebration of parts and Ahab's furious quest for the whole.

Complementing analyses of Eckert's *And God Created Great Whales* by Robert K. Wallace and Elizabeth Schultz in this volume, the last part of this essay will focus on an aspect of Eckert's chamber opera that resonates with Anderson's and Barrymore's *Moby-Dick*s: the struggle between Nathan and his Muse. They argue about Olivia's idea, evoked early in the performance, that Nathan add a part for her in his *Moby-Dick* opera: "Perhaps Ahab could have a vision. A dark woman appears to bring him a promise or a warning. Or maybe some heavenly creature at the end descending over Ishmael floating on his coffin. She could look just like me. Hanging there on a celestial wire, singing of redemption or love" (5). Although Nathan resists his Muse, Eckert scripts both of these scenes. They constitute the most extraordinary departures in *Great Whales*, departures that bring us back to *Moby-Dick*.

Olivia presses this "visitation" (15). Her diction suggests its significance: "visitation" as administering comfort or punishment, as exerting supernatural or spiritual influence. She explains the difference that her presence might make: "all those men harpooning, lancing, flaying, telling stories, sleeping the heavy sleep of whalemen on the swelling sea. Ahab in his cabin, pouring over his charts, glowering, obsessed. Then from nowhere I come in, sing some simple air. . . . Then I vanish as mysteriously as I appeared leaving a promise or a warning. A penultimate lightness before the groaning sea collapses on everything" (15).

Eckert takes the Muse's side in this debate. He conjures an alternative, which he figures as female and dark. The Muse and Olivia (both played by Nora Cole) bring to Nathan's Ahab a temporary calm. In some ways this female presence swerves from the text, in some ways not. We might view it as an enactment of the influences described in Melville's chapter entitled "The Symphony." There, as Ahab stands on deck, the "feminine air" and "man-like sea" seem joined (MD 542). During his exchange with Starbuck, Ahab speaks for the first time of his wife and child, whom he sees in Starbuck's eye. Yet Eckert's Muse seems more resistant and independent than the tremulous bride given by Melville's narrator to the masculine ocean in "The Symphony." She holds the possibility of imagining a different outcome, a break from the narcissism, masochism, and vengeance.

Such a possibility is pursued in the much derided plot inventions of the 1926 Sea Beast. Yes, the particular outcomes scripted are absurd. Ahab kills Moby Dick, rather than being garroted by the whale line that snaps around his neck. He returns to New Bedford to find that his beloved Esther has survived, and they embrace and kiss. (It is quite a kiss, though, celebrated in its time, combining several passionate takes.) Yet the happy endings—both the redemptive violence and sentimentality—have an illusory quality to them. Those who have read the book or know Melville's story are free to denounce the filmmakers' impiety or Hollywood's platitudes. Alternatively, viewers can savor the ways in which the celluloid discrepancies illuminate Melville's text.[13]

The most fantastic, and tender, moment in the film involves a female visitation. Alone on deck at night, Ahab sees an image of Esther come toward him from the clouds with welcoming arms. A cut to a medium-close shot shows Ahab with Esther's superimposed hands caressing his face and head. The scene fades to Ahab standing on deck in the morning light, still being caressed. The hands dissolve, and Ahab awakens and orders the ship to be turned toward home. One may quarrel with what follows—before home is reached, the ship will pick up a stranded Derek (remember, he is the captain's treacherous half brother), whom Ahab will throw overboard, and Ahab will encounter and dispatch Moby Dick—but the intervention here resembles Eckert's. Both the 1926 film and Eckert's chamber opera realize a female presence on board the Pequod and envision the difference it might make.[14]

In a surprising aria, Eckert has the Muse meditate on the dynamics of male projection. She laments her state, wondering, "Oh, lord, what am I? A sylph. A woman with no history. / Every man's dream" (19). As she sings a cappella, she imagines her own alternatives: "If only I were flesh and bone / I'd live a different life . . . Far from Nathan's mind / I'll find I'm really real / Far from Nathan's mind / My history will soon begin / The pain and pleasure flooding in" (19–20). At the beginning of *Great Whales*, Nathan's taped voice instructs him that the Muse is both "a product of your imagination" and "infallible" (1). Their relationship unfolds in rhythms of dependence and autonomy. Although the Muse yearns, she ultimately yields. Eckert's proposal that "a product of the imagination" may have a life of its own suggests that *Moby-Dick* may press on *Great Whales* in unexpected ways. It also suggests a way to understand the recalcitrance and vehemence of Melville's own *Pierre*. The Muse has her "Symphony" moment, which, like Ahab's glimpse of an alternative, soon lapses and is followed by steep collapse.[15]

In contrast to Anderson, who says that she cannot feel Ahab's rage, Eckert gives voice to it. For Eckert, though, rage and desire are bound together. Ahab's fixation on the whale fuels his passion for the divine. Eckert explains that his Ahab has "had a taste of the divine and he can't go back to his mundane life. He can't ever go back. So it's a sense of union. Spiritual union is really what he's after."[16] Eckert's Nathan, too, pursues his white whale in a quest for plenitude. His opera, he hopes, will be the way he masters his descent. In *Great Whales*, Eckert performs one of Melville's great themes: drowning and being saved. In the final vocalized duet, with Nathan, anguished and exhilarated, joining the Muse, Eckert suggests a "happy" ending. Not as happy as Hollywood's Ahab embracing his Esther (or, at the end of Barrymore's 1930 remake, his "Faith")—but Eckert's ending helps us to remember that Melville's epilogue, too, is absurd and affecting. Nathan's music, like Ishmael's language, buoys him. In art, possibly, time may be conserved and mind, if not identity, preserved.[17]

The Muse describes to Olivia a dream of Nathan's, in which Olivia praised him for "your sprawling mind. Your ability to pack the smallest gestures with significance . . . assign symphonic pretensions to a simple interval, the perfect fifth becoming the emblem of a nation of fifths, the natural energy of a vibrating string seen as proof against the ravaging entropy of it all" (10). We might read this passage as a musical epitome of *Moby-Dick:* its scope, density, democratic gestures, and resonant narrative voice. "The natural energy of a vibrating string seen as proof against the ravaging entropy of it all" describes not only the narrator of *Moby-Dick* but also the figure of Laurie Anderson, at the start of *Songs and Stories,* playing her violin before a huge screen, a great shroud, of waves. Listening to *Great Whales* helps us hear the musical, and especially operatic, qualities of Melville's book. Nathan's profession seems fitting. A piano tuner, his task is to make sure that the strings vibrate at the correct pitch and in unison, but the correct pitch is not the perfect pitch. His is an art of imperfection. He must temper the strings, make certain notes flat or sharp, since what the ear recognizes as true is not in tune. This discrepancy enables the music.

In describing the pull of Melville, Eckert warns that "you can get caught in Melville's vortex because it's so compelling. At some point I had to respectfully put him at arm's length and say the only way I'm going to do service to his book is if I absorb it and make it mine." Here Eckert alludes to the whirlpool toward which Ishmael ultimately is drawn and from which he is propelled by Queequeg's coffin. He evokes Melville's cautions about imitating Shakespeare in "Hawthorne and His Mosses."[18]

In *Moby-Dick,* Eckert and Anderson—and Orson Welles, John Huston, Charles Olson, Frank Stella, C. L. R. James, and so many others—see themselves and their cultures. They are absorbed and, in turn, they absorb the book. Such mirrorings suggest the uncanny properties of the alluring invitation stretched across the textual surface of *Moby-Dick.* They may indicate why the book has produced such a sustained and broad response from artists and readers in the twentieth and now twenty-first centuries. "Call me," the narrator invites, enjoins, and seduces, apprehending his readers. Anderson speaks of "how much we have in common with *Moby-Dick,* in terms of obsession, love of work, love of details . . . the concept of the crazy captain." Eckert tells his interviewer that *Moby-Dick* "reminded me of my culture . . . It seems quintessentially American to me . . . that grand and naive spiritual aspiration." An obsessed book about obsession, written in what Warner Berthoff has described as a style of "exceptional persistence and tenacity," its "sentences stamped with urgency," a book about a writer pursuing a sailor pursuing a captain pursuing a whale—a book about interpretation and creativity—has drawn many artists into its orbits.[19]

Melville's narrator invites his readers to share his reflections. In a series of complicated gestures—intimate and excessive, tantalizing and narcissistic—the images proliferate. *Moby-Dick* is mirror, magnifying glass, and whirlpool. Melville's book, of course, is not unique in these features. One might make similar claims about texts by, say, Faulkner or Morrison. Yet in *Moby-Dick* the conjunction of biography, history, plot, character, narration, and language intensifies these dynamics.

The mirror of *Moby-Dick* is on stage in *Songs and Stories* and *God Created Great Whales.* Eckert and Anderson are playful, ambitious, obsessive, aggrandizing, deprecating, and revealing. They are drawn into and draw out of Melville's vortex. Their performances are self-reflexively about incarnation and transcendence, the rhythms of past and present, and the meanings of repetition and originality. That is to say they are—they help us to recognize what is—peculiarly Melvillean.

NOTES

1. In this essay, I base my analysis of Laurie Anderson's *Songs and Stories* on a performance I attended in Berkeley, California, in October 1999; on a May 2000 performance at the Barbican Theater in London, broadcast by BBC radio; on lyrics provided to me by Anderson and lyrics published in RoseLee Goldberg's *Laurie Anderson* (New York: Harry N. Abrams, 2000); and on the three *Moby-Dick* songs on Anderson's 2001 CD release *Life on a String* (Nonesuch 79539–2). I base my analysis of Rinde Eckert's *And God Created Great Whales* on performances I attended in New York City in September 2000 and December 2001 and on materials shared with me by Eckert, including a script and a videotape of a June 2000 performance. Page numbers from this unpublished script will be given in parentheses in the body of the essay. The phrases quoted in this first paragraph are from page 17. My essay could not have been written without the generosity of Anderson and Eckert and also Robert K. Wallace, all of whom gave me access to unpublished materials and have allowed me to quote from them. There have been four American film versions of *Moby-Dick*: *The Sea Beast* in 1926 and *Moby Dick* in 1930 and 1956 (all three from Warner Brothers) and *Moby Dick* in 1998 (from Hallmark).

2. Buchman, "*The Sea Beast*," x–xi. Grosset and Dunlap also published a "photoplay" edition in conjunction with the 1930 film version of *Moby-Dick*. Each edition is illustrated with movie photographs, showing scenes nowhere described in Melville's text. Gene Fowler describes the working relationship between Barrymore and Meredyth in *Good Night, Sweet Prince: The Life and Times of John Barrymore* (New York: Viking Press, 1943), 236–38. On *The Sea Beast* and Barrymore's sound remake, *Moby Dick* (1930), see Thomas Inge, "Melville in Popular Culture," 696–70; on the ways in which the early filmmakers sought to open Melville's text to a popular audience, see Edward Stone, "Ahab Gets Girl" (1975), rpt. in Hayes, *The Critical Response*, 170–82. Barrymore, the proud owner of a first edition of *Moby-Dick*, had insisted that the first of the three major films he signed to do with Warner Brothers would be based on Melville's book; see Martin F. Norden, *John Barrymore: A Bio-Bibliography* (Westport, Conn.: Greenwood Press, 1995), 15. Franc Roddam, the director of the 1998 *Moby Dick*, provides a glimpse of Ahab's wife and child at the beginning of his film. The early films (1926, 1930) wreak revenge on Moby Dick, scripting and depicting his death. In Orson Welles's play *Moby Dick—Rehearsed* (1955), Ahab and Moby Dick kill one another. Thus several of Melville's adaptors fulfill Ahab's fantasy.

3. Laurie Anderson, interviewed by BBC radio, May 24, 2000. For reviewers who noted Anderson's kinship with Melville, see Stacey Kors, "Call Me Laurie," Salon.com, Oct. 5, 1999, and Mark Swed, "Pursuing the Great White," *Los Angeles Times*, Oct. 22, 1999. RoseLee Goldberg surveys Anderson's career and catalogs her performances, recordings, and books, in *Laurie Anderson*. Anderson writes about her interest in Melville in the *Stagebill* for the show (Oct. 1999), 12A–12C. She discusses Melville in an interview with Clifford Ross in *BOMB: The Arts and Culture Quarterly* 69 (Fall 1999): 60–66. In her *Stagebill* essay, Anderson estimates that 10 percent of the words in her script for *Songs and Stories* are taken from *Moby-Dick*.

4. For details on the Alabama skeleton and its fate, see Vincent, *The Trying-Out of Moby-Dick*, 349–51, and Mansfield and Vincent, "Notes," 810.

5. In her interview with Clifford Ross, Anderson describes her dilemma: "you can't really represent the book on stage without making it 50 hours long . . . There were so many heartbreaking decisions to make . . . I decided to throw up a white flag and say, 'I'm just going to touch on some of the things that I love and not try to tell the whole story because it's too long" (*BOMB* 63). In an unpublished interview with Robert K. Wallace (Nov. 9, 2001), Eckert makes a similar point: "I think everybody who approaches a great work has to be anchored in some kind of specific take. You don't tackle a work of the manifold dimensions of *Moby-Dick* by trying to deal with it whole" (12). Melville and Anderson's talk of parts alludes to Exodus 33:23, in which God tells Moses that he shall see His back parts but not his face.

6. In deciding which parts of *Moby-Dick* to extract, Bess Meredyth, the screenwriter of *The Sea Beast,* also turned her attention to passages from "The Tail." Both the 1926 and 1930 versions begin with a page on screen, purporting to represent the first few paragraphs of the book: "There never was, nor ever will be, a braver life than the life of a whaler. Compared to the game they hunted, the mightiest land beast was but a poodle dog." It is unclear why Meredyth, or Rupert Hughes, the writer of the title cards, felt it necessary to change "terrier" in Melville's original (378) to "poodle dog," thus rendering Melville's analogy even odder.

7. Interviewed by Clifford Ross, Anderson calls *Moby-Dick* "one of the most bizarre things I've ever read" (*BOMB* 62). In her BBC radio interview, she says, "I just was astounded. It's an incredibly strange book, and so beautiful." Anderson's words recall the responses of the initial British reviewers of *Moby-Dick,* and her performance and stagecraft seem designed to defamiliarize the book.

8. Anderson discusses the musicality of *Moby-Dick* in her *Stagebill* essay, 12A–12B, and in her *BOMB* interview, 62.

9. *Stagebill,* 12A; BBC radio interview; *BOMB* interview, 62. On Ishmael as narrative presence, see Sedgwick, *Herman Melville;* Vincent, *Trying-Out of* Moby-Dick; and Bezanson, "*Moby-Dick:* Work of Art." William V. Spanos emphasizes Ishmael's decentering absence, in *The Errant Art of* Moby-Dick.

10. See Harrison Hayford, "Unnecessary Duplicates."

11. Anderson mentions her six readings of *Moby-Dick* in her *Stagebill* essay, 12A. She recounts her difficulties with the show in her *BOMB* interview, 63, 65; in an interview with Keith Phipps on the Web site theonionavclub.com (accessed Nov. 26, 2001); and on the Web site laurieanderson.com (accessed Apr. 12, 2001). In a review of *Songs and Stories,* Scott Saul analyzes her recitals of failure and notes her allegiance to Ishmael and distance from Ahab; see "Mysteries of the Postmodern Deep: Laurie Anderson's *Songs and Stories from Moby Dick,*" *Theater* 30.2 (2000): 160–63. Rumor has it that a DVD recording of a performance of *Songs and Stories* at the London Barbican, filmed by the director Mike Figgis, may one day be released.

12. See Orson Welles, *Moby Dick—Rehearsed.* In his setting of *Moby-Dick,* Eckert, like Welles, makes spare use of props and costumes. Anderson, too, thought of framing her *Moby-Dick:* "I initially wanted my piece to be a dream about the book" (*BOMB* 65). Eckert thanks Anderson in the playbill for *Great Whales.*

13. John Kobler describes the final embrace between Ahab (John Barrymore) and Esther (Dolores Costello) in *Damned in Paradise: The Life of John Barrymore* (New York: Atheneum, 1977), 216.

14. John Barrymore ends his early autobiography, *Confessions of an Actor* (Indianapolis: Bobbs-Merrill, 1926), with some thoughts about the industry's resourcefulness and about Ahab's possible sexual and species orientations: "What we are going to do for a love interest, I don't quite know. He might fall in love with the whale. I am sure, however, Hollywood will find a way." *The Sea Beast* imagines not only a female influence (Esther) and a fantasy of vengeance

(the death of Moby Dick) but also a human location of betrayal and redemption: Derek, responsible for pushing his half brother into the jaws of the whale, is bested and himself cast into the ocean by Ahab. In an unpublished interview with Robert K. Wallace (Nov. 9, 2001), Wallace asked Eckert about the parallels between the female "visitations" in *Great Whales* and *The Sea Beast,* as I had described them in a talk given at the *Moby-Dick* sesquicentennial conference at Hofstra University in October 2001. He expressed delight at the connection and said that he had been unaware of the 1926 film (12).

15. Eckert explains in interviews that the part of the Muse/Olivia was expanded as he collaborated with Nora Cole. See Wallace, "Avoiding Melville's Vortex," 87; unpublished interview with Robert K. Wallace (Nov. 9, 2001), 3.

16. Wallace, "Avoiding Melville's Vortex," 100. See also 99: "I forgave and understood Ahab when he took Pip in. That's when I felt like this is something different. This isn't some blind revenge. And I started thinking about the nature of revenge, and the nature of this kind of antipathy, seeming antipathy for the whale, and I saw it in the context of a spiritual pursuit. It's very difficult to come up with terms, the motivational terms, that will encourage a relationship with the divine. And so one chooses, one looks for the kinds of mundane human motivations that will draw us into these larger passions. My feeling is that revenge for Ahab is that agency that puts him in the way of the divine."

17. In his unpublished interview with Robert K. Wallace (Nov. 9, 2001), Eckert speculates on Nathan's fate: "Maybe the opera—maybe he's saved by his opera. Maybe he's saved, maybe not; I don't know" (14).

18. Wallace, "Avoiding Melville's Vortex," 95; Melville, "Hawthorne and His Mosses" (*PT* 244–48).

19. Ross, interview with Laurie Anderson, in *BOMB,* 65; Wallace, "Avoiding Melville's Vortex," 102; Warner Berthoff, *The Example of Melville,* 206, 208. M. Thomas Inge considers the appeal of *Moby-Dick,* in "Melville and Popular Culture," 696; Jeffrey Insko considers its "high" art enticements, in "Art After Ahab," *Postmodern Culture* 12.1 (Sept. 2001). For examples of intensely self-reflexive artistic and critical responses to *Moby-Dick,* see Elizabeth A. Schultz, *Unpainted to the Last;* Robert K. Wallace, *Frank Stella's* Moby-Dick: *Words and Shapes;* D. H. Lawrence, *Studies in Classic American Literature;* Charles Olson, *Call Me Ishmael;* and C. L. R. James, *Mariners, Renegades, and Castaways,* with its insistent subtitle *Herman Melville and the World We Live In.*

Feminizing *Moby-Dick*

Contemporary Women Perform the Whale

Elizabeth Schultz

In discussing *Moby-Dick* in her 1990 book *Sexual Personae*, cultural critic Camille Paglia argues that Melville's novel emphasizes masculinity at the expense of femininity: "The novel's cognitive data are cognitive data shored against male ruin. Again and again, Melville elevates the masculine principle above the feminine, driving back and limiting female power." Her argument regarding *Moby-Dick*'s androcentricism receives ostensible validation not only by its inclusion in Norton's second edition of the novel in 2002[1] but also by feminist critics of the 1970s and 1980s who condemn the novel for its paucity of women characters and its lack of attention to women's experience.[2]

On the scholarly front, essays by more recent feminist critics, however, counter the perpetuation of the perception that *Moby-Dick* is a work driven by "the masculine principle" by demonstrating the novel's concern with issues of sentimentality, domesticity, and maternity—issues germane to women's life and culture in the nineteenth as well as the twentieth centuries.[3] On the cultural front, since the 1950s, a startling number of dramatic and multimedia performances have feminized *Moby-Dick*. What I term the feminizing of *Moby-Dick* is based on the cultural impetus generated by twentieth-century dramatists and multimedia artists to revise Melville's novel so that women may claim it as their own. Such revisions not only include women characters, but increasingly insist on the importance of "female power" in *Moby-Dick*. They embrace a vision of women's experiences and women's concerns, a vision supporting the more encompassing hopes for a pluralistic and equal society.[4]

Manifestations of this cultural impetus revise Melville's text as a way to comment on American gender politics in general. Several of these performance pieces introduce cross-dressing into their scripts, implying the permeability of gender in *Moby-Dick*. The assignment of women to roles taken by men in the novel also positions them as central to the narrative. With few exceptions, most of these feminizing adaptations depend on the use of multiple media—the integration of music, dance, and visual elements into the narrative script, not as mere background elements but as intrinsic to the performance—to reinforce this vision of an open and dynamic society. Notably, both men and women artists have contributed to the feminizing of *Moby-Dick*—as dramatists, choreographers, painters, actors, musicians, and dancers.

Melville's two references to Ahab's wife have been the specific stimulus for several of these performances (*MD* 79, 544), while other artists have found Pip's sympathetic characterization and Ishmael's fluid persona to have inspired them to perceive the feminine in *Moby-Dick*. However, the growing prominence of women in American public life as well as the attention to "female power" in feminist theory in the late twentieth century underlie the representation of women in these feminized versions of *Moby-Dick*. Increasingly, women appear in these works, not as stereotypes or as victims but as creative agents. I argue that the feminizing of *Moby-Dick* intensified in the 1990s, reaching a culmination during the millennium years—from 1999 to 2001—with three remarkable performance pieces: Ellen Driscoll's *Ahab's Wife or the Whale*, Laurie Anderson's *Songs and Stories from Moby Dick*, and Rinde Eckert's *And God Created Great Whales*. All three of these works, in their celebration of women's lives, addressed a millennial dream of reinvigorating a pluralistic vision of American democracy. In this volume, the discussions of *Songs and Stories from Moby Dick* and *And God Created Great Whales* by Samuel Otter and Robert Wallace, which reflect on the works' openness and contemporary resonance, complement my discussion.

Women make their first appearance in adaptations of *Moby-Dick* in the novel's first two cinematic versions—*The Sea Beast* (1926) and *Moby Dick* (1930), both produced by Warner Brothers and starring John Barrymore, with the screenplay for *The Sea Beast* written by Bess Meredyth and that for *Moby Dick* by J. Grubb Alexander. Both are revised to give Ahab a sweetheart, and it is possible that Meredyth's script calculated that a woman in the *Moby Dick* narrative might provide the hot romantic interest that would not only showcase the range of the flamboyant Barrymore's acting skills but also appeal to a female audience and thereby create a more commercially lucrative film.[5] The 1930 film also added a number of minor women's roles—Whale Oil

Rosie, Fat Fannie, Old Maid, Mother of Many Children—to swell the crowd scenes on shore and to continue to attract women viewers' attention. However, these women are stereotyped and caricatured, with Ahab's sweetheart cast literally as an Angel in the House, appearing to him in a dream where she welcomes him into her arms. The long-suffering heroine is rewarded in the conclusion by welcoming Ahab home after he has heroically killed both his rivals—his jealous brother-in-law and Moby Dick. With their distorted, romantic conclusions, these early cinematic versions of *Moby-Dick* are more antifeminist than feminizing.

Gilbert Wilson is the first (and, to this day, the only) artist to represent Ahab's wife (*Unpainted* 162–85). From the early 1950s, she appeared in Wilson's touring film and slide show renditions of *Moby-Dick*, both based on his paintings and drawings of the novel. From 1949 until his death in 1991, Wilson cherished the dream of producing a grand opera, titled *The White Whale*. He wrote a fifty-five-page libretto for his projected opera, tried to convince Shostakovich to write its score, and created detailed stage sets. In his libretto as well as in his paintings and drawings, Wilson foregrounds the novel's diverse ethnic crew as well as Ahab's wife and child. His repeated evocations of these characters, while lamentably reinforcing degraded and conventional racial and gender stereotypes, are nonetheless evidence of a passionate commitment to assigning them a significant position in *Moby-Dick*. Wilson associates Ahab's wife as well as Pip with redemptive possibilities of innocence and tenderness. Had Ahab turned to them, Wilson believed, the *Pequod* would have been saved. In four sketches, he draws Ahab's wife as a young girl, always in relation to pastoral and domestic scenes, usually with her arm around her child. However, in Wilson's psychological and political reading of *Moby-Dick*, Ahab's ostensible castration inhibits his return to the peace and love of her sphere and necessitates his continued "war upon the horrors of the deep" (*MD* 543). In Wilson's film and opera script, thus, Paglia's interpretation appears plausible: the conventional masculine principle is elevated over the conventional feminine principle

Orson Welles's *Moby Dick—Rehearsed: A Drama in Two Acts* (1955) can be said to begin the feminizing of *Moby-Dick*. Welles's drama, perhaps more than any other theatrical adaptation of *Moby-Dick*, continues to play to acclaim worldwide—on TV, radio, and stage. Acknowledging the seeming absence of women in Melville's novel, Welles creates a definitive space for one woman on board the *Pequod*. The Young Actress, who appears in the metadrama which begins the play, announces that "'Lear's' what I was called to rehearse; but if you're doing this 'Moby Dick' instead, there aren't any women's parts, so I guess I'm only needed for some music."[6] In his actual dramatization of *Moby-Dick*, however, Welles has an important role for his Young Actress: Pip. Identified with the *Pequod*'s least powerful crew member, but one of the novel's most appealing characters, the Young Actress is able to step forward in the drama as both an African American and a woman to protest oppression.

Thirty years after Wilson had envisioned Ahab's wife and Welles had assigned the Young Actress to Pip's role, Patty Lynch radically revised *Moby-Dick* with *Wreck of the Hesperus*, which played to supportive audiences in Minneapolis in 1987 and received largely enthusiastic reviews. Directly addressing both masculine and feminine gender issues, Lynch's play explicitly protests the oppression of women. *Wreck of the Hesperus* rewrites Melville's narrative to place it in contemporary America, specifically at Moby Dick's, "a sleazy strip joint" operated by one Captain Ahab. This version of Ahab is obsessed not with the White Whale[7] but with white women, in particular with his wife and his daughter. As the White Whale taunts Ahab, thereby drawing him to his doom, Ahab's wife in Lynch's drama curses him by giving birth to his daughter, who becomes a stripper in his club and who, as the subject of his incestuous desires, torments him even further. One critic explains, "The women in *Wreck of the Hesperus* are quite literally prisoners of the male imagination. And the men, locked into their own romantic notions of women, the sea and love, are imprisoned as well."[8] Lynch's drama, more emphatically than other feminized versions of *Moby-Dick*, uses Melville's novel as a serious vehicle with which to challenge oppressive patriarchy.

In the 1990s, with postmodern feminist scholarship examining women's lives from multiple perspectives, several adaptations, using diverse genres and strategies, opened *Moby-Dick* to women. In all these works, women assume agency. However, in Robert Longden and Hereward Kaye's 1992 rock musical and Sena Jeter Naslund's 1999 novel, women overwhelm the whale. Despite retaining vestiges of *Moby-Dick*'s characters and plot, these works obliterate the novel's capacious philosophical, psychological, political, and aesthetic concerns in becoming dominated by women, who are converted into caricatures in one and propagandists in the other. Performance works of the nineties—Bill Peters' *Hunting for Moby Dick* (1996), JoAnne Spies' "Melville & Me" (1997), Ellen Driscoll's *Ahab's Wife, or the Whale* (1998), and Laurie Anderson's *Songs and Stories from Moby Dick* (1999), followed by Rinde Eckert's *And God Created Great Whales* (2000)—however, explore and expand on Melville's novel to raise compelling questions regarding women, their identities, and their lives. In these works, women discover and express themselves.

Moby Dick! The Musical, with book, lyrics, and music by Longden and Kaye, features the attempt of students at a British girls' academy to produce a version of Melville's novel in the school's swimming pool. Although *Moby Dick!* sank under mixed reception in both London and New York, the musical has been revised and revived multiple times. Through the summer of 2005, it has continued to play globally from Japan to Ireland, Massachusetts to Arizona, in multiple venues from dinner theaters to high school auditoriums. Its all-female cast subverts feminist scholarship that condemns *Moby-Dick* for its lack of major women characters. As if in imitation of the early *Moby-Dick* films, *MobyDick! The Musical* also introduces Ahab's wife as well as romance into the narrative. In astonishing convolutions of the novel's plot in this version, however, Ahab, unable to bear children because of his ostensible castration by Moby Dick, proposes to his wife that they adopt Pip as their child; when "Esta" refuses, he curses her in such dire terms that she is driven to suicide. Ahab's hunt for Moby Dick thus becomes an excuse for him to assuage his guilt for his wife's death, while the rest of the cast has a rollicking good time (and exposes a lot of campy leg). Following Ahab's death in the conclusion, the crew gleefully boast in song that they have "Save[d] the Whale." With posters advertising it as "The Butch New Musical" and proclaiming, "Stuff Art. Let's Dance," *Moby Dick! The Musical* mocks *Moby-Dick* the novel, as well as women.

Naslund's bestselling, Book-of-the-Month Club novel *Ahab's Wife, or the Star-Gazer*, while not a performance piece, was critically highlighted along with Anderson's *Songs and Stories from Moby Dick*, which appeared in the same year, as part of the national millennial hype. In her novel, Naslund has clear feminist intentions regarding *Moby-Dick:* she is determined to "'redeem the territory' of [Melville's novel] by providing a place in it for women."[9] With her protagonist, Una, she creates a female Ishmael, an imaginative and independent woman who goes a-whaling and becomes both a castaway and a cannibal. Naslund's Una also self-consciously takes up domestic tasks, like other nineteenth-century heroines, and develops an interest in a range of social issues critical to both her time (suffrage and racism) and ours (homophobia). Thus while Naslund succeeds in evocatively feminizing *Moby-Dick* through her characterization of Una, her narrative, by becoming a vehicle for blatant social commentary, turns self-righteous. In addition, no White Whale looms for Una in *Ahab's Wife;* unlike Ishmael, her pursuit is only of herself and a good marriage partner. Naslund's goal of "revising American literature and critiquing traditional masculinity" consequently is diminished, as if she were saying to her readers, as one critic has suggested, "'There, there. Such a fuss about a fish.'"[10] Una's marriage to Ahab is brief, and her marriage at the novel's conclusion to Ishmael a surprise to readers, as Naslund, in the process of creating her feminist bildungsroman, seems gradually to have written both the White Whale and *Moby-Dick* altogether out of *Ahab's Wife*.

Bill Peters' *Hunting for Moby Dick*, however, feminizes *Moby-Dick* while simultaneously illuminating it.[11] Throughout the ninety-minute drama, both women and men are cast in all the roles of the novel's dramatis personae. The seven members of the cast—four women and three men—take the role of Ahab, even as, by playing diverse other crew members, they also become cogs in Ahab's scheme. Finding that the slogan, "Blood for Oil," popularized during the first Gulf Crisis, reminded him of *Moby-Dick*, Peters interprets the novel as both criticizing and celebrating individuality—in leaders as well as artists.[12]

The only position in the play not taken by a woman is that of Melville, which Peters himself takes. As a figure desperately engaged in searching for the means to initiate his novel, Melville opens the play, scattering pages from a box about the stage in a blizzard of white. The author's obsessive hunt for *Moby-Dick*, as compared to Ahab's hunt for the White Whale, subsequently becomes the play's organizing principle. The drama is done when "Melville" takes a copy of the book from the same box and intones, "Call me Ishmael."

The dramatic trajectory of *Hunting for Moby Dick* focuses on the whale, the search for it, and the attempts to kill it, and with his adaptable cast and a minimum of props—an enormous white sheet, four long poles, red and white paint—Peters recreates a diversity of scenes and moods from the novel. Immediately after "Melville's" appearance, a woman actor appears before the white sheet to introduce the audience to Whale by spouting water about the stage and quoting passages from "The Fountain" chapter; throughout the drama, she repeatedly spouts off—as Whale—representing the novel's life force. Although Lynch, through analogy, explicitly identifies Moby Dick with women, Peters, in anticipation of Spies and Driscoll, associates the Whale not with conventional masculine attributes of aggression and dominance but with nurturing attributes usually associated with "female power."

During the drama, both male and female members of the cast assemble and reassemble themselves into the *Pequod* and whale boats with the ease of dancers, simultaneously singing a variety of chanteys to convey the hunt's compelling nature. In the course of this simulated pursuit, Peters evokes the butchering of the blind whale, the near drowning of Pip, the insanity generated by the try-works fire, and "The Symphony." He ends with "The Masthead," Father Mapple's sermon, and "the great shroud of the sea [that] rolled on as it rolled five thousand years ago" (*MD* 572), returning to "Melville," whose last word, "Call me Ishmael," suggests that he can begin the novel. While focused on *Moby-Dick*'s quest narrative, *Hunting for Moby Dick*, with its multimedia effects of song and dance, releases the performance from the confines of a constricting linear play. In its open-endedness and gender fluidity, it implies that the novel's questions of individuality, obsession, and exploitation concern men and women.

In Peters' play, the creator's search, however, belongs to men, a notion denied by JoAnne Spies' "Melville & Me," Ellen Driscoll's *Ahab's Wife or The Whale*, Laurie Anderson's *Songs and Stories from Moby Dick*, and Rinde Eckert's opera, *And God Created Great Whales*. Each of these works, based on their creators' intimate readings of Melville's novel; their integrations of music, drama, and dance with stunning visual effects; and their merging of original scripts with Melville's text, finds, as Driscoll explains in discussing her work, "a space for the female imagination within [*Moby-Dick's*] framework."[13] They reveal women extending their creative abilities, imaginations, and souls in searching beyond boundaries of conventional culture and even geography. The women in these performance pieces move beyond the stereotypes of women represented in the work of Wilson and the early filmmakers and beyond the oppressions alluded to by Welles and condemned by Lynch. Unlike *Moby Dick! The Musical* and *Ahab's Wife*, they locate women and their stories within Melville's words and his capacious vision. They thereby envision American democracy anew and become transcendent, contemporary works, meaningful for both women and men.

Spies first presented her one-woman, multimedia work "Me & Melville" at the Berkshire Women Performing Arts Festival, taking it later to diverse venues throughout New England and New York—from colleges and museums to Arrowhead and senior centers. Although several one-man *Moby-Dicks* have recently garnered critical attention, Spies' "Me & Melville" is the only comparable work created by a woman. Her work, unlike that of Christopher Moore and Carlo Adinolfi,[14] does not attempt a straightforward adaptation of *Moby-Dick's* narrative, but, like later multimedia revisions of the novel, melds her narrative with other aesthetic expressions and arranges her material to emphasize a woman's perspective. On being invited to participate in the festival, Spies considered her "reverence for Melville" as well as her desire to challenge a productive process that has valorized male artists: "I wanted to look at a male icon . . . [and claim] that greatness for [my]self in a way, saying 'yes, we can all be great.'" "Here is this big man writer . . . [writing about] such man things—whaling and the sea." Thus the creation of "Me & Melville" became a way for her "'to claim these things' for her own."[15]

Concerned to make both Melville and *Moby-Dick* accessible to all contemporary viewers through "Me & Melville," Spies attempts several tactics with varying degrees of success: 1) song lyrics and recitations, which make Melville an ordinary person rather than the great artist; 2) a focus on

Melville's relationships, especially those with Nathaniel Hawthorne and his wife, Elizabeth; 3) melodic, folksy music, imagistic poetry, and a backdrop of shifting slides, which generate an open-ended and free-flowing narrative, simulating the fluidity of *Moby-Dick* itself. Accompanying herself on guitar and often joined by a cello or a bass and fiddle, Spies integrates her retelling of *Moby-Dick* with Melville's biography, songs, music, and art. The slides, representing Spies' own sculpture and painting, drawings by children from workshops she has given in schools and women's shelters, and portraits of Melville and his family, as well as historical whaling scenes, move from simplistic cartoons of smiling whales to swirling abstractions.

Spies' opening lyric draws on Melville's language to address the actuality as well as the mystery of whales:

Whales in paint and teeth and wood
Whales in stones and stars . . .
Whale of light and whale of snow
Goin' where no one can go
Whale of light and whale of snow
Speakin' what no one can know.

Like Melville, she touches on the multiple ways in which whales have been represented. She also evokes his description of the mother whale in "The Grand Armada," noting that the female whale has milk as "sweet as early grass butter in April" and explicitly connecting her biologically and spiritually to her personal life and to women's identities and lives:

Woman, mother, life at sea
Roll me to infinity.[16]

Spies most strongly, however, identifies with Ishmael. His ability to transcend boundaries and to continue searching, she believes, is explicitly associated with the feminine.[17]

In Driscoll's *Ahab's Wife, or the Whale,* Ahab's wife is specifically depicted as capable of transcending boundaries and searching—as is both Ahab and the Whale. Created as the centerpiece for a group of installations and performances at Staten Island's Snug Harbor Cultural Center, Driscoll's work embraces a variety of forms—more than thirty drawings, monoprints, sculptures, and a multimedia theatrical performance. Her inspiration for *Ahab's Wife, or the Whale* derived from her discovery of a connection between her father's aphasia (which inhibited his communication and divided his perceptions, preventing the coordination of the right and left sides of his body) and Melville's description of the sperm whale's eyes: "The peculiar position of the whale's eyes, effectually divided as they are by many cubic feet of solid head, which towers between them like a great mountain separating two lakes in valleys; this, of course, must wholly separate the impressions which each independent organ imparts. The whale, therefore, must see one distinct picture on this side, and another distinct picture on that side" (*MD* 330). The dominance of eyes in much of Driscoll's work reflects her interest in perception—in its physical, psychological, and cultural complexities—while the dominance of doubles in her work suggests the potential for fissures in our lives. Driscoll explains the connection explicitly: "This condition of living with split vision/split body is the condition that the surrogate persona of Ahab's Wife explores in the theater piece [in] her own relationship with the whale/man."[18] The title for her performance piece—*Ahab's Wife, or the Whale*—underscores her consciousness of these problems: it refers not only to the title of Melville's novel, but also to her two principal characters, both characters in *Moby-Dick*, both estranged from Ahab, and both voiceless—Ahab's wife, who is alluded to only twice in the novel, and the whale, who is ubiquitous in the novel.

In her sculpture *The Space Between*, Driscoll uses metal tubing to create the frames for a strange pair of spectacles. The two eye-shaped hemispheres are identically sized: a shining, mottled eyeball fills one, while a small androgynous figure crouches in the empty cup of the other. Melville underscores such bifurcation in *Moby-Dick*, Driscoll's work implies: all the men on board the *Pequod* are alienated from the life of whales and women, and whales and women are alienated from the men. In another sculpture, *The Eye of the Whale*, Driscoll again brings two hemispheres into relation; however, here the sphere holding the eyeball is set in an oval steel table suggesting, in its pattern of rusting, a whale's skin, while the sphere holding the small figure hovers over it. Critic Ken Johnson believes *The Eye of the Whale* "comes close to capturing the viscerally cosmic imagery" of *Moby-Dick*,[19] a perspective that Driscoll makes possible for Ahab's wife in the conclusion of her performance piece when she at last can perceive Ahab and Whale in relation to a full spectrum of life.

Among Driscoll's sculptures is a small, rough-hewn figure strapped into an enormous hoop skirt almost as if it were a parachute securing her to the ground; the figure in her skirt is then locked into a lucite case. This sculpture expresses an uncertain response to women's position: the skirt, while confining the figure just as whalebone corsets and full skirts confined antebellum American women, also buoys the figure and, through its multiple reflections in the case, suggests escape. With a full map of the globe inscribed on the skirt, Driscoll alludes to the world that a nineteenth-century woman might have access to if she could go to sea—as did some captain's wives. Several of Driscoll's ink drawings reveal a hoopskirted female figure. In one image, the skirt is immense, ballooning out, whalelike, underwater. Also whalelike, the skirt is literally waifed, keeping the small female figure wearing the skirt weighted in place and just barely above water. In several other images, the figure's head is tethered by a line to spheres resembling the globe or the heavens and implying her oscillation between fluidity and stasis,[20] the liberation of spirit and imagination on the one hand and the weight of society on the other.

Through the use of her visual designs, a poetic script,[21] and dance in *Ahab's Wife, or the Whale*, Driscoll envisions Ahab's wife as a character who journeys forth emotionally and imaginatively, leaving a woman's sheltered life on land for a man's adventurous life on the high seas. Program notes for the performance indicate that this journey occurs in three movements: first she "slips overboard in search of a sandal wood fan her lover [Ahab] gave her; [next] she meets the Whale down in the deep, [who] tells her what it knows about her missing lover, and then [she] returns from the shipwreck to the surface."[22] The role of Ahab's wife is taken by two dancers, one representing the young wife, the other the mature woman who challenges gender roles through costume and action and whose adventure propels the performance's movement. With a multiethnic dance troupe of nine men and women, Driscoll's narrative is one of continuous transformation, fusing classical and contemporary music and flowing among diverse worlds of meaning and dance—the violence and physicality of whaling evoked by jujitsu, humor by the ballroom dancing of 1930s and Marx Brothers slapstick, fantasy and dream by dramatically shifting shadows reminiscent of Balinese puppet theater.

Driscoll's hoopskirt, a wonderfully adaptable stage prop as it is manipulated by dancers using poles, is the barometer of these transformations. Initially Ahab's young wife appears in the skirt with, as Robert Wallace observes, her "semaphoric arm movements suggest[ing] a regimented stasis."[23] However, when she escapes to seek Ahab, she invites the sea into her soul, projecting herself into ocean reveries through a diving bell, whose form mirrors the skirt's shape. In the course of the production, the gray silk skirt comes to resemble a jellyfish, sails, and the billowing sea; in the conclusion, the skirt is inverted, with the round waist transformed into a porthole or a great eye.

Precipitating the life changes in Ahab's wife is her encounter with the Whale, performed by Robert Langdon Lloyd, whom she meets in the depths of the sea. As the wife's vision is dichotomized between her restricted position on land on the one hand, and her longing to explore the sea and to be at sea with her husband on the other, the Whale's vision is also double. The two hemispheres of the diving bell, which is split in two, are set on either end of the stage where they evoke the hoopskirt as well as the Whale's two bulging eyeballs, emphatically estranged. The script tells us that the Whale sees "the rigging in the one eye, the sea stretching out gray and flat in the other," indicating that he remembered the pain of countless encounters with whale ships as well as the continuity of his life in the sea. As Wallace notes, the pain of these divisions creates a "magnetic pull" between Ahab's wife and the Whale, "this being the verbal as well as the emotional crux of the play" (28).

At the performance's conclusion, puppets as well as male and female dancers representing Ahab and the *Pequod*'s crew spill out of the hemispheres, now turned magic lanterns, with their shadows looming large and tumbling across the stage in their deadly encounter with the Whale. In its last incarnation as a cosmic eye, the skirt rises to the flyspace above the stage. Its path leads the audience to observe this concluding action that Wallace describes as "the moment of ultimate magic, of unconscious stasis breaking into miraculous, freeform, ungraspable, multitudinous life" (29). Like Ishmael, both Ahab's wife and the Whale live on after the drama of Ahab's pursuit of Moby Dick is completed. At its conclusion, Driscoll's astonishing, multiple visualizations of the lives of woman and Whale demand that *Moby-Dick* be viewed from their complex—anguished, joyous, and unsettling—perspective.

In creating *Songs and Stories from Moby Dick*, a nonlinear, multimedia, high-tech extravaganza of sound and image that has played to crowds in major American and European cities, Laurie Anderson also reorganizes *Moby-Dick* in order to open the novel to women's participation. In conceptualizing her work, Anderson recognized Melville's novel's predominantly masculine orientation: "If you look at what's in quotation marks and the characters, it's certainly really a guy book, with all that blubber and blood around." Her challenge, thus, was to find space for herself in the narrative: "It's a guy thing. What would I be doing in this?"[24] With a cast of four men, in addition to herself, Anderson answers her own question, implicitly, by her full participation in *Songs and Stories from Moby Dick*. She not only gives herself the specific roles of a reader, Pip, and the Whale but also enters into her production as director and creator of the visual design, music, and lyrics.

Her perception of the often interchangeable position of Melville and Ishmael led her to discover the means of comprehending how to revise *Moby-Dick* most dramatically. She recognized that "as the book unfolds, it becomes virtually impossible to find the author. He's hundreds of people: accountant, botanist, lawyer, philosopher, dreamer, preacher, historian. And it's this daring approach to narrative voices that I've found most exciting and original about the book. Imagistic, concise, and associative, Melville built his world and inhabited it with a cast of the living and the dead. Spinoza, Noah, Job, and Jonah sailed on the doomed Pequod just as much as Ahab, Ishmael, Pip, Queequeg, and the crazy cook."[25] Understanding *Moby-Dick* as rich with "just hundreds of different voices," Anderson appreciates not only the power of Melville's language but also the impossibility of assigning a single voice or a single meaning to the novel. The significance of these diverse and changing voices and of Melville's words is kept before her audience by the songs and stories presented by the five actors as well as by their projection in overlapping and changing script on the backdrop.

Noting that Melville makes few references to the sounds of these voices themselves, Anderson took it upon herself to provide music for *Moby-Dick*. She also devised "a talking stick," a six-foot "microphone filled with digital processing equipment capable of producing a full orchestra of sounds,"[26] which she and the other actors carried about the stage like a harpoon and which, when stroked, mysteriously produced a range of tones. To further emphasize the wonder of sounds in Melville's natural world—sperm whales' clicks, ships' creaks, winds' moans, gulls' cries, rhythms of sailors' chanteys—she uses live music, played by herself on keyboard and a tiny violin as well as by others on drums, bass, guitar, and charango.

By not focusing on feminism per se, but by taking the stage herself as the embodiment of numerous voices, of adventurous possibilities, and of unanswered questions, Anderson liberates her *Songs and Stories from Moby Dick* to explore answers beyond most boundaries, including those of gender. However, she does see both *Moby-Dick* and her performance piece as tied to American culture: "I think Melville's Americans were very similar to us—very garrulous, . . . practical, mechanical. But also, there is this streak of transcendentalism that, in the middle of all our technology, there's still this need to understand why we're here."[27] Multiple voices, multiple answers, and multiple expectations haunt Anderson's open-ended revision of *Moby-Dick*: "I initially wanted my piece to be a dream about the book—a dream dealing with some of the ways it made me feel. But, once you bring in actors, they ask, 'Who am I?' And there is no single answer."[28]

Central to Rinde Eckert's revision of *Moby-Dick*, his transcendent opera *And God Created Great Whales*, is a woman, who not only challenges gender conventions but whose soaring voice lifts the audience to a new vision of society. Like Anderson, Eckert was attracted to *Moby-Dick* in part because of its American qualities: "It reminded me of my culture. It's a messy culture, it's an eclectic culture, and I thought: Melville is the first one to recognize exactly how messy and grandiose and wonderful this culture is. [*Moby-Dick*] seems quintessentially American to me."[29] Eckert's perception of the "messiness" of both American culture and Melville's novel is the means for his opening up the narrative to cross and to embrace a diversity of oppositions—male and female, black and white, young and old, sick and healthy, technology and spirituality. In Eckert's opera, which played on both American coasts in 2000 and 2001, this cultural diversity is compellingly expressed through multiple literary material and musical styles—from aria to folk song, from humorous rant to lyrical elegy.

Eckert's opera reinvents Melville's narrative in gender terms by focusing equally on a man and a woman: Nathan, a piano tuner and composer, who, in the last stages of a memory-threatening disease, persists in attempting to compose his operatic version of *Moby-Dick;* and Olivia, his muse, who, being "infallible" about "music or art or the dark night of the soul,"[30] persists in her attempts to ignite Nathan's memory. In performances of *And God Created Great Whales*, Eckert himself, a large, bald white man, sings the roles of Nathan, Ishmael, Father Mapple, Ahab, and Pip, among others, while Nora Cole, a small African American woman, is Olivia/Muse, Starbuck, Bulkington and the other members of the crew, including Queequeg, Daggoo, and Tashtego, as well as the spirit of the sea. Through their soliloquies and duets, Nathan and Olivia establish a reciprocity that reveals them to be passionately both independent and interdependent.

Although the female muse's traditional role has been to aid and abet the male creator, and although Eckert's Olivia is a projection of Nathan's desperate desire to complete his opera, rather than being subservient to him, she also sings her own rapturous vision. As diva, not as muse, Olivia explicitly voices the hope for American democracy in the significant moment when she interpolates an aria of her own into Nathan's opera. Here she envisions a society of full and gracious equality: "Come all . . . come all women and all men . . . All are welcome in this place." Nathan reprimands Nora severely at this point, insisting that they return to the man's world of the whaling ship, where "the stuck whale, lanced and bleeding, [runs] from [men,] those rancorous creatures."[31] Robert Wallace unpacks the significance of this moment which doubly subverts the prevalence of conventional gender relationships: "This contested aria allows Eckert to express in one extended melody not only Melville's implicit dream of an all-inclusive community . . . but also his awareness of the obstacles to actually achieving it."[32]

In the conclusion of *And God Created Great Whales*, Nathan, his struggle to pursue his opera as desperate and debilitating as Ahab's is to pursue Moby Dick, drifts into an abyss of meaningless voices of whalemen. Olivia, however, shifts to pursue her own struggle. She is determined to discover an identity "far from Nathan's mind." She is determined to discover an identity apart from myths of femininity created by convention and commerce, a process, her song implies, that resembles Nathan's, Eckert's, and Melville's readers' endeavors to discover Moby Dick for themselves. With the power of her vocalizations at the opera's conclusion, she reaches Nathan and lifts him up on the coffin of her ecstasy, inspiring him to join her in giving equal voice to the full and pure and wondrous sound of life. Through his rewriting of Melville's text, Eckert perceives that a woman's voice most meaningfully gives hope for the possibilities for achieving "that grand and naive spiritual aspiration," which characterizes the "best in American culture" and which he believes "underlies all of [Melville's] work."[33]

A 2001 lampoon on Garrison Keillor's *Prairie Home Companion* indicates, however, that *Moby-Dick* continues to be perceived in American culture as a novel antagonistic to women. Featuring the distinguished galaxy of mid-nineteenth-century writers living in the Berkshires, it focuses on a nagging Elizabeth Melville who complains about her husband's failures. Comparing him disparagingly to Hawthorne, she laments that if only he would write like Nathaniel, "we could buy more sheets and pillowcases" and fears that "women are not going to read an endless saga of men and the sea."[34] The feminizing of *Moby-Dick*, however, indicates that both women and men have not only continued to read this "saga of men and the sea" but are also engaged in revising it in response to women's rights to claim it. In 2004 an all-woman cast performed Welles's *Moby Dick—Rehearsed* in Philadelphia. Although reviewer David Anthony Fox maintains that the director of this production, Madi Distefano, offered no explanation for her casting decision, he believes that "the casting allows us to think about *Moby-Dick* in a new way, to recognize how much hangs on tensions between traditionally masculine characteristics—aggression, power, the need to conquer—and the more feminine virtues of care giving and compassion (the encounter between Captain Ahab and Captain Gardiner of the Rachel is a prime example)."[35] This new production of Welles's play, in addition to the work of Peters and Spies and the exuberant multimedia and multinuanced millennial works of Driscoll, Anderson, and Eckert, reveals *Moby-Dick*'s ongoing openness to women's identities, women as creators, and women's lives. Paglia's argument and Keiller's spoof notwithstanding, the persistent feminizing of *Moby-Dick* demonstrates that Melville constructed a narrative that continues to resist definitive interpretations, a narrative that can be interpreted not only to include but also to celebrate women.

NOTES

1. Camille Paglia, "*Moby-Dick* as Sexual Protest," in *Moby-Dick*, ed. Hershel Parker and Harrison Hayford, 2nd ed. (New York: W. W. Norton, 2002), 697. Paglia's essay, which first appeared in *Sexual Personae: Art and Decadence from Nefertiti to Emily Dickinson*, is the only one by a woman and the only one focused on gender in this edition.

2. See Ann Douglass, *The Feminization of American Culture* (New York: Knopf, 1977); Joyce W. Warren, *The American Narcissus: Individualism and Women in Nineteenth-Century American Fiction* (New Brunswick, N.J.: Rutgers Univ. Press, 1984); Wilma Garcia, *Mothers and Others: Myths of the Female and the Works of Melville, Twain, and Hemingway* (New York: Peter Lang, 1984). Gene Patterson-Black comments on Melville's hatred and distrust of women but credits this attitude and the apparent absence of women in his works to the construction of a Melville canon that "crystallized around works in which women do not figure, thereby producing a distorted concept of Melville's work as a whole and producing a general reading public that assumes that Melville did not write about women" ("On Herman Melville" 107–8).

3. See Elizabeth Schultz, "The Sentimental Subtext of *Moby-Dick*: Melville's Response to the 'World of Woe,'" *ESQ: A Journal of the American Renaissance* 42 (1996): 29–49; and Rita Bode, "'Suckled by the Sea': The Maternal in *Moby-Dick*," in *Melville and Women*, ed. Elizabeth Schultz and Haskell Springer (Kent, Ohio: Kent State Univ. Press, 2006).

4. Joyce Adler's dramatizations of three of Melville's works—*Moby-Dick*, "Benito Cereno," and *Billy Budd*—are not included in my discussion; although Adler does emphasize Melville's commitment to a racially and ethnically diverse society, in her careful adherence to Melville's texts, she does not revise them to acknowledge the possibility of women's presence (*Dramatization of Three Melville Novels*). In productions of Adler's *Moby-Dick*, however, at the 2003 Melville Society conference in Lahaina, the role of Queequeg was taken by a woman, and a woman also played both the role of one of the slaves and a judge in the 2005 production of "Benito Cereno" at the 2005 Melville Society conference in New Bedford.

5. *The Sea Beast*, a silent film, was directed by Millard Webb, and *Moby Dick*, with sound, was directed by Lloyd Bacon and adapted by Oliver H. P. Garrett. The roles of both Esther and Faith, who appear as Father Mapple's daughter in *The Sea Beast* and *Moby Dick*, respectively, were taken by Delores Costello, whom Barrymore later married, and Joan Bennett. In both movies a jealous brother causes Ahab to believe that his sweetheart will not love him after he has lost his leg to Moby Dick. In *The Sea Beast*, instead of a scar, he wears Esther's name as a tattoo and cherishes the heart-shaped locket she gives him. In both conclusions, Ahab kills both the brother and the whale and marries the girl.

6. Welles's only produced play, *Moby Dick—Rehearsed*, played in Long Island as recently as the summer of 2005 to good reviews. Orson Welles, *Moby Dick—Rehearsed: A Drama in Two Acts* (New York: Samuel French, 1965), 9. In the first production of *Moby Dick—Rehearsed*, actress Joan Plowright took the role of Young Actress/Pip. Eric Simonson, who adapted *Moby-Dick* for the Milwaukee Repertory Company's production in 2002, also used a woman for the part of Pip.

7. Vali Myers, known for her paintings of *Moby-Dick*, also understood the white whale to be female. Stating that "I identify with that whale 100%," she felt that the whalers' harpoons went into her own body. Letter to the author, Oct. 15, 1992; letter to Midori Oka, Aug. 3, 1992.

8. Robert Collins, "Ships and Quips," rev., *City Pages*, Dec. 2, 1987.

9. Quoted by Edward Rothstein, "Modern Hunts for the Great White Whale Leave Ahab Adrift," *New York Times*, Oct. 16, 1999.

10. Stacey D'Erasmo, "Call Me Una," rev., *New York Times Book Review*, Oct. 3, 1999.

11. Peters wrote and directed *Hunting for Moby Dick* in conjunction with San Francisco's Ghostlight Theatre. The production has had several runs on the West Coast as well as in New York, Canada, and Australia.

12. Bill Peters, telephone conversation with the author, Apr. 2, 2001.

13. Quoted in brochure for Newhouse Center for Contemporary Art, Snug Harbor Cultural Center, September 1998.

14. Adinolfi has presented his "One-Man 'Moby-Dick'" in New England and New York beginning in 2001; Moore did his first *Moby-Dick* in 2003 and continues to perform in New York and the Midwest.

15. See Judith Monachina, "Spies to Perform *Melville & Me* Four Times in Housatonic," *The Advocate*, July 16, 1997; *The Advocate*, Aug. 9, 2000.

16. JoAnne Spies, "Fabulous Shadow," *Me & Melville* (Dolce Music, 1997).

17. JoAnne Spies, telephone conversation with the author, Dec. 22, 2000.

18. Ellen Driscoll, Web site, *Ahab's Wife*, 2002–03.

19. Ken Johnson, "Ahab's Wife, Ignored in 'Moby-Dick,' Tries Again," *New York Times*, Aug. 28, 1998.

20. *Ahab's Wife, or the Whale*, special program for benefit night, Newhouse Center for Contemporary Art, Snug Harbor Cultural Center, Staten Island, N.Y., 1998.

21. Poet Tom Sleigh, Driscoll's husband, wrote the script for *Ahab's Wife, or the Whale*.

22. *Ahab's Wife, or the Whale, Harborbill*, The Music Hall at Snug Harbor, September 1998.

23. Ellen Driscoll, postplay discussion, video made by Robert K. Wallace, Snug Harbor Cultural Center, Sept. 20, 1998. Robert K. Wallace, rev., "Ahab's Wife or the Whale," *Melville Society Extracts* 116 (Feb. 1999): 28.

24. Quoted by Doug Ullen, "Whale of a Show," *The Flint Journal*, Sept. 8, 1999, and by Justin Davidson, "In the Belly of the Beast," *Los Angeles Times*, Oct. 17, 1999.

25. Laurie Anderson, "Program Notes," *Stagebill*, Brooklyn Academy of Music, Oct. 1999.

26. Roselle Goldberg, "Hitching a Ride on the Great White Whale," *New York Times*, Oct. 3, 1999.

27. Shermakaye Bass interview with Laurie Anderson, "Anderson's 'Moby-Dick' premiering in Dallas," *Austin American Statesman*, Apr. 22, 1999.

28. Clifford Ross interview with Laurie Anderson, http://www.laurieanderson.com/interview.html (July 1999).

29. Robert K. Wallace, "Avoiding Melville's Vortex: A Conversation with Performance Artist Rinde Eckert," *Leviathan: A Journal of Melville Studies* 3.1 (Mar. 2001): 102.

30. Robert K. Wallace, rev., "Carlo Adinolfi's *One-Man Moby-Dick* and Rinde Eckert's *And God Created Great Whales*," *Melville Society Extracts*, 120 (Feb. 2001): 19.

31. Quoted in Wallace, "Adinolfi and Eckert," 20.

32. Wallace, "Conversation," 80.

33. Quoted in ibid., 102.

34. *Prairie Home Companion*, dir. Garrison Keillor, National Public Radio, June 30, 2001.

35. David Anthony Fox, "*Moby-Dick—Rehearsed*," http://www.citypaper.net, June 3–9, 2004.

Fusing with the Muse

Eckert's *Great Whales* as Homage and Prophecy

ROBERT K. WALLACE

Rinde Eckert's *Moby-Dick* opera *And God Created Great Whales* opened at 45 Bleecker Street in New York City in September 2000. The opera returned to Bleecker Street in November 2001—one month after the *Moby-Dick* 2001 Conference at Hofstra and two months after the attack on the World Trade Center. By May 2002 Eckert and his co-performer Nora Cole were singing and acting *And God Created Great Whales* at the Center Stage Theater in Baltimore.[1] Although the show did not change appreciably when performed on these three separate occasions, its meaning did. Its meaning will continue to change—as will that of *Moby-Dick* itself—as long as American ideas and ideals, linked to American coercion and fears, hold forth on the world's stage.

The most obvious artistic context in which to locate Eckert's opera is within a remarkable sequence of theatrical adaptations of *Moby-Dick* beginning in 1998. Preceding Eckert's September 2000 Bleecker Street production of *And God Created Great Whales* were Ellen Driscoll's *Ahab's Wife* at the Snug Harbor Cultural Center in September 1998, Laurie Anderson's *Songs and Stories of Moby Dick* at the Brooklyn Academy of Music in October 1999, and Carlo Adinolfi's *One Man Moby Dick* at New York's Ensemble Studio Theater in August 2000.[2] Additional *Moby-Dick* theatrical works created after the September 2000 production of Eckert's opera include the May 2001 debut of *Moby Dick: An American Opera,* composed by Doug Katsaros, with a libretto by Mark St. Germain, at the New Repertory Theater in Newton, Massachusetts; the September 2002 premiere of Eric Simonson's theatrical adaptation of *Moby-Dick* by the Milwaukee Repertory Company; the American premiere of Robert Longden and Hereward Kaye's *Moby Dick! The Musical* by the Human Race Theater in Dayton, Ohio, in February 2003; the premiere of Christopher Moore's one-man *Moby-Dick* at the West End in New York in May 2003; a public reading from Joyce Adler's theatrical adaptation of *Moby-Dick* by Hawaiian actors in Kahului, Maui, in June 2003; the premiere of Sharon Butler's multimedia *dickathon* for the fringe festival The Edge in New Haven, Connecticut, in June 2003; a new version of Carlo Adinolfi's *One Man Moby Dick*, now with music by David Pinkard, at the Fringe Festival in Edinburgh in August 2003; and the premiere of *Call Me Ishmael*, a new *Moby-Dick* opera by Gary Goldschneider, in Amsterdam in May 2004.

The popularity of *Moby-Dick* in theatrical and musical adaptations at the end of the twentieth century and the beginning of the twenty-first century would itself prove a subject worthy of exploration. So would the fact that four of the stage adaptations mentioned above have been created by women—and that women have memorably taken on the roles of Melville's male whalers in a number of these productions.[3] (See Elizabeth Schultz's essay "Feminizing *Moby-Dick*" in this volume.) But the primary subject of this essay is Eckert's *And God Created Great Whales* as it had been created and performed in advance of the *Moby-Dick* 2001 Conference at Hofstra. In addition to the immediate context provided by the stage adaptations by Driscoll, Anderson, and Adinolfi, three major nonfiction trade books had recently anticipated Eckert's opera by using *Moby-Dick* as a reference for exploring the actual world of whaling. Tim Severin's *In Search of Moby Dick* (1999) and Robert Sullivan's *A Whale Hunt* (2000) sought out indigenous peoples on opposite ends of the Pacific who were still hunting the whale at the end of the twentieth century. Severin presents the peoples of Lamalera at the southwest edge of the Pacific Ocean as "the last community on earth where men still regularly hunt sperm whales by hand," whereas Sullivan documents the two-year process by which the Makah peoples of the northwest coast of the Olympic Peninsula recreated the tradition of hunting the gray whale after the practice had died out.[4] Whereas these two authors used *Moby-Dick* as a frame of reference for contemporary whale hunts by indigenous peoples, Nathaniel Philbrick in *In the Heart of the Sea* (2000) recreated the tragedy of the whale ship *Essex* in the middle of the Pacific on February 23, 1821—when the Nantucket whale ship was stove in by the whale it was hunting, after which the abandoned whalers literally became the bloodthirsty cannibals they were afraid of being hunted by.[5]

Eckert's libretto for *And God Created Great Whales* resembles each of the above nonfiction books by depicting the hunt of a whale through a modern consciousness for which Melville's *Moby-Dick* serves as a touchstone. His opera differs from these books in that its male-centered, whale-chasing story is embedded in the larger story of a man and a woman. The man is Nathan, a piano tuner who is writing an opera based on *Moby-Dick* in spite of suffering from a degenerative nerve disorder that is destroying his memory. The immediate drama pivots on whether Nathan will complete his opera before he loses his mind. The deeper drama involves whether Nathan can be humanized by Olivia, the diva who becomes his Muse. Selections from Nathan's opera-in-progress are framed and punctuated by Nathan's "real-life" interactions with Olivia/ Muse. Within the excerpts performed from the opera, Nathan is imprisoned in the world of the hunt, as unable as Ahab to see beyond the dimensions of the chase. In his interaction with Olivia as Muse, Nathan has the option of abandoning or transforming the chase. Her presence as his equal partner on stage makes the question of whether he will finish his opera secondary to the question of what kind of opera it will be—a tragic tribute to Ahab's nineteenth-century obsession or an unlikely amalgam of twenty-first-century inclusion. The dialogic voice in which Eckert dramatizes this question contrasts tellingly with the narrative voices in which Severin, Sullivan, and Philbrick had recently presented their nonfictional accounts of the hunt of the whale.

Severin narrates his story in the afterglow of the British empire on which the sun never set, in the voice of the resourceful adventurer who takes us into pre-civilized places whose remarkable peoples are preserving a fragile handmade tradition of hunting the whale that is now endangered by everything modern. He narrates in the jaunty, self-assured style of the solo performer, a Boomer without his Bunger. Sullivan takes on more the persona of a cub reporter, settling in alongside the Makahs for two dreary years between the Pacific shore and the Olympic rain forest, his persistence finally paying off as the successful hunt of one gray whale restores the missing link in an ancient culture. He narrates this story rather like the young Ishmael on the *Pequod,* but without a Queequeg for company in that rain-soaked shack. Philbrick recreates the story of the *Essex* as a disciplined, impassioned historian, the passion most often expressed in the cogent precision of the prose in which a nearly unendurable irony is conveyed. His narrative voice in this way resembles Melville's after *Moby-Dick,* and after *Pierre*—after Melville had lost his audience but still had much to say, and began to count on what was not said to convey much of its force. That a book as serious, cogent, and challenging as Philbrick's won the National Book Award for the year 2000 shows something very positive about our culture. So does the success of Eckert's opera in the same year.[6]

Contrasting Eckert's performative voice in the person of Nathan with the narrative voices of Severin, Sullivan, and Philbrick shows how poignant, vulnerable, and wildly Romantic Nathan is. He is Romantic not only in the nineteenth-century Ahabian dimension of hunting the whale but also in his twenty-first-century exposure to the cultural "other" as embodied by the Muse. Nathan is also Romantic in the deeper Melvillean dimension of going flat-out in the service of creativity itself. He is a piano tuner who is creating an opera that may never be performed. He is a man whose neurological disorder is gradually eradicating areas of his remembered experience at the same time that he continues to strive to shape his human fragility into words buoyed by song. In his highly Romantic, yet intensely postmodern race against time, Nathan is aided on the one hand by the battery of boxy tape recorders that hang from his neck and, on the other, by Olivia, his Muse. Olivia adds the element that lifts Eckert's opera into greatness.

Two performers, Eckert himself as Nathan and Nora Cole as Olivia/Muse, take all the roles in both the whaling story and the domestic one. In doing so, they achieve a gender, racial, and vocal equality that is rare on stage (see figure). He, a large, balding white male, and she, a taut, feisty African American female, embody an exceptionally rich mix of "unlike things" that "meet and mate" (in the language of Melville's poem "Art"). The "unlike things" in Melville's 1891 poem include: "A flame to melt—a wind to freeze; / Sad patience—joyous energies; / Humility—yet pride and scorn; / Instinct and study; love and hate; / Audacity—reverence." Together, "These must mate, / And fuse with Jacob's mystic heart, / To wrestle with the angel—Art."[7] The mystical fusion in Eckert's opera occurs at the very end, after "the great shroud of the sea" has silenced the "topmost grief" of Ahab's ultimate aria.

When the Muse returns to the stage, she sees Nathan staring blankly into space, possibly comatose, accompanied only by the sound track of John Huston's film of *Moby-Dick*. She asks him if he remembers how he had "planned to handle the ending—all that grand violence, the monolithic whale, the sinking ship." She recalls that, after the catastrophe as Nathan had imagined it, "all subsides, the leviathan, the cloth waves, the lonely coffin bobs in the center. Then I descend on a wire like a baroque angel to pull Ishmael from the sea." After the Muse speaks those words, Eckert's libretto indicates simply this: "She sings. Nathan joins her. They finish. Lights fade. The end."[8] What she sings, and they sing together, is a wordless vocalize in which the Baroque angel pulls the broken composer momentarily out of his ultimate oblivion. The vocal fusion of their hearts and souls lasts just long enough for us to be shocked by its sudden cessation as the song, and the opera itself, abruptly ends.

It goes without saying that very little of such a mystical, musical denouement can be captured in the silence of words on a page in an essay. The essence of such musical emotion is as "invisible" from the reader's eye as is music itself in Emily Dickinson's poem "This World is not Conclusion": "A Species stands

Nora Cole and Rinde Eckert sing "Promise and Warning" in *And God Created Great Whales* at the Dance Theater Workshop of the Foundry Theatre in New York City, June 2000. Photograph by Carol Rosegg.

beyond—/ Invisible—as Music—/ Positive, as Sound." The sung sound of the unconcluded closing duet recalls "death's outlet song of life" in Walt Whitman's "Out of the Cradle Endlessly Rocking."[9] Unfortunately, no recorded performance of *And God Created Great Whales* exists at the present. The words of this essay must suffice to suggest a few of the ways in which Eckert's opera is at once a homage to Melville and a prophecy for our nation.[10]

The September 2000 production of *And God Created Great Whales* at 45 Bleecker Street represented an homage to *Moby-Dick* in much the same way as the stage creations by Driscoll, Anderson, and Adinolfi that immediately preceded it. Eckert's combined talents as a dramatist, composer, and performer were richly documented in the Summer 2000 issue of the journal *Theater,* in which an extended interview about his performance activities was accompanied by the scripts of three plays he had already written and performed: *Romeo Sierra Tango, The Idiot Variations,* and *The Gardening of Thomas D.*[11] In spite of this extensive coverage of Eckert and his works, the issue of *Theater* did not mention his work-in-progress inspired by Melville's *Moby-Dick. And God Created Great Whales* is a breakthrough work in which Eckert has fused his versatile gifts in an entirely new way. His homage to Melville "fuses" the "audacity" and "reverence" in Melville's "Art." He achieves this fusion by "Avoiding Melville's Vortex" (as he recounted in a March 2001 interview in *Leviathan*): "You can get caught in Melville's vortex because it's so compelling.

At some point I had to respectfully put him at arm's length and say the only way I'm going to do service to his book is if I absorb it and make it mine."[12]

Anchoring the "reverence" side of Eckert's homage to Melville are the scenes from Nathan's opera-in-progress that are directly inspired by the plot and characters of *Moby-Dick* itself. Nathan begins the opera in a creative impasse, but as soon as Olivia gets him back on task he searchingly finds his way into his "Call me Ishmael" aria. With the help of the Muse, he then moves on to New Bedford, where they act out between them the Ishmael-Queequeg encounter, sing an inventive "Street Vendor" song, visit the Whaleman's Chapel, and enact a spellbinding version of Father Mapple's sermon. Delivering his Sermon aria with increasing passion over the rising crescendo of an angry ostinato, Nathan blacks out for the first of three times in the show as he repeats the words "drown or be saved."

Recovering from his first blackout, Nathan the piano tuner gets his everyday bearings by playing the prerecorded tape in which the doctors have mapped out the successive stages in the growth of his disease ("Your name is Nathan. You are suffering from memory loss"). When he gathers his creative wits about him again—after the Muse praises him for his "seagoing mind" in the words of Ishmael's "Lee Shore" chapter—Nathan and the Muse are ready to depart from the shore in a leave-taking duet that binds them to each other in meeting whatever fate will bring their way ("Well away from the crowded towns"). Not only the swelling of their voices but the swaying of their bodies creates an "elongated Siamese ligature" comparable to that between Ishmael and Queequeg in the "Monkey-Rope" chapter (*MD* 320). Their togetherness only deepens when the Muse moves from worded song into liquid vocalise, Nathan responding in kind, their side-to-side motion suggesting the rocking, nautical movement of a ship's figurehead through long, strong swells.

From this poignant leave-taking and shoreless motion, Nathan's nascent opera now slips into the business of the chase. Various members of Ahab's crew are introduced with quick vocal and musical characterizations until Pip is presented with a gravity indicating that he plays no mere cameo role. After the Muse announces Pip as "the cabin boy, the innocent, the black Alabama boy with the tambourine," Nathan ups the ante with this imperative injunction: "Boy, you Pip, give us an air to calm the drunken blood, ho, lullaby us, boy, put us in the arms of Morpheus, unnerve us, boy, so we drop like barrels into the dead water in the wake of sleep." Catching the tambourine tossed by the Muse, Nathan embodies Pip's essential castaway loneliness by singing "Shenandoah" in Eckert's fragile, unworldly falsetto (while standing as tall and motionless as Gilles in Watteau's painted portrait of the innocent fool among the Italian comedians). Eckert's plaintive, disembodied sound here is a far cry from the massive voice in which he had intoned the heavy rhetorical burden of Father Mapple's sermon—and in which he will soon be doing the same as Captain Ahab on the quarterdeck. Before, however, Captain Ahab can inject his particular brand of operatic terror into the musical proceedings, we have a quick interlude in which Eckert's inventive reverence for Melville's characters and situations is entirely displaced by an audacious digression in which Nathan expresses his deepest existential doubts and fears as a piano-tuning composer in a metropolitan city at the end of the twentieth century.

As soon as the second stanza of Pip's leave-taking "Shenandoah" has further "lullabied" us into "the arms of Morpheus" ("I long to hear you" becomes "I'm bound to leave you"), Nathan is jolted with a "yelp" from his "wake of sleep" to suddenly ask: "What if you jumped from a tall building and you discovered half way down that some sort of law, some physical law, some law of conservation? Call it Nathan's first law of conservation of time. . . ." The Muse, unnerved by this blatant digression from Nathan's *Moby-Dick* opera, tries to slow him down by saying, "Marginal note, Nathan." But he rolls right on to ask, "I mean, what if at moments of certain death, time is experienced as if one were traveling at velocities approaching the speed of light, time slowing to conserve itself? . . . What if nature doesn't let us escape, so that the terror of falling is preserved like a whale eye in a jar of alcohol. One would be perpetually staring at the up-rushing earth, unable to stop, and unable to stop. What if nature works that way?"

By asking these questions in the Bleecker Street production in September 2000, Nathan anticipated the terror of each individual who was to jump to certain death from the towers of the World Trade Center one year later. Moreover, he voiced the psychic terror that each of us was to feel as soon as we knew they had done so. That trauma was frozen pictorially in the photograph of one man plunging headfirst that was published in the *New York Times* on September 12, 2001.[13] That photo preserves the "terror of falling forever" by means of the lens of a camera distant from the observed body. Nathan's digression sees such terror from within the plunging body, where "one would be perpetually staring at the up-rushing earth, unable to stop, and unable to stop." Eckert imagines us into the very eye of the psyche, as Melville does with Pip in the "Castaway" chapter.

We shall return to the terrifying transition from Pip's aria to Nathan's digression, but first we must follow the flow of the music and the action through the next scene in the opera, "Ahab Smoking on the Quarter Deck." To bring Nathan to this scene, the Muse must abruptly cut off his accelerating meditation on the implications of the perpetual fall. Nathan is still asking himself, with escalating passion, "What if you knew this? You could maybe master that moment. A man drowns but uses his drowning, is ecstatic within the fury of it, ecstatic and preserved and. . . ." When the Muse does force Nathan's attention back to an "actual passage" from his *Moby-Dick* opera, she brings Ahab to the fore. Over swelling, portentous music, she enunciates these words: "He tossed the still lighted pipe into the sea. The fire hissed in the waves; the same instant the ship shot by the bubble the sinking pipe made. With slouched hat, Ahab lurchingly paced the planks." Given this cue, Nathan, as Ahab, "assembles the crew" and launches into his self-definition as "a man of deeps cut off at the knee."

Eckert's insight into Ahab's psyche creates a different kind of terror from what we feel when we experience either Pip's castaway aria or Nathan's existential digression: "Shipmates. Do ye see a man standing in the rain? A wounded man. A crippled man. Call him a man of courage, or a man of courage and intelligence, but no luck. . . . And somewhere there is another man, a whole man, a man with legs, a lucky fool, capering about. A man of little imagination and no daring, but all his limbs. All his limbs and no faculties. He walks about unencumbered and sees nothing, hears nothing. Senses not the running of the sea beneath; smells not the nearness of death; knows not the awful faces of fear. . . . The brave man is hobbled at his work, a man of deeps cut off at the knee." As Ahab's inspired rant intensifies, he calls "Nature" a "fool" for making "the dim-witted strong, the ambitious foolhardy, and the wise, slow to act." After commanding the harpooners to cross lances and be branded with his fire, Nathan's Ahab dictates this oath to the crew: "God hunt us all if we do not hunt this whale. Carve the white skin with our sharp knives. Spell our names in blood to be remembered by. . . . If it's blood or bedlam, boys, by God I choose blood!" After uttering these words, which are nearly inarticulate on stage owing to his ecstatic rage, Nathan's Ahab plunges into the second total blackout of the opera, a frightening replay of the one experienced by Father Mapple at the peak of his similarly overwrought sermon.

Pip's aria in the Shenandoan mode is poignant in its submerged terror. Nathan's existential digression converts an imagined terror into a living abstraction. Ahab's "Man of deeps cut off at the knee" converts personal loss to political coercion, consigning the entire crew to a destruction not only physical but metaphysical. Within Eckert's opera, this opens up an opportunity for transformation that the Muse seizes upon immediately after Nathan's recovery from the blackout. She proposes to Nathan that he make room in his opera for her to make a "visitation" to Ahab in his cabin. There, accompanied by "an oriental instrument, something exotic, a Koto perhaps," she could deliver "a promise or warning" that might divert him from his bloody oath. Her proposed visitation takes the form of a forgiving, inclusive aria in which "all is welcome to this plain; all is welcome save the shadows of forgotten things and vain regret." She imagines that during this visitation "the music changes," and "Ahab calms down." Nathan listens as she sings this aria, but he rejects it, and the "dark woman" who would sing it, from his opera. "She doesn't belong. It's a whaling ship, for God's sake," he exclaims excitedly. "It's not a magical place. It's a bloody business. There are no comforting visions. There is the ship and the whaleboats and the harpoons and the stuck whale, lanced and bleeding, running from these rancorous creatures, then the towing of the carcass, the slaughter, the men high on the kill, the water white with frenzied sharks tearing at the wounded obliging flesh. There are no visitations, no sculpted women appearing in the dark with prayers or promises."

Although Nathan excludes such "visitations" from his opera, Eckert includes them, three times over, in his. First we hear the long folk-song aria in which the Muse proposes to Nathan that "all is welcome." Then comes the duet of "The Promise and the Warning," introduced by the Muse but with Nathan becoming an active partner by the end. And then, after the third and last blackout, following Ahab's vengeful demise, the Muse does return "like a baroque angel" to pull Nathan, as Ishmael, from the sea, allowing them to fuse fully, though briefly, in the concluding vocalize. As Melville does in *Moby-Dick,* Eckert leaves us in a precarious balance between absolute loss (Ahab, Nathan, Nathan's opera) and spiritual transformation (Nathan, the Muse, Eckert's opera).

The talk I had planned to give at Hofstra in October 2001 would have highlighted the "audacity" and "reverence" of Eckert's homage to Melville's novel by emphasizing the degree to which his creation of the role of the Muse for Nora Cole allowed the performers on stage to infuse Melville's mid-nineteenth-century whaling story with a late twentieth-century exploration of gender, race, and representation. When 9/11 intervened a month before our conference, Eckert's opera acquired new dimensions that I felt compelled to address. Nathan's existential digression after Pip's "Shenandoah" aria was now no longer an abstract, contemporary, citified analog for Pip's castaway terror after being isolated at sea. Nathan's "marginal note" was now an anticipation of the real-life terror felt by living New Yorkers who had "jumped from tall buildings" during the destruction of the towers—and soon internalized by the entire nation. This plot-level similarity between Nathan's imagined fear and our nation's real-life trauma was stunning enough. But even more significant was the way in which the deeper dynamics of loss in which Eckert had embedded Nathan's fear spoke to deeper psychic issues resulting from the attack on the World Trade Center, especially to the tension between "love and hate," another pair of "unlike things" that must "meet and mate" in Melville's 1891 poem "Art." On this deeper, subterranean psychic level, too, Eckert's September 2000 opera anticipated realities we would be facing in September 2001—and beyond.

On the plot level, Nathan's "What if you jumped from a tall building" meditation is a total digression between Pip's "Shenandoah" aria and Ahab's "Quarter-Deck" aria. On the psychic level it links Nathan's present-day psychic terror with that of Pip and Ahab in the novel/opera. Whereas Pip and Ahab react to the terror by reaching out and striking out, respectively, Nathan is unconsciously seeking a way to "master the moment" by finding some "ecstasy in the fury of the thing." On the immediate plot level, Nathan's digressive plunge leads to Ahab's ecstatic call to fury on the quarterdeck. At a "little lower layer," it leads to the possibilities of redemptive love as embodied by the Muse. During the negotiations between Nathan and the Muse after Ahab's "blood"-versus-"bedlam" blackout, we hear two major musical pieces not related to Melville's *Moby-Dick* in any direct way. We have already considered the Muse's aria of inclusion in which "All is welcome." By rejecting this aria as inapplicable to the story he is compelled to tell about the "bloody business" and "the men high on the kill," Nathan emphatically chooses Ahab's retaliatory "hate" over the Muse's inclusive "love" as the only way to respond to the trauma of unendurable loss.

Not surprisingly, this is the way our nation immediately responded to the terrorist attack on the World Trade Center on September 11. By the time our *Moby-Dick* conference convened at Hofstra on October 18, our military forces had launched a retaliatory attack on the nation of Afghanistan whose Taliban leaders had harbored Osama bin Laden and other Al Qaeda operatives. This was the first act in the war on terror whose most immediate objective was to hunt down Osama himself. He was then the adversary upon whose "hump" we "piled the sum of all the general rage and hate felt by [our] whole race," so that, "if his chest had been a mortar," we could "burst [our] hot heart's shell upon it" (*MD* 184).

In Eckert's opera, the Muse's second musical digression is much more abstract than was the "visitation" aria so quickly rejected by Nathan. She announces that this new digression is being brought by a woman who comes as "an apparition . . . out of that provoking night." She leads the hesitant Nathan into a "Promise and Warning" duet whose "unlike things" prove as paradoxical as those in Melville's "Art." This is another moment in which the simple words on this page can give no hint of the drama on the stage as the musical accompaniment turns paradox into portent. This duet suspends the forward motion of the opera in a sonic oasis that is Eckert's equivalent to Ishmael's "insular Tahiti" from which we should never "push off" (*MD* 274). The first promise from the Muse, "The day will dawn," is answered by her warning that "Night will fall." Then "The night will be cool" is followed by "The day will be hot." Her promise "You will find what you seek" is followed by her warning that "You will find what you seek." Here Nathan immediately objects to her "irony," saying "It's on opera, for God's sake." But she tells him "It's not finished." When she prompts *him* to declare a promise, he declares "I will be innocent"—and repeats it as his warning. His second promise—"I will be a child again"—he also repeats as his warning, but this time he cannot stop repeating it, reverting into incoherence from which she is able to rouse him only for Starbuck's encounter with Ahab on the last day of the chase. The Muse as Starbuck declares to Nathan as Ahab that it is not "too late," even on the third day, "to desist. See! Moby Dick seeks thee not. It is thou that madly seekest him!" In spite of this last warning, Nathan's Ahab persists in his furious quest. Grandly declaring that "my topmost greatness lies in my topmost grief," he darts his harpoon one last time at the hated whale and blacks out forever.

The challenge of the "Promise" and the "Warning," followed by the encounter with Starbuck on the last day of the chase, presents Nathan/Ahab with a last chance to live for love in the place of hate. On the plot level of Nathan's opera, Ahab "finds" what he "seeks" in the fatal encounter he has continued to seek in spite of every possible warning. In the denouement of Eckert's opera, Nathan does perhaps find some of that subterranean love he seeks when the voice of the Baroque angel pulls him, if only momentarily, from the mindless, blank fixation in which we see him after Ahab's hateful demise. Any sense of salvation we may feel from this last-minute rescue of Nathan-as-Ishmael by the voice of the Muse, however, is immediately undercut by the abrupt cessation of their blended voices. The Muse's love has reached Nathan's soul without being able to save his life, much as Ishmael, in spite of having been saved by Queequeg's "lonely coffin," has lost Queequeg himself, and the rest of the crew, forever.

How does this dense, complex, prophetic fusion of love and hate, of promise and warning, of the saved and the wasted, play itself out in the "War on Terror" as the essays in this volume are to be published? Our new day "dawned" in this nation's unprovoked, unilateral, preemptive invasion of Iraq in March of 2003. The "night" of that day had "fallen" by early September—in the resistance to our occupation expressed by the bombings of the Jordanian Embassy, the U.N. Headquarters, the Baghdad police headquarters, and the Najaf Mosque.

In March 2003 those who designed the military campaign of "shock and awe" got what they "sought" in the "bloody business" in which our own soldiers were "high on the kill" as they "spelled our names in blood to be remembered by." By September 2003 we had gotten the inevitable reprisals and retaliation from Iraqis responding to the chaos into which we had plunged their nation. These Iraqis were saying, just as surely as Nathan's Ahab did, "If it's blood or bedlam, boys, by God I choose blood." Their instinctive wish to "Carve [our] white skin with [their] sharp knives" shows no special demonism on their part, so much as a natural response to the mayhem our intervention has unwittingly unleashed. In this sense it resembles Moby Dick's retaliation against Ahab (whether in Eckert's opera or Melville's novel), the instinctive response of a living creature to Ahab's unprovoked, murderous attack. It also resembles our nation's first, instinctive wish to retaliate against the terrorists who had attacked the Pentagon and the World Trade Center without apparent provocation.

Whereas a case could be made, and was made, that invading Afghanistan and overthrowing its Taliban leadership was a natural and appropriate response to the attack on the World Trade Center, and that the targeted pursuit of Osama bin Laden was an appropriate response to the trauma and mayhem he had visited upon New York City, no comparable case was ever made against Saddam Hussein or the nation of Iraq. Ignoring all warnings from friends and allies, we transferred our justified rage against the living "hump" we had so far failed to hunt down over to the new one we now substituted in its place. This time "bursting" our "hot heart's shell upon" Saddam rather than Osama, we once more missed our primary target but this time destabilized an entire nation in the process. In doing so, we have got what we "sought" in more ways than one. In the paradoxical, prophetic words of Melville's 1891 poem, we have "fused" both "A flame to melt" and "a wind to freeze."

Eckert's opera updates Melville's novel into our own day in two ways. On the plot level, it helps us to see how the coercive, murderous, retaliatory psyche of Melville's Ahab remains a powerful force in our national psyche 150 years after Melville published *Moby-Dick.* Spiritually, it helps us to see that the salvific potential of Ishmael's inclusive vision and Queequeg's buoyant coffin in Melville's novel, translated into Nathan's Muse and Baroque angel in Eckert's opera, are as essential to the salvation of this nation's soul as ever before. However this nation's "War on Terror" plays out in Iraq, in Afghanistan, and in the 2004 "Grand Contested Election for the Presidency of the United States" (*MD* 7), the psychic dynamics of Eckert's opera, like those of Melville's novel, will remain helpful in evaluating the choices we now face in seeking a creative fusion among the "love and hate" in our own souls, as well as in our relations with all those with whom we share the globe.

The Muse's wish to make a visitation in which "all" would be "welcome" may seem impossibly idealistic in its reliance on love, but the current results of this nation's calculated attempt to impose its will on Iraq through military intimidation and regulated hatred might well suggest that love is the more realistic of the two. At any rate, Rinde Eckert's *And God Created Great Whales* has audaciously transformed Melville's original whaling tale into a story that offers a driven man representing an aspiring but rapacious nation an opportunity of redemption through the intervention of an inspired, feisty, indispensable female Muse. If our nation, like Nathan, does, to some degree, dispense with the Muse in the short term, we can only hope that the redemptive work of the Baroque angel in the opera does chart a course that will be increasingly followed in the future. If her salvific voice and redemptive example are not to be heeded (along with those of such recent female adaptors of *Moby-Dick* as Ellen Driscoll, Laurie Anderson, Joyce Adler, and Sharon Butler), then our male-centered ship of state will run the danger of reverting even further into the condition of the *Indomitable* at the key moment in which Captain Vere delivers instructions to the officers he has called together to decide the case of Billy Budd. In cases such as this, he tells them, however our "hearts" may be "moved" by an impulse to love, "the feminine in man . . . must be ruled out" (*Billy Budd* 111).

On November 9, 2001, two weeks after our Hofstra conference, I interviewed Rinde Eckert about the return engagement of *And God Created Great Whales* at 45 Bleecker Street that was to begin the following week. After summarizing my interpretation of the opera at the conference, I asked whether he felt a relation between the dynamics of love and hate as embodied by the Muse and Ahab in his opera and the crisis facing our nation after the destruction of the World Trade Center two months earlier. I also asked, of course, whether he related Nathan's "What if you jumped from a tall building" digression to the trauma of those who had jumped from the towers.

In response to the latter question, Eckert expected that Nathan's meditation on "the terror of falling" would "take on a peculiar resonance" for audiences who would be seeing the work in these new circumstances. "I meant it back then the way that it's going to be interpreted now. The only difference is that everybody's going to perhaps see it with the clarity that I had envisioned from the beginning. You hope that people will understand that terror, and have an empathy and sympathy for that terror. [For] those of us who have been involved with tragedy, those of us who have the tragic sensibility, it's not that big a leap to take." Beyond seeing Nathan's "notion of loss as much more cogent" in response to the real-life terror, Eckert was hoping that his new audience might relate Nathan's consciousness to the "cultural crisis" that the terrorist act has provoked. For Eckert, this is a crisis "about the nature of belief, the nature of faith, and exactly what one becomes capable of. It's a negotiation with modern culture—things ancient and primitive but also things of great spiritual value." During Nathan's "protracted fall into the abyss," audience members "have time to think." You have "time to think on your way down of the consequences of your action, or to suddenly be struck by the possibility of something after death."[14] This opens up the possibility of a tragic recognition—for an individual character or for a culture as a whole.

When asked to comment on my reading of the "terror" of Nathan's "falling forever"—that it provokes the contrasting solutions to terror embodied by Ahab's bloody oath and the Muse's transformative visitation—Eckert felt that this was "a very good read." When presented with the idea that his *Great Whales* has it both ways, that the "purity of Ahab's revenge" (in Nathan's opera) is "overlaid by the transcendence of the Muse's visitation" (in Eckert's opera), he saw such dynamics at work. He related them to the epilogue of *Moby-Dick,* in which the *Rachel* materializes to save Ishmael. In his opera, as in Melville's novel, "We have to let it finish. We have to go down. And it has to be a finish. And then you say, 'Oh, by the way.' Redemption to a degree. Through this buoyancy, this wonderful airtight salvific agency, this coffin. And of course it's like the afterlife of Queequeg, who has basically in a sense tied himself to Ishmael—it's their monkey-rope that saves Ishmael, and he ultimately fulfills the promise of friendship at that moment. And so you have in my image too that notion of the fulfilled friendship, the promised friendship between these two characters." Although it was "very tricky and interesting to try and see what kind of analog would actually fit my purposes," it did "turn out" that the Muse "has that kind of buoyancy." Her bonding with Nathan at the very end does have "that salvific potential." This answer shows how fully Eckert's imaginative world has fused with that of Melville in the process of creating the opera. His artistic fusion of "Audacity-reverence" in responding to Melville seamlessly combines "instinct and study," another pair of "unlike things" in Melville's art.

The move from terror to recognition to empathy to love is the deepest abstract rhythm in *Moby-Dick* that Eckert answers in his opera—and that the "War on Terror" poses to the culture at large. Near the end of *Great Whales* that entire long-range motion is condensed in the Muse's remembered vision of how Nathan had planned to end his opera. He had pictured for her an apocalyptic scene in which the "stage is a sea of blue cloth" within which "a great chorus of doomed whalemen rises to frame the coming of the enormous whale, towering in the opera house as the orchestra swells" in an escalating tension until everything collapses and "subsides" in the aftermath of the chase, setting the scene for the redemptive return of the Muse as the "baroque angel" to "pull Ishmael from the sea." Eckert was asked to comment on the "uncanny" way in which the apocalyptic image of the "enormous whale, towering in the opera house," had formerly anticipated, and now looked back upon, the collapse of the real-life towers. I wondered if there was some kind of "collective imagination of the Western mind, or the American mind, that Melville was tapping into that you are also tapping into"—especially now that real-life events seemed to be making their own cogent commentary on the apocalyptic implications of the opera he had created earlier. Without trying evaluate his own contribution, Eckert's answer was that "artists are working to be in touch with forces, or a certain kind of resonance, or a certain kind of something that's broadcast almost on a cellular level. We don't know how to measure it, but certain people are aware of its effects. Melville was aware of these potentials somehow. They broadcast themselves. That sounds very mystical." Eckert has "no idea how much these things are just coincidence, and to what extent they represent an insight." But he does feel that it is the "job" of the artist to be attuned to those "larger resonances." The "best" responses to them are "perhaps arrived at unconsciously," while the artist, "steeped in images," is "obeying dreams and impulses."

Melville depicts such an unconscious state at the beginning of his poem "Art":

> In placid hours well pleased we dream
> Of many a brave unbodied scene.
> But form to lend, pulsed life create,
> What unlike things must meet and mate

Melville addresses the "mystical" side of Eckert's own creative process at the end of the poem when he declares that all of the "unlike things" specified in the body of the poem must "fuse with Jacob's mystic heart / To wrestle with the angel—Art." By fusing with his own muse, and wrestling with his own artistic "angel," Eckert has written an opera that relates to the psychic needs of our own age as much as it does to the psychological intensities of Melville's 1851 novel.

1. The September 2000 debut of Eckert's opera at 45 Bleecker Street was preceded by a June 2000 preview of the show by the Foundry Theatre in New York.

2. For my review of Eckert's production in the context of these three immediate predecessors, see *Melville Society Extracts* 120 (Feb. 2001): 18–19. For Laurie Anderson, see the essays by Samuel Otter and Elizabeth Schultz in this volume.

3. Notable among the productions I was able to see in 2003 were Katie Pees as Ishmael at the Human Race Theater in Dayton and Denise Fleetham as Queequeg in the Hawaiian reading in Kahulai.

4. Tim Severin, *In Search of* Moby-Dick: *Quest for the White Whale* (London: Little, Brown, 1999); Robert Sullivan, *A Whale Hunt: Two Years on the Olympic Peninsula with the Makah and Their Canoe* (New York: Scribner, 2000).

5. Nathaniel Philbrick, *In the Heart of the Sea: The Tragedy of the Whaleship* Essex (New York: Viking, 2000).

6. Reviews of *And God Created Great Whales* in 2000 included Don Shewey, "Not Moby-Dick but Whalish," *New York Times,* June 11, 4, 6; D. J. R. Bruckner, "A 'Moby-Dick' to Make All Opera Funny," *New York Times,* June 17, A15, 25; Michael Feingold, "About this Whale . . . ," *Village Voice,* June 20, 83; and Margo Jefferson, "As Melville Told Marlene, the Muse Leads the Music," *New York Times,* Sept. 18, B2.

7. For six successive versions of the poem as Melville himself wrestled with it, see John Bryant's edition of Melville's *Tales, Poems, and Other Writings,* 537–40.

8. I am grateful to Rinde Eckert for permission to quote from his unpublished libretto of the opera in the course of this essay.

9. Dickinson's poem is dated ca. 1862 in *The Complete Poems of Emily Dickinson,* ed. Thomas H. Johnson (Boston: Little Brown, 1960), no. 501. Whitman's "Out of the Cradle" was first published in the 1860 edition of *Leaves of Grass.*

10. I am grateful to Rinde Eckert for loaning me a production tape for study purposes and for use in my presentation.

11. See *Theater* 30.2 (2000): 83–127. The interview by Tom Sellar is entitled "Idiot's Paradise."

12. Robert K. Wallace, "Avoiding Melville's Vortex" (95). This interview was reprinted in part in the program for Baltimore's Center Stage production of *And God Created Great Whales,* May 20–June 16, 2002, pp. 3–5.

13. Credited to the Associated Press. Caption: "A person falls headfirst after jumping from the north tower of the World Trade Center. It was a horrific sight that was repeated in the moments after the planes struck the towers" (A7).

14. I am grateful to Rinde Eckert for permission to quote from this unpublished interview on November 9, 2001, conducted at the Seaport Suites on Water Street, a few blocks from what was then being called Ground Zero.

"Lying in Various Attitudes"

Staging Melville's Pip in Digital Media

WYN KELLEY

It started as a game. While preparing a presentation for a conference on games and narrative, I began to imagine an electronic *Moby-Dick* for players of all ages and levels. Without any experience of online games, without in fact the slightest aptitude for playing anything except solitaire, I mentally designed a *Moby-Dick* world where players could study winds and tides, chart voyages through the seven seas, soar on the wings of fancy, indulge their itch for things remote—and, oh, yes, slaughter large peace-loving mammals with razor-sharp weapons tempered in blood and dedicated to outrageous gods. It looked like a winner.

Imagining *Moby-Dick* as a game frees one to think of it nonlinearly and to see this familiar text as it might appear to a kindergartener, a ninth-grader, or a college freshman encountering it for the first time. For *Moby-Dick* to be a place where anyone might play, though, it would have to be conceived of not only as a structured narrative but also as an imaginative space where one could enter and engage at will. Fully convinced that *Moby-Dick* provides such a space—a web of words, images, dreams, and yarns knit together by the most fluid and plastic of narrators—I tried to think of a way to make reading the book more like playing games.

For many reasons, of course, this concept seems threatening to those of us involved in academic scholarship and teaching. Games, at least those in digital media, are addictive to some and a crashing bore to others. But many have been designed with extraordinary sophistication in uses of multimedia effects and with all the heady ambitions of a new art form. As Henry Jenkins boldly states: "Computer games are art—a popular art, an emerging art, a largely unrecognized art, but art nevertheless."[1] If we can acknowledge the common ground that print and electronic media, games and literary art share, then perhaps we can arrive at a similarly bold view of *Moby-Dick:* as part of a narrative tradition from which games and other multimedia forms emerge and as a novel that can be enriched by multimedia perspectives. Indeed, as many scholars have recently shown, Melville's fiction can and must be read in the context of other arts.[2] John Bryant's work on fluid texts makes it clear that Melville's narratives are well suited to analysis enabled by juxtaposing print text with other media, and Haskell Springer's scholarly electronic archives for "Bartleby, the Scrivener" and *Moby-Dick* make lavish use of multimedia annotation.[3] Melville's best-known book, these scholars have made clear, is especially hospitable to the possibilities of multimedia illumination.

I had some of these ideas in mind when I began working with a research group, MetaMedia, set up by members of the Comparative Media Studies Program at the Massachusetts Institute of Technology.[4] Dedicated to improving students' communication skills and media literacy, MetaMedia aims "to enable students to step outside the flow of media sounds and images within cultures, and to develop a better understanding of how media influences their lives and shapes their interpretations of those materials."[5] Working with CMS graduate students and faculty, I planned an electronic archive of images, music, and film to be used in teaching a single chapter of *Moby-Dick,* "Midnight, Forecastle." Although I expected to learn a great deal about digital media, more surprisingly the experience fundamentally altered and renovated my own more traditional scholarship. My game became serious business indeed.

I chose "Midnight, Forecastle" because race and ethnicity feature largely in my teaching of *Moby-Dick.* This chapter, where Melville showcases sailors of many ethnic identities, meshes well with Toni Morrison's readings of *Moby-Dick* in her "Unspeakable Things Unspoken: The Afro-American Presence in American Literature" and her book *Playing in the Dark: Whiteness and the Literary Imagination.*[6] Morrison's view of Melville's Ahab as haunted by whiteness in a culture where what she calls "the Africanist presence" is everywhere present but never acknowledged conveys the book's complex racial dynamics in accessible terms. Students, however, tend to have difficulty judging Melville's representations of race for themselves. How can one evaluate them without a rich context of nineteenth-century images and aids? A Web archive seemed a useful way to provide the visual and historical context to support Morrison's reading of the text.

A second aim, however, influenced this choice, namely the chapter's strongly visual and performative features. *Moby-Dick*'s Chapter 40 begins by alerting us to its theatricality: "*Foresail rises and discovers the watch standing, lounging, leaning, and lying in various attitudes, all singing in chorus*" (*MD* 173). Melville's stage direction focuses attention on the deck as stage, the sail as curtain, and the sailors in "various attitudes," assuming their positions in a tableau just as actors in nineteenth-century stage melodramas often began or ended a scene.[7] In particular, Melville recalls the nautical melodramas of his day, stories of sailor derring-do like those of Douglas Jerrold (whose *Mutiny at the Nore* Melville later consulted in writing *Billy Budd*).[8] In a shift from the high tragical style of the preceding Shakespearean chapters—"The Quarter-Deck," "Sunset," and "Dusk"—Melville signals that "Midnight, Forecastle" will perform itself as an *entr'acte* in the more popular idiom of sailor ballads, jigs, and jokes. However, Melville expands the boundaries of conventional nautical melodrama, which tended toward patriotic and nationalistic themes, by including sailors of all nations—not only the multiracial harpooneers and Pip, but also men from Europe, Asia, and the South Seas. He further bends the generic frame by shifting the sailors from their jolly opening, "singing in chorus," to a violent squall both natural and human, climaxing in the racially charged battle between Daggoo and the Spanish sailor. Melville's assault on sailor congeniality ends with an equally unsettling dénouement, Pip's soliloquy, delivered with chattering teeth from his hiding place beneath the windlass. In a final "attitude," Pip performs the fear—of the whale, of God, of Ahab, of whiteness—that the men have not dared give a name or recognize in themselves: "Oh, thou big white God aloft there somewhere in yon darkness, have mercy on this small black boy down here; preserve him from all men that have no bowels to feel fear!" (*MD* 178).[9] A multimedia archive might make students more sensitive to Melville's visual and dramatic effects and to the complicated levels of performance in the chapter.

A third aim was to offer students not only a database or set of resources in different media but also models of certain tasks expected in any literature class: close reading and annotation, writing, and oral presentations. The MetaMedia group was particularly interested in this aspect of the project, because they were looking for pedagogical tools and functions that would be useful in humanities classrooms. Thus, although the Melville archive began as a static model of these functions, the MetaMedia team was already thinking of ways to make them live and interactive. That stage of the project is still in development, but its possibilities are evident in the site we designed first.

Because the site was to be restricted to the MIT community, I had considerable freedom in choosing materials. Permission to use images from the Hart Nautical Collection at MIT and the Kendall Whaling Museum (now incorporated into the collection of the New Bedford Whaling Museum) for educational purposes made a wide range of resources available. I also scanned images from books, took songs from recordings, and made clips from videos. Unfortunately, current copyright laws make it impossible to display most of these materials on the World Wide Web without paying high prices for permission. As soon as these restrictions ease, it will be possible to share this work more freely. There are certain advantages, though, to keeping these materials, which will change from semester to semester, course to course as needs change, in a classroom database for educational and highly idiosyncratic use.

The "Midnight, Forecastle" site has three areas: an archive, an annotated text showing the archival materials in notes to the chapter, and a multimedia essay that I wrote to demonstrate more creative uses of archive materials. The home page, designed to suggest the curtain of a stage, features Anton Otto Fischer's illustration of a 1931 children's edition of *Moby-Dick,* an image of the *Pequod* under full sail.[10] The sound of sailors singing "John Kanaka" welcomes visitors to Melville's nautical world.[11] The viewer can then enter the archive, which features images, songs, and video clips. The image archive has about seventy-five items arranged according to a few topics: maps, sailors, whaling. Some of these are general enough to be useful for reading the whole book, but most relate to the themes of "Midnight, Forecastle." The audio archive has about a dozen chanteys and songs from different recordings and some excerpts from a radio recording of Laurie Anderson's "Songs and Stories from *Moby-Dick.*"[12] As Stuart M. Frank has pointed out, sailor songs survive in many different versions, and it would be hard to identify precisely which ones Melville would have known. Since the chapter, though, contains two songs familiar from many recordings, "Spanish Ladies" and "The Bold Harpooneer," they appear in the archive, along with other songs that suggest the range of nations contributing to nautical music of the period. The video archive contains clips from early nautical films or versions of *Moby-Dick: Down to the Sea in Ships* (1922), *The Sea Beast* (1926), *Moby Dick* (starring John Barrymore; 1930), and *Moby Dick* (starring Gregory Peck; 1956).

Research into these materials turned up some unexpected finds. For example, nineteenth-century visual portrayals of life in the forecastle were far more subtle and probing than one would assume. Images of rollicking tars often seem jolly enough, until closer inspection reveals the violence and frustration of the sailors in their tight quarters. An illustration, for example, from J. Ross Browne's *Etchings from a Whaling Cruise* clearly shows tensions erupting in the close confines of the forecastle, as the sailors pommel one another.[13] This image and others like it from the period suggest that even at leisure the sailors suffered violence and deprivation. More sinister representations of sailor life can be found in reform-minded and sensational sources: pictures of flogging and punishment, for example, from J. Ross Browne, William H. Meyers's journal, and William Comstock's *The Life of Samuel Comstock.*[14] Mainstream publications like *Harper's,*[15] on the other hand, produced fairly commonplace, even idealized illustrations of ordinary sailors, and scrimshaw etchings of sailors singing and dancing in the former Kendall Whaling Museum collection show surprising realism and attention to detail.[16] From the archive's visual images, then, one can get remarkably diverse representations of the American sailor.

The visual materials also emphasize the wide range of different national types recorded in popular media. One 1861 cartoon drawing by a sailor on board the bark *Abraham Barker* sketched twelve different nautical figures, including a "Yankee Captain" (who bears a startling resemblance to Ralph Waldo Emerson), "English First Mate," "Irish Third Mate" (see illustration p. 92) "Dutch Fourth Mate," a sailor from "The Far North" (seemingly Inuit or Icelandic), and a "Chinese Cook," to name only those nationalities that also appear in "Midnight, Forecastle."[17] Where students might see Melville's white characters as basically undifferentiated from each other, a contemporary observer saw many shades and distinctions. For images of African sailors, Jeffrey Bolster's *Black Jacks* is invaluable for showing stereotypes but also more unusual representations of prosperous African American captains and African sailors in Japan.[18] Because Melville's chapter also contains Polynesian sailors, I borrowed illustrations from Samuel Otter's *Melville's Anatomies* that display the richness of South Seas tattooing (Otter 29, 31, 37, 44). Rockwell Kent's 1930 drawings of "Midnight, Forecastle" and the sailors seemed indispensable as well, because Kent was one of the few early illustrators to focus on the men's class differences, as well as to produce a soulful portrait of Pip.[19] The Hart Nautical Collection at MIT also has numerous prints of whaling in different seas, fisheries, and nations. These graphically demonstrate that Melville's representation of the sailors' identities goes beyond racial and ethnic differences to the subtle distinctions between national styles of whaling and labor, a point elaborated fully in Richard Ellis's work on regional fisheries.[20]

Since the site was also intended as a model of certain pedagogical functions, a second area offers an example of multimedia annotation. This model shows the advantages of close reading and multimedia research, and the Comparative Media Studies graduate students wanted to devise a way for students to make annotations of their own and share them online. The annotated chapter includes notes in textual form, as well as music, images, and video clips. One can read the text linearly, calling up notes through the highlighted words, or one can wander through the information more fluidly, as Melville's narrative strategies throughout the novel encourage one to do. Furthermore, the different media work to convey very different kinds of information, from nautical facts, to the sounds of songs, to images of sailors and whaling life. The note for the title "Midnight, Forecastle," for example, includes some of the nineteenth-century illustrations of life in the forecastle mentioned above, a clip from *Down to the Sea in Ships* (1920), showing the men eating in their close quarters, and a discussion, drawing on Web reference sources and links, of the significance of the sailors' watches. Other thematic notes comment on Melville's references to different religions (Christian, Chinese, Hindu, pagan), to sexuality (as elsewhere in the novel this chapter explores sexual tensions between the men—in the figure of Pip, for example—but also celebrates female sexuality with great frankness),[21] and to national traits and differences. These verbal notes, along with the songs and video clips, offer historical and thematic context for details in the text.

Annotating the chapter this closely led to the discovery that Melville has carefully mapped the world of whaling through the sailors' nationalities. The notes on the French Sailor, the Dutch, the Azorean, and the Chinese, for example, show that the chapter moves along the historical and geographical lines of the whaling industry itself. Thus the first sailors to speak are from Nantucket, the original home of Atlantic whaling; the next come from the major European whaling nations: the Netherlands, France, and Iceland, hence the Atlantic and North Seas fisheries. Next come the sailors who frequently outfitted American ships stopping in the Azores: the Azorean Sailor and possibly the Maltese and Sicilian. Then Melville moves to the Pacific and the South Seas fisheries, with the Chinese, Lascar, and Tahitian sailors. Other sailors appear, but Melville has so well established the national pattern that when the Spanish sailor challenges Daggoo, speaking of an "old grudge," we see that this grudge is nothing personal. It grows out of ancient competition between Europe and Africa, Spain and the Moors, over control of the Mediterranean.[22]

A further surprise was the discovery, when the chapter is approached through close reading and multimedia annotation, of how lively and rich a performance it offers. Of course, Ahab and the other characters perform dramatically throughout the novel, but here Melville seems to concentrate particularly on the ordinary lives of the men, their recreation and pleasure, in very specific—i.e., audible and visible—ways. Even when the men are not singing or dancing, the language is musical and onomatopoetic, the rhythms of the chapter palpable, the effects dramatic and vivid—not for the benefit of a single monomaniacal captain but for the pleasure of his underappreciated men.

The annotation, then, provides a model of research and close reading and of interpreting patterns of speech, sound, and movement as they perform the men's identities, so little recognized elsewhere in the text. Of particular interest is the bravura performance of Pip, whose appearance alone on the stage during the squall takes the scene in a wholly new and unexpected direction:

Jollies? Lord help such jollies! Crish, crash! there goes the jib-stay! Blang-whang! God! Duck lower, Pip, here comes the royal yard! It's worse than being in the whirled woods, the last day of the year! Who'd go climbing after chestnuts now? But there they go, all cursing, and here I don't. Fine prospects to 'em; they're on the road to heaven. Hold on hard! Jimmini, what a squall! But those chaps there are worse yet—they are your white squalls, they. White squalls? white whale, shirr! shirr! Here have I heard all their chat just now, and the white whale—shirr! shirr!—but spoken of once! and only this evening—it makes me jingle all over like my tambourine—that anaconda of an old man swore 'em in to hunt him! Oh! thou big white God aloft there somewhere in yon darkness, have mercy on this small black boy down here; preserve him from all men that have no bowels to feel fear! (*MD* 178)

His speech is the subject of my multimedia essay "Pip's Soliloquy," which occupies the third area of the site.

In the essay I look closely at Pip's address to the storm and the god who created it and collect the database materials in a new configuration that demonstrates how students might use the archive to construct their own presentations and essays. The first section, "Pip as Performer," for example, focuses on the soliloquy's musical language:

A close reading of Pip's soliloquy might start with a consideration of his dramatic presence on stage, and, in contrast with his "sulky" and reluctant playing earlier in the scene, his highly musical and onomatopoetic language. Whereas previously his tambourine provided, at the mariners' bidding, the banging, rattling, and jingling that excited the sailors to dance and song, here his speech expands and imitates the sounds of the storm, the ship, and his fear—"Crish, crash!" "Blang-whang!" "Jimmini, what a squall!" "White squalls? White whale, shirr! Shirr!" "It makes me jingle all over like my tambourine." The steady stream of exclamation points creates a squall of energy, like the snow in the "whirled woods, the last day of the year!" With the dashes and occasional question marks, Melville blends pure sound with Pip's perceptive questioning of the white men's and white God's actions. The white squalls, white whale, and white god make a white world (whirled?) where Pip struggles to find himself, a "small black boy down here" in the whiteness of a kind of lunacy, the lunacy of "all men that have no bowels to feel fear!" The extraordinary sound effects in this speech allow Pip to emerge as the scene's most successful and fully-realized performer of the men's emotions, especially the fear they have alluded to and danced around but not expressed.

Accompanying this section of the essay on Pip's onomatopoetic language are links to some of the chanteys and the scrimshaw images of dancing sailors.

Pip is also immensely powerful as a figure of his race, and so the next point focuses on "Pip as Slave"[23]:

Many images from the period, borrowing from popular representations of plantation slaves, show African or African-American sailors as violent and threatening. But Pip's speaking alone in the white vacuum created by the storm and the scattering of the sailors suggests Melville's commitment to voicing, with considerable dignity and drama, what Toni Morrison calls the Africanist presence. Unlike "Benito Cereno," where the slave Babo chooses silence as resistance, in "Midnight, Forecastle" Pip speaks, though alone and to himself in the second and third persons: "Duck lower, Pip, here comes the royal yard!" "this small black boy." How, though, does Pip's soliloquy represent a racial consciousness? How does it compare with the words of Daggoo and Tashtego earlier in the chapter? Unlike Tashtego, who smokes, grunts ("humph!"), and saves his sweat rather than engage in the fray, Daggoo and Pip clearly articulate their recognition of racial difference and the violence of racial conflict. But Pip is a coward, unlike Daggoo and Babo, and the chapter ends with him. Do we see this conclusion as affirming the identity of a dignified, reflective racial Other or as striking a blow at Pip's identity, reducing him to gibberish? Melville seems to position Pip somewhere between the stereotype of the cowering slave and the voice of reflection and conscience for the book.

This section of the essay emphasizes Melville's subversion of reductionist racial typing and uses contrasting images of African American sailors depicted as violent or menial.

The third section of the essay moves away from thematic and historical questions into those of performance and media, considering Pip in the Shakespearean context Melville establishes with the chapters around "Midnight,

Forecastle." Titled "Pip as Boy," this section argues that Pip's soliloquy suggests interesting parallels with that of Shakespeare's king in *Henry V;* video clips from Laurence Olivier's film version of *Henry V* support the comparison:

> Although Pip has most often been seen in terms of his race and of his role in *Moby-Dick*'s Shakespearean tragedy (as Fool to Ahab's Lear), he may also be seen as a boy and in the context of Shakespeare's history plays, specifically *Henry V.* The chapter, "Midnight, Forecastle," is reminiscent of *Henry V,* IV, i. It includes men of different nations, as Shakespeare does with his Welsh, English, Scots, and French characters. In both, the commander is at a distance—Ahab retired to his cabin, Henry in disguise—so that the men speak freely. And in both a fight breaks out of the tensions surrounding a larger violence—that of the whale hunt in *Moby-Dick* and of the war in *Henry V.* This fight among the men threatens the authority of those in power but is contained and suppressed. Interestingly enough, both scenes end with a soliloquy. In Shakespeare's, a king muses on the nature of his power, compares himself with the "wretched slave," and speaks to God, asking him to "steel my soldiers' hearts, / Possess them not with fear!"
>
> Pip is no king, but he reflects no less wisely. He too recognizes the fears of the men; he is experiencing them himself. And he too calls on God to assist him: "Oh, thou big white God aloft there somewhere in yon darkness, have mercy on this small black boy down here; preserve him from all men that have no bowels to feel fear!" Unlike Henry, who wants God to steel his men's hearts against fear, Pip is most afraid of such fearless men.
>
> A closer look at Olivier's version of this scene suggests a further nuance in this comparison. Olivier has the rebellious Williams challenge the king—"That's more than we know"—but he has Williams's more thoughtful and reflective speech spoken by an unnamed boy. This speech utters the conscience of the play. The boy asks how the king will face his "heavy reckoning" if the cause for which the men have died "be not good": "Now, if these men do not die well, it will be a black matter for the King that led them to it." Pip too alludes to Ahab's accountability at the end of the chapter: "that anaconda of an old man swore 'em in to hunt him [the whale]!" Like Olivier's boy, Pip is an innocent outsider in the men's world and hence privileged to speak the words of moral reproach.[24]

As a boy in the liminal space of adolescence, Pip is free to utter the men's fears and to challenge the great white God above.

My final point suggests another context for Pip, that of nineteenth-century whaling and the big money it generated from the labor of mostly poor and dispossessed men. This section grows out of Melville's reference to Ambroise Louis Garneray's painting, *La Pêche de la Baleine,* in Chapter 56, "Of the Less Erroneous Pictures of Whales, and the True Pictures of Whaling Scenes." Garneray's portrayal of the whale hunt is one of the few early nineteenth-century images to include an African or African European. Not only does Garneray's painting feature an African sailor, but, in an irony of which Melville may well have been aware, American seaport currencies included images of this multiracial crew inscribed on the emblems of their own wealth.[25] The bills tell a story, though very different from Garneray's painting. In a section entitled "Pip as Whaler," I argue that Melville might have been thinking of the more political and social implications of Pip's soliloquy, and indeed his presence on the ship:

Ambroise Louis Garneray's famous painting, *La Pêche de la Baleine* (1835) [fig. 1], which Melville describes at length in Chapter 56, appeared in many forms throughout the nineteenth century, especially in prints and reproductions, but also on American currency. Garneray's painting is unusual in representing so prominently in the foreground an African sailor (images of African or EuroAfrican or African American sailors are rare, unless they appear in ethnographical prints or as the subjects of mutiny). Garneray's sailor differs from the other rowers not only in his dark skin but in his eager and alert attitude. When Melville said in Chapter 56 that the French have "furnished . . . the only finished sketches at all capable of conveying the real spirit of the whale hunt," he may have been referring as much to Garneray's sympathetic portrayal of the African sailor as to his treatment of the whale and whalers.

If so, then the currency suggests another irony in Melville's allusion to Garneray. Various banknotes from the 1850s and later show Garneray's painting in different configurations. In a New Bedford one dollar bill, the brave whalers are central to the picture and are placed over an image of a Native American woman (June 1858) [fig. 2]. In a New Jersey five dollar bill (1856) [fig. 3], the heroic whaling scene is balanced by images of a proud ship and a romantic white sailor. Still, though, the racially mixed whaleboat is central to the scene. A Connecticut two dollar bill [fig. 4], however, has moved the working men to one side, elevating the figure of a prominent white bank president or statesman over the American sailor. Two other bills that bear no particular relation to Garneray's painting nevertheless show remarkable similarities and

Fig. 1. Ambroise Louis Garneray, *La Pêche de la Baleine*. Aquatint, Paris 1835. Courtesy of the New Bedford Whaling Museum.

Fig. 2. One-dollar bill. Mechanics Bank of New Bedford (June 1, 1858). Courtesy of the MIT Museum.

Fig. 3. Five-dollar bill. Commercial Bank of New Jersey (1856). Courtesy of the MIT Museum.

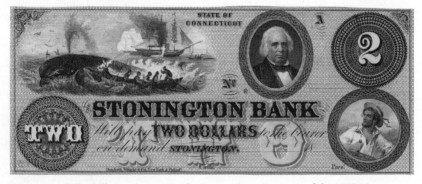

Fig. 4. Two-dollar bill. Stonington Bank, Connecticut. Courtesy of the MIT Museum.

significant differences. A Hawaiian five [fig. 5], while echoing Garneray's subject, shows no racially distinct sailors, though a single white mariner remains in a cartouche to the right. And in an 1864 New London dollar [fig. 6], the sailors are gone, the boat has disappeared, and a classical marble female nude presides over the scene.

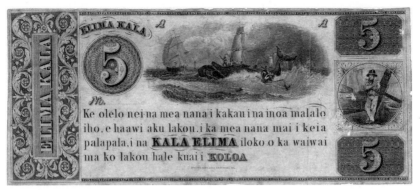

Fig. 5. Five-dollar bill from Hawaii (n.d.). Courtesy of the MIT Museum.

Fig. 6. One-dollar bill. The Whaling Bank, New London, 1864. Courtesy of the MIT Museum.

It is hard to know if Melville saw any of these bills, but if so, and especially if the Stonington bill or one like it was available earlier in the 1840s or 50s, it gives a spectacular image of the "big white God aloft there somewhere" above the single black sailor below. Pip in this context appears as an unstable sign of the whaling industry, shifting in its significance and its relationship to the American economy. Pip as African American sailor might be seen as an icon of American democracy, on the one hand, but eventually, on the other, a dispensable symbol of American prosperity and the fact that the whalers became slaves, oiling the industrial machine.

With this section, the essay concludes, inspiring readers, one hopes, to pursue further avenues of their own. Indeed, my work on the multimedia essay heightened my respect for this dynamic and innovative form of analysis. Each point in the essay is unthinkable without the visual, audio, or video materials from the archive; the reader follows the linear path of the argument but at the same time ranges visually and intellectually over a wealth of other materials. This use of multimedia, then, allows for a more flexible, less rigid and thesis-driven form of argument than usual. The supporting materials help make rhetorical points quickly and efficiently and render a bulky verbal structure unnecessary. The multimedia essay can combine the best features of traditional scholarship with the dazzling effects of multimedia presentations, as many online journals have already begun to demonstrate.

The "various attitudes" in which I was able to place Melville's chapter introduced me to new methods of research and lines of inquiry that made a palpable difference in my scholarly as well as pedagogical work. Rather than taking attention away from the text, as I at first feared they might, the multimedia materials brought me back to it again and again, with a deeper appreciation for Melville's knowledge of whaling, his strongly visual and dramatic imagination, and his power to reveal, even in a seemingly minor chapter, fresh details and nuances. In its next phase, the archive will develop sophisticated tools to make the site interactive and flexible. Eventually, users will be able to generate their own enhanced readings of the text in a form that others can share, discuss, and store. One can imagine, then, an ever-expanding archive growing out of classrooms and living rooms worldwide, a continuing encounter with *Moby-Dick* that reads the book in Melville's "just spirit of Equality."

Digital media have certain limitations, of course, but for many new readers of Melville's work, they can help recreate the visual and auditory world we have lost since Melville's time. In a sense, this project reveals how much Melville's plastic, voluminous, and abundantly sensual imagination anticipates the technologies with which we now read his novel more deeply. Like Stubb eating the whale by its own light (*MD* 299), we shine on Melville's work a lamp illumined by Melville's mind and art.

The game is afoot.

Notes

Special thanks to Peter S. Donaldson (Literature and Comparative Media Studies), Kurt Fendt (Foreign Languages and Literature and Comparative Media Studies), and Henry Jenkins (Film and Media Studies and Comparative Media Studies) at MIT for their guidance and inspiration; Candis Callison, for her superb design; Christopher York (Technical Director), Belinda Yung (Assistant Technical Director), and Daniel Huecker of the HyperStudio and MetaMedia for their work on and support of the project; Kurt Hasselbalch and Jennifer O'Neill of the Hart Nautical Collection at MIT, Stuart M. Frank, Michael Dyer, and Laura Perreira of the New Bedford Whaling Museum, Mary K. Bercaw Edwards, Shawn Waldron, and Suki Williams at Mystic Seaport: The Museum of America and the Sea, and Samuel Otter at the University of

California, Berkeley, for their help in locating, scanning, and reproducing materials; Julie Saunders for help producing the illustrations; Tom Clay for his astute assessment of the project in its testing phase; and Joaquin Terrones for outstanding ideas and wise counsel throughout.

1. Henry Jenkins, "Art Form for the Digital Age," *Technology Review* (Sept.–Oct. 2000): 117.

2. For one of the first treatments of *Moby-Dick* in multimedia, see Stuart M. Frank, *Herman Melville's Picture-Gallery: Sources and Types of Pictorial Chapters in* Moby-Dick (Mystic, Conn.: Mystic Seaport Museum Publications, 1986); see also Douglas Robillard, *Melville and the Visual Arts: Ionian Form, Venetian Tint* (Kent, Ohio: Kent State Univ. Press, 1997); Elizabeth A. Schultz, *Unpainted to the Last;* Christopher Sten, ed., *Savage Eye: Melville and the Visual Arts* (Kent, Ohio: Kent State Univ. Press, 1991); Robert K. Wallace, *Melville and Turner: Spheres of Love and Fright* (Athens: Univ. of Georgia Press, 1992); and *Frank Stella's* Moby-Dick.

3. My concept of *Moby-Dick* as a fluid text owes much to John Bryant's work, both on fluid text editing and as editor of the Melville Electronic Library. See his "Politics, Imagination, and the Fluid Text," *Studies in the Literary Imagination* 29.2 (Fall 1996): 89–105. See also his "Manuscript, Edition, Revision: Reading *Typee* with Trifocals," in *Melville's Evermoving Dawn: Centennial Essays*, ed. John Bryant and Robert Milder (Kent, Ohio: Kent State Univ. Press, 1997), 297–306; his introduction to *Typee: A Peep at Polynesian Life* (New York: Penguin Books, 1996), ix–xxxvii; his introductory essay, "Herman Melville: A Writer in Process," in *Herman Melville: Tales, Poems, and Other Writings* (New York: Modern Library, 2001), xvii–l; and *The Fluid Text: A Theory of Revision and Editing for Book and Screen* (Ann Arbor: Univ. of Michigan Press, 2002). Haskell Springer's "The Hypertext *Moby-Dick*" follows on his excellent hypertext "Bartleby, the Scrivener. A Story of Wall-Street," at *http://raven.cc.ukans.edu/~zeke/bartleby/* and is the basis for the proposed *Melville Electronic Library,* edited with John Bryant.

4. See *http://web.mit.edu/cms/index.html* (accessed Sept. 22, 2005) for a full description of the Comparative Media Studies Program. For MetaMedia, see *http://metamedia.mit.edu/* (accessed Sept. 22, 2005).

5. From MetaMedia, "Our Philosophy," at *http://metamedia.mit.edu/philosophy1.html.*

6. Toni Morrison, "Unspeakable Things Unspoken: The Afro-American Presence in American Literature," *Michigan Quarterly Review* 28.1 (1989): 1–34 and *Playing in the Dark: Whiteness and the Literary Imagination* (New York: Vintage Books, 1992).

7. On melodrama, see Peter Brooks, *The Melodramatic Imagination: Balzac, Henry James, Melodrama, and the Mode of Excess* (New Haven, Conn.: Yale Univ. Press, 1985; 1976) and Daniel C. Gerould, *American Melodrama* (New York: Performing Arts Journal Publications, 1983). On nautical melodrama, see *Melodrama: The Cultural Emergence of a Genre,* ed. Michael Hays and Anastasie Nikolopoulou (New York: St. Martin's Press, 1996), especially Marvin Carlson, "He Should Never Bow Down to a Domineering Frown: Class Tensions and Nautical Melodrama," 147–66; Jeffrey Cox, "The Ideological Tack of Nautical Melodrama," 167–89; and Harmut Ilsemann, "Radicalism in the Melodrama of the Early Nineteenth Century," 191–207.

8. See B. R. McElderry Jr., "Three Earlier Treatments of the *Billy Budd* Theme," *American Literature* 27 (May 1955): 252–57. Noted in Bercaw 158.

9. Although Pip's speech can be read as dignified, many of its elements—heavy use of sounds and onomatopoeia, or the shivering and cowering—might be seen as reminiscent of minstrel shows. See Eric Lott, *Love and Theft: Blackface Minstrelsy and the American Working Class* (New York: Oxford Univ. Press, 1993), 163. Melville is known to have visited minstrel shows. See Parker 1:174.

10. From Herman Melville, *Moby Dick, The White Whale,* The Children's Bookshelf series (Philadelphia: John C. Winston, 1931), facing 390. See Schultz 334.

11. From Stuart M. Frank, Stuart Gillespie, and Ellen Cohn, *Sea Chanteys and Forecastle Songs at Mystic Seaport* (Smithsonian Folkways Recordings, F-37300). I chose the song partly because Melville refers to the "Kanakers" in *Typee* and *Omoo* and partly because it is a working song and would suggest how much of sailor musical "performance" was associated with muscle and sweat.

12. For the audio archive, aside from the recording already noted, I consulted Paul Clayton's *Whaling and Sailing Songs* (Tradition Records, 1956) and Ewan McColl and A. L. Lloyd, *Blow Boys Blow* (Tradition Records). I have also benefited from Stuart M. Frank's knowledge and advice, as well as his numerous publications: "'Cheerly Man': Chanteying in *Omoo* and *Moby-Dick*," *New England Quarterly* 58.1 (Mar. 1985): 68–82; "'Boston': Two 'New' Texts of an Old Favorite Sea Song," *American Neptune* 45.3 (Summer 1985): 175–79; and "The King of the Boundless Sea: Selected Whaling Poems," from an unpublished manuscript. For Laurie Anderson's music, Samuel Otter taped a radio recording of her show and kindly sent it to me. He also gave good advice about acquiring the videotape of *The Sea Beast*.

13. "Life in the Forecastle," A. A. Schmidt and J. Halpin, illus. J. Ross Browne, *Etchings from a Whaling Cruise* (New York: Harpers, 1846). Scanned image courtesy of the Hart Nautical Collection, MIT. "A Scramble for Salt Junk," colored engraving (n.d.) also in the Hart Nautical Collection, shows sailors fighting over their meager rations. "Life in a Whaleship," Alonso Hartwell, illus., in Reuben Delano, *Wanderings and Adventures of Reuben Delano* (New York: H. Long and Brothers, 1846) shows a white cabin boy perched among a group of leering sailors. I am indebted to Michael Dyer at the Kendall Institute for showing me Delano's book.

14. "A Picture for Philanthropists," Schmidt and Halpin, illus., in *Etchings;* "Punishment," a watercolor by William H. Meyers, from his journal (1841–44) at the Bancroft Library, University of California, Berkeley, in Otter 69; illustration from William Comstock, *The Life of Samuel Comstock* (Boston: James Fisher, 1840), slide courtesy of the New Bedford Whaling Museum.

15. See, for example, D. H. Strother, "A Summer in New England," *Harper's New Monthly Magazine* 21 (June 1860): 1–19.

16. With Stuart Frank's help, I chose these images of dancing figures because they either portrayed or were carved by African American sailors.

17. Cartoon vignette by E. C. Snow on board the *Abraham Barker*, 1861. Slide courtesy of the Kendall Institute.

18. W. Jeffrey Bolster, *Black Jacks: African American Seamen in the Age of Sail* (Cambridge, Mass.: Harvard Univ. Press, 1997), especially W. Heath, "Cooking" (National Maritime Museum, London); Augustin Brunias, "Cudgelling Match between English and French Negroes," 1779 (Courtauld Institute of Art, London); "Head-butting in a Venezuelan Village," *Harper's Weekly,* Aug. 15, 1874; Anonymous, Japanese watercolor scroll showing African American sailors (Old Dartmouth Historical Society, New Bedford Whaling Museum); Anonymous, "Stove Boat" (Old Dartmouth Historical Society, New Bedford Whaling Museum); and "Oil Portrait of Captain Absalom" (Nantucket Historical Association); all facing page 112.

19. *Moby Dick, or The Whale*, illus. Rockwell Kent (New York: Random House, 1930), 248, 253, 257.

20. Richard Ellis, *Men and Whales* (New York: Lyons Press, 1991).

21. On sexuality in *Moby-Dick*, see Robert K. Martin, *Heroes, Captains, and Strangers: Male Friendship, Social Critique, and Literary Form in the Sea Novels of Herman Melville* (Chapel Hill: Univ. of North Carolina Press, 1986).

22. Richard Ellis's *Men and Whales* is particularly helpful in establishing this point.

23. Melville never makes it clear whether Pip is a slave or not. His history is that of a northern African American, born outside of slavery, but he shares many characteristics of the minstrel-show figure of plantation slavery.

24. I am indebted to Peter S. Donaldson for pointing out the significance of this scene and for modeling multimedia essays in his own work. See "Digital Archives and Sibylline Fragments: *The Tempest* and the End of Books," in *Postmodern Culture* 8 (Jan. 1998) at http://muse.jhu.edu/journals/pmc/v008/8.2donaldson.htm. (accessed Sept. 22, 2005).

25. Jennifer O'Neill, curator at the Hart Nautical Collection at MIT, pointed out this connection and led me to banknotes portraying American whalers.

General Works Cited

[The following list includes works generally cited throughout the volume; for more specialized citations, see notes to individual chapters.]

Works by Herman Melville

Unless otherwise indicated or modified, all references are to the standard Northwestern Newberry edition (NN), *The Writings of Herman Melville,* ed. Harrison Hayford, Hershel Parker, and Thomas Tanselle (Evanston and Chicago: Northwestern University Press and The Newberry Library).

Typee. Vol. 1, 1968. Cited as *T.*
Mardi. Vol. 3, 1970. Cited as *M.*
White-Jacket. Vol. 5, 1970. Cited as *WJ.*
Moby-Dick, or The Whale. Vol. 6, 1988. Cited as *MD.*
Pierre; or the Ambiguities. Vol. 7, 1971. Cited as *Pierre.*
Israel Potter: His Fifty Years of Exile. Vol. 8, 1982. Cited as *IP.*
The Piazza Tales and Other Prose Pieces 1839–1860. Vol. 9, 1987. Cited as *PT.*
Clarel: A Poem and Pilgrimage in the Holy Land. Also ed. Walter E. Bezanson and Alma A. MacDougall. Vol. 12, 1991. Cited as *Clarel.*
Correspondence. Also ed. Lynn Horth. Vol. 14, 1993. Cited as *Cor.*
Journals. Also ed. Vol. 15, 1989. Cited as *Journals.*
Billy Budd, Sailor. Ed. Harrison Hayford and Merton M. Sealts Jr. Chicago: University of Chicago Press, 1962.

Secondary Sources

Adler, Joyce. *Dramatization of Three Melville Novels.* Lewiston, N.Y.: Mellen, 1992.
Arvin, Newton. *Herman Melville.* 1950; New York: Viking, 1957.

Barnett, Louise K. "Speech in *Moby-Dick*." *Studies in American Fiction* 11 (1983): 139–51.

Bercaw, Mary K. *Melville's Sources.* Evanston, Ill.: Northwestern University Press, 1987.

Bersani, Leo. "Incomparable America." In *The Culture of Redemption,* 136–54. Cambridge, Mass.: Harvard University Press, 1990.

Berthoff, Warner. *The Example of Melville.* Princeton, N.J.: Princeton University Press, 1962.

Bezanson, Walter E. "Moby-Dick: Document, Drama, Dream." In *A Companion to Melville Studies,* 170–210, ed. John Bryant. Westport, Conn.: Greenwood Press, 1986.

———. "*Moby-Dick*: Work of Art." In *Moby-Dick Centennial Essays,* 30–58, ed. Tyrus Hillway and Luther S. Mansfield. Dallas: Southern Methodist University Press, 1953.

Bloom, Harold, ed. *Ahab.* Major Literary Characters. New York: Chelsea House, 1991.

Bode, Rita. "'Suckled by the Sea': The Maternal in *Moby-Dick*." In *Melville and Women,* ed. Elizabeth Schultz and Haskell Springer. Kent, Ohio: Kent State University Press, 2006.

Brodhead, Richard H., ed. *New Essays on "Moby-Dick."* The American Novel. New York: Cambridge University Press, 1986.

Brodtkorb, Paul. *Ishmael's White World.* New Haven, Conn.: Yale University Press, 1965.

Bryant, John, ed. *A Companion to Melville Studies.* Westport, Conn.: Greenwood Press, 1986.

———. *Melville and Repose: The Rhetoric of Humor in the American Renaissance.* New York: Oxford University Press, 1993.

Buchman, S. R. "*The Sea Beast*—the Picture: An Appreciation." In *Moby-Dick, or The White Whale; Photoplay Title: The Sea Beast,* ix–xi. New York: Grosset and Dunlap, 1925.

Buell, Lawrence. "*Moby-Dick* as Sacred Text." In *New Essays on "Moby-Dick,"* 53–72, ed. Richard H. Brodhead. New York: Cambridge University Press, 1986.

Chase, Richard. *Herman Melville: A Critical Study.* New York: Macmillan, 1949.

———, ed. *Melville: A Collection of Critical Essays.* Englewood Cliffs, N.J.: Prentice Hall, Inc., 1962.

Colatrella, Carol. "'I Hear America Singing': Multiple Voices in Melville's *Moby-Dick*." In *Other Americans, Other Americas: The Ethics and Politics of Multiculturalism,* 50–61, ed. Magdalena Zaborowska. Aarhus, Denmark: Aarhus University Press, 1998.

———. *Literature and Moral Reform: Melville and the Discipline of Reading.* Gainesville: University Press of Florida, 2002.

Cowan, Bainard. *Exiled Waters: Moby-Dick and the Crisis of Allegory.* Baton Rouge: Louisiana State University Press, 1982.

Dillingham, William B. *Melville's Later Novels.* Athens: University of Georgia Press, 1986.

Dimock, Wai-Chee. *Empire for Liberty: Melville and the Poetics of Individualism.* Princeton, N.J.: Princeton University Press, 1989.

Douglass, Ann. *The Feminization of American Culture.* New York: Knopf, 1977.

Dryden, Edgar. *Melville's Thematics of Form.* Baltimore, Md.: Johns Hopkins University Press, 1968.

Duban, James. "Chipping with a Chisel: The Ideology of Melville's Narrators." *Texas Studies in Language and Literature* 31 (Fall 1989): 341–85.

———. *Melville's Major Fiction: Politics, Theology, and Imagination.* DeKalb: Northern Illinois University Press, 1983.

Duquette, Elizabeth. "Speculative Cetology: Figuring Philosophy in *Moby-Dick.*" *ESQ: A Journal of the American Renaissance* 47 (2001): 33–57.

Duyckinck, Evert A. "Melville's *Moby-Dick, or The Whale.*" Reprinted in Harrison Hayford and Hershel Parker, eds., *Moby-Dick,* 613–16. New York: Norton, 1967. Originally published in *New York Literary World* 9 (Nov. 22, 1851): 403–4.

Feidelson, Charles Jr. *Symbolism and American Literature.* Chicago: University of Chicago Press, 1953.

Gale, Robert L. *A Herman Melville Encyclopedia.* Westport, Conn.: Greenwood Press, 1995.

Garcia, Wilma. *Mothers and Others: Myths of the Female and the Works of Melville, Twain, and Hemingway.* New York: Peter Lang, 1984.

Grejda, Edward S. *The Common Continent of Men: Racial Equality in the Writings of Herman Melville.* Port Washington, N.Y.: Kennikat Press, 1974.

Hayes, Kevin J., ed. *The Critical Response to Herman Melville's* "Moby-Dick." Westport, Conn.: Greenwood Press, 1994.

Hayford, Harrison. "Unnecessary Duplicates: A Key to the Writing of *Moby-Dick.*" In *New Perspectives on Melville,* 128–61, ed. Faith Pullin. Kent, Ohio: Kent State University Press, 1978.

Heimert, Alan. "*Moby-Dick* and American Political Symbolism." *American Quarterly* 15 (Winter 1963): 498–534.

Hilbert, Betsy. "The Truth of the Thing: Nonfiction in *Moby-Dick.*" *College English* 48 (1986): 824–31.

Hillway, Tyrus, and Luther S. Mansfield, eds. *Moby-Dick: Centennial Essays.* Dallas: Southern Methodist University Press, 1953.

Holstein, Jay. "Melville's Inversion of Jonah in *Moby-Dick.*" *Iliff Review* 42 (Winter 1985): 13–20.

Inge, Thomas. "Melville in Popular Culture." In *A Companion to Melville Studies,* 696–70, ed. John Bryant, Westport, Conn.: Greenwood Press, 1986.

James, C. L. R. *Mariners, Renegades, and Castaways: The Story of Herman Melville and the World We Live In.* New York: C. L. R. James, 1953.

Karcher, Carolyn L. *Shadow over the Promised Land: Slavery, Race and Violence in Melville's America.* Baton Rouge: Louisiana State University Press, 1980.

Ketterer, David. "The Time-Break Structure of *Moby-Dick.*" *Canadian Review of American Studies* 19 (1988): 299–323.

Kier, Kathleen E. *A Melville Encyclopedia: The Novels, Part Two.* 2nd ed. Troy, N.Y.: Whitston Publishing Company, 1994.

Lee, A. Robert. *Herman Melville: Reassessments.* London: Barnes and Noble, 1984.

———. "*Moby-Dick*: The Tale and the Telling." In *New Perspectives on Melville*, 86–127, ed. Faith Pullin. Kent, Ohio: Kent State University Press, 1978.

Levin, Harry. *The Power of Blackness: Hawthorne, Poe, Melville.* New York: Knopf, 1970.

Leyda, Jay. *The Melville Log: A Documentary Life of Herman Melville, 1819–1891.* 2 vols. New York: Harcourt, Brace, 1951.

Mansfield, Luther S., and Howard P. Vincent. "Notes" to *Moby-Dick,* by Herman Melville. New York: Hendricks House, 1952.

Matteson, John T. "Grave Discussions: The Image of the Sepulchre in Webster, Emerson, and Melville." *New England Quarterly* 74 (2001): 419–46.

Matthiessen, F. O. *American Renaissance: Art and Expression in the Age of Emerson and Whitman.* New York: Oxford University Press, 1941.

McCarthy, Paul. *"The Twisted Mind": Madness in Herman Melville's Fiction.* Iowa City: University of Iowa Press, 1990.

Murray, Henry A. "'In Nomine Diaboli.'" In *Moby-Dick: Centennial Essays*, 3–21, ed. Tyrus Hillway and Luther S. Mansfield. Dallas: Southern Methodist University Press, 1953.

New, Elisa. "Bible Leaves! Bible Leaves! Hellenism and Hebraism in Melville's *Moby-Dick.*" *Poetics Today* 19 (Summer 1998): 281–303.

Olson, Charles. *Call Me Ishmael.* San Francisco: City Lights Books, 1947. Reprinted with a new afterword by Merton M. Sealts Jr. Baltimore, Md.: Johns Hopkins University Press, 1997.

Otter, Samuel. *Melville's Anatomies.* Berkeley and Los Angeles: University of California Press, 1999.

Paglia, Camille. "*Moby-Dick* as Sexual Protest." In *Moby-Dick,* ed. Hershel Parker and Harrison Hayford, 2nd ed. New York: W. W. Norton, 2002.

Parker, Hershel. *Herman Melville: A Biography.* Vol. 1, 1819–1851, Vol. 2, 1851–1891. Baltimore, Md.: Johns Hopkins University Press, 1996, 2002.

Patterson-Black, Gene. "On Herman Melville." In *American Novelists Revisited: Essays in Feminist Criticism,* ed. Fritz Fleischmann. Boston: G. K. Hall, 1982.

Porter, Carolyn. "Call Me Ishmael, or How To Make Double-Talk Speak." In *New Essays on "Moby-Dick,"* 73–108, ed. Richard H. Brodhead. New York: Cambridge University Press, 1986.

Post-Lauria, Sheila. "'A Philosophy in Whales . . . Poetry in Blubber': Mixed Form in *Moby-Dick.*" *Nineteenth-Century Literature* 45 (1990): 300–316.

Rampersad, Arnold. "Melville and Race." In *Herman Melville: A Collection of Critical Essays,* 160–73, ed. Myra Jehlen. Englewood Cliffs, N.J.: Prentice Hall, 1994.

Renker, Elizabeth. *Strike through the Mask: Herman Melville and the Scene of Writing.* Baltimore, Md.: Johns Hopkins University Press, 1996.

Reynolds, David. *Beneath the American Renaissance: The Subversive Imagination in the Age of Emerson and Melville.* Cambridge, Mass.: Harvard University Press, 1989.

Robertson-Lorant, Laurie. *Melville: A Biography.* New York: Clarkson Potter, 1996.

Rogin, Michael Paul. *Subversive Genealogy: The Politics and Art of Herman Melville.* New York: Knopf, 1983.

Rollyson, Carl, and Lisa Paddock. *Moby-Dick. Herman Melville A to Z: The Essential Reference to His Life and Work.* New York: Checkmark Books, 2001.

Royster, Paul. "Melville's Economy of Language." In *Ideology and Classic American Literature.* 313–36, ed. Sacvan Bercovitch and Myra Jehlen. New York: Columbia University Press, 1986.

Sanborn, Geoffrey. *The Sign of the Cannibal: Melville and the Making of a Post-Colonial Reader.* Durham, N.C.: Duke University Press, 1998.

Schultz, Elizabeth A. "The Common Continent of Men: Visualizing Race in *Moby-Dick.*" *Leviathan: A Journal of Melville Studies* 3.1 (Mar. 2001): 19–36.

———. "The Sentimental Subtext of *Moby-Dick*: Melville's Response to the 'World of Woe.'" *ESQ: A Journal of the American Renaissance* 42 (1996): 29–49.

———. *Unpainted to the Last: "Moby-Dick" and Twentieth-Century American Art.* Lawrence: University Press of Kansas, 1995.

Sealts, Merton M., Jr. *Melville's Reading: A Check-List of Books Owned and Borrowed.* Madison: University of Wisconsin Press, 1966.

Sedgwick, William Ellery. *Herman Melville: The Tragedy of Mind.* Cambridge, Mass.: Harvard University Press, 1944.

Simpson, David. *Fetishism and Imagination: Dickens, Melville, Conrad.* Baltimore, Md.: Johns Hopkins University Press, 1982.

Simpson, Eleanor E. "Melville and the Negro: From *Typee* to 'Benito Cereno.'" *American Literature* 41 (1969–70): 19–38.

Smith, Henry Nash. "The Image of Society in *Moby-Dick.*" In *Moby-Dick: Centennial Essays,* 59–75, ed. Tyrus Hillway and Luther S. Mansfield. Dallas: Southern Methodist University Press, 1953.

———. "The Madness of Ahab." In *Democracy and the Novel: Popular Resistance to Classic American Writers,* 35–55. New York: Oxford University Press, 1978.

Spanos, William V. *The Errant Art of* Moby-Dick: *The Canon, the Cold War, and the Struggle for American Studies.* Durham, N.C.: Duke University Press, 1995.

Stanonik, Janez. "The Sermon to the Sharks in *Moby–Dick.*" *Acta Neophilologica* 4 (1971): 53–60.

Sten, Christopher. *Sounding the Whale: Moby-Dick as Epic Novel.* Kent, Ohio: Kent State University Press, 1996.

Stern, Milton. *The Fine Hammered Steel of Herman Melville.* Urbana: University of Illinois Press, 1963.

Stone, Edward. "The Other Sermon in *Moby-Dick.*" *Costerus* 4 (1972): 215–22.

Stuckey, Sterling. "The Tambourine in Glory: African Culture and Melville's Art." In *The Cambridge Companion to Herman Melville,* 37–64, ed. Robert S. Levine. Cambridge: Cambridge University Press, 1998.

Thompson, Lawrance. *Melville's Quarrel with God.* Princeton, N.J.: Princeton University Press, 1952.

Thomson, Shawn. *The Romantic Architecture of Herman Melville's Moby-Dick.* Madison, N.J.: Fairleigh Dickinson University Press; London: Associated University Presses, 2001.

Tolchin, Neal L. *Mourning, Gender, and Creativity in the Art of Herman Melville.* New Haven, Conn.: Yale University Press, 1988.

Vick, Marsha C. "'Defamiliarization' and the Ideology of Race in *Moby-Dick.*" *College Literature Association Journal* 35 (1992): 325–38.

Vincent, Howard. *The Trying Out of Moby-Dick.* Carbondale: Southern Illinois University Press, 1949.

Wallace, Robert K. "Ahab's Wife, or the Whale." *Melville Society Extracts* 116 (Feb. 1999): 28.

———. "Avoiding Melville's Vortex: A Conversation with Performance Artist Rinde Eckert." *Leviathan: A Journal of Melville Studies* 3.1 (2001): 83–103.

———. *Frank Stella's* Moby-Dick: *Words and Shapes.* Ann Arbor: University of Michigan Press, 2000.

Warren, Joyce W. *The American Narcissus: Individualism and Women in Nineteenth-Century American Fiction.* New Brunswick, N.J.: Rutgers University Press, 1984.

Watters, R. E. "The Meanings of the White Whale." *University of Toronto Quarterly* 20 (1951): 155–68.

Welles, Orson. *Moby Dick—Rehearsed: A Drama in Two Acts.* New York: Samuel French, 1965.

Woodruff, Stuart C. "Stubb's Supper." *ESQ: A Journal of the American Renaissance* 43 (1966): 46–48.

Wright, Nathalia. *Melville's Use of the Bible.* Durham, N.C.: Duke University Press, 1969.

Zirker, Priscilla Allen. "Evidence of the Slavery Dilemma in *White-Jacket.*" *American Quarterly* 18 (1966): 477–92.

Index

Baudissin, Wolf Graf, 257
Bavarian Public Radio, 270
Baym, Nina, 242
Beales, Thomas, 29
Bercaw, Mary K., 227
Berkshire Women Performing Arts Festival, 311
Berman, Antoine, 276, 279
Berthoff, Warner, 301
Bezanson, Walter E., xv, 52, 79n20, 176, 295
Bible, 173, 190, 234, 257; Elijah, 18; Exodus, 139, 144n19; Ezekiel, 124, 129, 187–88; Gospels, 41; Hebrew, 41; Israelites, 196n15; Jacob, 335; Jehoshaphat, 243, 250n12; Jehovah, 265; Jeremiah, 44; Jesus, 51, 120, 130n9; Job, 44, 156, 316; King Ahab, 83, 249, 250n12; King James Version, 48, 256, 257; Luke, 120, 130n9; Martin Luther's, 257, 268; Mary Magdalene, 124; Matthew, 44, 125; measuring temples in, 187; Nineveh, 40–41, 53; Noah, 20, 50, 316; Old Testament, 73, 196n15; Peter, 48, 49; Rachel, 44; renderings of, xv, 191, 263, 271, 284; Revelation, 187; Sermon on the Mount, 157; Zechariah, 187–88. *See also* Jonah, book of
biblical allusions, 139, 261; apocalypses, 182; Bunker Hill, 119; Flood, 260; Ishmael, 247; prophecy, 191, 192; readings, 39; references, 81; rhetoric, 190; scholars and Jonah, 54n4
Bildad, 40, 137, 268
bin Laden, Osama, 7, 330, 332
bipolar disorder, 82, 99n4. *See also* manic depression
blacks, 84, 85, 209, 210, 212–15, 221, 222, 349. *See also* African American culture; African American sailors; African American women; Daggoo; Fleece; Pip; speech, black
Blackstone, William, 139, 142, 143n5
Blackwell's Island, 168
Blake, William, 284
blankness, 27, 67, 74, 76; of white page, 29, 30, 36. *See also* Whiteness
Bleecker Street, no. 45 (theater), 321, 325, 327, 333, 336n1
Bolívar, Simón, 224, 227
Bolster, Jeffrey, 143n8, 341
Boomer, 177, 178

Booth, Wayne, 149, 152, 158–59, 161–62
Borges, Jorge Luis, 199, 200, 207n14
Bradbury, Ray, 292
Brazil, 3, 10, 274, 284, 287
British people, the, 191, 238–39, 242, 250n3
Brodhead, Richard, 10
Brooklyn Academy of Music, 321
Browne, J. Ross, 340–41
Browne, Sir Thomas, 257
Bryant, John, 256, 338, 351n3
Bryant, William Cullen, 118–19, 226
Büchergile Gutenberg edition, 258
Buchman, S. R., 292
Buhlert, Klaus, 270
Bulkington, 2, 27, 30, 122, 171, 296, 317
Bunker Hill, 118, 120–21, 125, 129
Burke, Kenneth, 53
Burkert, Walter, 52
Burnett, Graham, 185, 193
Burnham, Michelle, 242
Burns, Ken, 183
Burton, Robert, 257
Butler, Sharon, 322, 333
Byron, Lord, 257

Calderón de la Barca, Pedro, 230
Camões, Luis de, 230
cannibalism, 157–58, 171, 221
Cape Verde Islands, 265
Carlyle, Thomas, 128, 257
cartography, 182, 185, 191–92, 313, 340. *See also* measurement
cartoons and drawings, 99n8, 312, 341; of "Irish Third Mate," 92. *See also* television: cartoons; visuals
castration, 71, 73, 77n3, 79n22
Center Stage Theater, Baltimore, 321, 333n12
Centro Cultural de São Paulo, 287
cetology, 199–203, 205, 293; chapters on, 11, 26–28, 30, 33–34, 186, 207n5, 284, 294; and classification, 148, 207n6, 255
chance, 43, 155, 156
chanteys. *See* sailor songs
Chase, Richard, 212
Checkhov, Anton, 23
Chichester, Dan, 286
Child, Lydia Maria, 168
children. *See* adaptations, illustrated, for children

Quaker idiom, 23, 268
Quakers (the Society of Friends), 142, 144n20
Quartim Yone, 286
Queequeg, 4–5, 7–9, 27, 81, 99n15, 171, 174, 212, 214–15; coffin of, xii, 46, 50, 89–90, 123, 125–26, 332; and death, 51, 85, 155, 175, 179; and doubloon, 219–22, 229, 234; in Eckert, 331, 334; and the Golden Rule, 147; and Ishmael, xi, 17, 40–41, 157, 170, 173, 204–7, 244–47; and New Zealanders, 183, 195n5; played by Cole, 317; in Portuguese, 287; as symbolic character, 86–87, 95–98; and Tashtego, 35, 251n14, 295; tattooing of, 21, 127; X mark of, 248–49
Queiroz, Rachel de, 280

Rabelais, 211, 215, 216, 218, 266
race, xv, 166, 199–200, 207, 229, 242; currency, 346; domination, 210, 217, 219; and language, 7–9, 11; Melville and, 210, 222, 226, 249–50, 329; Parkman and, 247; and Pip, 217, 344–45; theories of, 204, 217; wars, 241, 244. See also African American
Rachel, the, 19, 56n19, 147, 153, 158, 163, 178, 318, 334
racial issues, 8, 204, 205, 209–10, 225–26, 307, 319n4, 324, 344
racism, 205, 213–14, 239, 248–49, 309
rage, 88, 95, 102–4, 300
Ramos, Graciliano, 287
Rampersad, Arnold, 209
Rathjen, Friedhelm, 262, 269, 272n11
readers, 26, 174–75, 178, 194, 222, 236, 288, 350; and assumptions and stereotypes, 213, 217, 225–26; of doubloon, 219–20, 233–35; and Ishmael, 154, 166–67, 170–71, 247; and web archive, 349
reading, 6, 86, 175, 229, 283, 296, 333n3, 339; of doubloon, 166, 171, 229, 231, 234–35; as a living activity, 129–30; and Melville, ix–x, 105, 111, 249; and moral rehabilitation, 6, 79n21, 164, 167–69, 172–73, 178–79
realism, 16, 75, 99n2, 226
reformers, 167, 168, 173, 175
regeneration, 220, 221
rehabilitation, 167–69, 172, 173, 175
religions, 52, 166, 234, 247, 251n16, 342

religious matters, 7, 128–29, 169, 189–92, 205, 249
Renker, Elizabeth, 4, 29–30
representation, 166, 233, 292, 329
revenge, 53, 55n10, 73, 79n23, 88, 138–40; Ahab and, 42, 45, 57n24, 66, 73, 102. See also vengeance
Revolutionary era, 121, 221
revolutionary tradition, 118–20, 121, 190, 210, 211, 214–15, 217–18
Revue des Deux Mondes, 257
Reynolds, Jeremiah, 183, 184
rhetoric, xv, 44, 70, 71, 102, 147–48, 152, 172, 256, 258; biblical, 190; in Rabelais, 216; Webster's, 119
Rich, John, 157
rights, 133–36, 143n10, 210, 214–16
Rimbaud, Arthur, 76
Rio de Janiero, 227
Robertson-Lorant, Laurie, 90, 239–40
Rocha, Francisco Manuel da, 285
Rochsteiner, Adalberto, 275, 282
Rockies, 190
Roman, 139; Catholic church, 226, 265; Law, 139, 140; Saturnalia, 218
Romance tradition, 81, 86–88, 99n1, 98n2, 99n6, 113n15, 269
Romanticism, 16, 66, 67, 70, 76, 79n18, 193, 257
Rosa, Guimarães, 275
Rousseau, Jean-Jacques, 139
Rowlandson, Mary, 44
Ryle, Gilbert, 149. See also thick description

sacred and violence, 37–38, 40–41, 44, 45, 51, 56n13, 56n19
sacrifice, 52–53, 55n5, 56n16, 57n24, 249. See also sacrificial crisis; sacrificial victim
Sacrifice Rock, 239, 241, 247, 249
sacrificial crisis, 37–38, 43, 49–50
sacrificial victim, 46–49
Saddam Hussein, 332
Sag Harbor (New York), 22–23
sailors, 143n3, 143n8, 166–67, 170, 338, 342, 346, 348. See also Slavery, of sailors
sailor songs, 339–40, 342, 352n11
Samuel Enderby, the, 177
Sanborn, Geoffrey, 86, 96

Walker, William, 225, 236n3

Wallace, Robert K., xvi, 7, 10–11, 298, 302n1, 304n16; and Driscoll production, 314, 315; and Eckert, 11, 303n5, 304n14, 306, 317

Warner Brothers, 291–92, 302n2

"War on Terror," 332, 334

wars of liberation, 231

Watteau painting, 326

weather, 226, 231–32

web, the. *See* World Wide Web

Webster, Daniel, 118–20, 125, 129

Welles, Orson, 11, 301, 311, 318, 319n6; production, xvi, 297, 302n2, 303n12, 307–8

Wertheimer, Eric, 226

whale, xiii, 30; in Anderson production, 293–94; body parts of, xii–xiv, 12, 97, 130n13, 148, 187, 190, 265, 294–95; classification of, 166, 200–204; hunt portrayed in painting, 346; oil leaking, 132, 136; readers' interpretations of, 171; sightings of, 166, 193, 196n21; trope of dead, 131n13. *See also* cetology

Whaleman's Chapel, 123–24, 129

whalemen, xiii, 231, 322, 303n6, 349

whalers, 176, 310. *See also names of individual ships*

whaling, 20, 23, 28, 33, 156, 167, 169, 173, 312, 346; dangers of, 17, 170, 174; in Eckert, 324, 329, 333; industry, 185, 349–50; life, xii, 21, 166, 322, 342; in web archive, 340–41

whiteness, 43, 74–76, 80n25, 217, 244, 338; hegemony of, 209, 222

Whitman, Walt, 325

Wilkes, Charles, 195n4, 195n5, 195n13, 228; botanists with, 227, 315; expedition of, 183, 185–86, 191–92, 194; letter of instructions to, 195n6, 227, 236n6; narrative of, 6, 184, 188–90, 192–93, 195n5, 225, 227–29, 233; to Bowditch Island, 188, 190–92

Williams College, 4

Wilmot Proviso, 217

Wilson, Gilbert, xvii, 307–8, 311

Wilson, James Q., 159

Winchester, Simon, 109

Winichakul, Thongchai, 185

Winthrop, John, 239

Women's issues, 305–6, 308, 311, 313–16, 319n2, 322. *See also* African American women; feminist criticism

Woodruff, Stuart, 213

Woolf, Virginia, 16

World Trade Center, New York, 269, 321, 327, 330, 332, 333

World Wide Web, 340, 343–44; adaptations, 10; audio in archive, 349

Wright, Nathalia, 39

Writing, 16–17; block 18, 28, 31, 36; and composition, xiv, 18–19. *See also* author

Xavier, Berenice, 274–80

Yeats, 199, 284

Yojo (god), 158, 244–47, 249, 251n15

Zansky, Louis, 284

Zeit, Die (Hamburg weekly), 269

Zirker, Priscilla Allen, 209, 222

Žižek, Slavoj, 61, 76, 77, 80n27

Zodiac signs on doubloon, 21, 234

Zotz, Werner, 286